You Never Forget Your First

Also by JOSH LEWIN

Getting in the Game: Inside Baseball's Winter Meetings

Also in the Potomac Books Baseball Lineup

Forging Genius: The Making of Casey Stengel, Steven Goldman

Wrigley Field: The Unauthorized Biography, Stuart Shea

The Baseball Rookies Encyclopedia, David Nemec and Dave Zeman

Chasing Steinbrenner: Pursuing the Pennant in Boston and Toronto,
Rob Bradford

The Baseball's Most Wanted™ Boxed Set, Floyd Conner and John Snyder

Deadball Stars of the National League, Society for American Baseball
Research, edited by Tom Simon

Bob Feller: Ace of the Greatest Generation, John Sickels

Paths to Glory: How Great Baseball Teams Got That Way,
Mark L. Armour and Daniel R. Levitt

Mickey Mantle: America's Prodigal Son, Tony Castro

You Never Forget **Your** First

JOSH LEWIN

Potomac Books, Inc.
Washington, D.C.

Published in the United States by Potomac Books, Inc. All rights reserved. No part of this book may be reproduced in any manner whatsoever without written permission from the publisher, except in the case of brief quotations embodied in critical articles and reviews.

Library of Congress Cataloging-in-Publication Data

ISBN 1-57488-961-3

(alk. paper)

Printed in the United States of America on acid-free paper that meets the American National Standards Institute Z39-48 Standard.

Potomac Books, Inc.
22841 Quicksilver Drive
Dulles, Virginia 20166

First Edition

10   9   8   7   6   5   4   3   2   1

To my dad, Edward,
who taught me the importance of
believing in projects, ideas, and ideals,
and seeing them all the way through.

CONTENTS

ACKNOWLEDGMENTS

The research for much of this project can best be summed up in one word: Google. Thanks, Internet trailblazers, for you made what could have been a horse-and-buggy ride a cruise along the autobahn.

Special recognition goes to a trio of websites whose contributors obviously love the game and its seemingly bottomless bowl of anecdotal information. First is www.baseballlibrary.com, which provided terrific support for much of the player and manager information included in these pages. I can only hope to write even half as beautifully and passionately as these biographers have. This site is, quite simply, a tour de force literary performance by a group of astute baseball historians. Second, kudos to the dynamic www.baseball-reference.com, which displays easy-to-follow summaries of who accomplished what, and when they did it. Third, a shout out to www.playerprofiles.com, a subscription service that is worth every penny for those who write or broadcast sports for a living.

Other research tools included Dan Epstein's *Twentieth Century Pop Culture*, *The Bill James Handbook*, Burt Solomon's *The Baseball Timeline*, Joel Whitburn's *Billboard Book of Top 40 Hits*, Donald Dewey and Nicolas Acocella's wonderful *New Biographical History of Baseball*, Baseball America's *Encyclopedia of Minor League Baseball*, The Sporting News' *Scouting Notebook: 2004*, John Thorn and Pete Palmer's *Total Baseball*, and Tim Brooks and Earle Marsh's *Complete Directory to Primetime Network and Cable TV Shows*. These are all great books to have in your library.

However, the star of the show, so to speak, is David Smith and his crew at the incomparable resource for anyone looking for baseball information, www.retrosheet.org, the alpha and omega of baseball Web sites, to which I am eternally grateful. Not only does the site provide a guilty pleasure treasure hunt of baseball minutiae you never knew existed, but it's the one-stop shop for box scores, both recent and retro. This book likely would have been out during the summer of 2007, rather than 2005, were it not for the point-and-click ease of this amazing site. Way to go, fellas—you've reached the pinnacle of baseball's stathead mountain, and I say that with hat-in-hand respect.

On the publishing side, Potomac Books is a terrific partner, and its baseball-crazy sports editor, Chris Kahrl, never fails to amaze me with her patience and talent. Much appreciation is extended to Potomac Books' production staff as well as Will Allison who faced a challenging copyedit.

Finally, sincere thanks to the dozens of players who so kindly agreed to be interviewed for this project. Only two players—both of them superstars on New York–based teams—failed to be cooperative, and most every player was at the very least thoughtful, and oftentimes elegant, in recounting what made his debut so special. This was truly a fun book to research and to write.

INTRODUCTION

There is nothing in baseball more romantic, if you will, than a rookie tasting the big time for the first time: All that hard work paying off, finally finding Albuquerque in his rearview mirror and the bright lights of Dodger Stadium shining on his clean new uniform. Welcome to *You Never Forget Your First: Ballplayers Recall Their Big League Debuts.*

The idea to compile major leaguers' recollections of their "first times" was born out of a casual conversation with a fellow named Don Kalkstein, the Texas Rangers performance enhancement coach. Kalkstein is, essentially, a sports psychologist, and at his core, he is curious about what makes athletes tick. At the batting cage one scorching afternoon in August 2003, Don related to me how thrilling it is to watch a young player take those first bold steps out of the dugout and onto a big league diamond. Don said he always wonders (as psychologists are inclined do) what goes through the player's mind.

Thanks for the idea, Don. Dinner's on me.

As I traveled with the Rangers and Fox Sports in 2004, I made it a point to seek out players who could relate their stories, even decades after the fact. What follows is a verbatim account of what they remember, sandwiched between biographical information and the box score from their maiden voyage.

I pared down my list to 120 or so players, in the interest of paper conservation; there are many more memorable debuts that could have been included. Marcus Thames, for instance, homered on the first big league pitch he saw—one thrown by Randy Johnson. A pair of St. Louis hitters—a Brown named Bob Nieman and a Cardinal named Keith McDonald—homered in their first two big league at bats. Nieman did it against Mickey McDermott at Fenway Park in 1951, and his next time out, beat out a bunt. He went on to enjoy a decent career, batting as high as .325 for the Orioles in '58. McDonald, on the other hand, had only seven more at bats, playing Triple-A each of the three years following his historic feat. But at least he left footprints— McDonald's nine big league at bats are nine more than the legendary "Moonlight" Graham ever got.

Other stories are ripe for the picking. Bert Campaneris homered twice in his first two big league games. The Royals' Mark Quinn debuted with a double and pair of long homers. Josh Bard and the late Billy Parker each debuted with walk-off home runs. The Angels' Tom Satriano homered in his first big league at bat, too, but the game was called due to rain in the fifth inning, so it didn't count. The Twins' Mike Ryan had two hits in his first two at bats, both in a nine-run second inning at Detroit, but the game was called due to rain in the fourth—from 2-for-2 to 0-for-0, thanks to Mother Nature. Kelly Heath got exactly one at bat with Kansas City in 1982, getting into the game only because Frank White's hemorrhoids flared up.

Some debuts are portents of things to come. Willie McCovey went 4-for-4 with a pair of triples in his first game, off Robin Roberts no less. Jack Morris debuted with a complete game 12-strikeout shutout, and in Bob Feller's debut, he fanned 15. Then again, the Red Sox' Ted Cox started off 6-for-6 in '77, then hit .236 during the rest of his inglorious career.

In the end, it's probably less about the results and more about that feeling in the pit of one's stomach, a feeling that only the players themselves can describe. *You Never Forget Your First* offers a forum for your favorite players to relate, in their own words, what it was like to hear that magic, life-changing sentence: "You're going up."

Photographs

Larry Andersen
Born: May 6, 1953
Debut: September 5, 1975

As Dennis Eckersley's minor league roommate in the Indians system, Larry Andersen picked up both the subtleties of a good slider and the importance of having fun. "The bottom line in baseball is maintaining your sanity," Andersen has said. "If I can say something stupid or do something stupid and get a couple laughs, then that's good." Overheard from Andersen through the years:

- "If we throw rice at weddings, do the Chinese throw hot dogs?"
- "Why is it when you send something by ship it's cargo, and when you send it by car, it's shipment?"
- "What do you pack Styrofoam in?"
- "If blind people wear glasses, why don't deaf people wear ear muffs?"

Now a broadcaster for the Phillies, the Oregon native has kept 'em in stitches while maintaining a healthy respect for the game that's made him his living.

As for the slider, it bought him a career-best 1.54 ERA for the Astros in 1989, second best in the league among pitchers with at least 80 innings of work. The following year, however, saw the right-hander acquire the epitaph for his tombstone. "When I die," he says, "it'll read 'Here lies the guy Houston traded even-up for Jeff Bagwell.'" At the time, it seemed to be an intelligent deal for the Red Sox. After all, they were in the playoff chase, and Bagwell was simply seen as an extra third baseman stuck behind Wade Boggs and a young power hitter named Scott Cooper. Andersen pitched in only 15 games for the Red Sox before moving along to San Diego; Bagwell, through 2004, has played in close to 2,100 games for Houston. "Yes," says Andersen. "But can he sustain a belch for up to a minute?"

I was in Oklahoma City, and my manager, Red Davis, told me, with Rick Manning and Dennis Eckersley, two of my good buddies already up with the big club. I was looking forward to seeing them as much as anything else. I joined the team in Milwaukee, and walking in there, it wasn't the nicest ballpark, obviously, but to me, it was a palace. My first big league ballpark. So, to me, old County Stadium always felt like the Taj Mahal.

Arch [Rick Manning] came right over to me, and he and Eck both made

2

it so nice . . . But, in my own head, wow, things were spinning. I got into my first game in Detroit . . . My first assignment was Willie Horton, Bill Freehan, and Aurelio Rodriguez, three real good players. I got Willie to pop up in foul ground . . . Freehan hammered one, but Manning went and made a great play on it for me, then I struck out Rodriguez. Frank Robinson was the player-manager, and I had heard he was real tough. He kind of expected everyone to be as good as he was. I was just hoping I could compete, and, fortunately, I did okay.

My sister and my mom back in Seattle were the first people I called, to tell 'em I had gotten in and done well. Two old, falling-down ballparks held such special memories for me, because it's where the first steps of my career were taken—County Stadium and Tiger Stadium.

Also on September 5, 1975
Mike Flanagan makes his major league debut for the Orioles in a 5–4 win over the Yankees.

AUTHOR'S NOTE: Not a bad day for the purveyors of one-liners: Flanagan is one of the few pitchers in big league history who could rival Andersen for memorable quips. When the Orioles Bird slipped and fell into the Baltimore dugout, it was Flanagan who stood over the fallen mascot saying, "Take two worms and call me in the morning."

BOXSCORE

Detroit Tigers 11, Cleveland Indians 2
Game Played on Friday, September 5, 1975 (Night) at Cleveland Stadium

Detroit	0	0	0	0	7	0	0	1	3	—	11	15	0
Cleveland	0	0	0	1	1	0	0	0	0	—	2	7	0

BATTING

Detroit Tigers	AB	R	H	RBI	BB	K	PO	A
Roberts rf	4	0	1	1	0	1	2	0
Sutherland 2b	3	1	0	0	2	0	3	6
Meyer 1b	4	2	2	3	0	1	13	1
Pierce 1b	0	0	0	0	0	0	0	1
Horton dh	5	2	3	4	0	0	0	0
Freehan c	5	1	2	1	0	1	2	0
Rodriguez 3b	4	1	1	0	1	2	0	3
Oglivie lf	5	1	2	0	0	1	2	0
LeFlore cf	5	1	1	0	0	1	3	0
Veryzer ss	4	2	3	2	0	0	0	5
Ruhle p	0	0	0	0	0	0	2	1
Totals	39	11	15	11	3	7	27	17

FIELDING
DP: 2

BATTING
2B: Meyer (17, off Waits); Veryzer (9, off Buskey)
HR: Horton 2 (23, 5th inning off Brown, 1 on, 1 out; 9th inning off LaRoche, 1 on, 1 out); Freehan (14, 9th inning off LaRoche, 0 on, 1 out)
SH: Roberts (5, off Waits)
HBP: Meyer (2, by LaRoche)
IBB: Sutherland (3, by Waits)

BASERUNNING
SB: Freehan (1, 2nd base off Waits/Ashby)

Cleveland Indians	AB	R	H	RBI	BB	K	PO	A
Kuiper 2b	3	0	1	0	0	1	2	3
Crosby 2b	1	0	0	0	0	0	0	1
Manning cf	4	0	1	0	0	1	2	1
Hendrick rf	4	1	2	1	0	0	3	0
Powell 1b	4	0	1	0	0	0	12	0
Carty dh	4	0	0	0	0	0	0	0
Gamble lf	3	0	0	0	1	0	0	0
Bell 3b	4	1	1	0	0	0	0	3
Ashby c2	0	0	0	1	0	7	0	
Duffy ss	3	0	1	1	0	0	1	4
Waits p	0	0	0	0	0	0	0	2
Brown p	0	0	0	0	0	0	0	0
Andersen p	0	0	0	0	0	0	0	0
Buskey p	0	0	0	0	0	0	0	0
LaRoche p	0	0	0	0	0	0	0	0
Totals	32	2	7	2	2	2	27	14

FIELDING
DP: 1

BATTING
2B: Duffy (19, off Ruhle)
HR: Hendrick (20, 4th inning off Ruhle, 0 on, 0 out)

PITCHING

Detroit Tigers	IP	H	HR	R	ER	BB	K
Ruhle W(11–10)	9.0	7	1	2	2	2	2

Cleveland Indians	IP	H	HR	R	ER	BB	K
Waits L(3–1)	4.1	8	0	6	6	1	3
Brown	1.2	2	1	1	1	2	1
Andersen	1.0	0	0	0	0	0	1
Buskey	1.0	2	0	1	1	0	0
LaRoche	1.0	3	2	3	3	0	2
Totals	9.0	15	3	11	11	3	7

WP: Ruhle (2), Brown (5)
HBP: LaRoche (2, Meyer)
IBB: Waits (5, Sutherland)
Umpires: Hank Morgenweck, Marty Springstead, Don Denkinger, Dale Ford
Time of Game: 2:18   Attendance: 4,108

JEFF BAGWELL
Born: May 27, 1968
Debut: April 8, 1991

Jeff Bagwell can lay claim to being one of the best and most popular Astros players of all time, but, strangely, he may not be able to lay claim to being the best first baseman born on May 27, 1968. Bagwell shares a birthday with Frank Thomas but not much of anything else. Whereas Thomas has always been seen as moody and a teammate of questionable character, Bagwell has always been lauded for his unwavering devotion to his fellow Astros and for fighting his way through pain to contribute.

Few Astros have contributed as much (or as selflessly) as the strapping Connecticut native. Learning to play first base at the tail end of his first big league spring training, Bagwell diligently learned "on the job" and went on to have a Rookie of the Year campaign. In 1994, he was a runaway train, hitting .368 with 116 RBI in his first 100 games. However, just as the nation was beginning to fully appreciate the young slugger, the players' strike hit and wiped out the rest of the season. Bagwell, with 39 home runs and a Gold Glove in tow, won the National League MVP.

A rather unaccomplished minor league player, he had only six home runs in 700 minor league at bats. Toying with his stance, "Baggy" finally jettisoned his pale imitation of his boyhood hero, Carl Yastrzemski, and picked a bizarre crouch that made him appear as though he were sitting on an invisible chair. With his unmistakable bat waggle, Bagwell has blistered as many as 149 RBI in a single season. However, until 2004, he was known for an almost spectacular lack of postseason success, having gone his first 50 playoff at bats without an extra-base hit. That stigma was vaporized in 2004 when his two-run, seventh-inning homer cemented the deciding game of the NLDS in Atlanta.

What is sometimes forgotten about Bagwell is what a complete player he was in his prime; in 1997, he became the first-ever first baseman with a season of 30 homers and 30 steals. He is a four-time All-Star, and a Gold Glove winner who led National League first baseman in assists five times. If he has a fault, it's his penchant for cigars. "I keep five small fans in my locker," says his teammate and friend, Brad Ausmus. "That stuff stinks."

I had made the team out of spring training. What was so memorable to me was that the Reds had just won the World Series the year before, and the opener was at Riverfront Stadium there in Cincinnati. So there was the emotion

4

of that, but also, it was when the first troops had just come back from the Gulf War, so there was that emotion, too. [The troops] were on the field, Opening Day in the best Opening Day city in baseball. It doesn't get much more big league than that.

The hairs were standing up on my arms and neck when Lee Greenwood came out there and sang that song about "proud to be an American." I was proud to be in the major leagues, but it was so much more than that, that day. I went out there and went 0-for-3, but one of the outs was a line-out to short with the bases loaded off Rob Dibble. Barry Larkin was standing right behind the bag at second and caught it—I couldn't believe he had been positioned there. I remember the pitch just before that Dibble threw right at my forehead—imagine that. But I lined out to end the game, and the place went crazy.

After the game, me, my dad, and a couple of players all went to dinner. My dad was retired by then, and I think the whole day was just as special for him as it had been for me.

Also on April 8, 1991
Darryl Kile makes his big league debut in the same game, pitching an inning of two-hit shutout relief.

AUTHOR'S NOTE: Kile and Bagwell would become best friends, and Kile's tragic death during the summer of 2002 continues to haunt his buddy. "Not a day goes by I don't think about him," says Bagwell, whose cleats now have Kile's #57 sewn on the side, in his honor.

BOXSCORE

Cincinnati Reds 6, Houston Astros 2
Game Played on Monday, April 8, 1991 (Day) at Riverfront Stadium

Houston	0	0	0	1	0	0	0	0	1	—	2	5	1
Cincinnati	0	0	0	5	1	0	0	0	x	—	6	10	0

BATTING

Houston Astros	AB	R	H	RBI	BB	K	PO	A
Yelding ss	4	1	1	0	0	0	3	1
Finley cf	3	0	0	1	0	1	2	1
Biggio c	4	1	2	1	0	0	5	1
Gonzalez lf	3	0	0	0	1	2	3	0
Caminiti 3b	3	0	1	0	1	0	2	2
Bagwell 1b	3	0	0	0	1	0	7	0
Rhodes rf	3	0	1	0	0	0	1	1
McLemore 2b	3	0	0	0	0	0	1	5
Scott p	1	0	0	0	0	0	0	0
Rohde ph	1	0	0	0	0	1	0	0
Clancy p	0	0	0	0	0	0	0	0
Ramirez ph	1	0	0	0	0	0	0	0
Kile p	0	0	0	0	0	0	0	0
Totals	29	2	5	2	3	4	24	11

FIELDING
DP: 1
E: McLemore (1)

BATTING
3B: Yelding (1, off Browning)
HR: Biggio (1, 4th inning off Browning, 0 on, 1 out)
SF: Finley (1, off Browning)

Cincinnati Reds	AB	R	H	RBI	BB	K	PO	A
Hatcher lf	4	0	0	0	0	0	1	0
Larkin ss	4	2	2	1	0	0	4	2
O'Neill rf	4	1	1	0	0	1	2	0
Davis cf	4	0	2	0	0	1	4	0
Morris 1b	4	0	1	1	0	1	9	0
Sabo 3b	4	1	1	1	0	0	1	4
Reed c	2	0	1	0	2	0	4	0
Duncan 2b	1	1	0	0	0	0	1	1
Doran 2b	2	0	1	0	0	0	1	2
Browning p	3	0	1	3	0	0	0	1
Myers p	0	0	0	0	0	0	0	0
Dibble p	0	0	0	0	0	0	0	0
Totals	32	6	10	6	2	3	27	10

FIELDING
DP: 2

BATTING
2B: O'Neill (1, off Scott); Sabo (1, off Scott); Browning (1, off Scott)
HR: Larkin (1, 4th inning off Scott, 0 on, 0 out)
HBP: Duncan (1, by Scott)
IBB: Reed (1, by Scott)

BASERUNNING
SB: Hatcher (1, 2nd base off Scott/Biggio)

PITCHING

Houston Astros	IP	H	HR	R	ER	BB	K
Scott L(0-1)	4	5	1	5	5	1	1
Clancy	3	3	0	1	1	1	1
Kile	1	2	0	0	0	0	1
Totals	8	10	1	6	6	2	3

Cincinnati Reds	IP	H	HR	R	ER	BB	K
Browning W(1-0)	8.1	5	1	2	2	1	4
Myers	0	0	0	0	0	2	0
Dibble SV(1)	0.2	0	0	0	0	0	0
Totals	9.0	5	1	2	2	3	4

HBP: Scott (1, Duncan)
IBB: Scott (1, Reed)
Umpires: Frank Ballina, John Floras, Randy Bruns, Dick Urlage
Time of Game: 2:21   Attendance: 55,205

Dusty Baker
Born: June 15, 1949
Debut: September 7, 1968

Three-time National League Manager of the Year Dusty Baker had a falling out with the San Francisco Giants but landed on his feet in Chicago, where Cubs fans asked him to lead them to the promised land. "My name is Dusty, not Messiah," he said at his introductory press conference, but that failed to stop the production of T-shirts that read, "In Dusty We Trusty."

In his first year as Cubs skipper, Baker led the team to just their fourth postseason appearance in 57 years and had them within five outs of their first World Series appearance since 1945. (After the Cubs' Game Seven NLCS loss, Baker received a package from a fan containing a Cubs jacket and cap with a note reading, "Here. I can't take it anymore.")

Still, wristband-wearing, toothpick-chewing Dusty Baker continues to stay positive in the face of negativity. He has navigated two of the game's most mercurial superstar sluggers in Barry Bonds and Sammy Sosa, and he continues to see proverbial glasses as half-full, rather than half-empty. (*Chicago Tribune* columnist Mike Royko once pegged Cub fans as those who looked at the glass and simply asked, "When's it gonna spill?") It's been said that Baker has a knack for getting everyone on his roster to play hard for him; if a guy has one competitive vein in his body, Baker will tap it.

As a player, he was a career .278 hitter, known as "Dr. Scald" for hitting wicked line drives. As a one-time 26th-round pick of the Braves, he exceeded all expectations, totaling 242 home runs and playing for 16 years, never spending a day on the disabled list. Hank Aaron (who hit in front of Baker the night of Aaron's record-breaking 715th home run) once said, "Dusty has more potential than any outfielder I've ever seen in all my years with the Braves." After three subpar seasons in Atlanta, however, he was shipped to the Dodgers, where he had some huge postseason hits, hammering eight RBI in the '77 NLCS. In 1981, he finished third in the league in hitting (.320) and made an outstanding catch in that year's All-Star Game, perhaps helping him win his only Gold Glove.

He never had a 100-RBI season and had only one 30-homer season, but it always seemed he could be scripted in for 25 of the latter and 80 of the former, while stealing ten to 20 bases. He ended his career in the Bay Area, with the Giants and Athletics, near his childhood home of Sacramento.

Lou Fitzgerald, my minor league manager, told me the good news, just after we had won the championship game, and I called home collect. I'd had a good year in the low minors, but that was a heck of a jump, being 19 years old and going from Greenwood, in the Western Carolinas League, up to Atlanta.

I got a hit off Juan Marichal soon after my first game, in San Francisco, close to where I grew up, in Sacramento. My mom and dad were there, my girlfriend, all my home boys . . . They all saw me get that hit off Marichal, and I can't imagine a prouder moment. My dad and I hadn't always gotten along, but he was there for me to see that first base hit. My mom and dad were newly divorced, so they weren't sitting anywhere near each other, but I remember finding both of them in their seats, making eye contact. That was special.

Also on September 7, 1968
The trial of Black Panther founder Huey Newton comes to an end in Oakland. He will be found guilty later in the week of voluntary manslaughter of a white police officer.

AUTHOR'S NOTE: Baker has spoken passionately about what it meant to him growing up around the militant black movement in Northern California.

BOXSCORE

Houston Astros 6, Atlanta Braves 3 (10)
Game Played on 9/7/1968 at Atlanta-Fulton County Stadium

Houston	1	0	0	0	0	1	0	1	0	3	—	3
Atlanta	0	0	0	0	0	0	1	2	0	—	7

Houston	AB	R	H	RBI
Menke 2b	4	3	2	0
Miller rf	3	0	1	0
Wynn cf	3	2	2	3
Staub 1b	4	0	1	1
Rader 3b	5	1	2	1
Aspromonte lf	5	0	1	0
Adlesh c	4	0	0	0
Thomas ph	1	0	1	1
McFadden c	0	0	0	0
Lemaster p	2	0	0	0
Shea p	2	0	0	0
Dukes p	0	0	0	0
Coombs p	0	0	0	0
Buzhardt p	0	0	0	0
Totals	37	6	10	6

FIELDING
E: Adlesh

BATTING
2B: Wynn (off Raymond), Rader (off Raymond)
HR: Wynn (21)
Sac: Miller
SF: Wynn
Team LOB: 8

Atlanta	AB	R	H	RBI
Alou cf	5	1	2	0
Millan 2b	5	0	1	0
H.Aaron rf	4	0	1	1
Torre 1b-c	4	0	1	0
B.Johnson 3b	2	0	0	0
Jackson ss	2	1	2	1
T.Aaron lf	3	0	0	0
Lum lf	1	0	0	0
Tillman c	3	0	1	0
Francona 1b	2	0	0	1
Martinez ss-3b	5	0	1	0
Niekro p	2	0	1	0
Baker ph	1	0	0	0
Upshaw p	0	0	0	0
Kelley p	0	0	0	0
Garr ph	0	1	0	0
Raymond p	0	0	0	0
Reed p	0	0	0	0
D. Johnson ph	0	0	0	0
Totals	39	3	10	3

FIELDING
E: Martinez
DP: 1

BATTING
2B: Martinez, Jackson, H. Aaron

BASERUNNING
Team LOB: 14

PITCHING

Houston	IP	H	R	ER	BB	K
Lemaster	6.2	7	0	0	3	1
Shea	1.1	1	3	3	2	0
Dukes	0.2	2	0	0	1	0
Coombs W (4–2)	0.2	0	0	0	1	0
Buzhardt	0.2	0	0	0	0	0
Total	10.0	10	3	3	7	1
Atlanta	**IP**	**H**	**R**	**ER**	**BB**	**K**
Niekro	7.0	6	2	1	0	4
Upshaw	0.1	1	1	1	1	1
Kelley	1.2	0	0	0	1	3
Raymond L (3–5)	0.1	2	3	3	2	0
Reed	0.2	1	0	0	0	0

HBP: by Upshaw (Wynn), by Coombs (Lum)
Umpires: Unknown
Time of Game: 3:00   Attendance: 6,429

Rocco Baldelli
Born: September 25, 1981
Debut: March 31, 2003

The name sounds like it's straight out of *The Sopranos*, but the face looks like it's straight out of *Up With People*. Much more Bambino than Gambino, the soft-spoken and unfailingly polite Baldelli is the kid you would have wanted to take your daughter to the prom. He was a straight-A student, recruited by both Princeton and Yale, though the Ivy League campus closest to his heart was Brown, just 15 miles from his Woonsocket, Rhode Island, driveway. Although he excelled at baseball, his true loves in junior high were volleyball and basketball. It wasn't until his sophomore year of high school, when he broke his leg trying to push off for a dunk, that he realized baseball, not the other sports, would be his ticket out of Rhode Island.

Nicknamed "The Woonsocket Rocket," he honed his swing in the basement of his dad's business, a combination coffee house/check cashing service/pawn shop. Hava Java Coffee House is believed to be the only coffee and donut joint in the state with a batting cage underneath.

Baldelli's dad, a retired firefighter, was flattered by all the comparisons being made between his son and another graceful, long-legged Italian-American, Joe DiMaggio. It had nothing to do with DiMaggio's association with Mr. Coffee and everything to do with his being a talented, right-handed hitting Italian center fielder who also wore number five. But one got the sense as the Baldelli bandwagon gathered speed that maybe everyone ought to stand back and take a breath before anointing the kid as the next Joe D. That included Devil Rays owner Vince Naimoli, who reportedly asked if Baldelli could wear #56, to mark DiMaggio's record hitting streak.

Baldelli kept both his humility and his sanity during that first major league spring training of 2003 and would ultimately finish third in the balloting for American League Rookie of the Year, hitting safely in all but one of his first 24 big league games. Thankfully, no one asked him to change his uniform number to the fraction 23/24.

Most of the first inning, when we were in the field, I just don't remember; it was all going by so fast. But we came in to hit and Pedro [Martinez] was on the mound for Boston. That you don't forget. I doubled against him for my first-

8

big league hit, and later C.C. [Carl Crawford] hit the home run in the ninth to win the game. That part will stay with me forever; that was just so cool.

I had left tickets for my two brothers, my mom, and dad, and they were thrilled . . . They knew I had made the team halfway through spring training, and it was weird because I was hitting around .220 at the time that they made that decision. But Lou [Piniella] told me I was going to be his Opening Day center fielder, and it took a little bit for that to really sink in.

Getting in the box for the first time against Pedro is probably when it truly sank in. Even when you're on the foul line being introduced before the game, it's like it's happening to someone else . . . But then you're facing Pedro in front of 40,000 fans, and wow, it's happening to you.

Also on March 31, 2003
Day 13 of the War in Iraq, news of the SARS outbreak in Hong Kong, a killer landslide in Bolivia, and a killer mudslide in Indonesia made March 31 one of the darkest days of the entire calendar year. However, there was joy in Syracuse, New York, as Jim Boeheim's Syracuse University Orange finally won a men's basketball title, and there was joy in Woonsocket, Rhode Island, as the Woonsocket Rocket had officially taken flight.

BOXSCORE

Tampa Bay Devil Rays 6, Boston Red Sox 4
Game Played on Monday, March 31, 2003 (Night) at Tropicana Field

Boston	3	0	0	0	1	0	0	0	0	—	4	8	1
Tampa Bay	0	0	0	0	0	0	1	0	5	—	6	7	2

BATTING

Boston Red Sox	AB	R	H	RBI	BB	K	PO	A
Damon cf	4	0	0	0	1	0	4	0
Walker 2b	4	2	1	0	1	0	2	3
Garciaparra ss	5	1	2	0	0	1	2	3
Ramirez lf	4	1	1	0	0	0	0	0
Millar 1b	3	0	1	0	0	2	8	1
Mueller 3b	0	0	0	0	0	0	0	0
Hillenbrand 3b-1b	4	0	1	3	0	0	1	1
Giambi dh	4	0	0	0	0	2	0	0
Nixon rf	4	0	0	0	0	0	1	0
Varitek c	4	0	2	0	0	1	7	0
Martinez p	0	0	0	0	0	0	1	1
Mendoza p	0	0	0	0	0	0	0	1
Embree p	0	0	0	0	0	0	0	0
Fox p	0	0	0	0	0	0	0	0
Totals	36	4	8	3	2	6	26	10

FIELDING
DP: 1
E: Hillenbrand (1)

BATTING
2B: Hillenbrand (1, off Kennedy); Varitek 2 (2, off Kennedy 2)
HBP: Millar (1, by Kennedy)

Tampa Bay Devil Rays	AB	R	H	RBI	BB	K	PO	A
Crawford lf	5	1	1	3	0	1	1	0
Baldelli cf	4	0	1	0	0	1	1	0
Huff 3b	4	0	1	0	0	0	0	2
Lee 1b	4	1	1	0	0	1	9	2
Martin dh	2	1	1	0	0	1	0	0
Shumpert ph-dh	1	1	1	2	0	0	0	0
Grieve rf	3	0	1	0	0	1	3	0
Rolls pr	0	0	0	0	0	0	0	0
Hall c	4	0	0	0	0	1	7	1
Abernathy 2b	4	1	0	0	0	0	1	6
Ordonez ss	2	0	0	0	1	1	3	0
Anderson ph	0	1	0	0	1	0	0	0
Kennedy p	0	0	0	0	0	0	2	1
McClung p	0	0	0	0	0	0	0	0
Totals	33	6	7	5	2	7	27	12

FIELDING
E: Huff (1), Abernathy (1)

BATTING
2B: Baldelli (1, off Martinez)
HR: Shumpert (1, 9th inning off Embree 1 on, 0 out); Crawford (1, 9th inning off Fox, 2 on, 2 out)
HBP: Martin (1, by Martinez); Grieve (1, by Martinez)

BASERUNNING
SB: Abernathy (1, 2nd base off Fox/Varitek)

PITCHING

Boston Red Sox	IP	H	HR	R	ER	BB	K
Martinez	7	3	0	1	0	1	6
Mendoza	1	0	0	0	0	0	0
Embree	0	3	1	3	3	0	0
Fox L (0–1)	0.2	1	1	2	2	1	1
Totals	8.2	7	2	6	5	2	7
Tampa Bay Devil Rays	**IP**	**H**	**HR**	**R**	**ER**	**BB**	**K**
Kennedy	7	8	0	4	1	0	3
McClung W(1–0)	2	0	0	0	0	2	3
Totals	9	8	0	4	1	2	6

HBP: Martinez 2 (2, Martin, Grieve); Kennedy (1, Millar)
Umpires: Charlie Reliford, Mike Everitt, Hunter Wendelstedt, Dan Iassogna
Time of Game: 2:35   Attendance: 34,391

Josh Beckett
Born: May 15, 1980
Debut: September 4, 2001

Brimming with Texas-sized confidence, young Josh Beckett shut out the Yankees at the storied House that Ruth Built, winning the 2003 World Series for Florida. At 23, Beckett was the owner of not a single major league complete game entering the '03 postseason. Then he coolly ripped one off in the Bronx, to the chagrin of 56,000 Yankee fans. The last time a starter had gone all the way to clinch the World Series was Orel Hershiser, some 15 years prior—and Beckett turned in his masterpiece on (gulp) just three days' rest, and was named Series MVP.

While Hershiser was (and still is) known for his modesty, the immodest Beckett isn't shy about speaking his mind. In 2004, he referred to a Marlins trainer as "an ass" and criticized manager Jack McKeon on the record. Back in high school, Beckett once threw not at an opponent, but at the opponent's father—because the old man was giving away pitch location from his seat behind the plate. For Beckett, at least in high school and the minors, it wasn't about just *dominating* the hitters; he wanted to *embarrass* the hitters.

He entered the 2003 season, however, with a middling 17–17 big league record. Enter 2003 Marlins pitching coach Wayne Rosenthal, who lectured Beckett on the notion of "easy cheese," a great fastball that comes with minimum strain on the arm. Curt Schilling may be the best modern example of "easy cheese," and to drive home his point, Rosenthal showed Beckett tapes of Schilling, the man who would be the following year's World Series hero for Boston.

A Texan to the bone, Beckett says he is almost as proud of what he accomplished on November 11, 2002, as he is of his Series performance. Hunting with his dad, he bagged a 14-point buck that scored 401 Muy Grande points, giving him the award for largest deer shot in the state of Texas that year. More importantly for Marlins fans, "muy grande" is how they described Beckett's magical run in October of 2003.

They had called me up a week before I got my first start . . . I had to go to New York, so the first big league stadium I ever stepped in was Shea Stadium, of all places. It was cool, kind of exciting, watching big league games from the dugout. Coming from Portland, Maine, Double-A, it was all a pretty big change. Blaine Neal and I had taken a puddle jumper from Altoona, Pennsylvania, to get to New York . . . something I would recommend you never do if you can help it.

We cabbed it right to Shea, but the big one was later, at home against Chicago. I had 15 or so people come in from Texas—my dad, mom, grandparents, a few friends. I got Delino DeShields leading off . . . He swung at my very first major league pitch, and he grounded out, thank you very much, Delino. I got Sammy [Sosa] that inning too, so I was feeling pretty good. Preston Wilson hit a three-run homer and Kevin Millar had a grand slam in that game, so I was set for run support.

Everything else fell into place real nice . . . [Catcher] Charles Johnson and I got into a nice rhythm, and the only hit I allowed [in six innings] was to Rondell White. I had as many hits as I gave up, because I doubled later in the game against Jon Leiber. Yeah, that's a pretty good way to get yourself going.

Also on September 4, 2001
The Yankees suffer their most humiliating defeat in more than 11 years, getting rolled in Toronto, 14–0. The losing pitcher is Houston native Andy Pettitte.

AUTHOR'S NOTE: Pettitte and Beckett, a pair of Houston natives, would hook up in what would prove to be even more of an embarrassment for the Yankees two years later. Beckett outdueled Pettitte in Game Six of the 2003 World Series, which led to the surreal scene of the underdog Marlins partying on Yankee Stadium's pitcher's mound, smoking cigars, drinking champagne, and generally putting their feet on some very expensive furniture. Marlins owner Jeffrey Loria did a victory lap around the bases in his thousand-dollar shoes, accomplishing something no Yankee player had done all game: touch home plate.

BOXSCORE

Florida Marlins 8, Chicago Cubs 1
Game Played on Tuesday, September 4, 2001 (Night) at Pro Player Stadium

Chicago	0	0	0	0	0	0	0	1	0	—	1	6	0
Florida	3	0	0	0	5	0	0	0	x	—	8	8	0

BATTING

Chicago Cubs	AB	R	H	RBI	BB	K	PO	A
DeShields 2b	3	0	0	0	1	0	4	1
Tucker cf-lf-rf	4	0	1	0	2	1	0
Sosa rf	4	0	0	0	0	1	3	0
Van Poppel p	0	0	0	0	0	0	0	0
McGriff 1b	2	0	0	0	1	0	4	0
Mahay p	0	0	0	0	0	0	0	0
Meyers cf	1	0	0	0	0	0	1	0
White lf	2	0	1	0	1	1	3	0
Patterson cf-lf	1	0	0	0	0	0	0	0
Gutierrez ss	4	0	2	0	0	0	1	2
Coomer 3b	4	0	1	0	0	0	1	1
Girardi c	4	1	1	0	0	2	6	0
Lieber p	2	0	0	0	0	1	0	1
Stairs 1b	1	0	0	0	0	1	0	0
Totals	**32**	**1**	**6**	**1**	**3**	**8**	**24**	**5**

BATTING
3B: Tucker (4, off Nunez)

Florida Marlins	AB	R	H	RBI	BB	K	PO	A
Castillo 2b	3	0	0	0	0	0	1	4
Lee 1b	3	1	1	1	0	0	8	0
Floyd lf	3	2	1	0	1	1	1	0
Wilson cf	4	2	2	3	0	0	3	0
Lowell 3b	2	1	0	0	1	0	0	0
Millar rf	4	1	3	4	0	0	3	0
Johnson c	4	0	0	0	0	2	8	0
Gonzalez ss	4	0	0	0	0	2	3	4
Beckett p	2	1	1	0	0	0	0	0
Owens ph	1	0	0	0	0	1	0	0
Nunez p	0	0	0	0	0	0	0	0
Acevedo p	0	0	0	0	0	0	0	0
Totals	**30**	**8**	**8**	**8**	**2**	**6**	**27**	**8**

FIELDING
DP: 1

BATTING
2B: Beckett (1, off Lieber)
3B: Millar (3, off Lieber)
HR: Wilson (18, 1st inning off Lieber, 2 on, 1 out); Millar (17, 5th inning off Lieber, 3 on, 2 out)
SH: Castillo (4, off Lieber)
SF: Lee (5, off Lieber)
HBP: Lowell (9, by Lieber)

PITCHING

Chicago Cubs	IP	H	HR	R	ER	BB	K
Lieber L (17–6)	5	7	2	8	8	2	2
Mahay	2	0	0	0	0	0	3
Van Poppel	1	1	0	0	0	0	1
Totals	**8**	**8**	**2**	**8**	**8**	**2**	**6**
Florida Marlins	**IP**	**H**	**HR**	**R**	**ER**	**BB**	**K**
Beckett W (1–0)	6	1	0	0	0	3	5
Nunez	2	3	0	1	1	0	2
Acevedo	1	2	0	0	0	0	1
Totals	**9**	**6**	**0**	**1**	**1**	**3**	**8**

HBP: Lieber (3, Lowell)
Umpires: Dale Scott, Jim Joyce, Bill Miller, Tim Timmons
Time of Game: 2:21   Attendance: 13,401

Carlos Beltran
Born: April 24, 1977
Debut: September 14, 1998

A buried treasure in Kansas City, Beltran was dusted off and displayed on a national stage when his new team, Houston, bombed its way into (and almost out of) the 2004 NLCS. Beltran was a one-man wrecking ball, smashing four home runs in the Division Series vs. Atlanta. He followed with four more as the Astros took a 3–2 lead in the best-of-seven LCS with St. Louis, but many other Houston bats stayed silent, and the Cards rallied for a trip to the Fall Classic.

Beltran blazed his way to American League Rookie of the Year in Kansas City, taking 26 of 28 first-place votes in 1999. The Royals had seen only three 20-homer/20-steal seasons from one of their own in franchise history until Beltran's arrival (two by Bo Jackson, one by Amos Otis.) Beltran proceeded to rip off 20/20s in four of his first five seasons while playing electric defense in Kauffman Stadium's spacious center field.

Dealt to Houston, which has an even more spacious outfield to cover, he took flight that summer of 2004, helping the Astros go 36–10 down the stretch to catch and pass the Cubs for the wild card spot. Beltran had always been a near-perfect stolen base artisan; heading into the '04 season, he'd been successful on 89 percent of his attempts, the best in big league history with a minimum of 100 attempts. Once he got to Houston, he crafted a consecutive steal streak at which Tim Raines, Eric Davis, and others could only marvel: 28-for-28 in the regular season, 6-for-6 in the playoffs.

Although a menace on the bases, Beltran is laid back off the field. When the Royals asked him to list his favorite hobby on a questionnaire, he wrote "sleeping." The "speak softly but carry a big stick" approach is one he gleaned from fellow Puerto Rican center fielder Bernie Williams. The two were teammates in winter ball when Williams was at the height of his career and postseason success with the Yankees. Williams taught Beltran the value of appreciating what you have, and Beltran has had plenty to appreciate. In a 72-hour stretch in '99, he a) got married, b) vacationed in Orlando, and c) got that Rookie of the Year Award. And, in the spirit of appreciating all of life's pleasures, Beltran reports that high up on the list in that 72 hours of bliss was the chance to see Shamu, the killer whale, up close. Bobby McFerrin sang it; Beltran has lived it—simple pleasures are the best.

With his recently found riches, Beltran has moved his parents into their dream home, and his dad has been able to retire from his job in the pharmaceutical sales business. Beltran hit the free agent market after his eye-opening 2004 season and now makes enough for *everyone* in the pharmaceutical sales business to retire. With his best years still in front of him, Beltran could be one of the top three all-around players in the game today.

I faced Buddy Groom, pinch-hitting. I got an infield hit, in a game where our team was winning big. I scored two runs, on the infield hit and a walk. Both my mom and dad made it to the game, because they had been in Wichita, where I had been playing Double-A. We drove from Wichita to Kansas City together, and my dad looked very proud the whole way there, that his son was going to the big leagues. That was his dream. When I got that first hit, I gave him the ball, and he still has it at his home. I had a lot of great days in Kansas City, but that one was the first.

My dad still comes and sees me play sometimes, usually on my birthday, in April. I always seem to have good games when he's there.

Also on September 14, 1998
One-time "can't miss" five-tool prospect Melvin Nieves plays his final major league game, for the Cincinnati Reds.

AUTHOR'S NOTE: Nieves was supposed to have been what Beltran would ultimately become—a "do it all" switch-hitting 6'1" 190-pound outfielder from Puerto Rico. Nieves debuted as an Atlanta Brave, at the beginning of the Braves' run of NL East dominance. Many now believe that run is over—and if that's the case, look no further than Beltran, who led the Astros past Atlanta in the 2004 postseason.

BOXSCORE

Kansas City Royals 16, Oakland Athletics 6
Game Played on Monday, September 14, 1998 (Night) at Kauffman Stadium

												R	H	E
Oakland	1	0	0	0	5	0	0	0	0	—		6	10	2
Kansas City	1	1	3	1	1	3	2	4	x	—		16	19	0

BATTING

Oakland Athletics	AB	R	H	RBI	BB	K	PO	A
Henderson lf	4	2	3	1	1	0	4	0
Christenson cf	5	1	1	2	0	1	4	0
Ja. Giambi 1b	3	1	1	3	1	0	2	0
McDonald ph	0	0	0	0	0	1	0	0
Stairs dh	5	0	2	0	0	0	0	0
Blowers 3b	3	0	1	0	1	1	2	1
Grieve rf	2	0	0	0	2	1	5	0
Spiezio 2b	4	0	0	0	0	2	0	0
Velandia ss	0	0	0	0	0	0	1	1
Tejada ss	3	1	1	0	0	1	2	0
Chavez ph	1	0	0	0	0	0	0	0
Bournigal 2b	0	0	0	0	0	0	0	0
Macfarlane c	4	1	1	0	0	2	4	0
Haynes p	0	0	0	0	0	0	0	0
Stein p	0	0	0	0	0	0	0	0
Groom p	0	0	0	0	0	0	0	0
Holzemer p	0	0	0	0	0	0	0	0
Totals	**34**	**6**	**10**	**6**	**6**	**8**	**24**	**2**

FIELDING
DP: 1
E: Grieve (2), Tejada (23)

BATTING
HR: Henderson (14, 1st inning off Rosado 0 on, 0 out); Ja. Giambi (25, 5th inning off Rosado, 2 on, 1 out)

BASERUNNING
SB: Henderson 2 (62, 2nd base off Whisenant/Sweeney, 3rd base off Service/Sweeney)

Kansas City Royals	AB	R	H	RBI	BB	K	PO	A
Damon cf-rf	4	3	2	1	2	0	1	0
Brown pr-rf	0	1	0	0	0	0	0	0
Sutton rf	4	0	2	1	0	0	0	0
Beltran cf	1	2	1	0	1	0	1	0
Offerman 2b	5	2	2	0	0	1	1	3
Febles ph-2b	1	0	0	0	0	0	0	0
Palmer 3b	4	0	2	4	0	1	0	1
Leius ph-3b	1	0	1	0	0	0	1	0
Je. Giambi dh	2	1	0	1	3	0	0	0
King 1b	6	3	2	3	0	0	10	1
Halter 1b	0	0	0	0	0	0	2	0
Morris lf	3	1	1	0	1	0	1	0
Conine ph-lf	1	0	0	0	0	1	0	0
Sweeney c	5	2	4	4	0	1	8	0
Ortiz c	0	0	0	0	0	0	0	0
Lopez ss	5	1	1	1	0	0	1	5
Rosado p	0	0	0	0	0	0	0	1
Bones p	0	0	0	0	0	0	0	0
Whisenant p	0	0	0	0	0	0	0	0
Service p	0	0	0	0	0	0	1	1
Totals	**42**	**16**	**19**	**16**	**7**	**4**	**27**	**12**

FIELDING
DP: 2

BATTING
2B: Damon (26, off Haynes); Sutton (14, off Haynes); Sweeney 2 (18, off Stein, off Holzemer); Palmer (25, off Groom); Lopez (9, off Holzemer)
HR: Sweeney (8, 3rd inning off Haynes, 2 on, 2 out); King (24, 6th inning off Haynes, 2 on, 2 out)
SF: Palmer (11, off Haynes); Je. Giambi (1, off Holzemer)

PITCHING

Oakland Athletics	IP	H	HR	R	ER	BB	K
Haynes	4	7	1	6	3	3	3
Stein L (5–9)	2	5	1	4	4	2	0
Groom	1	2	0	2	1	1	1
Holzemer	1	5	0	4	4	1	0
Totals	**8**	**19**	**2**	**16**	**12**	**7**	**4**

Kansas City Royals	IP	H	HR	R	ER	BB	K
Rosado	4.1	9	2	6	6	2	4
Bones W (2–1)	2	1	0	0	0	1	2
Whisenant	0.1	0	0	0	0	1	0
Service SV (4)	2.1	0	0	0	0	2	2
Totals	**9.0**	**10**	**2**	**6**	**6**	**6**	**8**

WP: Stein 2 (13), Holzemer (1), Service (9)
Umpires: Drew Coble, Dale Ford, Ted Hendry, Larry Young
Time of Game: 3:16   Attendance: 12,103

Lance Berkman
Born: February 10, 1976
Debut: July 16, 1999

When Derek Bell departed for Pittsburgh, the Astros "Killer B" brigade took a hit, but only b-riefly. The next "B" on the conveyor belt was the beefy, switch-hitting Lance Berkman, who settled in with Craig Biggio, Jeff Bagwell, and, later, Carlos Beltran to form a sinister top half of the Houston batting order.

Of all those bashing Bs, Berkman is the only Astro with the built-in bonus of being a native Texan. For all the pomp and circumstance surrounding the signings of supposed native Texans Roger Clemens and Andy Pettitte, the two Houston residents were actually born in Ohio and Louisiana, respectively. Berkman, born in Waco and raised in Austin, keeps a picture of The Alamo in his locker at Minute Maid Park.

Growing up in Austin, he worked on his swings and his strength simultaneously. His dad, an attorney, hung a tire from the Berkman's backyard tree, and Lance would take his bat to it 100 times daily, from the age of six. Fifty hacks from the right side, then 50 from the left. The senior Mr. Berkman had grown up a huge Mickey Mantle fan, and by golly, little Lance was going to be a switch-hitter, too, just like The Mick!

Not only is Berkman powerful (in 2001, he became the first switch-hitter with a 50-double/30-homer season), but he isn't afraid to take a walk (nearly 100 in his first minor league season and 127 in 2004). The onetime Rice University Owl soared to a .316 batting average in '04, helping the Astros come within a game of their first World Series. Those who have followed his career figure the Fall Classic is only a matter of time. Rice made the College World Series on his watch, and minor league New Orleans made the Triple-A World Series, winning it when Berkman smashed three home runs in the deciding game.

It seemed like I was going to play for the Olympic qualifying team in Canada. I had flown to Tucson from New Orleans; my wife, Karen, had gone with me, and we're there about eight hours when I'm tracked down by [Astros GM] Gerry Hunsicker, who says, "Uh, listen, we've had to put Moises Alou on the disabled list up here, so I'm sorry to dash your Olympic dreams, but we'd like to bring you to the big leagues today." He gave me my flight information, so Karen and I settled down for the night, went to a nice dinner, and got ready to make the first flight out to Houston. Trouble is, I couldn't fall asleep! I was just too excited.

So having stayed up pretty much all night, I got the flight out but was real tired when I showed up. I hadn't really expected to get in the game, so I figured no big deal . . . But midway through the game, Larry Dierker, our manager, told me I'm going to pinch-hit for the pitcher, who was due up third that inning. I could barely stand. My knees were just weak, I was so nervous. Justin Thompson was pitching, and the first two guys in the inning got on against him, so now I'm ready. Obvious bunting situation, and I'm so zoned in, I didn't realize they were trying to call me back to get a better bunter up there! I kept walking into the batter's box, they announced me, and Dierker figured, "Well, I'd better let him stay in there, and we'd better have him swing away; he's going to be too nervous to get a bunt down." So, second pitch, I bang into a double play and kill the rally. This is after a major Justin Thompson curveball that just buckled me for strike one on the first pitch. Welcome to the big leagues. I ended up 0-for-my-first-10, 2-for-my-first-21.

Also on July 16, 1999
John F. Kennedy Jr. (age 38), his wife, Carolyn Kennedy, and her sister, Lauren, are killed when the Piper Saratoga he was piloting crashed off Martha's Vineyard.

BOXSCORE

Houston Astros 2, Detroit Tigers 1
Game Played on Friday, July 16, 1999 (Night) at Astrodome

Detroit	0	0	0	0	1	0	0	0	0	—	1	4	1
Houston	0	1	0	0	0	0	0	0	1	—	2	8	0

BATTING

Detroit Tigers	AB	R	H	RBI	BB	K	PO	A
Encarnacion lf	4	0	1	0	0	2	1	0
Easley 2b	4	0	1	0	0	1	4	3
Higginson rf	4	0	0	0	0	1	3	0
Palmer 3b	4	0	1	0	0	1	0	0
Clark 1b	3	1	1	1	1	1	7	1
Catalanotto pr-1b	0	0	0	0	0	0	0	0
Kapler cf	2	0	0	0	1	1	2	0
Haselman c	3	0	0	0	0	1	6	0
D. Cruz ss	3	0	0	0	0	0	3	4
Thompson p	2	0	0	0	0	1	0	2
Polonia ph	1	0	0	0	0	1	0	0
Brocail p	0	0	0	0	0	0	0	0
Totals	30	1	4	1	2	10	26	10

FIELDING
DP: 2
E: D. Cruz (7)

BATTING
2B: Palmer (16, off Elarton)
HR: Clark (9, 5th inning off Elarton, 0 on, 0 out)

BASERUNNING
SB: Encarnacion (24, 2nd base off Powell/Knorr)

Houston Astros	AB	R	H	RBI	BB	K	PO	A
Biggio 2b	5	0	1	1	0	1	0	2
Johnson 3b	3	0	0	0	1	0	1	1
Bagwell 1b	4	0	2	0	0	1	6	0
Hidalgo cf-lf	3	0	0	0	1	2	2	0
Mieske lf	2	0	0	0	1	0	5	0
Powell p	0	0	0	0	0	0	0	0
Spiers ph	1	0	1	0	0	0	0	0
Cabrera p	0	0	0	0	0	0	0	1
Bell rf	4	1	1	0	0	1	2	0
Eusebio c	2	0	2	0	1	0	8	0
Barker pr-cf	0	1	0	0	0	0	1	0
Bogar ss	4	0	1	1	0	0	0	1
Elarton p	1	0	0	0	0	0	0	1
Berkman ph	1	0	0	0	0	0	0	0
Knorr c	1	0	0	0	0	1	2	0
Totals	31	2	8	2	5	6	27	6

BATTING
2B: Bagwell (18, off Thompson)
SH: Elarton (1, off Thompson)

BASERUNNING
SB: Barker (12 2nd base off Brocail/Haselman)

PITCHING

Detroit Tigers	IP	H	HR	R	ER	BB	K
Thompson	7	6	0	1	1	3	3
Brocail L (2–3)	1.2	2	0	1	1	2	3
Totals	8.2	8	0	2	2	5	6

Houston Astros	IP	H	HR	R	ER	BB	K
Elarton	7	3	1	1	1	1	8
Powell	1	1	0	0	0	0	2
Cabrera W (2–0)	1	0	0	0	0	1	0
Totals	9	4	1	1	1	2	10

Umpires: Charlie Williams, Greg Bonin, Frank Pulli, Ed Rapuano
Time of Game: 2:48   Attendance: 36541

Craig Biggio
Born: December 14, 1965
Debut: June 26, 1988

On the one hand, Craig Biggio has stayed put in his career. Through 2004, he's played 2,409 games, all with the team that drafted him, the Houston Astros. On the other hand, Biggio's been (to borrow Steve Martin's late-seventies phrase) a "ramblin' guy." He broke in as a catcher, and after making the All-Star team at that position, he made it again at second base (six times) before being pinballed to center field and, ultimately, left.

Like his longtime Astros running mate, Jeff Bagwell, Biggio had to deal with a multitude of postseason failures heading into 2004. Biggio's career playoff batting average was .130 with just one lonely RBI in 61 trips to the plate, all of that scarring an otherwise gorgeous body of work. Through 2004, Biggio had stolen 400 bases and hit close to 250 home runs. He led the National League in doubles three times and in runs scored twice, including a whopping 146 in 1997.

Although he's only had one 200-hit season, his career bating average of .290 has made him a steady and trustworthy member of the National League's upper crust. Although he's been a magnet for getting drilled (257 HBP in a 17-year career), Biggio has rarely missed more than a handful of games each season. Having shifted from catcher to save his knees, Biggio sprinted through the 1997 season without hitting into a single double play, playing all 162 games. (Naturally, in his very first at bat of the following season, he rapped into a 6-4-3.)

A standout wrestler in his high school days, he gave up the sport because, in his words, "There's no running in wrestling." He was also a football quarterback who scrambled so much he was eventually turned into a running back and recruited by Penn State. The choice to play baseball has served him (and the Houston community) well.

I was in Triple-A and my mom was visiting at the time. My manager was Bob Didier, and that one day, I happened to be playing left field, which I had never played. Funny, 16 years later, I'd be asked to move there permanently, but back then I was a catcher and just happened to be playing left the day Didier told me. He said, "Congrats, you're going to Houston." My mom was still sitting in the seats right next to the dugout, so I ran back out there and was able to tell her, just seconds after I had gotten the news myself. I had signed

16

in '87; I'm going to the big leagues in '88. We were pretty happy about that. No flights out of Tucson that night, so my mom and I had dinner, celebrated, I called a lot of people, and tried to sleep but just couldn't do it.

[Houston manager] Hal Lanier asked me the next day when I got to the Astrodome if I was ready to play. And even though I'd only had a couple hours sleep, I said absolutely. So he put me in there, catching Jim Deshaies. San Francisco was who we played . . . and a few days later, I got my first hit when we played L.A. It was off Orel Hershiser. Not bad.

Also on June 26, 1988

A boffo first weekend at the box office closes for the animated/live action crossover *Who Framed Roger Rabbit*.

AUTHOR'S NOTE: A very different kind of Roger would finally lead Biggio's Astros to a postseason series win 16 years later. Clemens, along with Oswalt, Backe, and Lidge, pitched his heart out for Houston, but the Astros fell to St. Louis in the LCS, four games to three.

BOXSCORE

Houston Astros 6, San Francisco Giants 0
Game Played on Sunday, June 26, 1988 (Day) at Astrodome

San Francisco	0	0	0	0	0	0	0	0	0	—	0	7	2
Houston	1	4	0	1	0	0	0	0	x	—	6	3	0

BATTING

San Francisco Giants	AB	R	H	RBI	BB	K	PO	A
Butler cf	3	0	0	0	0	0	3	0
Youngblood ph	1	0	0	0	0	1	0	0
Price p	0	0	0	0	0	0	0	0
Thompson 2b	4	0	1	0	0	1	0	2
Clark 1b	4	0	1	0	0	0	6	0
Maldonado rf	3	0	0	0	1	1	0	0
Mitchell 3b	2	0	0	0	0	0	0	1
Garrelts p	0	0	0	0	0	0	0	0
Nixon ph-cf	1	0	0	0	1	1	2	0
Aldrete lf	4	0	3	0	0	0	1	0
Uribe ss	4	0	2	0	0	0	2	2
Manwaring c	3	0	0	0	0	2	7	1
Riles ph	1	0	0	0	0	1	0	0
LaCoss p	0	0	0	0	0	0	0	1
Bockus p	1	0	0	0	0	0	0	1
Speier 3b	1	0	0	0	2	0	2	0
Totals	32	0	7	0	4	7	24	8

FIELDING
E: Uribe (8), Manwaring (3)

BATTING
2B: Uribe (4, off Deshaies); Aldrete (8, off Deshaies)

BASERUNNING
CS: Uribe (6, 3rd base by Deshaies/Biggio)

Houston Astros	AB	R	H	RBI	BB	K	PO	A
Young cf	2	2	1	1	2	0	4	0
Hatcher lf	2	0	0	1	1	0	4	0
Doran 2b	4	0	1	3	0	1	2	3
Davis 1b	4	0	0	0	0	0	6	1
Bass rf	3	1	0	0	1	1	2	0
Reynolds 3b	4	0	0	0	0	1	1	1
Ramirez ss	4	1	1	1	0	2	0	1
Biggio c	2	1	0	0	1	1	7	1
Deshaies p	2	1	0	0	1	1	1	0
Andersen p	0	0	0	0	0	0	0	0
Totals	27	6	3	6	6	7	27	7

FIELDING
DP: 1

BATTING
HBP: Hatcher (4, by Bockus)

BASERUNNING
SB: Young 2 (43, 2nd base off LaCoss/Manwaring 2); Bass (19, 2nd base off LaCoss/Manwaring); Biggio (1, 2nd base off Bockus/Manwaring)
CS: Hatcher (12, Home by Bockus/Manwaring)

PITCHING

San Francisco Giants	IP	H	HR	R	ER	BB	K
LaCoss L (5–6)	1.2	2	0	5	4	4	0
Bockus	1.2	1	0	1	0	2	1
Garrelts	2.2	0	0	0	0	0	4
Price	2	0	0	0	0	0	2
Totals	8	3	0	6	4	6	7
Houston Astros	IP	H	HR	R	ER	BB	K
Deshaies W (5–5)	6.2	5	0	0	0	4	3
Andersen	2.1	2	0	0	0	0	4
Totals	9.0	7	0	0	0	4	7

WP: LaCoss (5)
HBP: Bockus (1, Hatcher)
Umpires: Jerry Crawford, Bob Davidson, Doug Harvey, Frank Pulli
Time of Game: 2:47   Attendance: 25,754

Hank Blalock
Born: November 21, 1980
Debut: April 1, 2002

He is blessed with a perfect, tough guy baseball name. The anti-Juan Eichelberger and anti-Van Lingle Mungo may be the Rangers' Hank Joe Blalock. (Not Henry Joseph Blalock—he was christened, by a tough guy baseball father, "Hank Joe." His younger brother, a Phillies prospect, is named Jake Willie.) It is a name perfect for no-nonsense North Texas baseball fans, who appreciate players who simply shut up and play hard. Could he have been destined, by name, for the Metroplex? Note that he was born the night we all learned who shot JR on the TV drama *Dallas*.

The blond-haired Californian got out slowly with the Rangers, going 2-for-30 at the age of 21 to begin his career. After a couple of trips back to Triple-A, he reemerged for good in 2003, blistering his way through spring training and into the All-Star Game, where he swung World Series home-field advantage for the AL by homering off Eric Gagne in Chicago.

He cemented his stature as a Texas tough guy in August, 2004. Stuck in a 21-for-135 slump, the lefty learned just before game time that his wife was headed to the hospital, in labor with the couple's first child. Insisting on playing before leaving to join her, Blalock rammed a double off the right-center wall in his first at bat, then homered in each of his next two trips to the plate—his first two homers in 42 days. He lined to the warning track in his final at bat, narrowly missing his fourth extra-base hit of the game, then rushed to the hospital in time to witness the birth.

Although the stats will never quite compare, a brush cut left-handed power hitter who hails from San Diego and wears number nine also roamed Arlington, Texas, when the Rangers first relocated from Washington: Texas's first manager was none other than Ted Williams. "I think Ted would have liked the way Hank approaches the game," says Ranger broadcaster Tom Grieve. "When I played for Ted, as long as you cared about working on your hitting, you were in good standing. And there are few players who work harder on their hitting than Hank Blalock." His hard work paid off in 2004, with his second consecutive trip to the All-Star Game and a team-high 38 doubles. He made just two errors in his first 49 games at third and ended up logging more innings at that position than any other player in baseball. With 32 home runs and 110 RBI at the age of 24—and signed through 2009—he will continue a tradition of popular blond-haired Ranger third basemen (Buddy Bell, Steve Buechele) whose last names start with "B" and whose bats are capable of greatness.

It was a cool, foggy morning in the Bay area. I woke up, I ate breakfast, I faced Mark Mulder. How's that? My dad was there, and that was the best part . . . He worked awfully hard, he and my uncle both, to make sure I was prepared as possible for my career . . . It meant a lot that they were there to see that first game. The first thing I did when I signed my [five-year] contract was I called my dad and told him he only has to work now if he wants to and when he wants to. My family gave up a lot for me and my brother, and the least I can do is give back to them. When I singled off Mulder, up the middle, first at bat, I know those guys were proud. I'll be there for my son's big league debut someday too.

Also on April 1, 2002
An 1897 Michigan law against swearing in front of women and children is declared unconstitutional.

AUTHOR'S NOTE: After the birth of his son, Trey, Blalock promised he'd do his level best to clean up his language, regardless of constitutionality.

BOXSCORE

Oakland Athletics 8, Texas Rangers 3
Game Played on Monday, April 1, 2002 (Night) at Network Associates Coliseum

Texas	0	0	1	0	0	0	0	0	2	—	3	7	0
Oakland	0	1	3	0	0	4	0	0	x	—	8	13	0

BATTING

Texas Rangers	AB	R	H	RBI	BB	K	PO	A
Catalanotto dh	4	1	1	0	0	1	0	0
Everett cf	4	1	1	2	0	0	1	0
A. Rodriguez ss	4	0	0	0	0	0	3	4
Gonzalez rf	4	0	2	0	0	1	1	0
Palmeiro 1b	4	0	0	0	0	2	8	1
I. Rodriguez c	3	0	0	0	0	0	6	0
Haselman c	0	0	0	0	0	0	0	0
Kapler lf	3	1	2	0	0	0	3	0
Blalock 3b	3	0	1	1	0	2	0	2
Young 2b	3	0	0	0	0	2	1	4
Park p	0	0	0	0	0	0	1	0
Van Poppel p	0	0	0	0	0	0	0	0
R. Rodriguez p	0	0	0	0	0	0	0	0
Lewis p	0	0	0	0	0	0	0	0
Woodard p	0	0	0	0	0	0	0	0
Totals	32	3	7	3	0	8	24	11

FIELDING
DP: 2

BATTING
2B: Kapler (1, off Mulder); Catalanotto (1, off Mulder)
HR: Everett (1, 9th inning off Mulder, 1 on, 0 out)

Oakland Athletics	AB	R	H	RBI	BB	K	PO	A
Giambi lf	4	1	3	1	0	0	0	0
Colangelo pr-lf	1	0	0	0	0	0	0	0
Velarde 2b	0	0	0	0	0	0	0	1
Menechino 2b	2	1	2	1	1	0	0	1
Hatteberg dh	4	0	0	0	0	0	0	0
Justice rf	4	2	3	2	0	0	3	0
Chavez 3b	4	2	2	2	0	1	0	3
Tejada ss	4	1	1	1	0	1	2	3
Long cf	4	1	1	1	0	1	3	0
Hernandez c	4	0	1	0	0	1	9	1
Pena 1b	4	0	0	0	0	2	10	0
Mulder p	0	0	0	0	0	0	0	1
Bradford p	0	0	0	0	0	0	0	0
Totals	35	8	13	8	1	6	27	10

FIELDING
DP: 2

BATTING
2B: Hernandez (1, off Park); Menechino (1, off Park); Chavez (1, off Park); Tejada (1, off Van Poppel)
HR: Chavez (1, 2nd inning off Park, 0 on, 0 out); Justice (1, 3rd inning off Park, 1 on, 1 out)
HBP: Velarde (1, by Park)

PITCHING

Texas Rangers	IP	H	HR	R	ER	BB	K
Park L (0–1)	5	9	2	6	6	0	5
Van Poppel	0.1	2	0	2	2	0	1
R. Rodriguez	0.1	1	0	0	0	0	0
Lewis	1.1	1	0	0	0	1	0
Woodard	1	0	0	0	0	0	0
Totals	8	13	2	8	8	1	6

Oakland Athletics	IP	H	HR	R	ER	BB	K
Mulder W (1–0)	8	6	1	3	3	0	8
Bradford	1	1	0	0	0	0	0
Totals	9	7	1	3	3	0	8

WP: Lewis (1)
HBP: Park (1, Velarde)
Umpires: Rick Reed, Tim Tschida, Mark Wegner, Bill Welke
Time of Game: 2:46   Attendance: 43,908

Barry Bonds
Born: July 24, 1964
Debut: May 30, 1986

There is perhaps no player as talented—and no player as polarizing—as Barry Lamar Bonds. Is he the egotistical, arrogant narcissist the media portray him to be, or is he simply the Dr. Pepper of athletes—"So misunderstood?" Most agree, as one teammate has put it, "Bonds was born on third base and assumed he hit a triple."

There is no denying the presence of a chip on Bonds's shoulder; it may actually be closer in size to an entire sequoia tree. The son of the often-overlooked Bobby Bonds, Barry approaches the game as if he has set out to single-handedly avenge whatever slights his old man suffered. But if indeed he is without many close friends in the game, Bonds is also without peers. His statistics are so staggering that one must travel back in time to find anyone who even somewhat compares. Babe Ruth and Ted Williams may be the only two.

"MVP" hardly seems to be enough to describe what he's been in his thirties—in several seasons, Bonds all but lapped the field. His 2001 included a record 73 home runs. His 2003 included a .341 batting average, 45 more homers and 90 more walks than strikeouts, which actually made it his *worst* season since 2000. The 2004 season was another treasure trove of almost blindingly gaudy stats, featuring his 700th career home run and a record 232 walks against 41 strikeouts. The American League leader in walks that year had 95; Bonds doubled that total before Labor Day. He was walked intentionally 120 times; next most in baseball was 26, bringing into sharp focus how perfectly the man's initials suit him. As it was written in *Sports Illustrated*, Bonds changes baseball's standard rules of engagement. "If baseball's a chess game, Bonds is the only queen on the board, influencing every move with the breadth of his power." The old bromide, "Don't let this guy beat you," has been taken to absurd new heights. One look at the 2004 stat sheet tells you all you need to know. Bonds's record on-base percentage of .609 was a cool 140 points higher than the runner-up. His .812 slugging percentage won out by 155 points. He has been a man—albeit quite possibly a steroid-aided man—among boys.

The taint of the steroid charges will perhaps always be his legacy, which seems a shame, since the man is already a seven-time MVP (and no one else in the history of the sport has won more than three). The specter of the BALCO steroids scandal notwithstanding, the lefty has become Must

See TV every time he leaves the batter's box. Now, if he could only enjoy himself.

Syd Thrift was the Pirates GM, and he was standing there during batting practice being really cryptic. I hit a bunch of balls out to right, and he seemed to like that. Then he said, "You're closer than you think," and I was trying to figure out what he meant. I get in the cage and he says, "I want to see you hit a home run to left." So I did. Then he says, "I want to see you do it in the game." So I did. And I hit one to right, too, in my next at bat. Sixth or seventh inning, I saw Syd come down to the dugout to talk to Tommy Sandt, our manager. So I'm thinking, I guess maybe I am pretty close, if they're talking about me. Sure enough, Tommy Sandt pulled me out of the game at that point and said, "Okay, you're going to the big leagues tomorrow." And Syd was standing there smiling when I looked at him. I went from Phoenix to Pittsburgh, playing with the Hawaii team in Triple-A . . . I got to Pittsburgh but had to sit around for five days waiting for Trench Davis to clear waivers. Syd had a lot of explaining to

Also on May 30, 1986
Eighteen-year-old Juan Gonzalez signs with the Texas Rangers.

AUTHOR'S NOTE: Barry Bonds's first seven seasons in the majors produced 222 home runs and 679 RBI, compared to Gonzalez's first seven full seasons of 296 home runs and 928 RBI. After winning his second MVP in 1998, Gonzalez appeared to be the far superior player. Since 1999 through 2004, however, the breakdown is as follows:
Bonds: 292 HR, 627 RBI, 945 walks
Gonzalez: 133 HR, 457 RBI, 164 walks

BOXSCORE

Los Angeles Dodgers 6, Pittsburgh Pirates 4
Game Played on Friday, May 30, 1986 (Night) at Three Rivers Stadium

Los Angeles	1	3	0	0	0	0	0	0	0	2	—	6	9	1
Pittsburgh	0	0	4	0	0	0	0	0	0	0	—	4	7	1

BATTING

Los Angeles Dodgers	AB	R	H	RBI	BB	K	PO	A
Sax 2b	6	0	3	2	0	0	4	2
Landreaux cf	5	1	1	1	1	1	4	0
Madlock 3b	6	0	0	0	0	1	0	1
Pena p	0	0	0	0	0	0	0	1
Reuss p	0	0	0	0	0	0	0	0
Marshall rf	4	0	2	1	1	0	0	0
Scioscia c	5	0	1	0	0	0	10	1
Brock 1b	3	0	0	0	1	2	5	0
Williams pr-lf	0	1	0	0	0	1	0	0
Stubbs lf-1b	4	2	1	0	0	1	5	0
Duncan ss	3	1	1	0	2	0	5	1
Hershiser p	1	1	0	0	0	0	0	0
Vande Berg p	0	0	0	0	0	0	0	1
Cabell ph	1	0	0	0	0	0	0	0
Howell p	0	0	0	0	0	0	0	0
Matuszek ph	1	0	0	0	0	1	0	0
Niedenfuer p	0	0	0	0	0	0	0	0
Cedeno ph	1	0	0	0	0	1	0	0
Anderson 3b	0	0	0	0	0	0	0	0
Totals	40	6	9	4	6	7	33	7

FIELDING
E: Stubbs (2)

BATTING
2B: Landreaux (7, off Bielecki)
SH: Hershiser (4, off Bielecki)
HBP: Stubbs (1, by DeLeon)

BASERUNNING
SB: Sax (5, 2nd base off Bielecki/T. Pena); Duncan (21, 2nd base off Guante/T. Pena); Williams (1, 2nd base off DeLeon/Ortiz); Stubbs (3, 2nd base off DeLeon/Ortiz).
CS: Sax (6, 2nd base by Bielecki/T. Pena)

Pittsburgh Pirates	AB	R	H	RBI	BB	K	PO	A
Bonds cf	5	0	0	0	1	3	4	0
Orsulak rf	3	0	0	0	1	0	0	0
Winn p	0	0	0	0	0	0	0	0
Diaz ph	1	0	0	0	0	0	0	0
Guante p	0	0	0	0	0	0	0	0
Brown ph	1	0	0	0	0	1	0	0
DeLeon p	0	0	0	0	0	0	0	0
Clements p	0	0	0	0	0	0	0	0
Rhoden ph	1	0	0	0	0	0	0	0
Ray 2b	5	1	3	0	0	0	0	3
Reuschel pr	0	0	0	0	0	0	1	0
Ortizc	0	0	0	0	1	0	1	0
Bream 1b-lf	4	1	1	0	2	1	12	1
Reynolds lf-rf	5	1	1	0	0	1	5	0
T. Pena c-1b	3	1	0	1	2	0	6	1
Morrison 3b	2	0	0	1	3	0	0	2
Belliard ss	1	0	0	0	0	1	4	4
Mazzilli ph-lf	3	0	0	0	0	1	0	0
Khalifa ss-2b	1	0	0	0	0	0	2	1
Bielecki p	1	0	0	0	0	1	0	1
Almon ph-ss-lf-ss	3	0	2	2	1	1	2	3
Totals	39	4	7	4	10	10	33	16

FIELDING
DP: 1.
E: Bream (6)

BATTING
2B: Ray (14, off Niedenfuer)
IBB: Bream (3, by Niedenfuer); Morrison (2, by Niedenfuer)

BASERUNNING
SB: Almon (3, 2nd base off Pena/Scioscia)
CS: Bream (2, 2nd base by Vande Berg/Scioscia)

PITCHING

Los Angeles Dodgers	IP	H	HR	R	ER	BB	K
Hershiser	3.1	4	0	4	4	4	3
Vande Berg	2.2	1	0	0	0	2	2
Howell	2	1	0	0	0	0	1
Niedenfuer W (3–2)	2	1	0	0	0	2	3
Pena	0.2	0	0	0	0	2	1
Reuss SV (1)	0.1	0	0	0	0	0	0
Totals	11.0	7	0	4	4	10	10

Pittsburgh Pirates	IP	H	HR	R	ER	BB	K
Bielecki	4	6	0	4	3	1	1
Winn	3	1	0	0	0	0	4
Guante	2	1	0	0	0	2	1
DeLeon L (1–2)	1.2	1	0	2	2	2	1
Clements	0.1	0	0	0	0	1	0
Totals	11.0	9	0	6	5	6	7

WP: Pena (1), DeLeon (1)
HBP: DeLeon (1, Stubbs)
IBB: Niedenfuer 2 (8, Bream, Morrison)
Umpires: Dutch Rennert, Fred Brocklander, Ed Montague, Lee Weyer
Time of Game: 2:16   Attendance: 25,320

the media to do about that. My plane ticket was the 25th. I was in uniform on the 30th.

When I got in that game on the 30th, my dad drove over to see it from Cleveland. He was the Indians hitting coach, and Pat Corrales told him to go ahead and get on over there to see his son play. I know my dad wouldn't have missed it.

I went 0-for-5 with three punch-outs, playing center field. Extra inning game, we lost. I faced Orel Hershiser and he threw a lot of stuff off the plate, but they were called strikes. I knew to get up there hacking, but the couple that I took, sure enough they were strikes if they were or not. I was wearing number seven then, I remember . . . I wanted number 24, but some other dude [Denny Gonzalez] had it. As soon as they released him, I grabbed it.

Courtesy Pittsburgh Pirates

Bret Boone
Born: April 6, 1969
Debut: August 19, 1992

If you're looking for the poster child for the old "Love him if he's your teammate/hate him if he's not" cliché, look no further than Bret Boone. Aggressive and always looking for an extra edge, Boone has sometimes rubbed opponents the wrong way with his "flair." This is especially evident after he hits a home run and engages in what's come to be known as the "Boonie Bat Flip," whereby his lumber is summarily discarded like a used tooth pick as he begins a leisurely home run trot.

There's no denying his on-field success, however. Boone had an unworldly 2001 season (.331 with 141 RBI and an AL-record 36 homers as a second baseman). The following year, his offensive numbers dipped, but he won the second of his three Gold Gloves.

A third-generation major leaguer, Boone broke in with the Mariners in 1992, was peddled to Cincinnati soon after, then, after forgettable seasons in Atlanta and San Diego, reunited with his ex-Reds skipper, Lou Piniella, back in Seattle. While Piniella left for Tampa Bay after the 2003 season, Boone stayed behind and slowly watched the Mariners crumble around him. Despite the presence of Boone, Ichiro, and Edgar Martinez, the M's went from 93 wins in 2002 down to 63 by 2004.

As the Mariners have faded lately, Boone at least has one World Series experience from which to draw; he was 7-for-13 for the Braves when they lost to the Yankees in '99. More recently, the slugging second baseman has watched brother Aaron homer his way into the World Series (see the 2003 ALCS). In fact, Bret had the best seat in the house for that blessed event, as a guest color commentator on FOX's national telecast.

I was in Triple-A and got a base hit to right field and a guy came out to pinch-run for me. I asked him what he was doing out there, and he said pinch-running, and I said, "No way, I'm not coming out." He said, "Skip [manager Keith Bodie] told me you were." I said, "No. Go back." So Bodie comes out and tells me, "Hey, I told him to come out for you, let's go." So I ask why, and he says, "You didn't hustle to first." And I'm like, "What? Did too!" "Did not." "Did too!" We're standing there at first base, arguing with each other in front of everybody. He says, "You're out of the game. I'm the manager, you're the player. I didn't think you were hustling, so you're sitting down, that's it." I was

BOXSCORE

Seattle Mariners 10, Baltimore Orioles 8

Game Played on Wednesday, August 19, 1992 (Night) at Oriole Park at Camden Yards

Seattle	0	3	0	4	0	2	1	0	0	—	10	12	0
Baltimore	2	0	0	1	0	3	2	0	0	—	8	12	1

BATTING

Seattle Mariners	AB	R	H	RBI	BB	K	PO	A
Cotto lf	4	2	3	2	1	1	5	0
E. Martinez 3b	5	2	3	4	0	0	0	2
Griffey cf	5	0	1	1	0	3	2	0
Parrish dh	4	0	1	0	0	2	0	0
O'Brien ph-dh	1	0	0	0	0	0	0	0
Buhner rf	4	1	1	0	1	2	3	0
T. Martinez 1b	4	2	1	1	1	2	8	1
Boone 2b	4	2	1	1	1	1	2	3
Valle c	2	1	0	0	1	0	5	0
Vizquel ss	3	0	1	0	0	0	2	5
Grant p	0	0	0	0	0	0	0	0
Jones p	0	0	0	0	0	0	0	0
Schooler p	0	0	0	0	0	0	0	0
Swan p	0	0	0	0	0	0	0	0
Totals	36	10	12	9	5	11	27	11

FIELDING

DP: 3

BATTING

2B: E. Martinez (37, off Rhodes); Cotto (8, off Rhodes); Parrish (6, off Rhodes); Griffey (30, off Mills)
HR: E. Martinez (16, 4th inning off Frohwirth, 3 on, 1 out); T. Martinez (10,7th inning off Mills, 0 on, 2 out)
SH: Valle (6, off Rhodes); Vizquel (7, off Rhodes)

BASERUNNING

SB: Cotto (16, 2nd base off Mills/Hoiles)

Baltimore Orioles	AB	R	H	RBI	BB	K	PO	A
Anderson lf	3	2	2	3	2	0	1	0
Devereaux cf	4	1	1	2	1	1	0	0
C. Ripken ss	5	0	1	0	0	0	2	4
G. Davis dh	5	0	0	0	0	0	0	0
Milligan 1b	5	0	2	0	0	2	8	0
C. Martinez rf	3	3	2	0	1	0	1	1
Gomez 3b	4	1	1	2	0	1	1	2
Hoiles c4	0	0	0	1	1	0	1	1
B. Ripken 2b	2	1	1	1	1	0	4	2
Segui ph	1	0	1	0	0	0	0	0
Hulett 2b	0	0	0	0	0	0	0	0
Rhodes p	0	0	0	0	0	0	0	2
Frohwirth p	0	0	0	0	0	0	0	0
Mills p	0	0	0	0	0	0	0	0
Flanagan p	0	0	0	0	0	0	0	0
Olson p	0	0	0	0	0	0	0	0
Totals	36	8	12	8	5	5	27	12

FIELDING

DP: 1
E: Martinez (2)

BATTING

2B: Martinez (7, off Grant); B. Ripken (14, off Grant)
HR: Devereaux (18, 1st inning off Grant, 0 on, 0 out); Anderson (17, 6th inning off Grant, 1 on, 2 out); Gomez (15, 7th inning off Jones, 1 on, 2 out)
HBP: Martinez (2, by Grant)

PITCHING

Seattle Mariners	IP	H	HR	R	ER	BB	K
Grant W (2–3)	5.2	9	2	6	6	3	3
Jones	1	1	1	2	2	2	1
Schooler	0.1	1	0	0	0	0	0
Swan SV (9)	2	1	0	0	0	0	1
Totals	9	12	3	8	8	5	5
Baltimore Orioles	**IP**	**H**	**HR**	**R**	**ER**	**BB**	**K**
Rhodes L (4–3)	3.1	5	0	6	6	4	4
Frohwirth	0	1	1	1	1	0	0
Mills	3.2	3	1	3	1	1	5
Flanagan	0.2	3	0	0	0	0	0
Olson	1.1	0	0	0	0	0	1
Totals	9.0	12	2	10	8	5	11

WP: Rhodes (2)
HBP: Grant (2, Martinez)
Umpires: Larry Barnett, Greg Kosc, Dale Ford, Al Clark
Time of Game: 3:34   Attendance: 41,149

pissed. I threw my helmet down and stormed off the field, and he kept a straight face the whole time. He comes back to the dugout and tells me why I was really coming out—because I was headed to Baltimore to meet up with the Mariners. The whole bench had been in on it, and they just busted up laughing.

So I called my folks, let 'em know, and it was off to Baltimore. My fiancée, my grandpa, everyone was real happy. Getting to Camden Yards, I can honestly say it was a much different feeling walking into a big league ballpark as a player as opposed to a coach's or player's kid. I wasn't really nervous, though. It felt right. There was a lot of media attention though. I was nervous in the field, actually. Not at the plate. I wasn't worried about a getting a hit—I did. Against Arthur Rhodes, who would become my teammate a few years later. What I didn't want to do was to screw up a double play ball. And sure enough, last play of the game—double-play ball right to me, but we turned it and won the game. I think it was 10–8.

Also on August 19, 1992
The third night of the Republican National Convention in Houston is family values night, featuring first lady Barbara Bush and Marilyn Quayle, wife of Vice President Quayle, as speakers.

AUTHOR'S NOTE: The Boone family's value to baseball is impeccable—with Bret's debut, the Boones became the first three-generation big league family, with father Bob having played 1972 through 1990 and grandfather Ray having played from 1948 through 1960.

Bob Brenly
Born: February 25, 1954
Debut: August 14, 1981

A dead ringer for Pittsburgh Steelers coach Bill Cowher, family man Bob Brenly enjoyed a nine-year big league playing career but struck gold as manager of the world champion Arizona Diamondbacks in 2001. Second-guessed in virtually every game of the series against the Yankees, he was ultimately vindicated when the Snakes rallied past Mariano Rivera with two in the ninth in Game Seven. He became just the fourth skipper with no prior managerial experience to win a World Series, the first since Ralph Houk in 1961.

Brenly had gone to the dugout from the broadcast booth when Arizona fired Buck Showalter after the 2000 season. Once Brenly was fired himself in 2004, he went back to the booth for FOX, where he had buoyed the network's baseball coverage from 1996 to 2000.

A guitar and motorcycle enthusiast, Brenly best exemplified baseball's ups and downs by his performance in a 1986 game against Atlanta. In the fourth inning, Brenly tied a big league record, committing four errors (three fielding, one throwing). However, he also collected four RBI in the game, including the game-ending, game-winning home run. His best all-around season had come two years earlier, with a .291 average, 20 home runs, and an invitation to play in the All-Star Game in the Giants' home ballpark.

They pretty much closed down my hometown of Coshocton, Ohio, because I think everyone made the two-hour drive down to Riverfront Stadium in Cincinnati. All my family, friends, college buddies, friends I didn't know I had, they all showed up for the game. First at bat, I got jammed badly and grounded out. It was my third at bat when I finally got a hit off a guy named Scott Brown. Mike LaCoss started and kept carving me up, throwing me sinkers in on my knuckles, but then Brown left one over the plate, and I hit it into center field. Big reaction! Not a big crowd that night, so you could really hear all those people from Coshocton.

I had come up immediately after the strike was settled in '81. Frank Robinson, the Giants manager, and Tom Haller, our GM, had come to watch the Triple-A Phoenix team play for a week during the strike, and it coincided with probably the hottest week I ever had in the minor leagues.

So here's how I found out I was going up: My mom, my aunt, and uncle

BOXSCORE

Cincinnati Reds 7, San Francisco Giants 6
(Game 2 of a Doubleheader)

Game Played on Friday, August 14, 1981 (Night) at Riverfront Stadium

San Francisco	2	1	0	0	0	0	3	0	0	0	—	6	16	2
Cincinnati	0	0	3	2	0	0	1	0	0	1	—	7	10	0

BATTING

San Francisco Giants	AB	R	H	RBI	BB	K	PO	A
Morgan 2b	5	1	2	0	1	0	4	5
Minton p	0	0	0	0	0	0	0	0
Bergman 1b	4	1	3	0	0	0	12	0
Stennett ph	1	0	0	0	0	0	0	0
Holland p	0	0	0	0	0	0	0	1
Pettini 2b	0	0	0	0	0	0	0	0
Clark rf	4	2	2	1	0	0	2	0
Evans 3b	4	1	2	2	0	0	2	4
Leonard lf	5	0	3	3	0	0	1	1
Martin cf	4	0	1	0	0	2	0	0
Brenly c	5	0	1	0	0	1	6	2
LeMaster ss	5	1	2	0	0	0	1	2
Ripley p	1	0	0	0	0	0	0	0
Breining p	1	0	0	0	0	1	0	1
Cabell ph-1b	2	0	0	0	0	1	1	0
Totals	41	6	16	6	1	5	29	17

FIELDING

E: Evans (10), LeMaster (6)

BATTING

2B: Clark (10, off LaCoss); Evans (8, off LaCoss)
SH: Ripley (2, off LaCoss)
SF: Evans (3, off LaCoss); Clark (2, off LaCoss).
HBP: Martin (3, by LaCoss)

Cincinnati Reds	AB	R	H	RBI	BB	K	PO	A
Collins rf	4	1	1	0	0	0	4	1
Oester 2b	5	1	2	0	0	1	0	4
Concepcion ss	4	0	0	0	0	2	3	2
Foster lf	4	2	2	3	0	0	6	0
Driessen 1b	2	0	0	0	1	0	6	0
Biittner 1b	1	0	0	0	1	0	3	0
Knight 3b	4	1	1	0	0	1	0	2
Mejias cf	5	1	3	1	0	0	2	0
O'Berry c	4	0	1	1	0	1	6	0
LaCoss p	2	0	0	0	0	0	0	0
Brown p	0	0	0	0	0	0	0	0
Griffey ph	0	1	0	0	1	0	0	0
Price p	0	0	0	0	0	0	0	0
Landestoy ph	1	0	0	0	0	0	0	0
Hume p	0	0	0	0	0	0	0	0
Totals	36	7	10	5	4	5	30	9

FIELDING

DP: 2

BATTING

2B: Mejias (2, off Ripley); Collins (13, off Ripley); Knight (11, off Ripley); O'Berry (2, off Ripley)
HR: Foster (16, 3rd inning off Ripley, 2 on, 2 out)
SH: Collins (2, off Breining); Knight (3, off Holland)
HBP: Concepcion (1, by Holland)
IBB: Foster (4, by Holland)

BASERUNNING

SB: Concepcion (3, 2nd base off Holland/Brenly)
CS: Driessen (2, 2nd base by Breining/Brenly)

PITCHING

San Francisco Giants	IP	H	HR	R	ER	BB	K
Ripley	4	7	1	5	4	0	1
Breining	3	2	0	1	0	2	2
Holland L (3–4)	2.1	0	0	1	1	2	2
Minton	0.1	1	0	0	0	0	0
Totals	9.2	10	1	7	5	4	5
Cincinnati Reds	IP	H	HR	R	ER	BB	K
LaCoss	6	12	0	6	6	1	4
Brown	1	2	0	0	0	0	0
Price	2	2	0	0	0	0	1
Hume W (5–2)	1	0	0	0	0	0	0
Totals	10	16	0	6	6	1	5

HBP: Holland (2, Concepcion); LaCoss (1, Martin)
IBB: Holland (4, Foster)
Umpires: Steve Fields, Doug Harvey, Eric Gregg, Nick Colosi
Time of Game: 3:13   Attendance: 22,404

were all out visiting me in Phoenix, and on a scheduled off-day, we took a trip up to the Grand Canyon. My wife and I took them up, drove up, spending the whole day at the Grand Canyon. Driving back, we picked up a Phoenix station, and the announcer was saying, "Two of our local boys got called up to the Giants today—pitcher Bob Tufts and catcher Bob Brenly." In the car, we all looked at each other, trying to figure out if we really just heard what we thought we heard. I pulled over and called [Phoenix manager] Rocky Bridges from a pay phone, and he says, "Where the hell have *you* been? Get your ass to San Francisco!"

Well, then the adventure really started. My wife and I had been given permission to drive to San Francisco, so we get in our '77 Dodge van, and it breaks down about 50 miles outside the Bay Area. I babbled to the policemen that came up on us, stranded at the side of the highway, that I had been called up by the Giants and had to get to San Francisco right away. Luckily, they were fans, and asked, "Are you the pitcher or the catcher?" They pushed the van up the ramp to a gas station, helped me get a guy to fix the alternator, and I finally got in at 8 A.M. for a 10 A.M. workout on pure adrenaline.

Also on August 14, 1981

Mike Schmidt connects for his 300th career home run as the Phillies beat up on the Mets, 8–4.

AUTHOR'S NOTE: In college, Schmidt held the Ohio University record for home runs in single season—that is, until the record was tied in '76 by Bob Brenly.

George Brett
Born: May 15, 1953
Debut: August 2, 1973

If Major League Baseball had a high school yearbook, George Brett may have perennially been voted "Most Popular." The blue-eyed, perpetually tan Californian took little time before charming Kansas Citians off their collective feet. Within 30 years and 3,000 hits of his debut, he would have his name on car dealerships, restaurants (try the burgers), and even bridges (the one that runs by Kaufmann Stadium is named in his honor).

Brett, to this day, comes across as a big, friendly puppy, occasionally doing something harmlessly goofy. When he retired, he went to work in the Royals front office, announcing to the media that his title was "Vice President of Deferred Payment." A brief stint in the FOX Game-of-the-Week broadcast booth saw him freak out producers by showing up for meetings with fake "Billy Bob" teeth in his mouth, then getting flummoxed on-air when the producer would try to talk to him in his earpiece. (Producer, off-air: "Hey, George?" Brett, on-air: "Hey, what's up?")

Displaying quick, self-deprecating wit, he charmed the national media during the summer of 1980 as he chased the elusive .400 batting average (he finished at .390 with a late slump). This was just a couple years after he was forced to miss playoff games due to, um, something for which Preparation H is very good. (Reporter's question: "George, will you play with your hemorrhoids?" Brett: "Frankly, sir, it's none of your business what I do with my hemorrhoids.") Brett will also be forever remembered for the "Pine Tar Home Run" at Yankee Stadium in 1983, a game that was successfully protested and saw Brett perform a flip-out for the ages.

Mostly, Brett will be remembered as one of the two greatest third basemen of all-time. Through the '70s and '80s the debate raged: Who was best, Brett or Mike Schmidt? It probably comes down to a matter of geography: If you grew up anywhere close to Kansas City, the popular, people's choice is the blond-haired slugger with the twinkle in his eye—and the bridge in his name.

I was in my apartment in Omaha that I shared with Mark Littell and Buck Martinez. There was a knock on our door, and it was our manager, Harry Malmberg. He said, "One of you guys is getting called up," and Buck and I both figured it was Littell. We were both wrong. Paul Schaal had sprained an ankle, so they needed an infielder for a couple weeks up in Kansas City . . . I was told I'd just be there as insurance, that I wouldn't be playing.

27

BOXSCORE

Kansas City Royals 3, Chicago White Sox 1

Game Played on Thursday, August 2, 1973 (Night) at Comiskey Park

Kansas City	2	0	0	0	0	0	0	1	—	3	8	0
Chicago	0	0	1	0	0	0	0	0	0	—	1	9	2

BATTING

Kansas City Royals	AB	R	H	RBI	BB	K	PO	A
Patek ss	3	1	0	0	1	0	7	1
Rojas 2b	4	0	3	0	0	0	4	5
Otis cf	4	1	1	1	0	0	3	0
Mayberry 1b	2	0	1	0	2	0	4	1
Hopkins dh	4	0	0	0	0	1	0	0
Piniella lf	4	1	1	0	0	1	0	0
Kirkpatrick rf	3	0	0	0	0	0	2	0
Brett 3b	4	0	1	0	0	1	2	1
Healy c	4	0	1	1	0	1	3	1
Drago p	0	0	0	0	0	0	1	0
Garber p	0	0	0	0	0	0	1	4
Totals	32	3	8	2	3	4	27	13

FIELDING

DP: 2

BATTING

SH: Kirkpatrick (3, off Bahnsen)

Chicago White Sox	AB	R	H	RBI	BB	K	PO	A
Kelly rf	4	0	2	0	0	0	0	0
Orta 2b	4	0	1	0	0	1	3	4
Hairston lf	4	0	2	0	0	2	3	0
Melton 3b	4	0	1	0	0	0	0	2
May dh	3	0	1	0	0	0	0	0
Jeter pr-dh	1	0	0	0	0	0	0	0
Bradford cf	3	0	0	0	0	0	2	0
D. Allen ph	1	0	0	0	0	0	0	0
Muser 1b	3	0	1	0	0	0	11	1
Alvarado ss	2	1	1	0	0	0	2	5
Henderson ph	1	0	0	0	0	0	0	0
Leon ss	0	0	0	0	0	0	1	1
Herrmann c	2	0	0	1	0	0	4	0
Bahnsen p	0	0	0	0	0	0	1	2
Totals	32	1	9	1	0	3	27	15

FIELDING

DP: 2

E: Melton (17), Leon (16)

BATTING

2B: Muser (9, off Drago)
3B: Alvarado (2, off Drago)
SF: Herrmann (5, off Drago)

BASERUNNING

SB: Melton (1, 2nd base off Drago/Healy)
CS: Kelly (11, 2nd base by Drago/Healy)

PITCHING

Kansas City Royals	IP	H	HR	R	ER	BB	K
Drago W (12–10)	5	6	0	1	1	0	2
Garber SV (10)	4	3	0	0	0	0	1
Totals	9	9	0	1	1	0	3
Chicago White Sox	**IP**	**H**	**HR**	**R**	**ER**	**BB**	**K**
Bahnsen L (14–11)	9	8	0	3	2	3	4

Umpires: Red Flaherty, Bill Deegan, Marty Springstead, Bill Kunkel
Time of Game: 2:28   Attendance: 11,775

I flew to Chicago where the Royals were playing the White Sox. Low-key flight, low-key cab ride. Really, no nerves. I get there, six o'clock, batting practice is going on, and I walk into the clubhouse and check the bulletin board, and my name is in the starting lineup. Not so low-key anymore. In fact, I suddenly had to go to the bathroom really bad. I went at least twice before the game—the sit-down kind. My nerves had shown up pretty good.

At 20 years old, you can imagine, I was pretty fired up. Kemmer [brother Ken] had already made it, so the family had already been through the thrill of a Brett in the big leagues . . . But they were happy for me, too. I remember I batted in front of Fran Healy, and the White Sox had Stan Bahnsen on the mound. I ended up 1-for-4, and the guys took me out on the town that night. I know, I was only 20, but the drinking age then was 18! Joe Hoerner was a pitcher on that team, and he really took me under his wing. Until the day he died, I sent him a Father's Day card every year. That's how much he meant to me, making a 20-year-old kid feel like he belonged. I'll never forget or repay his kindness.

Also on August 2, 1973
The cover of *Rolling Stone* hails "J. Geils— The Big Time Boogie from Boston."

AUTHOR'S NOTE: The band's first hit, receiving plenty of airplay that summer, was called "Looking For Love." Exactly the plight of Royals fans, who were stuck with a team of Bob Floyds and Richie Scheinblums at that point. Brett didn't disappoint; Royals fans swooned over Brett for the next 20-plus years. As for Geils? Far fewer hits than Brett's 3,154.

Kevin Brown
Born: March 14, 1965
Debut: September 30, 1986

Supremely talented but seemingly unable to control his volatility, Kevin Brown has alternately thrilled and frustrated managers and teammates since 1986. The son of a chalk miner in rural Georgia, Brown always had a sharp intellect and a keen desire to succeed, but as a chemist or marine biologist, not as a baseball player. It wasn't until he was made a first-round pick out of Georgia Tech that he tabled those plans and began what would be a 200-win career as a right-handed starter with a menacing sinker. Mel Hall once said that trying to hit Brown's sinker was like trying to hit a brick. His Rangers battery mate, Mike Stanley, called him "Chainsaw" for the way he carved up opponents' bats.

But mostly, Brown carved up his own performances, his perfectionism threatening to swallow him whole, often on live television. Wound as tight as the spin on that sinker, his high-strung nature would occasionally lead to public (and private) tantrums that often resulted in the dismantling of everything from water coolers to furniture to toilets.

Fiercely independent, Brown claims to have had no mentors—and this is a guy who pitched with Nolan Ryan for five years. Say what you will about the perception of Brown as a guy "on his own program"; in the 1996 season, he led the majors in ERA and it wasn't even close. At 1.89, his was a full run lower than that of Greg Maddux. Brown had walked only 33 batters in 233 innings—the precursor to helping the Marlins win the 1997 World Series. In the NLCS against the Braves that October, he pitched a gutsy 142-pitch complete game while fighting both a stomach virus and a manager (Jim Leyland) who wanted to take him out.

In 1998, it was on to World Series–bound San Diego, where he went 18–7 with a second-best NL ERA of 2.38. In '99, he was wooed north to L.A., where he bought singer John Fogarty's old house after signing for a cool $105 million over seven years. (The Dodgers also threw in use of a private jet to get his family back and forth from Georgia, and a *Star Wars* poster signed by producer George Lucas.)

His resume includes a no-hitter and consecutive World Series appearances with two different teams. The six-time All-Star has finished among the top six in Cy Young balloting five times, and he has had as many as 21 wins in a single season. "Still," says his former manager, Kevin Kennedy, "he may be the most self-destructive player I've ever met."

BOXSCORE

Texas Rangers 9, Oakland Athletics 5
Game Played on Tuesday, September 30, 1986 (Night) at Arlington Stadium

											R	H	E
Oakland	1	0	1	0	0	0	1	0	2	—	5	8	0
Texas	0	0	7	0	0	0	0	2	x	—	9	7	4

BATTING

Oakland Athletics	AB	R	H	RBI	BB	K	PO	A
Davis rf	5	0	1	1	0	1	3	0
Murphy cf	5	0	0	0	0	4	2	0
Canseco lf	3	1	1	0	1	0	2	0
Bochte 1b	4	0	1	1	0	1	5	0
Kingman dh	4	0	0	0	0	2	0	0
Lansford 3b	4	2	1	0	0	0	0	0
Hill 2b	4	0	0	0	0	2	1	3
Willard c	3	1	2	0	1	1	10	0
Javier pr	0	1	0	0	0	0	0	0
Griffin ss	4	0	2	2	0	0	1	1
Rodriguez p	0	0	0	0	0	0	0	0
Plunk p	0	0	0	0	0	0	0	0
Mooneyham p	0	0	0	0	0	0	0	0
Bair p	0	0	0	0	0	0	0	0
Totals	36	5	8	4	2	11	24	6

FIELDING
PB: Willard (3)

BATTING
2B: Canseco (29, off Brown); Willard (7, off Brown); Griffin (23, off Loynd)

BASERUNNING
SB: Davis (25, 2nd base off Brown/Slaught); Lansford (16, 2nd base off Loynd/Mercado)
CS: Griffin (15, 2nd base by Brown/Slaught)

Texas Rangers	AB	R	H	RBI	BB	K	PO	A
McDowell cf	4	2	1	0	1	1	2	0
Fletcher ss	4	0	0	0	0	0	3	2
Wilkerson ss	1	1	0	0	0	0	0	1
O'Brien 1b	1	1	0	0	3	0	4	0
Paciorek 1b	1	0	1	2	0	0	2	0
Incaviglia rf	3	1	0	1	1	2	0	1
Brower lf	0	0	0	0	0	0	0	0
Sierra lf-rf	4	1	1	3	0	1	2	0
Parrish dh	3	1	0	0	1	3	0	0
Slaught c	2	1	1	0	1	0	4	1
Mercado c	1	0	0	0	0	0	7	0
Buechele 3b	3	0	1	1	0	1	0	1
Stanley 3b	0	0	0	0	1	0	0	0
Browne 2b	4	1	2	1	0	1	0	4
Brown p	0	0	0	0	0	0	0	1
Loynd p	0	0	0	0	0	0	0	0
Totals	31	9	7	8	8	9	27	11

FIELDING
E: Sierra (6), Stanley (1), Browne (1), Loynd (1)
PB: Slaught (13)

BATTING
HR: Sierra (16, 3rd inning off Rodriguez, 2 on, 2 out)
HBP: Incaviglia (4, by Plunk)

BASERUNNING
SB: O'Brien (3, 3rd base off Plunk/Willard); Incaviglia (3, 2nd base off Plunk/Willard); Stanley (1, 2nd base off Mooneyham/Willard); McDowell (32, 2nd base off Bair/Willard); Wilkerson (9, 2nd base off Bair/Willard)

PITCHING

Oakland Athletics	IP	H	HR	R	ER	BB	K
Rodriguez L(1–2)	2.2	3	1	5	5	3	1
Plunk	1.1	3	0	2	2	2	2
Mooneyham	3.1	0	0	2	2	3	5
Bair	0.2	1	0	0	0	0	1
Totals	8.0	7	1	9	9	8	9

Texas Rangers	IP	H	HR	R	ER	BB	K
Brown W(1–0)	5.0	6	0	2	2	0	4
Loynd SV(1)	4.0	2	0	3	0	2	7
Totals	9.0	8	0	5	2	2	11

WP: Loynd (2)
BK: Rodriguez (1)
HBP: Plunk (4, Incaviglia)
Umpires: Jim Evans, Durwood Merrill, Derryl Cousins, Ted Hendry
Time of Game: 3:06   Attendance: 6,908

Kenny Rogers and I both broke in around the same time, and here we are both still cooking, huh? I remember my debut well . . . I gave up a hit to Jose Canseco with two out and gave up a single after that, and I was down 1–0, but then I settled in. The guys [Rangers] scored, like, seven runs for me in the third, so it was pretty easy from there.

I remember the heat. Texas is just flat-out brutal, even in September. I remember looking at Jose Canseco and thinking how incredibly large of an individual he was. I struck out Dwayne Murphy a bunch of times in that game. I faced Kingman, Dave Kingman . . . Carney Lansford wiggling that bat around . . . Stan Javier . . . I remember almost that entire Oakland lineup. I pitched five innings, then Bobby Valentine told me I was done. He said, "Nice job," and that was it. Mike Loynd finished up. I didn't walk anyone in my big league debut, I remember that . . . I was proud of that.

Also on September 30, 1986
Having allowed home runs 47, 48, and 49 of the season the day before, Twins pitcher Bert Blyleven tells reporters he'll make his final scheduled start of the season, even if it means surrendering an unheard-of 50th home run of the season. (He does, to the White Sox's Daryl Boston.)

AUTHOR'S NOTE: Six years later, Brown would set a career high with 21 wins by beating Blyleven—on the anniversary of the game in which Blyleven surrendered that record 50th homer.

Steve Busby
Born: September 29, 1949
Debut: September 8, 1972

Johnny Carson used to joke about *The Tonight Show* emanating from "beautiful downtown Burbank." On a night when Johnny had a very mediocre guest list (Phyllis Newman, Buddy Rich, and Dr. Jean Rosenbaum), Burbank's very own Steve Busby made the first of his 150 big league starts, against the Minnesota Twins.

The fact that the right-hander made only 150 starts was due to a frayed shoulder that could have been fixed up fairly easily with today's modern procedures. Within Busby's first 65 big league starts, he had already thrown two no-hitters and was the first player ever to have a no-hitter in each of his first two major league seasons. However, the shoulder began acting up in 1976, and a forlorn Busby had to watch from the dugout as his Royals lost Game Five of the best-of-five ALCS on Chris Chambliss's homer off Mark Littell.

Busby had a remarkable three-year run when he was healthy. An All-Star in both '74 and '75, he won 56 games in his first three full seasons, including 22 in '74 for manager Jack McKeon, who had been Busby's Triple-A skipper the year before.

The 1974 no-hitter (against Detroit) was followed by six innings of one-hit ball in his next start, but McKeon removed him due to a growing total of walks. His 1975 no-hitter (against Milwaukee) was nearly a perfect game—a second-inning walk to George Scott provided the Brewers with their only base runner. His following start was another gem, as he retired the first nine White Sox batters, giving him an AL-record run of 33 consecutive batters set down.

By 1980, however, his shoulder had shut down on him completely, and he walked away from the mound for good and into the broadcast booth.

Jack McKeon called me in and gave me the good news—well, good for me anyway. Dick Drago had been hit by a Carl Yastrzemski line drive and broke his jaw, so they needed someone to get up there in a hurry. From all I know, then and now, there was really no plan to get me up there that September . . . If Yaz hadn't hit that ball off Drago, I probably would have had to wait until spring training to try and make the team.

I had already been up a few days and was able to see the Twins up close . . . Carew and Tovar at the top of the order were plenty scary, and sure

BOXSCORE

Kansas City Royals 3, Minnesota Twins 2
(Game 2 of a Doubleheader)

Game Played on Friday, September 8, 1972 (Night) at Municipal Stadium

Minnesota	1	0	0	0	0	0	0	1	0	—	2	5	0
Kansas City	0	0	0	1	0	2	0	0	x	—	3	6	0

BATTING

Minnesota Twins	AB	R	H	RBI	BB	K	PO	A
Tovar cf	4	2	2	0	0	1	2	0
Carew 2b	3	0	1	1	0	0	4	1
Holt lf	3	0	0	1	0	1	2	0
Darwin rf	4	0	0	0	0	2	1	0
Reese 1b	3	0	0	0	1	0	10	1
Thompson ss	3	0	0	0	0	1	2	2
Granger p	0	0	0	0	0	0	0	0
Killebrew ph	0	0	0	0	1	0	0	0
Brye pr	0	0	0	0	0	0	0	0
Monzon 3b-ss	3	0	1	0	0	0	1	3
Manuel ph	1	0	0	0	0	0	0	0
Borgmann c	3	0	1	0	0	0	2	0
Corbin p	1	0	0	0	0	1	0	1
Braun ph-3b	1	0	0	0	0	1	0	1
Totals	**29**	**2**	**5**	**2**	**2**	**7**	**24**	**9**

FIELDING
DP: 1

BATTING
3B: Tovar (5, off Busby)
SH: Corbin (1, off Busby)
SF: Holt (1, off Busby); Carew (2, off Busby)

Kansas City Royals	AB	R	H	RBI	BB	K	PO	A
Otis cf	4	0	0	0	0	0	3	0
Rojas 2b	4	1	1	0	0	1	1	0
Hovley rf	3	1	2	1	1	0	1	0
Mayberry 1b	4	1	1	2	0	0	6	1
Piniella lf	3	0	0	0	0	1	4	0
Taylor c	3	0	0	0	0	0	7	1
Schaal 3b	3	0	1	0	0	0	1	3
Patek ss	2	0	1	0	0	0	4	1
Busby p	3	0	0	0	0	0	0	1
Totals	**29**	**3**	**6**	**3**	**1**	**2**	**27**	**7**

FIELDING
PB: Taylor (2)

BATTING
2B: Rojas (23, off Corbin)
HR: Mayberry (17, 6th inning off Corbin, 1 on, 2 out)
HBP: Patek (2, by Corbin)

PITCHING

Minnesota Twins	IP	H	HR	R	ER	BB	K
Corbin L (8–7)	7	5	1	3	3	1	1
Granger	1	1	0	0	0	0	1
Totals	**8**	**6**	**1**	**3**	**3**	**1**	**2**

Kansas City Royals	IP	H	HR	R	ER	BB	K
Busby W (1–0)	9	5	0	2	2	2	7

HBP: Corbin (5, Patek)
Umpires: Larry McCoy, Jim Honochick, Lou DiMuro, Bill Deegan
Time of Game: 2:00   Attendance: 7,541

enough, once I got out there, they both greeted me with base hits. But we ended up winning 3–2, and I had a complete game. My dad was there, my wife was there, which made it even more special. To be quite honest, I remember nothing at all except the game. Couldn't tell you what the weather was, what I did for breakfast or lunch . . . Anytime I think about that first game, all I can really remember is getting up on that mound and Rod Carew looking back at me.

But it all went well . . . It was the second game of a doubleheader, and Tom Murphy had thrown a shutout for us in game one. I had given up a run in the top of the first, so I knew I wouldn't be able to repeat that aspect of it . . . but I think we both ended up throwing complete games. I know mine, I went the distance, and I was awfully proud, seeing my dad there in the stands at the end.

Also on September 8, 1972
Ferguson Jenkins wins 20 for the sixth consecutive year as the Cubs beat the Phillies 4–3.

AUTHOR'S NOTE: Busby became a TV announcer for the Texas Rangers, signing on in December 1981. That same month, Jenkins left the Rangers to go back to the Cubs, where he finished his Hall of Fame career.

Eric Byrnes
Born: February 16, 1976
Debut: August 22, 2000

At first, no one knew exactly what to make of Oakland's Eric Byrnes. With long blond hair and a "Valley dude" California accent, he conjured up images of Jeff Spicoli, the stoned surfer Sean Penn portrayed in *Fast Times at Ridgemont High*. Byrnes was likable, outgoing, and constantly hustling, and the only question was whether or not he could chisel together enough actual talent to be an everyday player. Through his first three seasons, the right-handed swinger was a part-timer, playing a wall-banging outfield and occasionally being used to pinch-run or even pinch-hit. Finally, when Jermaine Dye's injury opened the door in 2003, he got his chance to prove himself and began that season on fire.

Starting April 24, 2003, Byrnes hit .352 over a 59-game stretch, culminating June 29 when he hit for the cycle against San Francisco. Having grown up an avid Giants fan, it was, in his own words, "the ultimate." (Or, as his doppelganger, Mr. Spicoli, might have said, "bodacious.")

Byrnes fast became a fan favorite in Oakland, and even when he slumped late in the '04 season, the fans delighted to his anthem, "Disco Inferno," whenever his name was announced. Byrnes finished 2004 with a career-high 20 homers and stole 17 bases in 18 attempts. The A's missed the '04 postseason, but he was at the epicenter of both their 2001 and 2003 division series experiences. In '01, it was Byrnes, said detractors, who should have been pinch-running for Jeremy Giambi when Derek Jeter made the amazing relay shovel pass to the plate, turning the series. In 2003, Byrnes's collision with the Red Sox's Jason Varitek (and failure to touch home plate) stood as the turning point of that ALDS.

One of the league's best interviews, Byrnes is thought to be the only current big leaguer who can name all 43 U.S. presidents in order. He insists he memorized them in less than an hour while at a friend's house, when he noticed a placemat that had all of the presidents' pictures on it. "Everyone's gotta be known for something," he says. "If I wash out in baseball, I've got a good chance on *Jeopardy.*"

I took a red-eye flight from Sacramento to make it to my first game in the big leagues. I must have made 50 phone calls to let people know.

My first game was in Cleveland, and I was doing really well. A couple of hits early on, we were scoring a bunch of runs, but Steve Reed came in and took

33

BOXSCORE

Cleveland Indians 14, Oakland Athletics 6

Game Played on Tuesday, August 22, 2000 (Night) at Jacobs Field

Oakland	0	2	0	0	1	1	2	0	0	—	6	12	1
Cleveland	0	5	2	4	2	0	1	0	x	—	14	16	1

BATTING

Oakland Athletics	AB	R	H	RBI	BB	K	PO	A
Menechino 2b	3	1	2	1	2	0	3	5
Long cf	6	0	2	1	0	0	3	0
Tejada ss	4	0	0	0	1	0	2	1
Stanley 1b	4	1	1	0	0	1	7	1
Christenson ph-rf	0	0	0	0	1	0	0	0
Piatt rf-1b	3	0	1	0	2	2	2	0
Grieve lf	5	1	1	1	0	2	1	1
Byrnes dh	4	2	2	0	0	0	0	0
Chavez 3b	5	0	2	2	0	2	2	1
Hernandez c	5	1	1	0	0	1	4	0
Heredia p	0	0	0	0	0	0	0	0
Olivares p	0	0	0	0	0	0	0	2
Tam p	0	0	0	0	0	0	0	0
Totals	39	6	12	5	6	8	24	11

FIELDING

DP: 1
E: Heredia (1)

BATTING

2B: Menechino (8, off Finley); Stanley (10, off Finley); Hernandez (11, off Martin); Chavez (18, off Reed)
3B: Long (4, off Finley)
HBP: Menechino (1, by Martin); Byrnes (1, by Reed)

BASERUNNING

SB: Byrnes (1, 2nd base off Finley/S. Alomar)

Cleveland Indians	AB	R	H	RBI	BB	K	PO	A
Lofton cf	6	1	2	0	0	1	7	0
Vizquel ss	4	2	2	0	0	0	1	1
Cabrera ss	2	0	0	0	0	1	1	0
R. Alomar 2b	1	2	0	0	2	0	1	1
Selby ph-2b	1	1	1	0	0	0	1	1
M. Ramirez rf	3	2	2	3	2	0	1	0
Thome 1b	2	1	1	3	3	1	4	1
Segui dh	5	1	2	1	0	0	0	0
Fryman 3b	5	2	3	1	0	1	1	3
Cordero lf	4	2	2	1	1	0	2	0
S. Alomar c	4	0	1	3	0	0	8	0
Finley p	0	0	0	0	0	0	0	1
Martin p	0	0	0	0	0	0	0	0
Reed p	0	0	0	0	0	0	0	0
Shuey p	0	0	0	0	0	0	0	0
Karsay p	0	0	0	0	0	0	0	0
Totals	37	14	16	12	8	4	27	8

FIELDING

E: R. Alomar (13)

BATTING

2B: Segui (32, off Heredia); Cordero 2 (9, off Heredia 2); Thome (28, off Olivares); M. Ramirez (18, off Olivares)
HR: M. Ramirez (26, 2nd inning off Heredia, 0 on, 0 out)
SF: S. Alomar (4, off Heredia)
HBP: R. Alomar (5, by Olivares)

BASERUNNING

SB: R. Alomar (29, 2nd base off Heredia/Hernandez)

PITCHING

Oakland Athletics	IP	H	HR	R	ER	BB	K
Heredia L (13–9)	3	8	1	7	6	2	2
Olivares	4	8	0	7	7	6	2
Tam	1	0	0	0	0	0	0
Totals	8	16	1	14	13	8	4
Cleveland Indians	IP	H	HR	R	ER	BB	K
Finley W (10–9)	5	7	0	3	3	3	5
Martin	1	1	0	1	0	0	1
Reed	1	1	0	2	2	1	0
Shuey	1	1	0	0	0	1	1
Karsay	1	2	0	0	0	1	1
Totals	9	12	0	6	5	6	8

HBP: Olivares (6, R. Alomar); Martin (1, Menechino); Reed (1, Byrnes)
Umpires: Marvin Hudson, Gary Cederstrom, Rob Drake, Dale Scott
Time of Game: 3:45 Attendance: 43,299

offense that I was taking such big swings. He said something to me, which I swear I didn't hear . . . Then he turned and said something to our dugout, but I didn't think anything of it. Next thing I know I'm getting hit by his next pitch. I go on down to first base, but I was still oblivious. Our dugout was screaming, but I had no idea what was going on. But before long, we had retaliated and there was a big brawl. Welcome to the big leagues. Two veteran teams, Oakland and Cleveland going at it, and all because I had taken a big swing against Steve Reed, I guess. Whoops.

My mom, my sister, and one of my best friends were there. We went back to the hotel to drink a little bit and celebrate . . . and once we were done, Matt Stairs pulled me back in there so I could hang out with the guys. That was very cool of him to do. They all thought I was nuts because I had no interest in keeping the ball from my first hit . . . Seriously, I'd rather have a Will Clark autographed baseball than any of my own stuff. I'm a fan first. A ball that I've gotten a base hit with can't be distinguished from any other random ball I would put in some trophy case . . . That's not for me. Get me a Willie Mays and a Will Clark ball though, and that I'd put on display.

Also on August 22, 2000
Americans debate who will win tomorrow's final episode of the new hit reality show *Survivor.*

AUTHOR'S NOTE: Byrnes, a fan of the reality genre, wears his hair much like a male *Survivor* contestant—that is to say, in need of a trim.

Sean Casey
Born: July 2, 1974
Debut: September 12, 1997

One of the most giving and caring players in baseball, Sean Casey has become a fan favorite in Cincinnati. His agent, Ron Shapiro, has written a book called *The Power of Nice*, and although it is not a treatise on his client, Casey indeed possesses the qualities Shapiro espouses.

The Reds traded for Casey at the end of 1998's spring training, and then-Reds GM Jim Bowden boldly told reporters, "You watch. This will be the best trade this franchise has made since Joe Morgan arrived in the early '70s." He may not have been far off.

Straight up for Dave Burba, the Reds received a public relations machine who could also crank doubles and homers while hitting in the low .300s. And while his stats were always impressive during his first several years with the team, the stories of his kind off-field behavior seemed to generate more buzz. Case in point: In 2001, Casey became friendly with a 23-year-old autograph seeker from Dayton. In July of that summer, Casey noticed the young fan seemed withdrawn, and when Casey asked if he was okay, the fan said that his dad had just died, and the family was having a tough time paying for the funeral. Casey volunteered to write a check to cover the cost, but the fan said, "No way." The next day, Casey organized a fund-raising autograph session with a few of his teammates, and every dime went to the funeral home.

Growing up in Pittsburgh, Casey studied the swings of Stargell, Parker, and the other Pirate greats, but he ultimately picked a bizarre stance of his own, which features an elongated between–pitch routine of stepping out and adjusting his batting gloves while fidgeting like a man with sand in his bathing suit. No one's complaining in Cincinnati. In fact, Little League games across southern Ohio are now routinely delayed by kids imitating his mannerisms themselves. The former University of Richmond standout hit .324 in 2004, driving in 99 runs while striking out only three dozen times.

Mark Shapiro—now the Indians GM, but then the farm director for the Indians—was in our clubhouse just after we had won the Triple-A championship . . . I had just hit the game-winning home run to win the championship, and then he told me I was getting called up, so I ran outside of the clubhouse in Des Moines, Iowa, to find a pay phone . . . [I] found it in theconcourse of the

BOXSCORE

Cleveland Indians 9, Chicago White Sox 0
Game Played on Friday, September 12, 1997 (Night) at Comiskey Park

Cleveland	0	2	0	0	4	1	0	0	2	—	9	14	0
Chicago	0	0	0	0	0	0	0	0	0	—	0	3	0

BATTING

Cleveland Indians	AB	R	H	RBI	BB	K	PO	A
Roberts 2b	4	2	1	0	0	0	1	3
Vizquel ss	3	1	1	1	2	0	0	1
Branson ss	0	0	0	0	0	0	0	0
Ramirez rf	5	1	2	3	0	0	4	0
Aven lf	0	0	0	0	0	0	0	0
Thome 1b	5	2	3	1	0	2	8	1
Justice dh	4	0	2	0	0	2	0	0
Casey ph-dh	1	1	1	0	0	0	0	0
Williams 3b	4	2	2	2	1	0	0	4
Manto 3b	0	0	0	0	0	0	0	0
Giles lf-rf	2	0	0	2	1	1	5	0
Borders c	5	0	2	0	0	0	7	0
Wright p	0	0	0	0	0	0	0	0
Shuey p	0	0	0	0	0	0	1	0
Totals	**38**	**9**	**14**	**9**	**4**	**5**	**27**	**9**

BATTING
2B: Roberts (18, off Levine); Borders (7, off J. Darwin)
3B: Williams (2, off J. Darwin)
HR: Thome (39, 2nd inning off Drabek, 0 on, 0 out); Williams (32, 2nd inning off Drabek, 0 on, 1 out); Ramirez (25, 5th inning off Drabek, 2 on, 1 out)
SF: Giles 2 (7, off Levine, off J. Darwin)
HBP: Roberts (3, by Drabek)
IBB: Giles (2, by Drabek)

BASERUNNING
SB: Roberts (17, 2nd base off Drabek/Fabregas)

Chicago White Sox	AB	R	H	RBI	BB	K	PO	A
Durham 2b	3	0	1	0	0	0	1	3
Fonville 2b	0	0	0	0	1	0	1	1
Martinez 1b	1	0	0	0	2	0	6	0
Valdez 1b	1	0	0	0	0	0	0	0
F. Thomas dh	3	0	0	0	1	2	0	0
Belle lf	3	0	0	0	0	0	3	0
Abbott lf	1	0	0	0	0	0	3	0
Ventura 3b	3	0	0	0	0	0	0	3
Norton 3b	1	0	0	0	0	1	0	0
Cameron cf	4	0	0	0	0	3	4	0
Fabregas c	4	0	2	0	0	0	5	0
Ordonez rf	3	0	0	0	0	1	2	0
Guillen ss	3	0	0	0	0	0	1	1
Martin ss	0	0	0	0	0	0	1	0
Drabek p	0	0	0	0	0	0	1	0
Levine p	0	0	0	0	0	0	0	0
J. Darwin p	0	0	0	0	0	0	0	0
Totals	**30**	**0**	**3**	**0**	**4**	**7**	**27**	**8**

FIELDING
DP: 1

BATTING
2B: Durham (24, off Wright)

PITCHING

Cleveland Indians	IP	H	HR	R	ER	BB	K
Wright W(7–3)	7	3	0	0	0	2	5
Shuey	2	0	0	0	0	2	2
Totals	**9**	**3**	**0**	**0**	**0**	**4**	**7**

Chicago White Sox	IP	H	HR	R	ER	BB	K
Drabek L(10–11)	4.1	7	3	6	6	3	1
Levine	1.2	3	0	1	1	1	2
J. Darwin	3	4	0	2	2	0	2
Totals	**9**	**14**	**3**	**9**	**9**	**4**	**5**

WP: Drabek (12)
HBP: Drabek (4, Roberts)
IBB: Drabek (5, Giles)
Umpires: Dan Morrison, Greg Kosc, Ted Hendry, Ted Barrett
Time of Game: 2:56   Attendance: 31,249

stadium, and while the ushers and clean-up crew are all milling around, walking past me, I'm bawling my eyes out, telling my family what's just happened . . . game-winning home run, championship, called up to the big leagues, all in ten minutes' time. What a night. We went out to a team party that night, flew back to Buffalo, recovered a little bit, then flew out to Chicago to meet the Indians at Comiskey.

I remember not having a bat, a helmet, or batting gloves. It was absolute panic. I used Manny Ramirez's bat, Tony Fernandez's helmet, and Jeff Manto's batting gloves. I was on the end of the bench; Richie Sexson and I were sitting there, and our bench coach, Johnny Goryl, came down and stood in front of me in the dugout in Chicago, and he says, "Hey, Grover [manager Mike Hargrove] wants you to pinch-hit for Dave Justice." And I actually got a hit.

My mom and dad, four of my best friends flew in, they were all there, and it was great.

Also on September 12, 1997
Michael Jackson opens up to ABC's Barbara Walters in an exclusive *20/20* interview regarding his own life and that of the recently deceased Princess Diana.

AUTHOR'S NOTE: Casey has gained fame in the Reds clubhouse for his postgame victory dances, which are to Michael Jackson's moves what Pauly Shore is to high culture.

Eric Chavez
Born: December 7, 1977
Debut: September 8, 1998

Dark-haired and cat-like, Oakland's young third baseman has cut a popular swath through the East Bay. Of course, the Athletics have recently had other charismatic players in their employ, but they have paraded right past the adoring masses on their way out of town, to bigger East Coast riches. Jason Giambi—gone, to New York. Miguel Tejada—gone, to Baltimore. And most everyone assumed Eric Chavez would simply be the latest to walk off into a sunset that beckoned three time zones away. Instead, A's fans got a reprieve. Chavez, before his walk year was to begin, inked a six-year, $66-million deal that would keep him in the gaudy green and gold his predecessors had torn from their bodies. The man who signed him to that contract graduated from the same Southern California high school—like Chavez, A's GM Billy Beane was a Mt. Carmel Sundevil. "Blood brothers," Beane has said, with a wink.

Who cares if Chavez always has bad Aprils and mediocre Mays? From June 1 on, he's a lean, green, hitting machine. Who cares if he went 1-for-22 in the 2003 playoffs? With the A's great young pitching, assuredly there will be other playoff battles to be waged.

Chavez has also turned into a vacuum cleaner at third base, winning a Gold Glove at the age of 21, just like Brooks Robinson, whom he had never heard of at the time. That, too, merits a "Who cares?" Chavez admitted before the 2002 season opener that he had also never heard of Paul McCartney. With McCartney performing that night in the Jewel Box, next door to Oakland's Coliseum, Chavez, when prodded, had no clue which band McCartney had made famous in the sixties. "Dude, I wasn't even born then," he reasoned.

The ultimate "Who cares?" regarding Chavez is the pronunciation of his family's name. Diehard Latinos insist it should, of course, be CHA-vez, as in labor activist Cesar Chavez. Anglos have casually called him "cha-VEZ," as in the Chavez Ravine by Dodger Stadium. "Hey, dude, whatever," he has said on the topic. "I know who you're talking about, so either way, you know?"

CHA-vez, cha-VEZ, potato, po-tah-to—what you know you're going to get is 30 home runs, 100 RBI, and Gold Glove caliber defense alongside the even younger Bobby Crosby. Six years of *that* is, indeed, something worth caring about in Oakland.

BOXSCORE

Baltimore Orioles 5, Oakland Athletics 2

Game Played on Tuesday, September 8, 1998 (Night) at Oakland-Alameda County Coliseum

Baltimore	1	0	0	0	2	0	0	0	2	—	5	11	1
Oakland	0	0	0	2	0	0	0	0	0	—	2	7	1

BATTING

Baltimore Orioles	AB	R	H	RBI	BB	K	PO	A
Alomar 2b	5	0	0	0	0	0	6	5
Anderson cf	4	0	1	1	0	0	0	0
Baines dh	3	1	1	1	0	0	0	0
Kingsale pr-dh	0	0	0	0	0	0	0	0
Davis rf	4	0	1	0	0	1	1	0
Palmeiro 1b	4	0	1	0	0	1	4	1
Ripken 3b	4	1	2	0	0	1	4	0
Surhoff lf	4	1	3	0	0	1	1	0
Hoiles c	3	0	1	1	0	1	7	1
Clyburn pr	0	1	0	0	0	0	0	0
C. Greene c	0	0	0	0	0	0	3	0
Bordick ss	3	1	1	2	0	0	1	3
Johns p	0	0	0	0	0	0	0	0
Rhodes p	0	0	0	0	0	0	0	0
Mills p	0	0	0	0	0	0	0	0
Benitez p	0	0	0	0	0	0	0	0
Totals	34	5	11	5	0	5	27	10

FIELDING
DP: 1
E: Hoiles (3)

BATTING
2B: Bordick (24, off Heredia); Hoiles (11, off Mathews)
HR: Baines (9, 1st inning off Heredia 0 on, 2 out)
SH: Hoiles (4, off Heredia)
SF: Bordick (4, off Mathews)
HBP: Baines (1, by Holzemer)

BASERUNNING
CS: Surhoff (5, 2nd base by Heredia/Hinch)

Oakland Athletics	AB	R	H	RBI	BB	K	PO	A
Henderson lf	4	0	0	0	1	2	1	0
Christenson cf	5	0	2	0	0	2	7	0
Giambi 1b	4	0	1	0	0	0	9	1
Stairs dh	3	0	1	0	1	0	0	0
Blowers 3b	2	0	0	0	1	0	0	3
Chavez ph-3b	1	0	0	0	0	1	1	0
Grieve rf	4	0	0	0	0	2	0	0
Spiezio 2b	3	0	1	0	1	0	3	2
McDonald pr	0	0	0	0	0	0	0	0
Bournigal ss	0	0	0	0	0	0	0	0
Tejada ss	2	1	1	1	1	1	0	2
Roberts ph-2b	1	0	0	0	0	0	0	0
Hinch c	2	1	1	1	1	0	4	1
Sprague ph	1	0	0	0	0	1	0	0
Heredia p	0	0	0	0	0	0	1	0
Groom p	0	0	0	0	0	0	0	0
Worrell p	0	0	0	0	0	0	0	0
Holzemer p	0	0	0	0	0	0	0	0
Mathews p	0	0	0	0	0	0	0	0
Totals	32	2	7	2	6	9	27	9

FIELDING
DP: 2
E: Spiezio (12)
PB: Hinch (7)

BATTING
HR: Tejada (8, 4th inning off Johns 0 on, 2 out); Hinch (8, 4th inning off Johns, 0 on, 2 out)

BASERUNNING
SB: Henderson (59, 2nd base off Johns/Hoiles)
CS: Giambi (2, Home by Rhodes/Hoiles)

PITCHING

Baltimore Orioles	IP	H	HR	R	ER	BB	K
Johns	4.2	6	2	2	2	4	1
Rhodes W (4–4)	2.1	1	0	0	0	1	3
Mills	1	0	0	0	0	1	2
Benitez SV (20)	1	0	0	0	0	0	3
Totals	9	7	2	2	2	6	9
Oakland Athletics	IP	H	HR	R	ER	BB	K
Heredia L (3–1)	5.2	8	1	3	3	0	4
Groom	0	1	0	0	0	0	0
Worrell	1	0	0	0	0	0	0
Holzemer	1.1	0	0	0	0	0	0
Mathews	1	2	0	2	1	0	1
Totals	9	11	1	5	4	0	5

HBP: Holzemer (1, Baines)
Umpires: Terry Craft, Al Clark, Jim Joyce, Jim McKean
Time of Game: 3:11   Attendance: 7,924

I was in Canada and thought maybe the week before I'd get the call, but then we made the playoffs and I had to spend another week waiting, not knowing, yes or no. We lost and my manager, Mike Quade, called me in . . . He says, "To be honest with you, I don't think you're ready, but the guys up there, they seem to think you're worth a look." He was trying not to smile. He gave me a ticket right there in Edmonton's clubhouse. I flew through Salt Lake first thing in the morning and got to the hotel by noon. My parents met me there for lunch . . . I had called them the night before, and they flew up from San Diego first thing in the morning.

I was told at the ballpark that I wouldn't start right away but to be ready to pinch-hit. Sure enough, Alan Mills is pitching that night and they ask me to get up there . . . He threw me three heaters—two I swung and missed, the third one I took, and that was that. Three pitches and done.

Still, I was pumped. Everyone wants to do something that first at bat . . . I didn't. I just went back out in the field, watched some Oriole [Chris Hoiles] hit a home run, and I figured, that's me, next time.

Also on September 8, 1998

Both the debut of Eric Chavez and the more-heralded Cardinals outfielder, JD Drew, are completely overshadowed on this night by the enormity of Mark McGwire's 62nd home run of the season. A nationally televised lined shot, it breaks Roger Maris's long-standing single-season record and is hailed as one of the many feel-good stories of that summer.

AUTHOR'S NOTE: Chavez says he and his Oakland teammates watched it happen in between batting practice and game time, on the big TV in the A's home clubhouse.

Roger Clemens
Born: August 4, 1962
Debut: May 15, 1984

Roger Clemens hates the phrase "all hat and no cattle." Where he's from (outside Houston, Texas), the phrase connotes a man who's all talk, no action; all style, no substance; all pomp, no circumstance. His hero, cattleman Nolan Ryan, was the embodiment of how a man should carry himself, relying on his own hard work and confidence to over-deliver in every walk of life.

Certainly, on the mound, Clemens did his best to never back down from a challenge. Chipper Jones has said, "Clemens is the pitcher I most respect, because even if I'd homered in my last at bat against him, next time up, he'd throw me the exact same pitch. The guy simply never gives in." It seemed that the more powerful the opponent, the more Clemens was able to ratchet up his own game. To wit, Mark McGwire was 4-for-47 lifetime against him, and Cecil Fielder 2-for-46 with 21 strikeouts.

Through intimidation and incredible conditioning, Clemens pitched his way to an unprecedented seventh Cy Young in 2004, helping his hometown Astros to within a game of their first World Series. Lured out of retirement by his buddy (and fellow Houstonian) Andy Pettitte, "The Rocket" went 18–4 for the '04 Astros, helping them win 23 of their final 24 home games, including the postseason.

He had debuted and spent his first 13 seasons with the Red Sox, chalking up a pair of record-setting 20-strikeout games while he was there. Signing with Toronto after a fallout with the Sox front office, he posted back-to-back Triple Crown seasons, leading the league in wins, ERA, and strikeouts. In 2000, he moved onto his third AL East team, the Yankees. In 2001, at the age of 39, he started out 20–1, best out of the gate in history, finishing second in the league in both wins and strikeouts for Cy Young number six.

Through 2004, he had led his league in wins five times and in ERA and strikeouts six times. Like his hero, Ryan, he was still pitching at a high level in his forties, and like Ryan, won more than 300 games. The two tough Texans are 1–2 all-time in strikeouts, with more than 10,000 between them. While Clemens made 26 postseason starts, Ryan made only seven in his own Hall of Fame career and, shockingly, never won the Cy Young Award. Not only has Clemens won seven, he was also MVP in 1986, when the Red Sox fell to the Mets (the team for whom Ryan had first pitched).

BOXSCORE

Cleveland Indians 7, Boston Red Sox 5
Game Played on Tuesday, May 15, 1984 (Night) at Cleveland Stadium

Boston	0	0	0	4	0	1	0	0	—	5	10	2
Cleveland	1	0	0	3	0	1	0	2	x	—	7	12	0

BATTING

Boston Red Sox	AB	R	H	RBI	BB	K	PO	A
Boggs 3b	3	1	1	1	2	0	1	2
Evans rf	4	0	2	2	1	1	0	0
Rice lf	3	0	1	1	1	0	3	0
Armas dh	4	0	1	0	0	0	0	0
Easler 1b	4	0	0	0	0	0	6	1
Nichols cf	3	0	0	0	0	0	1	0
Miller ph-cf	1	0	0	0	0	0	1	0
Barrett 2b	4	1	2	0	0	1	2	4
Gutierrez ss	3	1	1	0	0	1	1	1
Remy ph	0	0	0	0	1	0	0	0
Hoffman pr	0	0	0	0	0	0	0	0
Allenson c	2	1	1	0	0	1	5	0
Gedman ph-c	2	1	1	1	0	1	2	0
Clemens p	0	0	0	0	0	0	1	1
Johnson p	0	0	0	0	0	0	0	0
Clear p	0	0	0	0	0	0	1	0
Totals	33	5	10	5	5	5	24	9

FIELDING
DP: 1
E: Easler (6), Gutierrez (8)

BATTING
HR: Gedman (6, 7th inning off Waddell, 0 on, 1 out)

BASERUNNING
SB: Barrett (2, 2nd base off Heaton/Hassey)
CS: Armas (1, 2nd base by Heaton/Hassey)

Cleveland Indians	AB	R	H	RBI	BB	K	PO	A
Butler cf	5	1	2	1	0	1	3	0
Bernazard 2b	3	1	1	2	1	2	2	4
Tabler lf	3	1	1	0	2	0	1	0
Castillo pr-rf	0	1	0	0	0	0	0	0
Thornton dh	3	0	2	3	1	1	0	0
Hargrove 1b	4	0	1	0	1	1	6	2
Franco ss	4	1	1	1	0	1	2	5
Hassey c	3	1	1	0	1	0	2	0
Nixon pr	0	0	0	0	0	0	0	0
Willard c	0	0	0	0	1	0	2	0
Jacoby 3b	5	0	1	0	0	2	2	0
Vukovich rf-lf	4	1	2	0	0	0	5	1
Heaton p	0	0	0	0	0	0	0	1
Waddell p	0	0	0	0	0	0	1	0
Camacho p	0	0	0	0	0	0	0	0
Totals	34	7	12	7	7	7	27	13

FIELDING
DP: 2

BATTING
2B: Bernazard (3, off Clemens); Vukovich (7, off Clemens)
SF: Thornton (3, off Clemens); Franco (2, off Clear)
HBP: Bernazard (1, by Clemens)
IBB: Hassey (2, by Clemens); Tabler (1, by Clemens)

BASERUNNING
SB: Tabler (1, 2nd base off Clemens/Allenson); Thornton 2 (3, 2nd base off Clemens/Allenson 2); Butler 2 (15, 2nd base off Clemens/Allenson 2); Franco (7, 2nd base off Clemens/Allenson); Nixon (7, 2nd base off Johnson/Gedman)

PITCHING

Boston Red Sox	IP	H	HR	R	ER	BB	K
Clemens	5.2	11	0	5	4	3	4
Johnson L(0–1)	1.1	1	0	2	2	3	2
Clear	1.0	0	0	0	0	1	1
Totals	8	12	0	7	6	7	7
Cleveland Indians	IP	H	HR	R	ER	BB	K
Heaton	4.2	7	0	4	4	3	1
Waddell W(1–1)	3.1	2	1	1	1	1	2
Camacho SV(5)	1.0	1	0	0	0	1	2
Totals	9.0	10	1	5	5	5	5

HBP: Clemens (1, Bernazard)
IBB: Clemens 2 (2, Hassey, Tabler)
Time of Game: 2:55 Attendance: 4,004

It was Rac Slider who told me I was going up. He was our manager at Pawtucket, and we were playing in Tidewater. As soon as I came out of the game there at old Met Park, he said, "Go in, shower and ice up, and then you're out of here." Not a lot of drama there. He just said, "Get going, you're flying to Cleveland." I got in a day before the start, which was enough time for my parents to come up from Texas.

A lot of things happened in that game. Man, they tried everything, figuring I'm just a kid rookie. Bunting, hit and run, suicide squeeze, you name it—they were trying to get in my head. But I think I showed where my head was right away . . . Right after I walked Brett Butler to lead off the game, I picked him off. I remember thinking that I had met the challenge, win or lose. Mike Hargrove was my first strikeout . . . I gave up a few hits, though . . . I came out with the game 4–4. Everyone seemed pretty happy with how it went, but I would have liked to have gotten the win. But I'm glad I won that next one. That's when I felt like I had really made it.

Also on May 15, 1984
Don Sutton wins his 275th game as the Brewers rally past Texas, 3–2.

AUTHOR'S NOTE: In 2004, Clemens caught and passed Sutton's eventual win total of 324, but he was more proud to have caught and passed the other major leaguer who'd ended his career with that total—his childhood hero, Nolan Ryan.

Bobby Crosby
Born: January 12, 1980
Debut: September 2, 2003

As a kid, Bobby Crosby missed out on his dad's big league exploits. Ed Crosby had been a utility infielder on the Reds' 1973 National League pennant-winning team and had enjoyed an otherwise unremarkable six-year big league career. By the time Bobby was born, Ed had retired to scouting, and young Bobby would occasionally follow dad on his assignments, holding the radar gun for him and getting a feel for what to look for.

As a high schooler, Bobby was able to put what he saw into action. Growing from 5'9" his junior year to 6'2" his senior year, Bobby began to garner notice from scouts besides his dad, and the A's made him their first-round pick after three years at Long Beach State. He was signed not by his dad, but by Rick Magnante. Ed Crosby had already landed the A's a big fish out of Long Beach a few years prior, a guy named Jason Giambi.

While Crosby wasn't asked to replace Giambi's newly departed bat in 2003, he was given the huge task of filling the shoes of the popular Miguel Tejada. When the 2002 MVP signed with Baltimore for 2004, Crosby was anointed the new A's shortstop, with no "plan B" in place. He scorched seven home runs in spring training but got out of the gate slowly come April. He hit his stride in midseason and was a landslide pick for Rookie of the Year, having led all American League rookies with 22 homers, 64 RBI, and 70 runs scored. A late-season slump dropped his batting average to .239, but he had laced 34 doubles and played solid defense as well. Manager Ken Macha compared him favorably to the shortstop he had coached in the Red Sox's minor league system, Nomar Garciaparra.

"As a big [6'3", 195-pound] shortstop, I guess I'll always be compared to other big shortstops," Crosby says. "Cal Ripken was my favorite player growing up, so that's fine with me. I just hope people don't expect me to do all the things those guys did right away." At the very least, he's off to a heck of a start.

My mom and dad were visiting me on a road trip, in Vegas. Fifth or sixth inning, I've already had a nice game with a couple of hits including a home run, and my manager, Tony DeFrancesco, pulls me aside after the single and says, "Hey, you're done for the night." I had no idea why, but I figured, okay, that's cool, so I just went and sat at the end of the dugout there at Cashman Field in Vegas. I figured he was resting me for the playoffs we were about to

41

BOXSCORE

Oakland Athletics 2, Baltimore Orioles 0

Game Played on Tuesday, September 2, 2003 (Night) at Oriole Park at Camden Yards

Oakland	0	0	0	0	0	0	0	0	0	2	—	2	5	0
Baltimore	0	0	0	0	0	0	0	0	0	0	—	0	7	0

BATTING

Oakland Athletics	AB	R	H	RBI	BB	K	PO	A
Long lf	4	0	0	0	0	3	0	0
Dye lf	2	0	0	0	0	0	0	0
Guillen rf	4	0	0	0	1	2	2	0
Chavez 3b	5	0	1	0	0	1	0	2
Tejada ss	3	1	1	0	2	1	4	5
Hatteberg 1b	2	1	1	0	3	0	13	2
Hernandez c	5	0	0	0	0	0	9	2
Durazo dh	3	0	0	0	0	0	0	0
Crosby ph-dh	1	0	0	0	1	0	0	0
Ellis 2b	4	0	1	1	0	0	4	3
Singleton cf	5	0	1	1	0	3	2	0
Zito p	0	0	0	0	0	0	1	1
Bradford p	0	0	0	0	0	0	0	2
Mecir p	0	0	0	0	0	0	0	0
Rincon p	0	0	0	0	0	0	0	0
Foulke p	0	0	0	0	0	0	0	0
Totals	**38**	**2**	**5**	**2**	**7**	**10**	**36**	**17**

FIELDING
DP: 2

BATTING
2B: Hatteberg (28, off Hentgen); Ellis (27, off Hentgen)
SF: Ellis (4, off Julio)

BASERUNNING
SB: Tejada (8, 3rd base off Ryan/Machado)

Baltimore Orioles	AB	R	H	RBI	BB	K	PO	A
B. Roberts 2b	5	0	1	0	0	2	4	1
Mora lf	5	0	1	0	0	6	1	1
Matos dh	5	0	1	0	0	0	0	0
Gibbons rf	4	0	1	0	1	1	3	0
Batista 3b	5	0	0	0	0	2	0	0
Surhoff 1b	4	0	1	0	1	1	9	0
Fordyce c	3	0	2	0	0	0	7	0
Morban pr	0	0	0	0	0	0	0	0
Machado c	2	0	0	0	0	1	5	0
Cruz ss	2	0	0	0	1	0	0	3
Bigbie ph	1	0	0	0	0	1	0	0
Raines cf	4	0	0	0	0	2	2	0
Hentgen p	0	0	0	0	0	0	0	2
Ligtenberg p	0	0	0	0	0	0	0	0
Ryan p	0	0	0	0	0	0	0	0
Julio p	0	0	0	0	0	0	0	1
Groom p	0	0	0	0	0	0	0	0
Carrasco p	0	0	0	0	0	0	0	0
Totals	**40**	**0**	**7**	**0**	**3**	**10**	**36**	**8**

FIELDING
DP: 2

BATTING
SH: Cruz (6, off Zito)

BASERUNNING
CS: Batista (3, 2nd base by Zito/Hernandez)

PITCHING

Oakland Athletics	IP	H	HR	R	ER	BB	K
Zito	8	4	0	0	0	2	7
Bradford	2	2	0	0	0	1	0
Mecir	0.2	2	0	0	0	0	0
Rincon W(8–4)	0.1	0	0	0	0	0	0
Foulke SV(38)	1	1	0	0	0	0	3
Totals	**12**	**7**	**0**	**0**	**0**	**3**	**10**

Baltimore Orioles	IP	H	HR	R	ER	BB	K
Hentgen	8	3	0	0	0	3	6
Ligtenberg	0.1	0	0	0	0	0	1
Ryan	1.2	0	0	0	0	2	2
Julio L(0–7)	1.2	1	0	2	2	2	1
Groom	0	1	0	0	0	0	0
Carrasco	0.1	0	0	0	0	0	0
Totals	**12.0**	**5**	**0**	**2**	**2**	**7**	**10**

Umpires: Marvin Hudson, Scott Nelson, Jerry Layne, Gary Darling
Time of Game: 3:43   Attendance: 19,517

start in a couple days. Then he comes over an inning later and says, "You think we've got a chance in the playoffs?" And I say, "Sure," but then he says, "Well, you're not going to be playing in them." And I'm like, "What? Why not?" He says, "No, you're going to Oakland." I say, "No way, dude," but he says, "Go get dressed and tell your folks." So that's what I did. Before they knew what was going on, I'm in the stands telling 'em . . . I had a couple family friends there, too. They drove me to the airport so I could red-eye out.

My first game I got in, I was sitting on the bench in Baltimore, and a bat broke. The head came flying into the dugout off the broken bat and I got smoked. Got hit in the back on a ricochet. This is the first few innings—I still haven't played yet, but I've already got to go to the trainer's room because I'm hurt. I got a pretty rough time about that, but later I got into the game and walked to set up our winning rally, so at least I was able to say I contributed.

Also on September 2, 2003
The Padres call up shortstop Khalil Greene from Triple-A and announce he'll start at shortstop the following night.

AUTHOR'S NOTE: The two 23-year-old Southern California shortstops, Crosby and Greene, would both make runs at Rookie of the Year honors in 2004. (Crosby won the AL award, and Greene finished second to the Pirates' Jason Bay in the NL.)

Johnny Damon
Born: November 5, 1973
Debut: August 12, 1995

He has a name that sounds like it's straight out of an action-hero comic book: The Adventures of Johnny Damon, and his Wonder Dog, Poochie! Actually, Damon is the son of a onetime army staff sergeant who served in the Vietnam War. His mother is Taiwanese and worked double shifts at a Disney World hotel to support the family.

He wallowed in obscurity in Kansas City and, to a lesser extent, in Oakland, then found his true inner Johnny once he moved along to Boston. The Red Sox have recently become the anti-Yankees; while the New Yorkers are all very cool, clean-shaven, professional, and well-spoken, the Red Sox are best summed up by Damon himself: "We're just a bunch of idiots." If ignorance is bliss, then the Red Sox clubhouse is Nirvana. The merry band of modern-day Red Sox souls are loud, outlandish, and occasionally even loutish. Damon fits right in, although he's light on the loutish.

During the 1999 season, a fan sent him a letter asking him to please help him buy a car on eBay. The fan wanted five grand and chose Damon as his benefactor because he simply seemed to be a good, approachable guy. Damon never did pony up, but it strikes you that Damon does come across as the kind of guy who just might lend a stranger $5K for a '94 Escort. By contrast, there is no record of anyone ever having approached Albert Belle for a car loan.

Damon had arrived for 2004 spring training sporting a look that some described as caveman chic, others described as Charles Manson 2.0, and still others described as Jesus-like. "I gotta be me," Damon explained, and his folically challenged manager, Terry Francona, gave his blessing (to the man who looked like maybe *he* should be doing the blessing). Heading into that 2004 season, Damon seemed like a man on a mission. He had trained rigorously during the winter, running wind sprints in his gated Orlando community, scaring the heck out of the neighbors. "I'd lurk in the bushes, then race the drivers as they came through on the 25-mile-per-hour speed limit," he said. "They'd speed up pretty quick, because all of a sudden, some berserk caveman-looking guy is running just off their right bumper."

He enjoyed a tour-de-force 2004 regular season, then smashed out of a postseason slump by cranking a pair of Game Seven home runs that tilted the ALCS out of New York and into New England. The next day, he jumped on stage with the band Godsmack at Boston's Lucky Strike Lanes,

BOXSCORE

Kansas City Royals 7, Seattle Mariners 2

Game Played on Saturday, August 12, 1995 (Night) at Kauffman Stadium

Seattle	0	0	0	0	0	0	2	0	—	2	3	0
Kansas City	0	1	0	2	1	2	0	1	x	—	7	12	1

BATTING

Seattle Mariners	AB	R	H	RBI	BB	K	PO	A
Cora 2b	4	1	1	0	0	0	1	3
Diaz cf	4	0	1	1	0	0	2	0
E. Martinez dh	3	0	0	1	1	0	0	0
T. Martinez 1b	3	0	0	0	1	0	8	1
Buhner rf	4	0	0	0	0	2	1	0
Blowers 3b	4	0	0	0	0	2	2	0
Newson lf	3	0	0	0	1	1	3	0
Wilson c	3	0	1	0	0	1	3	1
Fermin ss	2	1	0	0	1	0	3	1
Belcher p	0	0	0	0	0	0	0	0
Torres p	0	0	0	0	0	0	1	1
Totals	30	2	3	2	4	6	24	7

FIELDING
DP: 1

BATTING
2B: Cora (11, off Meacham)

Kansas City Royals	AB	R	H	RBI	BB	K	PO	A
Damon cf	5	1	3	1	0	0	2	0
Lockhart 2b-3b	4	0	0	1	1	1	2	0
Joyner 1b	4	1	2	2	0	0	10	1
Gaetti 3b	4	2	2	0	0	0	1	0
Howard 2b	1	0	0	0	0	0	0	1
Nunnally rf	3	0	0	0	0	1	4	0
Gagne ss	2	1	2	1	2	0	0	8
Cookson dh	2	0	1	2	1	1	0	0
Caceres pr-dh	1	0	0	0	0	0	0	0
Tucker lf	3	1	1	1	0	0	1	0
Mayne c	4	1	1	0	0	0	6	0
Appier p	0	0	0	0	0	0	1	0
Meacham p	0	0	0	0	0	0	0	1
Totals	33	7	12	7	4	3	27	11

FIELDING
E: Lockhart (4)

BATTING
2B: Gaetti (21, off Belcher); Cookson (1, off Belcher); Tucker (4, off Torres)
3B: Damon (1, off Belcher)
SH: Nunnally (3, off Belcher)
SF: Joyner (6, off Belcher)
HBP: Tucker (1, by Belcher)
IBB: Gagne (2, by Belcher)

BASERUNNING
SB: Lockhart (3, 2nd base off Belcher/Wilson)

PITCHING

Seattle Mariners	IP	H	HR	R	ER	BB	K
Belcher L (8–7)	5	6	0	6	6	4	2
Torres	3	6	0	1	1	0	1
Totals	8	12	0	7	7	4	3
Kansas City Royals	**IP**	**H**	**HR**	**R**	**ER**	**BB**	**K**
Appier W (12–7)	6	2	0	0	0	3	3
Meacham SV (1)	3	1	0	2	2	1	3
Totals	9	3	0	2	2	4	6

HBP: Belcher (3, Tucker)
IBB: Belcher (4, Gagne)
Umpires: Al Clark, Larry Barnett, Greg Kosc, Dan Morrison
Time of Game: 2:35   Attendance: 20,572

belting out their hit song, "I Stand Alone." The triumph of Captain Caveman.

I was 3-for-5 off Salomon Torres and some other dude [Tim Belcher]. I had a triple into the right-field corner, past Tino Martinez at first. We won, I know that. I had come up from Wichita . . . [The Royals] had just gotten rid of Vince Coleman and made a bunch of other moves. So me, Michael Tucker, Brent Cookson—a bunch of us went up. Ron Johnson was our manager at Wichita . . . and I was kind of upset I wasn't playing that day. He had given me the day off before, so here I am not playing again and I'm like, "What's the deal here?" And he said, "Oh, poor Johnny's whining and complaining that he's not playing, whoopee-doo, poor guy." And as I'm standing there getting angry, he goes, "It's 'cuz you're going to the big leagues." I thought he was kidding, because the next step from Double-A is Triple-A, not the big leagues. But he told me, "Yeah, go up there and go get 'em."

They wanted to bring up some

Also on August 12, 1995
Mickey Mantle's last day alive. The following morning, he would succumb to liver cancer in a Dallas hospital, at the age of 63. Later, at the Hall of Famer's funeral, Bob Costas would eulogize, ". . . God knows, no one's perfect. But God knows there's something special about heroes."

AUTHOR'S NOTE: Johnny Damon would be the first to admit that he, too, is far from perfect. But he himself would become a hero of sorts when he belted the Game Seven grand slam in the 2004 ALCS. He punched it into Yankee Stadium's right-field bleachers, where Mantle used to hit 'em, too.

kids to give 'em some energy . . . Bob Boone told us we'd play right away. The team clicked there for a while . . . We actually took a four-game lead in the wild card for a bit. We couldn't hold it, but what a great experience, man. All three of us got in the game that first day we were there . . . and it worked out great for me with three hits, but Cookie [Cookson] got hurt though. He hurt his ankle in that game and never played much after that.

Courtesy Kansas City Royals

Carlos Delgado
Born: June 25, 1972
Debut: October 1, 1993

Growing up in Puerto Rico, Carlos Delgado idolized the late Roberto Clemente, who died the year Delgado was born. Delgado's dad, an athlete himself, made sure the young man embodied the altruistic traits of the Pirates' legendary outfielder. And although Carlos wanted to play right field just like Clemente had, his Little League coaches made him a catcher, since he was so much bigger than the other boys. Signed as a catcher by the Blue Jays (who had become quite adept at identifying Latin American talent), Delgado swatted home runs at various minor league stops, then found a home at Skydome in 1994. After a couple of false starts (a .215 batting average found him retooling his stroke at Triple-A later that same year), he settled in for good in '95, shifting from catcher to first baseman/DH.

Delgado steadily increased his home run totals in the mid-to-late 90s, going from 25 to 30 to 38 to 44 by 1999. Although his 2000 season produced "only" 41, his other numbers skyrocketed, keeping the Jays in wild card contention for much of the year. Delgado, in fact, made a run at the Triple Crown before petering out down the stretch, but he had walloped a team record 57 doubles and hit a robust .344.

His injury-marred 2004 season would be his last in Toronto, as his salary was no longer viable for the Jays. (In 2003, Delgado was, believe it or not, the second-highest-paid player in the game, behind Alex Rodriguez.) He left the Blue Jays with a team-record 336 home runs and more than 1,000 runs batted in (knocking in 145 alone in his spectacular '03 season).

With leadership skills oozing from every pore, it was Delgado who was named team captain on those late-90s teams, despite the presence of veterans like Roger Clemens, Pat Hentgen, and Juan Samuel. Delgado made it a habit of inhaling scouting reports on every pitcher, dutifully arriving by 2:15 for 7:00 games, home and away, to work out and take rounds and rounds of private batting practice. Clemente would have been proud.

I got called up all the way from Double-A and was asked to go all the way to Minneapolis. But it was a long, long wait before that. See, they had actually told me I was going up 17 days before. But they said, "You won't go up until the team is done with the playoffs." And as much as I wanted to win in the playoffs and all, I knew that every day we won was another day in Double-A . . . another day missing major league service time, and missing the chance to show everyone what I could do. It was a battle . . . in my head, a battle. I knew the right thing to do was just do my best and help our team win at Double-A, but the Blue Jays were on their way to winning another World Series, remember . . . Who wouldn't have wanted to be a part of that? We had a great team at Double-A, too, and beat the Braves' team in the semifinals three games to two, with a couple rainouts in there I think that delayed things even more. Then we played Terry Francona's team in Birmingham, the White Sox farm team . . . and that series went long, too. Finally, finally, I was told, "Okay join the team in Minneapolis."

Me and Huck Flener went up together. I finally got in against Baltimore, and I walked against a right-hander. The next day, I popped out, and that was it for my first big league season! I had to wait all winter to try and make the team again in the spring and get my first hit.

Also on October 1, 1993
Mark McGwire celebrates his 30th birthday.

AUTHOR'S NOTE: McGwire (and his onetime Bash Brothers teammate Jose Canseco) were the two right-handed sluggers most capable of bouncing home runs off Skydome's upper deck. Delgado proved to be the most effective lefty.

BOXSCORE

Baltimore Orioles 7, Toronto Blue Jays 2
Game Played on Friday, October 1, 1993 (Night) at Oriole Park at Camden Yards

Toronto	0	0	1	0	0	0	1	0	0	—	2	8	1
Baltimore	1	0	2	2	1	0	0	1	x	—	7	12	0

BATTING

Toronto Blue Jays	AB	R	H	RBI	BB	K	PO	A
Henderson lf	3	0	1	0	0	0	2	0
Butler lf	2	0	0	0	0	1	0	0
White cf	2	0	0	1	0	0	1	0
T. Ward cf	2	1	1	0	0	0	2	0
Molitor dh	4	0	2	0	1	0	0	0
Carter rf	3	0	0	0	0	1	0	0
Canate rf	0	0	0	1	0	0	0	0
Olerud 1b	3	0	1	0	1	0	4	3
Fernandez ss	0	0	0	0	0	0	0	0
Schofield ss	3	0	1	0	1	0	5	2
Sprague 3b	3	0	0	0	0	0	0	0
Martinez 3b	1	0	0	0	0	0	0	0
Knorr c	2	0	1	0	1	0	3	0
Delgado c	0	0	0	0	1	0	2	0
Griffin 2b	4	1	1	0	0	0	3	2
Stottlemyre p	0	0	0	0	0	0	0	1
Williams p	0	0	0	0	0	0	1	0
Flener p	0	0	0	0	0	0	1	0
Totals	**32**	**2**	**8**	**2**	**5**	**2**	**24**	**9**

FIELDING
DP: 1
E: Fernandez (7)

BATTING
2B: T. Ward (4, off Valenzuela)
SF: White (3, off Valenzuela); Canate (1, off Valenzuela)

Baltimore Orioles	AB	R	H	RBI	BB	K	PO	A
Anderson cf	5	3	2	1	0	0	2	0
McLemore rf	3	1	2	1	0	0	2	0
Buford ph-lf	2	0	0	0	0	1	0	0
Ripken ss	5	1	2	1	0	0	3	4
Baines dh	5	0	2	2	0	1	0	0
Alexander pr-dh	0	0	0	0	0	0	0	0
Pagliarulo 3b	4	0	0	1	1	0	0	2
Voigt lf-rf	3	1	1	0	1	0	7	0
Carey 1b	3	0	0	0	1	1	6	0
Segui 1b	0	0	0	0	0	0	2	0
Reynolds 2b	2	1	2	0	2	0	2	3
Parent c	3	0	1	1	0	2	3	0
Valenzuela p	0	0	0	0	0	0	0	0
Frohwirth p	0	0	0	0	0	0	0	0
Mills p	0	0	0	0	0	0	0	0
Totals	**35**	**7**	**12**	**7**	**5**	**5**	**27**	**9**

FIELDING
DP: 1

BATTING
2B: Reynolds (20, off Stottlemyre); Baines (22, off Flener)
SH: Parent (3, off Stottlemyre)

BASERUNNING
SB: Anderson (23, 2nd base off Stottlemyre/Knorr); Voigt (1, 2nd base off Stottlemyre/Knorr)

PITCHING

Toronto Blue Jays	IP	H	HR	R	ER	BB	K
Stottlemyre L(11–12)	5	10	0	6	5	3	3
Williams	2	0	0	0	0	2	1
Flener	1	2	0	1	1	0	1
Totals	**8**	**12**	**0**	**7**	**6**	**5**	**5**

Baltimore Orioles	IP	H	HR	R	ER	BB	K
Valenzuela W(8–10)	6.2	8	0	2	2	4	2
Frohwirth	1.1	0	0	0	0	1	0
Mills	1	0	0	0	0	0	0
Totals	**9**	**8**	**0**	**2**	**2**	**5**	**2**

WP: Valenzuela (8)
Umpires: Tim Tschida, Gary Cederstrom, Don Denkinger, John Shulock
Time of Game: 2:57   Attendance: 45,881

Jim Deshaies
Born: June 23, 1960
Debut: August 7, 1984

The rare player known more for his Chris Berman–sanctioned nickname than for his pitching, Jim "Two Silhouettes On" Deshaies was actually a highly regarded Yankees prospect who ended up winning 84 big league games, including a 15–10 campaign with the Astros in 1989.

His debut with the Yankees gained him some fleeting fame as the 1,000th man to have played in a regular season game as a member of the storied franchise. Dealt to a much less storied franchise in Houston (26 World Series titles to zero), he blossomed under managers Hal Lanier and Art Howe. His career continued into 1994, when he led the American League in starts but had an ungainly ERA of 7.39.

He was an unlikely candidate for the Hall of Fame, but thanks to a fanciful PR campaign, he actually finagled a single vote in his lone year of eligibility. To get the PR machine rolling, he told reporters, "I struck out the first eight batters I faced in a game, which is a record. I set the record for pickoff attempts to first base in a season, which I think is still standing. I set the major league record for most at bats without an extra-base hit, which I think still stands. I managed to pitch nine years in the majors with an 84 mph fastball that was straight," he said. "That has to count for something."

A rain delay and Harold Baines hitting an upper tank home run, that's what I remember most. It was August of '84, Yankees vs. White Sox in a doubleheader at Yankee Stadium . . . The Yankee pitchers were the great Ron Guidry and, well, me. The White Sox had reigning Cy Young Award winner LaMarr Hoyt and Jerry Don Gleaton, and, of course, I drew not Jerry Don Gleaton but reigning Cy Young Award winner LaMarr Hoyt. The outcome was predictable.

I had gotten the call while our [Triple-A] Columbus team was in Syracuse, which is pretty close to my hometown of Massena, New York. My girlfriend, now my wife, [and] my parents were there with my little brother and sister, and we had all gone out to lunch. They dropped me off at the hotel and then they all skipped off to the mall. Stump Merrill, our manager, called me into his hotel room and gave me the news that I was being called up, so I was frantically trying to get ahold of my family at the mall—no cell phones of course. We called mall security and had them paged. Wow, did they have a nice party at the old Pepper Mill restaurant in Syracuse that night.

48

Originally, I was supposed to start on a Sunday, on Lou Piniella Day. Somebody thought I'd have a panic attack pitching on such a big day in front of a huge crowd, so they bumped me to a Tuesday double-header, and I still panicked anyway. Long rain delay, and I had a bad-fitting uniform with a terrible number, 67. I was 66 in spring training. I guess somehow I had gotten worse between March and August. Hard to feel confident when they give you the pulling guard's number. My pants were too short. Phil Rizzuto was on the air saying, "Now this kid is an old time ballplayer with respect for the game. Look at how he wears his pants up high like that." My parents knew it was just because the pants were too short.

Anyway, I got through the first inning or two okay, but then the rain delay [came] . . . and Harold Baines hit a ridiculous home run. First game's over, I've lost, and I'm sitting there as game two is starting, and I asked the clubhouse guy for a new uniform so I could go back out there and watch. But he kind of growled at me and never did give me a uniform, so I just walked out of the clubhouse in my street clothes and went and sat in the camera well to watch Guidry beat Gleaton in game two. At least my pants fit.

Also on August 7, 1984
The U.S. Olympic baseball team drops the gold medal game to Japan.

BOXSCORE

Chicago White Sox 6, New York Yankees 3
(Game One of Doubleheader)

Game Played on Tuesday, August 7, 1984 (Night) at Yankee Stadium

Chicago	0	0	0	0	4	1	1	0	0	—	6	14	1
New York	0	2	0	0	0	0	0	0	1	—	3	7	0

BATTING

Chicago White Sox	AB	R	H	RBI	BB	K	PO	A
R.Law cf	5	1	1	0	0	0	3	0
Paciorek 1b	5	2	3	1	0	0	13	0
Squires 1b	0	0	0	0	0	0	1	1
Baines rf	5	1	3	3	0	0	1	0
Luzinski dh	5	2	3	1	0	0	0	0
Walker pr-dh	0	0	0	0	0	0	0	0
Kittle lf	3	0	1	0	2	1	4	0
Hill c	1	0	0	0	1	0	0	0
Hairston ph	0	0	0	0	1	0	0	0
Fisk c	2	0	0	0	0	1	1	1
V.Law 3b	3	0	1	0	1	0	0	4
Dybzinski ss	4	0	1	0	0	0	2	3
Cruz 2b	4	0	1	0	0	2	1	7
Hoyt p	0	0	0	0	0	0	1	2
Agosto p	0	0	0	0	0	0	0	0
Totals	37	6	14	5	5	4	27	18

FIELDING
DP: 2
E: Baines (5)

BATTING
2B: Baines (24, off Deshaies); R. Law (8, off Deshaies); Paciorek (14, off Shirley); Kittle (11, off Shirley)
3B: Baines (5, off Shirley)
HR: Baines (18, 5th inning off Deshaies, 1 on, 0 out); Luzinski (12, 7th inning off Shirley, 0 on, 0 out)

New York Yankees	AB	R	H	RBI	BB	K	PO	A
Randolph 2b	4	0	1	0	0	0	3	6
Meacham ss	4	0	1	0	0	0	4	3
Kemp lf	4	0	0	0	0	0	2	0
Winfield rf	3	2	1	0	1	0	4	0
Baylor dh	4	1	2	2	0	0	0	0
Griffey 1b	4	0	0	0	0	1	7	1
Wynegar c	3	0	0	0	1	0	6	0
Pagliarulo 3b	3	0	2	1	0	0	0	1
Moreno cf	3	0	0	0	0	0	1	2
Deshaies p	0	0	0	0	0	0	0	0
Armstrong p	0	0	0	0	0	0	0	0
Shirley p	0	0	0	0	0	0	0	1
Totals	32	3	7	3	2	1	27	14

FIELDING
DP: 2

BATTING
2B: Baylor 2 (21, off Hoyt 2); Winfield (25, off Hoyt)

PITCHING

Chicago White Sox	IP	H	HR	R	ER	BB	K
Hoyt W(10–11)	8.1	7	0	3	3	2	1
Agosto SV(5)	0.2	0	0	0	0	0	0
Totals	9.0	7	0	3	3	2	1

New York Yankees	IP	H	HR	R	ER	BB	K
Deshaies L(0–1)	4.0	8	1	4	4	3	3
Armstrong	1.0	0	0	0	0	2	0
Shirley	4.0	6	1	2	2	0	1
Totals	9.0	14	2	6	6	5	4

Time of Game: 2:48   Attendance: 25,422

AUTHOR'S NOTE: The Olympians were led by a young (and then skinny) Mark Mc-Gwire, who would have many of his home runs later detailed by Deshaies from the broadcast booth.

Darin Erstad

Born: June 4, 1974
Debut: June 14, 1996

An immensely likable outfielder-turned-first baseman, Darin Erstad talks of the "privilege" of wearing a big league uniform. His humility and work ethic belie the fact he was the number one pick in the 1995 draft. Stories of his willingness to get his hands and uniform dirty abound; none is more telling than the one about his experience in the amateur Cape Cod summer league in 1993. To make a few bucks for spending money, Erstad and his teammates were given part-time summer jobs; only Erstad walked away with an "employee of the month" award, from the department store, Bradlees.

Erstad grew up in the small town of Jamestown, North Dakota, and is now a North Dakota treasure, somewhere in between Roger Maris and Lawrence Welk. He is now the most famous entity from Jamestown, edging the "World's Largest Buffalo," a 60-ton structure the townsfolk erected to be visible from the I-94 expressway, which runs just outside of town.

At the University of Nebraska, he was known as the Cornhuskers' left-footed soccer-style kicker and punter. By the time he reached the World Series for the 2002 Angels, Erstad had already been in possession of his national championship ring from college football a full eight years—and he was quick to point out the pressure of playing in the World Series was similar to (and as enjoyable as) playing in that national title game at the Orange Bowl against Miami.

We were in Edmonton . . . I remember taking a really, really bad batting practice, and Donny Long, our manager, walked out to center field and I thought I was going to get yelled at for not hitting good. He told me, "You're getting called up," so I'm like, "Whoa, I better find my swing in the next 24 hours." I flew back to Vancouver, got in around 2 A.M., got maybe two hours' sleep, flew to Anaheim, did a press conference, was in the starting lineup, went out there and proceeded to punch out three times and hit a nubber back to the pitcher. Erik Hanson was pitching with that good change-up . . . Shoot, I was geared up to hit a 120-mph fastball I was so excited, but I kept getting the 70-mile-per-hour change-up, so I pretty much got it shoved up my butt. Did we win or lose? I can't even remember. [Won, 7–4.]

The press conference was embarrassing, but that comes with the territory when you're a number one pick, I guess. The fact that the Angels made such a big deal out of it took the pressure off me being the one to get the word out. I walked into the clubhouse, and there's a note of congratulations from Tom Osborne and my football coaches back at Nebraska—really nice.

My family had made it in, they were all there . . . and I didn't do much those first two games, 0-for-8, but then I ripped off an 11-game hitting streak from there, and those thoughts of "What I am I doing here, I can't hit in the big leagues" pretty much stopped. Then just when I started feeling all confident, I went something like 4-for-60 and got sent down.

But, you know, I believed it then, I believe it now, you just gotta go out there and do what you do—first day, last day in the big leagues, all of 'em in between . . . I'm sure my manager and coaches all had some very wise advice for me those first few weeks, but I really don't remember what it was. Coaches can talk 'til they're blue in the face, but there's no substitute for going out there and experiencing it.

Also on June 14, 1996
Cal Ripken Jr. breaks the world record for consecutive games played—2,215—when he plays against the Royals in Kansas City. Japan's Sachio Kinugasa is in attendance to see his record fall.

AUTHOR'S NOTE: Erstad, like Ripken, is known for his desire to be out there for every inning. Erstad went so far as to lead the majors in at bats in 2000, yet even in that season, he missed five games. Ripken, whom Erstad has long admired, set the standard with 2,632 consecutive games played. Erstad, with his all-out style, has yet to have a streak of 100.

BOXSCORE

California Angels 7, Toronto Blue Jays 4

Game Played on Friday, June 14, 1996 (Day) at Anaheim Stadium

Toronto	4	0	0	0	0	0	0	0	0	—	4	8	0
California	2	2	2	0	1	0	0	0	x	—	7	10	1

BATTING

Toronto Blue Jays	AB	R	H	RBI	BB	K	PO	A
Brumfield cf	4	1	0	0	0	2	3	0
Cedeno 2b	5	1	1	0	0	1	3	0
Delgado dh	4	1	1	1	0	1	0	0
Carter lf	3	1	1	3	1	0	0	0
Olerud 1b	3	0	0	0	1	0	6	0
Green rf	4	0	1	0	0	1	3	0
Martinez c	3	0	1	0	0	0	7	1
Sprague ph	1	0	0	0	0	1	0	0
O'Brien c	0	0	0	0	0	0	0	0
Gonzalez ss	4	0	1	0	0	1	2	3
T. Perez 3b	3	0	2	0	1	1	0	1
Hanson p	0	0	0	0	0	0	0	0
Spoljaric p	0	0	0	0	0	0	0	0
Risley p	0	0	0	0	0	0	0	0
Totals	34	4	8	4	3	8	24	5

BATTING
HR: Carter (14, 1st inning off Grimsley, 2 on, 0 out)
HBP: Brumfield (1, by Grimsley)

California Angels	AB	R	H	RBI	BB	K	PO	A
Erstad cf	4	1	0	0	1	3	2	0
Slaught c	5	1	1	1	0	1	8	0
Anderson lf	5	1	2	2	0	1	1	0
Salmon rf	4	0	1	1	1	0	0	0
Davis dh	3	0	1	0	1	1	0	0
Snow 1b	1	1	0	0	3	0	8	2
Wallach 3b	4	1	1	2	0	1	1	2
Easley 3b	0	0	0	0	0	0	0	0
Velarde 2b	4	2	3	1	0	0	1	3
Disarcina ss	4	0	1	0	0	0	4	2
Grimsley p	0	0	0	0	0	0	2	0
McElroy p	0	0	0	0	0	0	0	0
Percival p	0	0	0	0	0	0	0	0
Totals	34	7	10	7	6	7	27	9

FIELDING
DP: 1
E: Disarcina (5)

BATTING
2B: Anderson 2 (14, off Hanson 2); Velarde (8, off Hanson)
HR: Wallach (7, 3rd inning off Hanson, 1 on, 1 out); Velarde (5, 5th inning off Hanson, 0 on, 1 out)

BASERUNNING
SB: Salmon (4, 2nd base off Hanson/Martinez)

PITCHING

Toronto Blue Jays	IP	H	HR	R	ER	BB	K
Hanson L (6–9)	5	8	2	7	7	5	5
Spoljaric	2	2	0	0	0	1	2
Risley	1	0	0	0	0	0	0
Totals	8	10	2	7	7	6	7
California Angels	IP	H	HR	R	ER	BB	K
Grimsley W (4–5)	7.2	8	1	4	4	2	4
McElroy	0.1	0	0	0	0	0	1
Percival SV (17)	1	0	0	0	0	1	3
Totals	9	8	1	4	4	3	8

HBP: Grimsley (4, Brumfield)
Umpires: Tim Welke, Joe Brinkman, Ken Kaiser, Derryl Cousins
Time of Game: 2:33   Attendance: 18,503

Steve Finley
Born: March 12, 1965
Debut: April 3, 1989

Paducah, Kentucky, native Steve Finley has made it a habit of bucking the odds. A 14th-round draft pick, he made the Orioles Opening Day roster in 1989 despite fewer than 200 minor league games' experience. Upon arrival in Arizona—and apparently on a career downturn at 33—he began putting up better numbers than he had when he was 23. All the while, he played with an on-field passion and lived with an off-field gentleness. Padres owner John Moores, when asked what he'd do if he had just one wish, said, "Simple. I'd clone Steve Finley."

For a long time, the book on "Fins" was that he was a good breaking-ball hitter who couldn't quite get to a quality fastball. But oddly, as Finley grew older, his bat got quicker. In 1999 and 2000, he had back-to-back 30-home-run seasons. Keep in mind, great players like Roberto Clemente and Al Kaline never had *one* 30-home-run season.

Scouts learned that the one thing you can never do with Finley is to pigeonhole him. When he first came up, he was labeled a "spare part," a fifth-outfielder type. Then he outgrew that and was supposed to become an everyday player, but only a singles hitter. Then he morphed into a Gold Glove center fielder with doubles power. Finally, he became a Gold Glove fielder with home run power.

Traded in midseason from Arizona to the Dodgers in 2004, he hit the walk-off grand slam that pushed L.A. into the postseason, against the rival Giants.

As a Kentucky native, he developed an affinity for horses, having spent summers in the stables at his grandparents' farm. Upon moving to San Diego, he and his family bought Kentmere Farm, with ten acres for horse breeding. Finley dabbles in the breeding of thoroughbreds, raising them for sale. "They're such powerful beings," he has said, and the same has been said about Finley himself. Few players know more tricks for getting more out of their bodies than Finley, who was a kinesiology major in college. Indeed, he seems to have gotten better with age.

I remember going into Frank Robinson's office at the end of spring training, and I didn't figure it to be good news. They had made the trade for Brady Anderson, and I knew he was going to play. We had, like, six outfielders, and I just figured I was the odd man out. So I sat there just dreading what he was going to say next, and for a minute, he didn't really say anything, so I was getting a little anxious. Then he says, "Finley, you made the club." And when you're not expecting to hear that, it doesn't register right away, but all of a sudden, a big grin came over my face. I didn't even know what to say. So finally Frank just said, "You can go now." So I went out and called my parents, who made their reservations to fly out to Baltimore for Opening Day.

Brady and I ended up rooming together at the Cross Keys Inn near the old ballpark while we looked for apartments.

The game was climactic and anticlimactic at the same time. It was amazing to get the start, the realization of everything I'd worked for, but then, three innings into the game, I ran into the outfield wall and separated my shoulder. So my parents came all that way to see me play for three innings. First at bat, I faced Roger Clemens and just missed a hanging slider; I flew out. That would have been the ultimate, homering off the Rocket in my first big league at bat!

Also on April 3, 1989
Seton Hall falls to Michigan 80–79 in OT in the NCAA men's basketball title game.

AUTHOR'S NOTE: Finley would later play with, and become close to, a Seton Hall athlete while in Houston—Craig Biggio, who attended the Hall with Mo Vaughn and John Valentin.

BOXSCORE

Baltimore Orioles 5, Boston Red Sox 4
Game Played on Monday, April 3, 1989 (Day) at Memorial Stadium

Boston	0	0	0	0	3	1	0	0	0	—	4	10	0
Baltimore	0	0	1	0	3	0	0	0	1	—	5	12	0

BATTING

Boston Red Sox	AB	R	H	RBI	BB	K	PO	A
Boggs 3b	4	1	2	0	1	0	1	1
Barrett 2b	3	0	0	0	0	0	3	4
Evans rf	5	1	1	1	0	1	5	0
Greenwell lf	4	1	2	2	1	0	0	0
Burks cf	5	0	0	0	0	1	2	0
Rice dh	5	0	1	0	0	0	0	0
Esasky 1b	4	1	2	0	1	0	10	2
Gedman c	5	0	1	0	0	2	7	2
Reed ss	5	0	1	1	0	1	1	3
Clemens p	0	0	0	0	0	0	2	1
Smith p	0	0	0	0	0	0	0	0
Murphy p	0	0	0	0	0	0	0	0
Stanley p	0	0	0	0	0	0	0	1
Smithson p	0	0	0	0	0	0	0	0
Totals	40	4	10	4	3	5	31	14

FIELDING
DP: 2

BATTING
2B: Boggs (1, off Schmidt); Evans (1, off Schmidt); Esasky (1, off Schmidt)
HR: Greenwell (1, 6th inning off Schmidt, 1 on, 1 out)
SH: Barrett 2 (2, off Schmidt,off Holton)
IBB: Greenwell (1, by Holton)

BASERUNNING
SB: Greenwell (1, 2nd base off Holton/Tettleton)
CS: Esasky (1, 2nd base by Holton/Tettleton)

Baltimore Orioles	AB	R	H	RBI	BB	K	PO	A
Anderson cf	4	2	3	0	1	0	3	0
Bradley lf	4	1	0	0	1	2	4	0
Finley rf	1	0	0	0	0	0	1	0
Orsulak rf	4	0	1	1	0	1	1	0
C. Ripken ss	5	1	1	3	0	2	4	2
Sheets dh	5	0	1	0	0	1	0	0
Tettleton c	3	1	1	0	2	0	4	4
Traber 1b	3	0	1	0	0	1	10	0
Milligan ph-1b	2	0	2	0	0	0	1	0
Worthington 3b	5	0	2	1	0	0	1	5
Gonzales 2b	4	0	0	0	0	0	4	0
Schmidt p	0	0	0	0	0	0	0	2
Hickey p	0	0	0	0	0	0	0	0
Holton p	0	0	0	0	0	0	0	0
Totals	40	5	12	5	4	7	33	13

FIELDING
PB: Tettleton (1)

BATTING
2B: Anderson 2 (2, off Clemens 2)
HR: C. Ripken (1, 6th inning off Clemens, 2 on, 1 out)

BASERUNNING
SB: Anderson (1, 2nd base off Clemens/Gedman)
CS: Worthington (1, 2nd base by Clemens/Gedman)

PITCHING

Boston Red Sox	IP	H	HR	R	ER	BB	K
Clemens	7	7	1	4	4	3	4
Smith	1	0	0	0	0	0	2
Murphy	0.1	1	0	0	0	0	1
Stanley L (0–1)	2	3	0	1	1	1	0
Smithson	0	1	0	0	0	0	0
Totals	10	12	1	5	5	4	7

Baltimore Orioles	IP	H	HR	R	ER	BB	K
Schmidt	6.1	7	1	4	4	1	3
Hickey	0.1	0	0	0	0	0	0
Holton W (1–0)	4.1	3	0	0	0	2	2
Totals	11.0	10	1	4	4	3	5

IBB: Holton (1,Greenwell).
Umpires: Don Denkinger, Larry McCoy, Steve Palermo, Durwood Merrill
Time of Game: 3:52   Attendance: 52,161

Nomar Garciaparra
Born: July 23, 1973
Debut: August 31, 1996

All of New England seemed to fall in love all at once with the mantis-like shortstop with the quick bat and the funky name. Nomar Garciaparra weighed only 147 pounds his senior year of high school but is now a buff 190, with the body fat of a barbell. The native Californian stormed to AL Rookie of the Year honors, winning unanimously after hitting .306 with 30 home runs, 98 RBI, and 22 steals. In August, he fashioned a 30-game hitting streak (a rookie record) and ended up with more hits and total bases than any Boston rookie in history.

A first round pick out of Georgia Tech two years prior, Garciaparra shimmied up the minor league ladder, whetting the appetite of a still-cautious Red Sox Nation, which had been burned in the past by the promised greatness of Phil Plantier, Scott Cooper, and Sam Horn. Garciaparra, however, was the genuine article—a smooth fielder who emerged as the third corner of the AL shortstop triumvirate, joining Derek Jeter and Alex Rodriguez as the cream of the crop.

His torrid hitting continued the following year as he batted .323 with 35 jacks and a team-leading 122 RBI. When Mo Vaughn left Boston for Anaheim as a free agent, the 25-year-old inherited the role of team leader and continued to pile up big numbers. He had entered 2003 with the highest batting average by a shortstop in major league history (.328 to Honus Wagner's .327) but suffered through a down season, highlighted by perceived postseason failure (two extra base hits and one RBI in 12 games). Disaffected by his contract situation and the rumors of Alex Rodriguez being traded in from Texas, he got out slowly in 2004 and was flipped to the Cubs at midseason, eschewing the second-worse curse for the first.

Garciaparra is also known for his quirky mannerisms and superstitions, which border on obsessive compulsive. He descends the dugout steps one at a time and always places his glove gently on the top step in the exact same spot. At the plate, he performs a fidgety Arthur Murray routine, with an elaborate series of tugs at his batting gloves and taps with his toes. However, as a notorious first-ball hitter, he's seldom at bat for very long.

Now married to soccer star Mia Hamm, Garciaparra has made the rounds in Hollywood and New York, appearing as himself on *Two Guysand a Girl* and *Saturday Night Live*. As Jimmy Fallon himself said, Garciaparra's time as a Red Sox was mostly "wicked awesome." The New England–

accented calls of "Nomah!" were muted when he was dealt to Chicago, but his time spent at Fenway will not be forgotten.

I was fortunate to have debuted in California, where my parents could see me play . . . It's a pretty long drive to Oakland from where I'm from, but they got in the car and made it in time to see the game. They were the first to know I had gotten the call—as soon as [Pawtucket manager] Buddy Bailey told me what was going on, I called 'em from my cell phone as I was leaving the parking lot.

The game itself wasn't that great . . . We got shut out there in Oakland, but I got in as a replacement for Jeff Frye and got in as an at bat . . . It was against a good friend of mine, a guy I had played with and against when I was a kid, Willie Adams. We're from the same hometown. I hit the ball pretty good but lined out to center. Willie pitched a complete game shutout, which was probably the best big league game he ever pitched. I was real happy for him.

BOXSCORE

Oakland Athletics 8, Boston Red Sox 0

Game Played on Saturday, August 31, 1996 (Night) at Oakland-Alameda County Coliseum

Boston	0	0	0	0	0	0	0	0	0	—	0	5	1
Oakland	2	2	3	0	0	1	0	0	x	—	8	8	1

BATTING

Boston Red Sox	AB	R	H	RBI	BB	K	PO	A
Bragg rf	4	0	0	0	0	1	1	0
Frye 2b	3	0	1	0	0	0	3	1
Garciaparra 2b	1	0	0	0	0	0	2	1
Vaughn 1b	3	0	1	0	1	1	8	1
Jefferson dh	4	0	1	0	0	3	0	0
Stanley c	4	0	0	0	0	1	3	0
O'Leary lf	4	0	1	0	0	1	0	0
Valentin ss	3	0	1	0	0	0	0	2
Manto 3b	3	0	0	0	0	1	1	2
Tinsley lf	3	0	0	0	0	1	5	0
Wakefield p	0	0	0	0	0	0	0	1
Eshelman p	0	0	0	0	0	0	1	0
Lacy p	0	0	0	0	0	0	0	0
Totals	32	0	5	0	1	9	24	8

FIELDING
DP: 1
E: Valentin (16)

Oakland Athletics	AB	R	H	RBI	BB	K	PO	A
Batista 2b-3b	5	1	2	2	0	1	0	2
Brosius 3b-1b	5	0	0	0	0	1	3	1
Giambi dh	3	1	1	0	1	0	0	0
McGwire 1b	2	2	1	2	1	0	6	0
Bournigal pr-2b	0	0	0	0	0	0	1	2
Berroa rf	4	1	3	3	0	0	1	0
Young pr-rf	0	0	0	0	0	0	0	0
Steinbach c	2	1	0	0	2	0	9	0
Lesher lf	4	1	1	1	0	0	2	0
Moore cf	4	0	0	0	0	1	4	0
Bordick ss	3	1	0	0	1	0	1	2
Adams p	0	0	0	0	0	0	0	1
Totals	32	8	8	8	5	3	27	8

FIELDING
DP: 1
E: Lesher (1)

BATTING
HR: McGwire (46, 1st inning off Wakefield, 1 on, 2 out); Berroa (35, 3rd inning off Wakefield, 2 on, 0 out); Lesher (2, 6th inning off Wakefield, 0 on, 0 out)
HBP: McGwire (5, by Wakefield)

BASERUNNING
SB: Batista (5,2nd base off Wakefield/Stanley)

PITCHING

Boston Red Sox	IP	H	HR	R	ER	BB	K
Wakefield L(11–12)	6	7	3	8	8	3	2
Eshelman	1	1	0	0	0	2	0
Lacy	1	0	0	0	0	0	1
Totals	8	8	3	8	8	5	3
Oakland Athletics	IP	H	HR	R	ER	BB	K
Adams W(2–2)	9	5	0	0	0	1	9

WP: Wakefield (4)
HBP: Wakefield (10, McGwire)
Umpires: Dale Scott, Dave Phillips, Rocky Roe, Durwood Merrill
Time of Game: 2:17 Attendance: 32,116

Also on August 31, 1996
Neifi Perez of the Rockies beats Garciaparra to the punch, becoming the first of the two 23-year-old shortstops to debut that night.

AUTHOR'S NOTE: Perez did an admirable job for the 2004 Cubs as interim shortstop but lost the job for good when the Cubs traded for Garciaparra.

Kirk Gibson
Born: May 28, 1957
Debut: September 8, 1979

It is hard to fathom that any one player has cared more about winning than Kirk Gibson. The gritty, almost Neanderthal persona was no act—it was merely a by-product of his intense desire to win at all costs, whether it meant stepping on toes or breaking hearts. Off the field and away from the prying eyes of the media, Gibson is a warm-hearted environmentalist, deeply devoted to his wife and children, coaching his boys' youth hockey teams every winter. But the lasting images of Gibson will likely be those of a snarling, surly, unapproachable warrior who always appeared as though he'd snap you in half if you dared to come within five feet.

Depending on whether a fan lived in L.A. or Detroit, Gibson's signature moment differs. For Tiger fans, it was his upper deck home run against Goose Gossage to cement Game Five of the '84 World Series. For Dodger fans, and perhaps for baseball fans in general, it was his courageous ninth-inning, two-out shot off Dennis Eckersley to steal Game One of the '88 Fall Classic. (The epic ten-pitch at bat was waged on one good leg; Gibson golfed a backdoor slider over the right-field wall, and next time you watch the video, note the parking lot in the background, where a car's brake lights go on as the driver hears the radio call.)

The tone for that '88 season had been set when Gibson was victimized by a practical joke the first day of spring training. Gibson went ballistic when he discovered someone [Jesse Orosco] had put eye black in his hat, and he told his teammates in no uncertain terms he hadn't signed on to (mess) around. Sure enough, L.A. won the NL West, upset the Mets in the NLCS, then shocked the A's to win it all.

We had just won the Triple-A championship in Springfield, Illinois. We partied pretty hard on the way back to Evansville, on the bus, and on the way, our manager, Jim Leyland, called me over and said, "When we get back, pack up and drive to Detroit, because they're calling you up." Well, I was planning on packing up and driving home anyway because that's home for me, Detroit.

We're playing the Yankees. Well, they're up by a run or two in the eighth inning the last night of the series. Gossage gets up to warm up, and I want in. He was the dominant closer of the time, and I wanted to get in there and try it out against the best. Ninth inning comes, Gossage goes to the mound, and I notice all the possible pinch hitters on our bench are suddenly excusing themselves to go pee. They want no part of him. Well, I picked up my bat and moved down towards [manager] Sparky [Anderson], clanking the bat around. Finally, he says, "What do you want?" I say, "I want Gossage." And Sparky says, "Okay, you got him, big boy." Place is going nuts as I step out of the dugout. I'm supposed to be the savior—the next Mickey Mantle, all-American, and a home-town kid, too. I take a couple practice swings and notice Gossage isn't even getting signs from the catcher. I know he's just gonna rear back and throw as hard as he can. He throws two fastballs, and both times, I swing out of my ass and just miss, fouling 'em straight back. Next pitch—strike three, outside corner. Game over. The whole at bat lasted maybe 40 seconds. [Elvis voice] "Thank you, thank you very much." But as I watched the Yankees come out of the dugout to congratulate Gossage, I said to myself, f—— it. He's the best, and you battled him. You're on your way. And that's what made the home run off Gossage in the '84 World Series so special. He had dominated me for five years starting with that first at bat. But when it counted, I got him.

Also on September 8, 1979
The singer/songwriter known as Pink is born in Doylestown, Pennsylvania.

AUTHOR'S NOTE: There may not be two more polar opposites on the planet than Kirk Gibson and Pink. (Although, some sportswriters might tell you the performer's singles, "Just Like a Pill" and "You Make me Sick," were written with Gibson in mind.)

BOXSCORE

New York Yankees 5, Detroit Tigers 4
Game Played on Saturday, September 8, 1979 (Night) at Tiger Stadium

	1	2	3	4	5	6	7	8	9	—	R	H	E
New York	1	2	1	0	0	0	0	1	0	—	5	8	3
Detroit	0	0	0	1	1	0	1	1	0	—	4	6	0

BATTING

New York Yankees	AB	R	H	RBI	BB	K	PO	A
Murcer cf	4	2	1	1	1	1	1	0
Chambliss 1b	4	0	1	1	0	0	9	1
Gamble lf	3	0	0	0	0	2	0	0
Piniella lf	1	0	0	0	0	0	0	0
Jackson rf	4	0	1	1	0	1	0	0
Spencer dh	3	1	2	0	1	0	0	0
Nettles 3b	3	1	1	1	1	0	0	5
Narron c	3	0	1	0	0	1	9	1
White ph	1	0	0	0	0	0	0	0
Gulden c	0	0	0	0	0	0	5	0
Doyle 2b	4	0	1	1	0	0	2	3
Dent ss	4	1	0	0	0	0	1	1
Guidry p	0	0	0	0	0	0	0	0
Gossage p	0	0	0	0	0	0	0	0
Totals	34	5	8	5	3	5	27	11

FIELDING
DP: 1
E: Nettles 2 (15), Narron (5)
PB: Narron (6)

BATTING
2B: Jackson (19, off Morris); Murcer (8, off Morris)
HR: Nettles (18, 8th inning off Underwood, 0 on, 2 out)
IBB: Spencer (7, by Morris)

BASERUNNING
CS: Spencer (2, 2nd base by Underwood/Parrish).

Detroit Tigers	AB	R	H	RBI	BB	K	PO	A
LeFlore dh	4	2	2	1	0	0	0	0
Brookens 2b	3	0	0	0	0	2	2	3
Summers ph	1	0	0	0	0	1	0	0
Trammell ss	0	0	0	0	0	0	0	0
Morales lf	3	0	1	0	1	0	2	0
Wockenfuss 1b	3	0	0	0	0	2	6	1
Thompson ph	1	0	0	0	0	1	0	0
Parrish c	3	0	1	0	0	1	6	1
Kemp ph	1	0	1	0	0	0	0	0
Jones rf	2	1	0	0	1	1	3	0
Greene ph	1	0	0	0	0	1	0	0
Stegman cf	3	1	1	2	0	0	3	0
Gibson ph	1	0	0	0	0	1	0	0
Rodriguez 3b	3	0	0	0	0	1	1	1
Wagner ss	2	0	0	0	0	2	2	2
Peters ph-2b	1	0	0	0	0	1	1	0
Morris p	0	0	0	0	0	0	0	0
Underwood p	0	0	0	0	0	0	0	0
Lopez p	0	0	0	0	0	0	1	0
Totals	32	4	6	3	2	14	27	8

BATTING
2B: LeFlore (20, off Guidry)
HR: Stegman (1, 7th inning off Guidry, 0 on, 2 out); LeFlore (5, 8th inning off Guidry, 0 on, 1 out)

BASERUNNING
SB: Morales (9, 2nd base off Guidry/Narron); Jones (7, 2nd base off Guidry/Narron)

PITCHING

New York Yankees	IP	H	HR	R	ER	BB	K
Guidry W(16–7)	7.1	5	2	4	3	2	10
Gossage SV(14)	1.2	1	0	0	0	0	4
Totals	9.0	6	2	4	3	2	14

Detroit Tigers	IP	H	HR	R	ER	BB	K
Morris L(13–7)	3	6	0	4	4	3	1
Underwood	5	2	1	1	1	0	3
Lopez	1	0	0	0	0	0	1
Totals	9	8	1	5	5	3	5

WP: Guidry (9), Morris (6)
IBB: Morris (4, Spencer)
Umpires: Larry McCoy, Joe Brinkman, Vic Voltaggio, Marty Springstead
Time of Game: 2:16   Attendance: 30,069

Brian Giles
Born: January 20, 1971
Debut: September 16, 1995

Brian Giles always dreamed of becoming a San Diego Padre, and it took him seven years as an Indians' minor leaguer, three years in Cleveland, then nearly five in Pittsburgh before the planets aligned for him. As the Pirates looked to shed payroll in 2003, he was dealt back home to San Diego, able to play in the last game at Jack Murphy/Qualcomm Stadium, then able to help open Petco Field in 2004.

Growing up in the city's suburbs, Giles always told his parents that if he never made it as a Padres player, he at least wanted to work on the grounds crew. His dad has told the story that when young Brian was asked to vacuum the family house, he somehow got the carpet to show the crisscross look one would see in a major league outfield. Brian first roamed a big league outfield in 1995, where he debuted against Roger Clemens with a hit, and ended a short audition hitting .556, 5-for-9. As a part-time player for the Indians, he never truly broke out, but when he was flipped to Pittsburgh for reliever Ricardo Rincon, he blazed to 39 home runs and a team-leading 115 RBI. His next three seasons, he averaged 38 home runs, tying Dave Parker's all-time record for total bases, when he piled up 340 in 1999.

Giles had a down season in 2004, playing his first full year for his beloved hometown team. Held to a .374 on-base percentage (down from .425 the year before), he struck out a career-high 80 times, although he did sting a career-best seven triples. Heading into 2005, his career batting average was .299, buoyed by back-to-back .315s in 1999 and 2000 for Pittsburgh.

Giles is never shy about participating in practical jokes, evidenced by the birthday celebration he and his Indians teammates once staged for Shawon Dunston. As stripper music played on the clubhouse stereo, a blindfolded Dunston was told a cake was being delivered to where he was sitting. Dunston removed the blindfold to find that, indeed, a birthday cake was being presented to him—by a nude Giles. "I was expecting something else," Dunston said.

Brian's more conventional younger brother, Marcus, has made his mark for the Atlanta Braves. Both brothers have exceeded expectations, as 17th and 53rd-round draft picks, respectively.

We had just gotten done with Game Five in the American Association playoffs, and the few of us getting called up drove over from Buffalo to Cleveland after we had wound down. Jeromy Burnitz, Billy Ripken, John Farrell, and I all in one car, after we lost that last game. It had been a busy week for Billy, because he had just been to Baltimore to see his brother break the Iron Man record. They had a 1:30 afternoon game, and I think we had pulled in at like four in the morning. I wasn't in the lineup originally, and was kind of relieved . . . dog tired, plus Roger Clemens was pitching. But then Manny Ramirez got sick, and they put me in last-minute.

So I got to face the Rocket, and I still have the ball from that first hit. Sellout at Jacobs Field, my nerves are all over the place, but somehow I got the Rocket. Davey Nelson was the first base coach, and I remember him congratulating me. Boy, what a way to break in. We jumped on Clemens pretty good that day . . . Eddie Murray had, like, four hits, and we hung on and won. I was exhausted afterwards, more mentally than anything else. From losing to Louisville in the Triple-A playoffs to beating Roger Clemens, in less than 24 hours.

Also on September 16, 1995
Greg Maddux sets a major league record with his 17th consecutive road win.

AUTHOR'S NOTE: Maddux would get strong defensive support from Giles's little brother, Marcus, when he won the last of his 224 games in a Braves uniform, beating the Phillies in the final game played at Veterans Stadium.

BOXSCORE

Cleveland Indians 6, Boston Red Sox 5
Game Played on Saturday, September 16, 1995 (Day) at Jacobs Field

Boston	0	0	4	0	0	0	0	1	0	—	5	7	1
Cleveland	0	3	2	0	0	1	0	0	x	—	6	11	0

BATTING

Boston Red Sox	AB	R	H	RBI	BB	K	PO	A
Hosey cf	3	2	2	0	1	0	2	0
Valentin ss	3	1	0	0	0	0	3	3
Vaughn 1b	4	0	2	2	0	1	6	1
Canseco dh	3	0	0	1	0	1	0	0
Greenwell lf	4	0	1	1	0	0	2	0
O'Leary rf	4	0	0	0	0	0	2	0
Donnels 3b	3	1	1	0	1	0	1	2
Haselman c	3	1	1	1	0	0	5	2
Stairs ph	1	0	0	0	0	0	0	0
Alicea 2b	3	0	0	0	0	1	2	3
Clemens p	0	0	0	0	0	0	1	0
Cormier p	0	0	0	0	0	0	0	1
Stanton p	0	0	0	0	0	0	0	0
Totals	31	5	7	5	2	3	24	12

FIELDING
E: Donnels (2)

BATTING
2B: Greenwell (23, off Clark)
3B: Haselman (1, off Clark)
SF: Canseco (5, off Clark)
HBP: Valentin (10, by Clark)

BASERUNNING
SB: Hosey (3, 2nd base off Clark/Pena)

Cleveland Indians	AB	R	H	RBI	BB	K	PO	A
Lofton cf	3	0	0	0	2	1	3	0
Giles rf	4	1	1	0	0	0	1	1
Amaro ph-rf	1	0	0	0	0	0	0	0
Thome 3b	4	1	1	2	0	1	1	0
Belle lf	3	1	0	0	1	1	6	0
Murray dh	4	1	4	0	0	0	0	0
Perry 1b	4	1	2	1	0	1	7	2
Levis c	1	1	1	1	1	0	3	0
Winfield ph	0	0	0	0	1	0	0	0
Pena c	0	0	0	0	0	0	1	0
B. Ripken 2b	4	0	1	0	0	0	2	1
Espinoza ss	4	0	1	1	0	1	1	2
Clark p	0	0	0	0	0	0	1	1
Assenmacher p	0	0	0	0	0	0	0	0
Tavarez p	0	0	0	0	0	0	0	0
Mesa p	0	0	0	0	0	0	1	0
Totals	32	6	11	5	5	5	27	7

BATTING
2B: Perry (12, off Cormier)
HR: Thome (23, 3rd inning off Clemens 1 on, 0 out)
SF: Levis (2, off Clemens)
IBB: Winfield (2, by Cormier)

BASERUNNING
CS: Espinoza (1, 2nd base by Clemens/Haselman); Lofton (13, 2nd base by Clemens/Haselman)

PITCHING

Boston Red Sox	IP	H	HR	R	ER	BB	K
Clemens L(8–5)	5.1	9	1	6	5	3	3
Cormier	1.2	2	0	0	0	2	1
Stanton	1	0	0	0	0	0	1
Totals	8	11	1	6	5	5	5

Cleveland Indians	IP	H	HR	R	ER	BB	K
Clark W(9–6)	7.1	6	0	5	5	2	2
Assenmacher	0	1	0	0	0	0	0
Tavarez	0.2	0	0	0	0	0	1
Mesa SV(44)	1	0	0	0	0	0	0
Totals	9	7	0	5	5	2	3

HBP: Clark (4,Valentin)
IBB: Cormier (2,Winfield)
Umpires: Greg Kosc, Dan Morrison, Al Clark, Larry Barnett
Time of Game: 2:50   Attendance: 41,765

Tom Glavine
Born: March 25, 1966
Debut: August 17, 1987

A high school hockey star, Tom Glavine was a fourth-round draft choice of the Los Angeles Kings but chose a career in baseball instead. A pair of Cy Young Awards lead one to believe it was a good call.

The lefty makes his living on the outside corner of the plate, pinpointing his fastball and change-up just on or off the edge, never giving in to the hitter, and occasionally breaking out a snapdragon curveball to ring up a strikeout when necessary. Greg Maddux would later teach him a cut fastball, which he used to paralyze righties, a pitch he ultimately took with him to the Mets in 2003.

He debuted for a horrendous Atlanta team in 1987 and was thrown to the wolves the following year, leading the league with 17 losses. Both Glavine and the Braves experienced their breakout years simultaneously—in 1991, Atlanta's "worst to first" year, Glavine started the All-Star Game and finished 20–11, becoming the first Atlanta pitcher (and the first Braves pitcher since Warren Spahn) to win the Cy Young. It was a poignant note for Glavine, whose dad had idolized Spahn and had constantly invoked the Hall of Famer's name when giving his son something for which to shoot.

The following year, Glavine won 19 of his first 22 decisions, started another All-Star Game, and pitched the Braves into their second straight World Series. The lefty cranked it up to 22 wins in '93, then watched things crumble slightly in '94. With a subpar ERA near four, Glavine's pitching was the least of his problems. As an outspoken players' union representative, he bore the brunt of the fans' anger. When baseball finally returned the following spring, Glavine heard catcalls every time he took the mound.

The 1995 season, however, would end up being his (and his team's) finest. Atlanta finally won a World Series, with Glavine pitching the decisive Game Six, tossing eight innings of one-hit shutout ball. For his efforts, he was named Series MVP. (Pitching well in the postseason had already become a Glavine staple—his career World Series ERA of 1.75 puts him in the company of Fall Classic heroes like Sandy Koufax and Lefty Grove.)

Over the next two seasons, he won 29 more games, and in '98 went 20–6 with a career-best 2.47 ERA to win his second Cy Young, edging the Padres' Trevor Hoffman. Through 2004, he had accumulated 262 wins, 53 complete games, and—more importantly, he insists—the unwavering respect of his peers.

My Richmond team was on the road in Toledo, and I had just pitched that night, and it was strange because I hadn't pitched that well and lost the game . . . You sure wouldn't expect to get good news after something like that, but my manager, Roy Majtyka, told me they had made the trade for Doyle Alexander, which opened a spot, and they were asking for me. I spent a sleepless night at a bad hotel in Toledo, pretty fired up that I was getting the call.

I met the team in Atlanta and immediately took off with them to Houston. First start, against a team in a pennant race, at the Astrodome, which is kind of overwhelming by itself . . . I was nervous but tried to maintain my composure best I could. It didn't go real well, but it was fun. My mom and dad, my high school coach came down, which was pretty cool . . . Second time out went much better in Atlanta. That first one was rough though . . . I kept giving up singles. It seemed like Billy Hatcher and Bill Doran were lining singles every couple minutes. I gave up maybe ten hits, and I think nine of them were singles, but I walked a bunch of guys too . . . I didn't deserve to win. But like I say, it was pretty cool just to have done it, knowing it would get better from there.

Also on August 17, 1987
Reggie Jackson hits the final home run of his Hall of Fame career, number 563, off the Angels' Mike Witt.

AUTHOR'S NOTE: On August 10, 2004, Jackson and Glavine would each experience a loss. Jackson lost his eighth-place standing on the all-time home run list to Sammy Sosa, and Glavine lost his two front teeth in a taxi accident.

BOXSCORE

Houston Astros 11, Atlanta Braves 2

Game Played on Monday, August 17, 1987 (Night) at Astrodome

Atlanta	0	0	0	0	0	1	1	0	0	—	2	7	0
Houston	2	0	2	2	0	1	0	4	x	—	11	16	1

BATTING

Atlanta Braves	AB	R	H	RBI	BB	K	PO	A
James cf	4	0	1	0	0	2	4	0
Oberkfell 3b	4	0	0	0	0	1	1	3
Perry 1b	4	0	0	0	0	1	7	0
Murphy rf	4	0	0	0	0	2	1	1
Griffey lf	4	1	2	1	0	0	3	0
Virgil c	4	0	1	0	0	2	4	0
Blauser ss	4	0	0	0	0	2	1	6
Hubbard 2b	3	1	1	0	0	1	3	0
Glavine p	1	0	0	0	0	0	0	0
Acker p	0	0	0	0	0	0	0	0
Hall ph	1	0	1	1	0	0	0	0
Mahler p	0	0	0	0	0	0	0	0
Nettles ph	1	0	1	0	0	0	0	0
Boever p	0	0	0	0	0	0	0	0
Totals	34	2	7	2	0	11	24	10

BATTING
2B: Hubbard (29, off Scott); Nettles (7, off Scott)
HR: Griffey (13, 7th inning off Scott, 0 on, 0 out)
HBP: Hubbard (6, by Scott)

Houston Astros	AB	R	H	RBI	BB	K	PO	A
Young cf	6	1	1	1	0	1	1	0
Hatcher lf	6	3	4	1	0	0	1	0
Wine c	0	0	0	0	0	0	1	0
Doran 2b	4	2	3	0	2	0	1	5
C. Reynolds pr-ss	0	0	0	0	0	0	0	0
Ashby c6	1	1	1	0	1	1	0	0
Childress p	0	0	0	0	0	0	0	0
Bass rf	3	2	1	2	0	0	2	0
Davis 1b	2	0	2	2	1	0	9	0
Walling 1b	1	0	0	0	0	0	1	0
Caminiti 3b	3	1	1	1	2	1	1	2
Berra ss-2b	2	0	1	1	3	0	0	2
Scott p	4	0	1	0	0	1	0	1
Cruz ph-lf	1	1	1	1	0	0	0	0
Totals	38	11	16	10	8	4	27	10

FIELDING
E: Bass (4)

BATTING
2B: Davis (28, off Glavine); Berra (1, off Mahler); Hatcher (21, off Boever)
3B: Young (1, off Boever)
HR: Hatcher (10, 8th inning off Boever, 0 on, 2 out)
SF: Bass (4, off Glavine)
HBP: Bass (4, by Mahler); Davis (3, by Mahler)
IBB: Berra 2 (2, by Glavine 2)

BASERUNNING
SB: Hatcher 2 (45, 2nd base off Glavine/Virgil 2)

PITCHING

Atlanta Braves	IP	H	HR	R	ER	BB	K
Glavine L(0–1)	3.2	10	0	6	6	5	1
Acker	1.1	0	0	0	0	1	2
Mahler	1	1	0	1	1	0	0
Boever	2	5	1	4	4	2	1
Totals	8	16	1	11	11	8	4

Houston Astros	IP	H	HR	R	ER	BB	K
Scott W(13–9)	8	6	1	2	2	0	10
Childress	1	1	0	0	0	0	1
Totals	9	7	1	2	2	0	11

WP: Boever (1)
HBP: Mahler 2 (2, Bass,Davis); Scott (3, Hubbard)
IBB: Glavine 2 (2, Berra 2)
Umpires: Bob Davidson, Harry Wendelstedt, Jerry Crawford, Terry Tata
Time of Game: 2:42   Attendance: 18,810

Luis Gonzalez
Born: September 3, 1967
Debut: September 4, 1990

It was *M★A★S★H*'s Frank Burns who once opined, "It's nice to be nice to the nice." In that vein, here are a few paragraphs on the man Curt Schilling dubbed "the male mother Theresa." For those claiming a dearth of "good guys" in modern day baseball, look no further than the Tampa native who's become the face of the Arizona Diamondbacks.

"Not much of a face at that," Gonzalez has said, in his typically self-deprecating fashion. "People think I got the nickname 'Gonzo' because it's short for Gonzalez. Actually, it's because Mark Grace used to say I looked like the character Gonzo from *The Muppet Show*. You know, the one with the big crooked beak."

Gonzalez played his high school ball with Tino Martinez and was a skinny kid who didn't fill out until well into his big league career. Not much of a home run hitter in the minors, and more of a line drive hitter while with the Astros, Cubs, and Tigers, he had an epiphany while in Detroit, at old Tiger Stadium. Teammate Bobby Higginson encouraged him to open his stance to take advantage of the ballpark's inviting right porch. It was a pivotal summer for Gonzalez; not only did he realize that maybe Higginson was right, he realized his life was about to change forever when his wife gave birth to triplets hours after a Tigers home game that June.

It was Higginson the D'backs first asked for, when discussing a trade for Karim Garcia. Arizona was told, "No, we're keeping Higginson, but we're pushing aside Gonzalez so we can bring in Gregg Jefferies, so would Gonzalez be an okay substitute for Higginson?" Resoundingly, the answer was yes. Gonzalez opened his stance even more upon arrival in Phoenix and hit 88 home runs his first two years there, as opposed to the 23 he had hit in his one year in Detroit.

The shining moment of his playing career was dunking the game-winning, ninth-inning hit into left-center off Mariano Rivera, beating the Yankees in the 2001 World Series. As was pointed out in *Sports Illustrated*, "Little celebrations broke out all across the country that it was Gonzalez." For all the checks he picked up at dinner, for all the clubhouse attendants he so handsomely tipped, for all the elevator operators and parking lot attendants whose names he thoughtfully remembered—it's as though Leo Durocher had been proven dead wrong. Nice guys don't necessarily finish last.

It was all pretty cool. Me and Andujar Cedeno flew in just in time from Double-A to get our uniforms and take infield. I ran out there and it was like *Bad News Bears in Breaking Training*, when the kids first walked into the Astrodome and they're turning around and around not quite believing where they are. We left right after that game for a road trip to L.A., and Glenn Davis did the coolest thing. He told me to ride with him in the cab to Dodger Stadium the next day and had the cabbie drop us off in center field, coming in through the center-field gate. We walked in, right onto the center-field grass, which I had seen so many times on TV, but now I was actually on it. And Davis said, "Remember this moment. Hopefully you'll be on fields like this a long, long time."

I was supposed to start at third base a couple days after that, but Davis got back spasms, so they scratched him, moved me to first base, and [Ken] Caminiti played third. I got my first hit in that game, off Steve Bedrosian. I doubled, got to second, and was so excited I said I wanted to keep the ball, and he said, "No, I won't do it," but he was just kidding.

I felt like I had finally arrived, and I've been fortunate enough to keep playing for all these years.

Also on September 4, 1990
Juan Gonzalez arrives from Triple-A and hits his first home run of the season for the Rangers.

AUTHOR'S NOTE: The two Gonzalezes, unrelated, couldn't be more different. Luis is lauded for his outgoing nature, while Juan has been criticized for his petulance and shyness. While Luis's career took flight immediately after he was traded away from Detroit, Juan's career went due south the moment he was traded *to* Detroit.

BOXSCORE

Houston Astros 10, Los Angeles Dodgers 8
Game Played on Tuesday, September 4, 1990 (Night) at Dodger Stadium

											R	H	E
Houston	0	0	0	4	2	2	1	1	0	—	10	12	0
Los Angeles	3	4	0	0	0	0	0	1	0	—	8	11	3

BATTING

Houston Astros	AB	R	H	RBI	BB	K	PO	A
Young cf	6	0	3	0	0	1	0	0
Oberkfell 3b	3	2	0	1	0	0	0	0
Meyer p	1	0	0	0	0	1	0	1
Agosto p	0	0	0	0	0	0	0	0
Smith p	0	0	0	0	0	0	0	0
Stubbs lf	4	1	0	0	1	0	1	0
Yelding pr-lf	0	1	0	0	0	0	2	0
Davis 1b	3	0	1	2	2	0	14	2
Rhodes rf	4	1	2	0	0	0	1	0
Candaele ph-rf	1	0	1	1	0	0	2	0
Ramirez ss	4	1	1	0	1	1	1	4
Gedman c	4	1	1	1	0	1	2	0
Biggio ph-c	1	0	0	0	0	0	1	0
Rohde 2b	5	2	2	0	0	0	0	7
Portugal p	0	0	0	0	0	0	2	0
Gonzalez ph	1	0	0	0	0	1	0	0
Hernandez p	0	0	0	0	0	0	0	0
Anthony ph	1	1	1	3	0	0	0	0
Osuna p	0	0	0	0	0	0	0	0
Davidson ph	1	0	0	0	0	1	0	0
Caminiti 3b	2	0	0	0	0	0	1	1
Totals	**41**	**10**	**12**	**8**	**4**	**6**	**27**	**15**

FIELDING
DP: 1

BATTING
2B: Rhodes (3, off Martinez)
3B: Davis (3, off Martinez)
HR: Anthony (8, 4th inning off Martinez, 2 on, 2 out)
HBP: Oberkfell (1, by Martinez)
IBB: Davis (13, by Gott & Aase); Ramirez (6, by Poole)

BASERUNNING
SB: Rhodes (2, 2nd base off Martinez/Scioscia); Yelding (52, 2nd base off Aase/Scioscia)

Los Angeles Dodgers	AB	R	H	RBI	BB	K	PO	A
Harris 2b	5	1	3	0	0	0	3	4
Javier cf	4	2	1	0	1	0	5	0
Daniels lf	5	2	2	6	0	0	1	0
Murray 1b	5	2	3	1	0	1	8	1
Brooks rf	5	0	1	0	0	1	0	1
Scioscia c	3	0	0	1	1	0	6	0
Sharperson 3b	2	0	0	0	2	0	2	0
Griffin ss	3	0	0	0	0	0	1	6
Gibson ph	0	0	0	0	0	0	0	0
Hatcher ph	1	0	0	0	0	0	0	0
Offerman ss	0	0	0	0	0	0	0	0
Martinez p	2	1	1	0	0	1	0	1
Crews p	0	0	0	0	0	0	0	0
Gott p	0	0	0	0	0	0	0	0
Vizcaino ph	1	0	0	0	0	0	0	0
Walsh p	0	0	0	0	0	0	1	0
Aase p	0	0	0	0	0	0	0	0
Poole p	0	0	0	0	0	0	0	0
Samuel ph	1	0	0	0	0	0	0	0
Holmes p	0	0	0	0	0	0	0	0
Totals	**37**	**8**	**11**	**8**	**4**	**3**	**27**	**13**

FIELDING
E: Harris (8), Murray (7), Brooks (9)

BATTING
HR: Daniels 2 (23, 1st inning off Portugal 1 on, 1 out; 2nd inning off Portugal, 3 on, 0 out); Murray (21, 8th inning off Meyer, 0 on, 0 out)

PITCHING

Houston Astros	IP	H	HR	R	ER	BB	K
Portugal	2	7	2	7	7	2	0
Hernandez	1	0	0	0	0	0	1
Osuna W (1–0)	2	1	0	0	0	0	1
Meyer	2.1	1	1	1	1	2	1
Agosto	0.2	0	0	0	0	0	0
Smith SV (22)	1	2	0	0	0	0	0
Totals	**9**	**11**	**3**	**8**	**8**	**4**	**3**

Los Angeles Dodgers	IP	H	HR	R	ER	BB	K
Martinez	4.1	8	1	6	5	0	2
Crews	0.2	0	0	0	0	0	0
Gott L (2–4)	1	2	0	2	1	1	1
Walsh	1.2	1	0	2	2	1	3
Aase	0	0	0	0	0	1	0
Poole	0.1	1	0	0	0	1	0
Holmes	1	0	0	0	0	0	0
Totals	**9**	**12**	**1**	**10**	**8**	**4**	**6**

WP: Portugal (4), Walsh (1)
BK: Walsh (1)
HBP: Martinez (3, Oberkfell)
IBB: Gott (2, Davis); Aase (3, Davis); Poole (2, Ramirez)
Umpires: Dana DeMuth, Eric Gregg, Jerry Crawford, Doug Harvey
Time of Game: 3:24   Attendance: 28,939

Danny Graves
Born: August 7, 1973
Debut: July 13, 1996

The word "closer" conjures up images of large, hulking, snarling tough guys who make you think twice before getting in the batters' box, just because they radiate such ferocity. Then there's ex-Red Danny Graves, who looks as though he's just begun puberty.

Graves has been nicknamed "The Baby Faced Assassin," and it fits him perfectly. The possessor of a wicked sinker and nasty 95-mile-per-hour heat, Graves may look like the front man for a boy band, but until 2005 he was a lights-out stopper for Cincinnati when they handed him the ball.

Curiously, the Reds attempted to move him into their starting rotation in 2003, and, hanging a few too many sliders, he gave up a staggering 30 home runs in 169 innings. Back in the closer's role in 2004, he picked up where he had left off, blowing hitters away while looking like the least likely guy on the field who could do so.

Graves is the first (and so far the only) major leaguer born in Vietnam; he is the son of a U.S. army serviceman and a Vietnamese mother and was conceived toward the end of the Vietnam War. He grew up stateside in Tampa, going to high school with Dwayne Johnson, who later went on to wrestling and acting fame as The Rock. Graves became a fan of the St. Louis Cardinals, watching them up close every spring training across the bridge in St. Petersburg. From Tampa, he went cross-state, to a distinguished collegiate career at the University of Miami. His senior season, he had an ERA of 0.89 but missed qualifying for the national ERA title by five innings.

With the Reds, he amassed 92 saves between 2000 and 2002, then broke through with a career-best 41 in 2004, walking only 13 batters in 68 games. Not bad for a guy who keeps getting mistaken for the batboy.

Brian Graham, my Triple-A manager, told me while our team, Buffalo, was playing in Indianapolis. I joined the [Indians] in Chicago. I joined the team right away, but I was way, way under the radar. Called up in late June, then I sat for 15 days. Never did anything but warm up a couple times. I mean, it was great to be in the big leagues, but we had all these stud starting pitchers: Nagy, Hershiser, Dennis Martinez . . . They were all pitching deep into games, so this so-called "emergency help" they thought they needed for the bullpen never really materialized. Finally, after the All-Star break, I got in a game in

Minnesota. It was a blowout, and from what I remember, I didn't exactly stop the bleeding.

They eased me in, you could say, no pressure, trying to pitch in something like a 13–2 game at the time. Tony Pena was my catcher and my first pitch is a strike. And I remember him giving me this big grin and yelling out to me, "I can't believe it! Strike on the first pitch!" After my couple innings, it was pretty much congratulations all the way around. I called everyone afterwards. It was a sigh of relief, finally getting in, to validate I was actually up there. I had gotten a whole big league paycheck, 15 days' service time, before I actually pitched in a game!

I got sent back down in August but got called up again in September. And it's funny . . . I haven't pitched in Minnesota much since I got traded [to Cincinnati] of course . . . but I still always think of that place real fondly, because that's where I first got in a game.

Also on July 13, 1996
Twins fans begin the post-Kirby Puckett era. The day before, the popular Minnesota outfielder announces early retirement, citing glaucoma in his right eye.

AUTHOR'S NOTE: It was appropriate that Graves's first big league appearance came at Minnesota. Through 2004, he is 28 for 29 lifetime in domed-stadium save opportunities

BOXSCORE

Cleveland Indians 19, Minnesota Twins 11
Game Played on Saturday, July 13, 1996 (Night) at Hubert H. Humphrey Metrodome

											R	H	E
Cleveland	3	0	0	4	5	6	1	0	0	—	19	22	2
Minnesota	1	1	1	0	3	3	0	2	0	—	11	15	0

BATTING

Cleveland Indians	AB	R	H	RBI	BB	K	PO	A
Lofton cf	4	2	3	3	0	0	1	0
Giles ph-lf	2	0	0	0	0	1	2	0
Vizquel ss	3	1	1	1	1	0	1	1
Espinoza ph-ss	2	0	1	1	0	0	0	0
Thome 3b	6	0	1	0	0	3	0	1
Belle lf	4	4	4	3	1	0	2	0
Leius 1b	1	0	1	0	0	0	2	0
Ramirez rf	5	3	2	2	1	1	3	0
Burnitz dh	5	3	2	5	1	1	0	0
Baerga 2b	5	4	3	0	0	0	2	2
Carreon 1b-cf	5	1	3	1	1	0	6	0
T.Pena c	6	1	1	3	0	0	9	0
Ogea p	0	0	0	0	0	0	0	1
Graves p	0	0	0	0	0	0	0	0
Embree p	0	0	0	0	0	0	0	0
Mesa p	0	0	0	0	0	0	0	0
Totals	48	19	22	19	5	7	27	5

FIELDING
E: Baerga (13), Carreon (1)

BATTING
2B: Lofton 3 (23, off Aguilera 2, off Trombley); Ramirez (22, off Aguilera); Burnitz (5, off Aguilera); Belle (20, off Trombley); Vizquel (23, off Trombley); T.Pena (3, off Hansell); Baerga (23, off Hansell); Carreon 2 (2, off Hansell 2); Leius (4, off Hansell)
HR: Belle (30, 1st inning off Aguilera, 2 on, 1 out); Burnitz (4, 5th inning off Trombley, 2 on, 0 out); Ramirez (22, 6th inning off Milchin, 1 on, 0 out)
HBP: Baerga (7, by Aguilera)

BASERUNNING
SB: Lofton (43, 3rd base off Aguilera/Myers); Vizquel (21, 2nd base off Aguilera/Myers)

Minnesota Twins	AB	R	H	RBI	BB	K	PO	A
Knoblauch 2b	2	3	1	0	1	0	1	1
Reboulet 2b	2	0	1	0	0	0	0	2
Becker cf	6	3	4	6	0	1	1	0
Molitor dh	5	0	1	1	0	0	0	0
Stahoviak 1b	4	1	1	0	0	3	4	0
Hale 1b	1	1	1	0	0	0	5	1
Cordova lf	5	1	1	1	0	2	2	0
Myers c	3	0	1	1	0	0	6	0
Walbeck c	2	0	1	0	0	0	1	0
Hollins 3b	3	1	0	0	0	1	1	1
Coomer 3b	2	0	1	0	0	0	0	0
Meares ss	5	1	1	0	0	1	2	4
Hocking rf	4	0	1	1	1	1	2	1
Aguilera p	0	0	0	0	0	0	0	0
Trombley p	0	0	0	0	0	0	0	0
Milchin p	0	0	0	0	0	0	0	0
Hansell p	0	0	0	0	0	0	1	0
Totals	44	11	15	11	2	9	27	10

BATTING
2B: Becker (18, off Ogea); Stahoviak (17, off Ogea); Meares (16, off Graves); Coomer (6, off Graves); Cordova (25, off Embree); Walbeck (4, off Embree)
3B: Becker (2, off Graves)
HR: Becker 2 (8, 3rd inning off Ogea, 0 on, 0 out; 5th inning off Ogea, 1 on, 0 out)
HBP: Knoblauch (9, by Ogea)

PITCHING

Cleveland Indians	IP	H	HR	R	ER	BB	K
Ogea W(5–1)	5.0	7	2	6	5	1	5
Graves	2.0	4	0	3	3	1	3
Embree	1.0	3	0	2	2	0	0
Mesa	1.0	1	0	0	0	0	1
Totals	9.0	15	2	11	10	2	9
Minnesota Twins	IP	H	HR	R	ER	BB	K
Aguilera L(2–4)	3.1	6	1	7	7	2	3
Trombley	1.1	5	1	5	5	1	1
Milchin	0.1	3	0	4	4	2	0
Hansell	4.0	8	0	3	3	0	3
Totals	9.0	22	3	19	19	5	7

WP: Ogea (1), Embree 2 (2), Aguilera (2), Trombley (1), Hansell (6)
HBP: Ogea (4, Knoblauch); Aguilera (1, Baerga)
Umpires: Tim Tschida, Derryl Cousins, Tim McClelland, Larry Young
Time of Game: 3:38   Attendance: 31,552

Ken Griffey Jr.
Born: November 21, 1970
Debut: April 3, 1989

Ken Griffey Jr. soared to superstardom as a precocious, do-it-all masher for the Seattle Mariners. He dazzled fans across the country with his glove, wowed them with his trophy left-handed swing, and melted them with his devil-may-care personality.

But all of that seemingly changed when he took a crowbar to his Seattle career, forcing the M's to deal him where he most wanted to go—back to his hometown of Cincinnati. From almost the moment he set foot on a field in a Reds cap, Griffey's world began to implode. A rash of injuries and subpar production made him chairman of the Careful What You Wish For department, class of 2001. While the Mariners won a record 116 regular season games, the Reds finished six games under .500, and the shine was off the Griffey Jr. star.

His dad, Senior, had carved out a 19-year career, spending several productive seasons on the powerful mid-70s Reds teams himself. Senior was known as a very selfless player, an ideal number two hitter who was nicknamed "KIP" for "Keep It in Play." Junior, however, was called out by both teammates and media as being a "me first" guy who had a special set of rules applying only to him. When called on the fact that he rarely stretched with his teammates before batting practice, he would sometimes wink and ask, rhetorically, "Does a cheetah need to stretch before chasing his prey?"

An 11-time All-Star, five-time RBI leader, and 1997's AL MVP, he would seem to be a lock for the Hall of Fame someday. He'd be the second person born in tiny Donora, Pennsylvania, to make it, following Stan Musial, with whom he shares a birth date. But for all his accomplishments, all his long home runs, all his early-career stolen bases, all his outfield flash, and all of his style, Griffey doesn't draw the attention he used to. As Barry Bonds said at the 2003 All-Star Game: "It's a shame nobody talks about Ken Griffey Jr. anymore."

Out of spring training, there was a lot of conjecture about whether or not I'd start the season with the big club or not . . . Jim Lefebvre was our [Seattle's] manager, and right at the end of spring training, he called me into his office. I'm 19, so I'm already thinking, "Hey, this probably isn't going to happen for me right now, and I guess that's okay, just try not too look too disappointed." He goes through, like, five minutes of stuff like "These decisions are so tough," "You know, we've got a lot of veterans that have earned their chance," then at the end, he sticks out his hand from across his desk and says, "You're my starting center fielder." So I go, "What?" And he had managed to keep a straight face the whole time.

So then we head to Vegas to play one last spring training game before opening the season in Oakland, and it's April Fool's Day, which I wasn't really aware of. I walk in the clubhouse and everyone's talking about a big trade we just made for Dale Murphy. Which would mean he's our new center fielder, not me. So I make that long walk to Lefebvre's office, and he says, "I guess you've heard about the big trade we made?" And again, he goes on and on, then finally he says, "Do you know today's date?" And I say "Yeah, April 1." Still didn't register. So he says, "Okay, just so you know what today is. April 1." And I sag my shoulders on out of there, and the whole team is standing outside the office saying, "gotcha!" then I remembered—April Fool's Day. At 19, you're gullible. Those guys were killing me all day in Vegas. The bus drove by Circus Circus and they insisted I get off there.

We got to Oakland, and man, I'm nervous. Dave Stewart's on the mound, and he could have rolled the ball up there, I would have swung. Somehow I got a hit.

Also on April 3, 1989
Omar Vizquel makes his big league debut for the Mariners as well.

BOXSCORE

Oakland Athletics 3, Seattle Mariners 2

Game Played on Monday, April 3, 1989 (Night) at Oakland-Alameda County Coliseum

Seattle	0	0	0	0	1	1	0	0	0	—	2	5	1
Oakland	1	0	2	0	0	0	0	0	x	—	3	6	1

BATTING

Seattle Mariners	AB	R	H	RBI	BB	K	PO	A
Reynolds 2b	4	0	0	0	0	1	2	2
Griffey cf	3	1	1	0	1	0	5	0
Davis 1b	4	0	0	0	0	1	13	0
Coles rf	4	0	1	1	0	2	1	0
Leonard dh	4	1	1	0	0	1	0	0
Briley lf	3	0	0	0	1	1	1	0
Valle c	4	0	1	0	0	0	2	1
E. Martinez 3b	3	0	1	1	0	0	0	5
Vizquel ss	3	0	0	0	0	0	0	5
Langston p	0	0	0	0	0	0	0	0
Totals	32	2	5	2	2	6	24	13

FIELDING
DP: 1
E: Vizquel (1)

BATTING
2B: Griffey (1, off Stewart)

Oakland Athletics	AB	R	H	RBI	BB	K	PO	A
Phillips lf	4	1	1	0	0	0	3	0
D. Henderson cf	3	0	1	0	0	0	5	0
Lansford 3b	4	1	1	0	0	0	1	1
McGwire 1b	3	1	2	3	0	0	3	0
Steinbach c2	0	0	0	1	0	6	0	
Parker dh	3	0	0	0	0	0	0	0
Hubbard 2b	3	0	0	0	0	0	2	2
Javier rf	3	0	1	0	0	2	6	0
Weiss ss	3	0	0	0	0	0	1	2
Stewart p	0	0	0	0	0	0	0	0
Nelson p	0	0	0	0	0	0	0	0
Honeycutt p	0	0	0	0	0	0	0	0
Eckersley p	0	0	0	0	0	0	0	0
Totals	28	3	6	3	1	2	27	5

FIELDING
DP: 1
E: Hubbard (1)

BATTING
2B: Phillips (1, off Langston)
HR: McGwire (1, 3rd inning off Langston, 1 on, 1 out)
SF: McGwire (1, off Langston)
HBP: D. Henderson (1, by Langston)

BASERUNNING
SB: Javier (1, 2nd base off Langston/Valle).

PITCHING

Seattle Mariners	IP	H	HR	R	ER	BB	K
Langston L(0–1)	8	6	1	3	3	1	2
Oakland Athletics	IP	H	HR	R	ER	BB	K
Stewart W(1–0)	5.1	4	0	2	1	2	2
Nelson	1.2	1	0	0	0	0	2
Honeycutt	0.2	0	0	0	0	0	1
Eckersley SV(1)	1.1	0	0	0	0	0	1
Totals	9.0	5	0	2	1	2	6

HBP: Langston (1, D. Henderson)
Umpires: Al Clark, Rick Reed, Mark Johnson, Dale Scott
Time of Game: 2:19   Attendance: 46,163

AUTHOR'S NOTE: Vizquel and Griffey first played together in Double-A in 1988, then played together in Seattle for four years before becoming rivals, opposing each other in the 1995 postseason. (Twice, Griffey was tagged out by Vizquel on stolen base attempts as the Indians beat the Mariners in six.)

Ozzie Guillen
Born: January 20, 1964
Debut: April 9, 1985

The White Sox drew criticism for trading Cy Young Award winner La-Marr Hoyt to the San Diego Padres in December 1984 in a seven-player deal. In fact, general manager Roland Hemond was fired not long after. But the trade netted a young prospect named Ozzie Guillen who a year later captured the AL Rookie of the Year Award. Guillen committed just 12 errors to lead AL shortstops in fielding and set a record for White Sox shortstops. His .273 batting average was higher than expected, and he was soon considered one of the better all-around middle infielders in the game. Knee surgery slowed him in the early '90s, but he never stopped competing and seemingly never stopped talking.

While stealing bases wasn't a problem for Guillen pre-surgery (he averaged 24 between 1987 and 1991), getting on base was. Guillen set a major-league record in 1996, walking only ten times in 150 games. His on-base percentage never rose above .325, and once even dipped to an astonishingly low .265. He had poor strike zone judgment, and though he didn't whiff as much as the heavy sluggers of the league, Guillen often swung at balls over his head or in the dirt. Still, playing in a "golden age" of American League shortstops (Ripken, Trammell, etc.) he managed to make three All-Star teams and play in three postseasons, winning a Gold Glove in 1990.

Following a 16-year playing career (including stops near the end with Baltimore, Tampa Bay, and Atlanta), he was asked to be a coach for his onetime Sox manager, Jeff Torborg, in Florida. After the Marlins won the 2003 World Series, the Sox invited him back to Chicago, where he became the first-ever Venezuelan big league skipper. Guillen is quite proud of his Venezuelan heritage and is part of a rich history of slick-fielding shortstops from that country. Guillen, in fact, chose uniform number 13 to honor Davey Concepcion.

As a manager, Guillen replaced the calm and orderly Jerry Manuel and immediately changed the culture of the Sox's previously morose clubhouse, injecting loud talking, loud music, and enough swear words to embarrass a longshoreman. His feisty personality occasionally rankled opposing managers, but just as in his playing days, he has yet to back down or change course.

I made the team out of spring training and knew I'd be playing Opening Day in Milwaukee, and I couldn't wait. The funniest thing is that all I really wanted was to have my family, my wife, and my kid there to see it, to come up from Chicago to Milwaukee, but it was snowing and cold, so they stayed home and watched on TV. Everyone else was freezing cold but me. I was hotter than hell because I was so excited. What an opportunity. Tom Seaver was breaking the record that day for most Opening Day starts, and I got to play.

Molitor and Yount, two people I admired so much, were playing against me, and I couldn't believe it. If you had asked me to name two players I'd buy a ticket to watch play back then, I'd have said those two guys. So professional, and they had fun too.

I got a bunt hit! But I also struck out. That guy, Haas, he got me good. He struck me out and I looked bad. But the bunt! I bunted then, and I bunted for 15 more years after that. I always liked to bunt when it was cold, make the other guy have to get off his ass and go get it.

Also on April 9, 1985
Shawon Dunston debuts for the Chicago Cubs.

BOXSCORE

Chicago White Sox 4, Milwaukee Brewers 2
Game Played on Tuesday, April 9, 1985 (Day) at County Stadium

Chicago	2	0	0	1	0	0	0	1	0	—	4 8 0
Milwaukee	0	0	0	0	0	0	2	0	0	—	2 6 5

BATTING

Chicago White Sox	AB	R	H	RBI	BB	K	PO	A
Guillen ss	5	0	1	0	0	1	2	3
Law lf	4	1	1	0	0	0	3	0
Paciorek ph	1	0	0	0	0	1	0	0
Fletcher 3b	0	0	0	0	0	0	0	0
Baines rf	3	1	1	0	2	0	2	0
Walker 1b	5	0	1	1	0	0	8	1
Kittle dh	4	0	0	1	0	2	0	0
Salazar 3b-lf	4	1	1	0	0	1	0	0
Boston cf	3	1	2	1	1	0	3	0
Hill c	3	0	0	0	0	1	7	0
Cruz 2b	3	0	1	1	0	0	1	5
Seaver p	0	0	0	0	0	0	1	0
James p	0	0	0	0	0	0	0	0
Totals	35	4	8	4	3	6	27	9

FIELDING
DP: 2

BATTING
2B: Boston (1, off Haas)
SH: Hill (1, off Haas)
SF: Cruz (1, off Haas)

BASERUNNING
SB: Cruz (1, 2nd base off Searage/Schroeder)

Milwaukee Brewers	AB	R	H	RBI	BB	K	PO	A
Molitor 3b	4	0	1	0	0	1	2	3
Yount lf	3	0	0	0	1	0	2	0
Romero ss	0	0	0	0	0	0	0	0
Cooper 1b	4	0	0	0	0	1	11	1
Oglivie rf-lf	4	0	0	0	0	1	1	0
Simmons dh	4	1	2	0	0	0	0	0
Loman cf-rf	4	1	1	0	0	1	2	0
Schroeder c	2	0	1	0	1	1	5	1
Gantner 2b	3	0	0	0	0	1	2	5
Giles ss	2	0	1	0	0	0	1	3
Manning ph-cf	1	0	0	0	0	0	0	0
Haas p	0	0	0	0	0	0	1	1
Searage p	0	0	0	0	0	0	0	0
Totals	31	2	6	0	2	6	27	14

FIELDING
DP: 2
E: Molitor (1), Cooper (1), Gantner 2 (2), Haas (1)

BATTING
2B: Loman (1, off Seaver); Simmons (1, off James)

BASERUNNING
SB: Molitor (1, 2nd base off Seaver/Hill); Giles (1, 2nd base off Seaver/Hill)

PITCHING

Chicago White Sox	IP	H	HR	R	ER	BB	K
Seaver W(1–0)	6.2	5	0	2	2	2	3
James SV(1)	2.1	1	0	0	0	0	3
Totals	9.0	6	0	2	2	2	6

Milwaukee Brewers	IP	H	HR	R	ER	BB	K
Haas L(0–1)	8	6	0	4	1	2	5
Searage	1	2	0	0	0	1	1
Totals	9	8	0	4	1	3	6

WP: Seaver 2 (2)
Time of Game: 2:35 Attendance: 53,027

AUTHOR'S NOTE: The two popular, happy-go-lucky Chicago shortstops would patrol their positions for their respective teams for the next dozen years, uninterrupted.

Tony Gwynn
Born: May 9, 1960
Debut: July 19, 1982

If there is such an animal as "Mr. Padre," that honor would have to go to the popular Tony Gwynn. A San Diego native, he went from high school to college to the big leagues all within a 15-mile radius and seldom disappointed the fans of the brown and gold (and later, the blue and orange).

Twice the Padres were all but completely dismantled out from under him, but rather than push for a trade, Gwynn stayed put both times, finishing a 20-year career as a lifetime Friar. He began his career as a singles hitter but emerged as much more than that as he grew into an eight-time National League batting champion. Gwynn hit as many as 17 home runs in a single season and coupled that total with 49 doubles in 1997.

His .394 batting average in 1994 was the highest in the National League since 1930, and the players' strike robbed the country of what could have been a sizzling ".400 watch" the rest of the summer.

Gwynn famously sliced base hits into what he referred to as the "5.5 hole," the gap in between the third baseman (position number 5) and the shortstop (6). Between 1993 and 1997, he never hit lower than .358, and for his career, ended at .338, the highest lifetime average since another native San Diegan, Ted Williams, hung up his spikes. When the Padres came through Cooperstown for the annual Hall of Fame game, Gwynn was handed a note left by Teddy Ballgame himself, reading, "I know you can do it [hit .400]." He never did get to four bills, but he did end up with 3,141 knocks; he successfully hit 23 different Cy Young winners before he retired and struck out three times in a game only once.

Known as much for his paunch as for his bat, Gwynn easily laughed off the fat jokes, saying, "I don't see a lot of skinny guys hitting .330 every year." The only thing light about Gwynn was his bat—30$^{1}/_{2}$ ounces of northern white ash, likely the lightest bat used by a big leaguer since Joe Morgan. Gwynn was a tireless student of his swing and would often make a beeline for the team's video room to watch his at bats upon arrival from a road trip, even if the arrival time was 2 or 3 A.M.

Eligible for the Hall of Fame in 2007, Gwynn is now the head coach at his alma mater, San Diego State.

The baseball field on campus is now named in his honor.

I still remember everything. Doug Rader was our Triple-A manager, and I had made a baserunning mistake that had cost us the game that night. I

70

thought for sure I was being called into his office so he could chew me out for that. He went through the whole thing, ripped my butt, then said, "Anyway, you're going to join the Padres tomorrow." And after that sunk in, he said, "And by the way, Steve Carlton will be pitching." Well, for six hours, I'm sitting around in Honolulu worrying to death about that, but when my plane got in, I found out it wasn't going to be Carlton after all, but Mike Krukow. Now, nothing against Krukie, but that was a big relief.

First at bat, sac fly . . . I ended up 2-for-4. I made it, and my first hit, Pete Rose trailed the play, shook my hand, and said, "Don't catch me all in one day, kid." Wow. My folks were there, my whole family, they saw it all.

After the game, all my buddies from San Diego State were there . . . It was a pass list of a couple dozen. To debut for your hometown team in your own hometown against a team with Rose on it, [Mike] Schmidt, Gary Matthews, Steve Carlton—you never forget that.

Also on July 19, 1982
At the first-ever "Old Timers' All-Star Game," 75-year-old Luke Appling homers at Washington's RFK Stadium. The AL wins, 7–2, and after the game, Appling quips: "I sure am glad the season is over."

AUTHOR'S NOTE: Gwynn, at 22, hit just one home run his first big league season and followed with none in the first 300 at bats of his sophomore season before taking one out in late September.

BOXSCORE

Philadelphia Phillies 7, San Diego Padres 6
Game Played on Monday, July 19, 1982 (Night) at Jack Murphy Stadium

Philadelphia	0	2	4	0	0	0	1	0	0	—	7	10 0
San Diego	2	1	0	0	0	0	0	3	0	—	6	12 1

BATTING

Philadelphia Phillies	AB	R	H	RBI	BB	K	PO	A
Dernier cf	4	1	1	0	1	0	3	0
Rose 1b	5	2	2	0	0	0	9	1
Matthews lf	5	1	1	2	0	2	2	0
Schmidt 3b	5	1	2	1	0	1	1	0
Diaz c	5	1	2	2	0	2	5	0
Robinson rf	3	0	1	1	0	1	0	0
Vukovich ph-rf	1	0	1	1	0	0	1	0
Trillo 2b	4	0	0	0	0	2	2	2
DeJesus ss	3	0	0	0	1	0	3	3
Krukow p	0	0	0	0	0	0	1	1
Monge p	2	1	0	0	1	1	0	1
Lyle p	0	0	0	0	0	0	0	0
R. Reed p	0	0	0	0	0	0	0	2
Totals	**37**	**7**	**10**	**7**	**3**	**9**	**27**	**10**

BATTING
2B: Robinson (5, off Show); Vukovich (6, off Show)
HR: Schmidt (13, 2nd inning off Curtis, 0 on, 0 out); Diaz (15, 2nd inning off Curtis, 0 on, 0 out)
SH: Monge (2, off Show)

BASERUNNING
SB: Matthews (14, 3rd base off Chiffer/Kennedy); DeJesus (14, 2nd base off Chiffer/Kennedy); Dernier (37, 2nd base off Show/Kennedy)

San Diego Padres	AB	R	H	RBI	BB	K	PO	A
Richards lf	4	1	2	0	1	0	0	0
Flannery 2b	2	1	1	1	1	0	2	1
Pittman ph-2b	1	0	0	0	0	0	0	1
Jones ph	1	0	0	0	0	0	0	0
DeLeon p	0	0	0	0	0	0	0	0
Templeton ss	5	0	1	0	0	1	1	4
Lezcano rf	4	1	2	1	0	0	1	0
Gwynn cf	4	1	2	1	0	1	5	0
Kennedy c	4	1	0	0	1	1	9	0
Perkins 1b	4	1	2	0	0	0	9	0
Salazar 3b	4	0	1	1	0	0	0	0
Curtis p	1	0	0	0	0	1	0	2
Chiffer p	0	0	0	0	0	0	0	0
Edwards ph	1	0	0	0	0	0	0	0
Show p	1	0	0	0	0	1	0	1
Bevacqua ph	1	0	1	1	0	0	0	0
Wiggins pr-2b	0	0	0	0	0	0	0	0
Totals	**37**	**6**	**12**	**6**	**3**	**5**	**27**	**9**

FIELDING
E: Flannery (8)

BATTING
2B: Lezcano (17, off Monge); Gwynn (1, off Monge)
HR: Lezcano (9, 8th inning off Monge 0 on, 0 out)
SH: Lezcano (2,off Krukow)
SF: Gwynn (1, off Krukow)

BASERUNNING
SB: Richards (20, 2nd base off Krukow/Diaz)

PITCHING

Philadelphia Phillies	IP	H	HR	R	ER	BB	K
Krukow	1.1	6	0	3	3	0	1
Monge W(4–0)	5.2	4	1	3	3	2	4
Lyle	0.2	1	0	0	0	0	0
R. Reed SV(2)	1.1	1	0	0	0	0	0
Totals	**9.0**	**12**	**1**	**6**	**6**	**3**	**5**

San Diego Padres	IP	H	HR	R	ER	BB	K
Curtis L(6–6)	2	5	2	6	6	1	1
Chiffer	2	1	0	0	0	1	1
Show	4	4	0	1	1	1	5
DeLeon	1	0	0	0	0	0	2
Totals	**9**	**10**	**2**	**7**	**7**	**3**	**9**

Umpires: Frank Pulli, Doug Harvey, Bob Davidson, Jerry Crawford
Time of Game: 2:48   Attendance: 33,558

Roy Halladay
Born: May 14, 1977
Debut: September 20, 1998

One of the billion Adam Sandler movies churned out in the mid-to-late '90s was called *Billy Madison*, a film about a grown man who is forced to go back to first grade (don't ask). Halladay, himself a Sandler fan, found himself living out a real-life version of the movie a few years later. Having washed out at Toronto with an ERA of 10.64 through 19 games (13 starts), he was sent by the Jays not to Triple-A, Double-A, or even their high-A affiliate, but all the way back to the Florida State League, the baseball equivalent of grade school.

He had daily sessions with Blue Jays' pitching coaches and weekly sessions with a sports psychologist, which was maybe most beneficial of all. Halladay learned to incorporate a modified Stuart Smalley approach ("I'm good enough, I'm smart enough," etc.), figuring out how to deal with (and come back from) failure. A helpful exercise in therapy was to write down ten things he liked about himself and two that he didn't. At first, it was easy to do it the other way around, but eventually he was able to come around and relate it to pitching. (As he explains it, "Instead of looking at Pedro Martinez and saying, 'Boy, I wish I could pitch like him,' I force myself to think that Pedro's maybe looking at me saying, 'Boy, I wish I was as tall as Halladay.' ")

The 6'4" Colorado native surged to a pair of huge seasons in 2002 and 2003, leading the AL in innings pitched both years. In '03, he was nearly unbeatable down the stretch, winning the Cy Young Award with a 22–7 record and sparkling 3.25 ERA. He led the league with nine complete games and finished third with 204 strikeouts.

Still, his best-ever game was his third-ever big league start, on the final day of the 1998 season. Against the Tigers at Skydome, he took a no-hitter into the ninth and, with two outs, needed only to retire Bobby Higginson to get it. Former Canadian Football League star Jim McKean was the home plate umpire, and he told Higginson as he approached the plate, "I've been umpiring 25 years and never had a no-hitter. Don't you dare mess this up." Higginson homered and did his best to suppress his laughter on his way around the bases.

We had finished the season in Syracuse, and I had spent a day packing up, just saying good-bye, gassing up the car and all, and had headed out on the

72

New York State Thruway, the first leg of the long drive back home to Colorado. Well, I got as far as Columbus, Ohio, and had stopped for dinner and to stay over at a hotel. I had a cell phone with me, but I guess I had been out of range on the drive, never heard it ring. When I remembered to check for messages, sure enough, I was told I had a message, so I hit a couple buttons, and there's our farm director, Tim McCleary's voice, saying, "Hey, don't veer off south . . . When you get to Cleveland, just stay there, because we're calling you up, and the team is at Jacobs Field." Shoot. So I had to double back to Cleveland, having just checked into the hotel, just having gotten into my hotel room.

I was supposed to just be in the bullpen, but they told me I'd actually be getting a start down in Tampa. So my folks flew in from Denver to see that. Five innings, three runs, I left with the lead, so I guess that's okay. I struck out Quinton McCracken on a bad pitch to start the game . . . I was real lucky. But I never felt too, too nervous . . . All the guys on the team made me feel real welcome that whole week before I got in. I probably would have been nervous had I gotten in a game in Cleveland right away. But it worked out real well.

Also on September 20, 1998
Jimmy Key makes his final major league appearance, pitching a scoreless inning for the Orioles against New York.

AUTHOR'S NOTE: Key was one of the Blue Jays' most successful pitchers in the 1980s and '90s. Halladay could be the team's best of the following decade.

BOXSCORE

Toronto Blue Jays 7, Tampa Bay Devil Rays 5
Game Played on Sunday, September 20, 1998 (Day) at Tropicana Field

Toronto	1	2	0	0	0	2	0	0	0	0	2	—	7	11	2
Tampa Bay	0	0	1	2	0	0	0	1	1	0	0	—	5	13	0

BATTING

Toronto Blue Jays	AB	R	H	RBI	BB	K	PO	A
Stewart lf	5	1	1	0	1	0	3	0
Green rf	5	2	3	2	1	0	3	0
Canseco dh	6	0	1	0	0	2	0	0
Delgado 1b	4	1	0	1	2	1	11	0
Cruz cf	4	1	2	0	2	0	2	0
Fernandez 3b	5	1	1	2	1	1	2	1
Evans 3b	0	0	0	0	0	0	1	1
Fletcher c	4	0	1	0	0	1	6	0
Samuel pr	0	0	0	0	0	0	0	0
Santiago c	2	0	1	0	0	0	5	0
Grebeck 2b	5	0	0	0	1	0	2	2
Gonzalez ss	5	1	1	0	0	1	2	1
Halladay p	0	0	0	0	0	0	0	1
Stieb p	0	0	0	0	0	0	0	0
Person p	0	0	0	0	0	0	0	0
Almanzar p	0	0	0	0	0	0	0	1
Sinclair p	0	0	0	0	0	0	0	0
Risley p	0	0	0	0	0	0	0	0
Totals	45	7	11	7	8	6	36	8

FIELDING
DP: 2
E: Cruz (4), Gonzalez (15)

BATTING
3B: Green (4, off Springer)
HR: Fernandez (8, 6th inning off Springer, 1 on, 0 out)
IBB: Delgado (12, by Lopez)

BASERUNNING
CS: Stewart (18, 2nd base by Yan/Flaherty)

Tampa Bay Devil Rays	AB	R	H	RBI	BB	K	PO	A
Winn cf	6	0	1	0	1	2	5	1
McCracken lf	5	1	3	0	0	2	0	0
Boggs 3b	2	0	1	0	0	0	1	0
Smith pr-3b	4	0	2	0	0	1	1	3
McGriff dh	4	1	3	2	2	0	0	0
Sorrento 1b	6	0	0	0	0	3	8	3
Ledesma ss	6	1	2	0	0	2	4	3
Butler rf	5	2	1	2	1	0	3	1
Flaherty c	5	0	0	0	0	1	8	1
Kelly ph	1	0	0	0	0	0	0	0
Silvestri 2b	3	0	0	0	0	0	3	3
Trammell ph	1	0	0	0	0	0	0	0
Cairo pr-2b	1	0	0	0	1	0	1	0
Arrojo p	0	0	0	0	0	0	1	0
Springer p	0	0	0	0	0	0	0	0
Aldred p	0	0	0	0	0	0	1	0
Mecir p	0	0	0	0	0	0	0	0
Yan p	0	0	0	0	0	0	0	0
Lopez p	0	0	0	0	0	0	0	0
Totals	49	5	13	4	5	11	36	15

BATTING
2B: McCracken (37, off Halladay)
HR: Butler (7, 4th inning off Halladay, 1 on, 0 out); McGriff (19, 9th inning off Person, 0 on, 0 out).
HBP: McCracken (3, by Person)

BASERUNNING
SB: Winn (26, 2nd base off Halladay/Fletcher); Smith (5, 2nd base off Halladay/Fletcher); Cairo (18, 2nd base off Stieb/Santiago)

PITCHING

Toronto Blue Jays	IP	H	HR	R	ER	BB	K
Halladay	5.0	8	1	3	2	2	5
Stieb	2.2	2	0	1	0	2	3
Person	1.1	2	1	1	1	0	1
Almanzar	1.0	1	0	0	0	0	1
Sinclair	0.2	0	0	0	0	0	1
Risley W(2–4)	1.1	0	0	0	0	1	0
Totals	12.0	13	2	5	3	5	11
Tampa Bay Devil Rays	**IP**	**H**	**HR**	**R**	**ER**	**BB**	**K**
Arrojo	1.1	1	0	1	1	2	0
Springer	4.2	4	1	4	4	3	2
Aldred	1.1	1	0	0	0	0	0
Mecir	0.2	1	0	0	0	1	1
Yan	2.0	2	0	0	0	0	1
Lopez L(7–4)	2.0	2	0	2	2	2	2
Totals	12.0	11	1	7	7	8	6

WP: Lopez (4)
HBP: Person (2, McCracken)
IBB: Lopez (4, Delgado)
Umpires: Derryl Cousins, Joe Brinkman, Tim Welke, Gary Cederstrom
Time of Game: 4:18   Attendance: 32,183

Keith Hernandez
Born: October 20, 1953
Debut: August 30, 1974

Keith Hernandez played 17 major league seasons, an appropriate number, considering how many players were inspired to adopt that same uniform number "Mex" had worn so successfully. Mark Grace, David Cone, Bobby Ojeda, and, briefly, Darryl Strawberry all requested that number themselves.

He was the soul of the 1980s Mets teams, having already been a co-MVP in 1979 for the Cardinals when he hit a league-best .344. He also set career bests, leading the league in on-base percentage (.421), doubles (48), and runs scored (116). His agility in the field bailed out an otherwise weak Mets infield, and he was summarily rewarded with 11 Gold Gloves. Known throughout his career as a fine clutch hitter, he had a huge two-out, bases-loaded single in the Mets' World Series Game Seven rally against the Red Sox. While it was recognized as an official statistic, no player had more "game-winning RBI" in a career (129) or in a season (24 in 1985).

In St. Louis, he had gotten a reputation as a soft, uninspired player, and it seemed that during his New York tenure he was bent on proving his skeptics wrong. His leadership abilities led to his being named Mets captain in 1987, his last productive season before suffering hamstring and knee injuries in '88 and '89. The five-time All-Star retired with close to 2,200 hits and nearly 1,100 RBI. He never had a 20-home-run season but finished among the National League's top five in doubles five times and in triples once. His career took an embarrassing turn in 1985, when he was among 21 players outed as users of illegal drugs, but for the most part, he handled the situation with grace and was heartily cheered by Mets fans upon his return from the infamous Pittsburgh cocaine trials.

After his retirement, Hernandez became a bit of a pop culture phenomenon, appearing in one of the most famous *Seinfeld* episodes, as a friend of Jerry's and potential love interest of Elaine's. He successfully debunked Kramer and Newman's assertion that he had spit on them during the summer of 1985, invoking a "second spitter," Roger McDowell.

Ken Boyer told me. I was playing in the minors for Tulsa, on the road at Oklahoma City, and he came and found me at the hotel, and all I could think was, "Great, but I've gotta go out and get some clothes to go to the big leagues with." All that was open in Oklahoma City . . . in fact, all they had was western wear stuff. But I needed travel clothes, so that's what I did. I looked like the polyester Roy Rogers heading off to the big leagues.

Of all places for the Cardinals to be playing, they were in San Francisco, my hometown. My family sat right behind home plate, near our dugout on a cold night at Candlestick. My first at bat was against Mike Caldwell. Joe Torre had sprained his thumb, but he didn't want to go on the DL, so they released Tim McCarver, and I got my chance to play right away, in a stretch run. They ended up losing the last day of the season to the Pirates. Joe and Lou Brock took me aside and made me feel welcome when I got there . . . I was 20, on a team of nothing but 33-year-old veterans. But the guys were nice enough to try and make me feel part of what they were doing.

Also on August 30, 1974
Willie Stargell, second in the league in slugging percentage, doubles in the winner in L.A. as the Pirates take a 1 1/2 game lead in the NL East over the Cardinals.

AUTHOR'S NOTE: Hernandez and Pittsburgh's Stargell won the only shared MVP in history five years later. Six years after that, Pittsburgh would be the site of Hernandez's testimony regarding cocaine use in baseball, leading to the conviction of Pittsburgh-based dealer Curtis Strong.

BOXSCORE

San Francisco Giants 8, St. Louis Cardinals 2

Game Played on Friday, August 30, 1974 (Night) at Candlestick Park

St. Louis	0	0	0	0	1	0	0	0	1	—	2	6	2
San Francisco	5	0	1	0	0	0	0	2	x	—	8	8	1

BATTING

St. Louis Cardinals	AB	R	H	RBI	BB	K	PO	A
Brock lf	5	0	1	0	0	0	1	0
Sizemore 2b	2	0	0	0	2	0	1	5
Smith rf	4	0	0	0	0	1	1	0
Simmons c	2	0	0	0	2	0	3	0
McBride cf	3	1	0	0	0	0	6	0
Reitz 3b	4	0	1	0	0	0	1	1
Hernandez 1b	2	0	1	1	2	1	9	1
Tyson ss	3	1	1	0	0	0	0	3
Dwyer ph	1	0	0	0	0	1	0	0
Siebert p	1	0	1	0	0	0	1	0
Folkers p	0	0	0	0	0	0	0	1
Melendez ph	1	0	1	1	0	0	0	0
Foster p	0	0	0	0	0	0	0	0
Godby ph	1	0	0	0	0	0	0	0
Osteen p	0	0	0	0	0	0	1	0
Cruz ph	1	0	0	0	0	0	0	0
Totals	30	2	6	2	6	3	24	11

FIELDING
E: Smith (6), McBride (3)

BATTING
HBP: McBride (11, by Caldwell)

BASERUNNING
SB: Melendez (2, 2nd base off Caldwell/Rader); Tyson (4, 2nd base off Caldwell/Rader)
CS: Brock (25, 2nd base by Caldwell/Rader)

San Francisco Giants	AB	R	H	RBI	BB	K	PO	A
Maddox cf	4	0	0	0	0	1	3	0
Fuentes 2b	3	1	1	0	1	0	6	4
Thomasson rf	4	1	1	0	0	1	1	0
Matthews lf	3	2	1	0	1	0	2	0
Goodson 3b	3	1	1	1	0	0	0	1
Miller 3b	1	0	0	0	0	0	0	1
Kingman 1b	3	2	2	3	1	0	11	2
Speier ss	3	1	0	1	1	0	1	6
Rader c	4	0	2	1	0	0	3	0
Caldwell p	4	0	0	0	0	1	0	3
Sosa p	0	0	0	0	0	0	0	0
Totals	32	8	8	6	4	3	27	17

FIELDING
DP: 2
E: Rader (8)

BATTING
2B: Kingman (13, off Osteen)
HR: Kingman (15, 1st inning off Siebert, 2 on, 1 out)
IBB: Kingman (2, by Folkers); Speier (6, by Osteen).

BASERUNNING
SB: Matthews (9, 2nd base off Folkers/Simmons)

PITCHING

St. Louis Cardinals	IP	H	HR	R	ER	BB	K
Siebert L(7–8)	2	5	1	6	6	2	0
Folkers	2	1	0	0	0	1	2
Foster	2	0	0	0	0	0	1
Osteen	2	2	0	2	1	1	0
Totals	8	8	1	8	7	4	3

San Francisco Giants	IP	H	HR	R	ER	BB	K
Caldwell W(13–3)	8	6	0	2	2	6	2
Sosa	1	0	0	0	0	0	1
Totals	9	6	0	2	2	6	3

HBP: Caldwell (3, McBride)
IBB: Folkers (8, Kingman); Osteen (3, Speier)
Umpires: Terry Tata, Dutch Rennert, Shag Crawford, John Kibler
Time of Game: 2:19   Attendance: 3,111

Orel Hershiser
Born: September 16, 1958
Debut: September 1, 1983

One look at Orel Hershiser and you'd figure the last thing he'd ever be called is "Bulldog." Sallow and bespectacled, Hershiser basically looks like six o'clock. "I've heard 'em all," he allows. "They say the only college from which I could have gotten a letter was Indiana, Illinois, or Iowa." Actually, Hershiser pitched at Bowling Green and at one point was close to washing out of school and off the team. True to his fighting spirit, he persevered, becoming a 17th-round pick of the Dodgers in 1979.

Manager Tommy Lasorda took it upon himself to fashion the nickname that would stick like flypaper to that sinewy body. "Take charge out there," he screamed. "Be aggressive! Be a bulldog! In fact, that's your new name from now on. Ninth inning, you're facing Dale Murphy, he hears 'Now pitching, Orel Hershiser,' he can't wait to hit you. But if he hears, 'Now pitching, *Bulldog* Hershiser,' he's going to be scared to death!"

"Orel," a family name passed down through generations of Hershisers, has now been passed to son Orel V, who is known around the family as "Quint." Hershiser says he began embracing his name when tennis star Martina Navratilova told him that in Czech, it translates directly to "Eagle." Whether a bird or a bulldog, Hershiser's lasting contribution to the game itself and to the Dodgers organization is undeniable. His dominance in 1988 catapulted the Dodgers to their most recent championship, and for his efforts he was named both Cy Young and World Series MVP. He was on the mound going the distance in Game Five against the Oakland A's, then days later, he was on the Johnny Carson show, singing hymns from the couch.

His '88 season will also be remembered for his record-setting scoreless-inning streak of 59. In his final start of the regular season, he needed a 10th shutout inning to cement it, and with previous record-holder Don Drysdale watching on like a proud father, Hershiser knocked it down, getting Keith Moreland on a fly out to set the new standard.

Battling back from major arm surgery in 1990, the New Jersey–raised righty ended his big league career with 204 regular season wins and three trips to both the World Series and the All-Star Game. He is now the well-respected pitching coach of the Texas Rangers.

Del Crandall was our Triple-A manager, and he called me into the office to tell me I was going up to L.A., as a September call-up. Big time phone tree . . .

I called my parents, they called everybody else. We were all real excited, but I had really felt I could have made the team out of spring training, but I was the only guy with an option left. I figured I could get called up any time, as soon as someone got injured, but no one ever did. April 'til September 1, they never changed a single pitcher. No one pitched badly, no one got hurt.

My first outing was my first night with the team. First batter I faced was Gary Carter, who became my first out on a groundball, Bill Russell to Greg Brock. I followed the path of Russell's throw, and the moment it hit Brock's mitt, I figured I was officially a big leaguer with an ERA and everything.

I can't say I even remember warming up or getting loose . . . I just remember that suddenly I was on the mound at Olympic Stadium, telling myself to keep the ball down to get some grounders . . . It was a three-up, three-down inning. Then the next inning I gave up, like, three doubles in a row, and I was out of the game. The game can turn on you quick.

Also on September 1, 1983
The KAL flight 007 is downed by a Soviet jet fighter after the airliner enters Soviet airspace. Two hundred and sixty-nine people are killed aboard the Korean Air Lines Boeing 747, including 61 Americans.

AUTHOR'S NOTE: Sixteen years later, Hershiser would be personally affected by an airline tragedy himself when his friend Payne Stewart and his agent and confidant, Robert Fraley, died aboard a private plane that malfunctioned over South Dakota.

BOXSCORE

Montreal Expos 8, Los Angeles Dodgers 3
Game Played on Thursday, September 1, 1983 (Night) at Stade Olympique

												R	H	E
Los Angeles	0	0	0	0	0	2	0	1	0	—	3	7	1
Montreal	1	0	3	0	0	0	0	4	x	—	8	11	1

BATTING

Los Angeles Dodgers	AB	R	H	RBI	BB	K	PO	A
S.Sax 2b	3	1	1	0	1	0	5	0
Russell ss	4	1	1	0	0	1	1	5
Baker lf	3	1	2	1	1	1	3	0
Guerrero 3b	2	0	0	1	2	1	1	1
Landreaux cf	4	0	1	1	0	2	1	0
Marshall rf	4	0	1	0	0	2	0	0
Brock 1b	4	0	1	0	0	1	8	0
Yeager c	3	0	0	0	0	1	5	2
Bream ph	1	0	0	0	0	0	0	0
Honeycutt p	1	0	0	0	0	0	0	4
Monday ph	1	0	0	0	0	1	0	0
Hooton p	0	0	0	0	0	0	0	0
Reynolds ph	1	0	0	0	0	0	0	0
Hershiser p	0	0	0	0	0	0	0	1
Beckwith p	0	0	0	0	0	0	0	0
Thomas ph	1	0	0	0	0	1	0	0
Totals	32	3	7	3	4	11	24	13

FIELDING
DP: 1
E: Baker (3)

BATTING
2B: S. Sax (14, off James)
HR: Baker (14, 8th inning off James, 0 on, 1 out)

BASERUNNING
SB: Baker (5, 2nd base off Lea/Carter)
CS: Guerrero (6, 2nd base by Reardon/Carter)

Montreal Expos	AB	R	H	RBI	BB	K	PO	A
Raines lf	3	2	2	0	2	0	0	0
Trillo 2b	5	1	2	1	0	0	2	1
Dawson cf	3	3	1	0	2	0	5	1
Carter c	5	0	1	2	0	0	11	1
Oliver 1b	4	0	1	1	1	0	3	0
Wallach 3b	3	0	1	0	1	1	1	0
Reardon p	1	0	0	0	0	1	0	0
Wohlford rf	4	1	1	0	0	1	3	0
Flynn ss	3	0	0	0	0	0	2	2
Lea p	2	0	0	0	0	1	0	1
James p	1	0	1	0	0	0	0	0
Schatzeder p	0	0	0	0	0	0	0	0
Speier 3b	1	1	1	1	0	0	0	0
Totals	35	8	11	5	6	4	27	6

FIELDING
DP: 1
E: Speier (12)

BATTING
2B: Raines (25, off Honeycutt); Dawson (28, off Honeycutt); Oliver (31, off Honeycutt); Wohlford (8, off Honeycutt)
SH: Flynn (4, off Hershiser)
IBB: Wallach (8, by Honeycutt); Dawson 2 (10, by Honeycutt, by Beckwith); Oliver (12, by Beckwith)

BASERUNNING
SB: Dawson (22, 2nd base off Honeycutt/Yeager); Raines (64, 2nd base off Honeycutt/Yeager)

PITCHING

Los Angeles Dodgers	IP	H	HR	R	ER	BB	K
Honeycutt L(2–1)	4.0	7	0	4	4	3	1
Hooton	2.0	1	0	0	0	1	1
Hershiser	1.0	2	0	3	1	0	1
Beckwith	1.0	1	0	1	0	2	1
Totals	8.0	11	0	8	5	6	4
Montreal Expos	IP	H	HR	R	ER	BB	K
Lea W(13–8)	5.0	5	0	2	2	3	7
James	2.1	2	1	1	1	1	1
Schatzeder	0.1	0	0	0	0	0	1
Reardon SV(20)	1.1	0	0	0	0	0	2
Totals	9.0	7	1	3	3	4	11

IBB: Honeycutt 2 (2, Wallach, Dawson); Beckwith 2 (11, Dawson, Oliver)
Umpires: Eric Gregg, Frank Pulli, Doug Harvey, Jerry Crawford
Time of Game: 2:52   Attendance: 30,428

Trevor Hoffman
Born: October 13, 1967
Debut: April 6, 1993

When the 1998 San Diego Padres shocked observers by reaching the World Series, it was generally agreed that it never would have happened were it not for their door-slamming closer, Trevor Hoffman. With a league-leading (and then league record) 53 saves, he blew only one opportunity all year, compiling an ERA of 1.48. Allowing just two home runs in 73 innings, the California native helped Bruce Bochy's team to a franchise-record 98 victories.

For his Padres career, he was successful on 89 percent of his save opportunities until shoulder surgery derailed him in 2003. He bounced back in 2004, recording 41 saves and walking just eight batters in 55 appearances.

Hoffman began his career as, of all things, a shortstop in the Reds organization. After hitting just .212 at short-season Charleston, he made the switch to the mound and pitched well enough to catch the eye of the brand-new Florida Marlins, who selected him fourth in the expansion draft. After a year with the Fish, he was dealt cross-country as part of the Marlins' trade for Gary Sheffield. Hoffman began his Padres career as a long man but by 1994 was anointed team closer, becoming a fan favorite as he successfully knocked down 20 out of 23 saves.

Before he gained fame on the mound, he had his fifteen minutes of fame at the 1993 Super Bowl, in Pasadena. His girlfriend was a Buffalo Bills cheerleader, and at the end of the third quarter, Hoffman held up a big sign from his seat, 30 rows behind her, proposing marriage. She saw it but assumed he was just kidding. Not until Hoffman bolted past an usher to get down on one knee did she (and a national TV audience) realize he was serious.

Hoffman's flair for the dramatic may have been inherited from a different usher, his dad, Eddie, who was known around Anaheim Stadium as "The Singing Usher." Eddie was occasionally called on to belt out the national anthem at Angels games and was known for peddling his products in a lilting sing-song voice.

As a kid, Trevor gravitated to baseball because of his dad and his brother, Glenn, who eventually played for the Red Sox and briefly managed the Dodgers. Trevor wasn't allowed to participate in contact sports due to a kidney he'd had removed when he was just six weeks old. To raise money and awareness for kidney disease, Hoffman has always donated $200 per save to the National Kidney Foundation.

I had made the team out of spring training, but I didn't get into a game until the second or third game. Everyone had been used on the team but me, but finally, the last guy out of the bullpen to see action . . . It was in that first home series against the Dodgers. Bases loaded, two outs, Rene Lachemann brought me in to face Eric Davis. I ran the count to 3-and-2 and was able to sneak one by him for strike three. We lost, but I felt I had done my job, keeping the game in check.

My mom and dad, my brothers were there . . . and of all teams to open up with, my hometown National League team, the Dodgers. Glenn was in their minor league system at that point, as a coach. It's kind of funny . . . There are pictures of the inaugural game showing Charlie Hough delivering the first pitch in Marlins history, kind of a panoramic view, and you can see my mom and dad's heads in the picture, barely in it there in the family section. Every time I see that picture, I always look for the two of them, just the tops of their heads.

Also on April 6, 1993
The Phillies' Mitch Williams changes his uniform number from 28 to 99, the highest number in Major League history. He picks up a save and vows to throw at 99 mph every outing.

AUTHOR'S NOTE: Hoffman racked up most of his saves dialing it well down from 99, using his change-up and seldom getting into the self-inflicted bases-loaded jams that made Mitch Williams famous.

BOXSCORE

Los Angeles Dodgers 4, Florida Marlins 2
Game Played on Tuesday, April 6, 1993 (Night) at Joe Robbie Stadium

Los Angeles	0	1	2	0	0	0	1	0	0	—	4	8	0
Florida	1	0	0	1	0	0	0	0	0	—	2	8	0

BATTING

Los Angeles Dodgers	AB	R	H	RBI	BB	K	PO	A
Offerman ss	4	0	0	0	1	1	2	3
Butler cf	3	0	1	1	2	0	1	0
Strawberry rf	4	0	0	0	1	0	0	0
Davis lf	4	1	0	0	1	1	2	0
Wallach 3b	4	2	2	0	0	0	0	1
Karros 1b	3	0	0	1	0	2	5	1
Piazza c	4	0	2	1	0	0	12	2
Reed 2b	3	0	1	0	1	1	4	3
R. Martinez p	1	0	0	1	0	1	0	0
Webster ph	1	1	1	0	0	0	0	0
Gott p	0	0	0	0	0	0	0	0
Harris ph	1	0	1	0	0	0	0	0
Worrell p	0	0	0	0	0	0	0	0
Totals	32	4	8	4	6	6	27	10

FIELDING
DP: 3

BATTING
2B: Piazza (1, off Armstrong); Butler (1, off McClure)
SF: R. Martinez (1, off Armstrong); Karros (1, ff Armstrong)

Florida Marlins	AB	R	H	RBI	BB	K	PO	A
Pose cf	4	0	2	0	0	1	2	0
Barberie 2b	1	0	0	0	3	1	2	1
Felix rf	4	1	1	0	0	1	0	0
Destrade 1b	4	0	1	1	0	2	9	0
Magadan 3b	2	1	0	0	2	1	2	2
Santiago c	4	0	0	0	0	3	6	0
Conine lf	4	0	2	0	0	1	4	0
Weiss ss	4	0	2	1	0	0	1	2
Armstrong p	2	0	0	0	0	2	0	2
McClure p	0	0	0	0	0	0	0	0
Lewis p	0	0	0	0	0	0	0	0
Carr ph	1	0	0	0	0	1	0	0
Aquino p	0	0	0	0	0	0	1	1
Hoffman p	0	0	0	0	0	0	0	0
Briley ph	1	0	0	0	0	1	0	0
Totals	31	2	8	2	5	13	27	8

FIELDING
DP: 1

BATTING
2B: Felix (1, off R. Martinez); Pose (1, off R. Martinez)

BASERUNNING
CS: Pose (2, 2nd base by R. Martinez/Piazza); Magadan (1, 2nd base by R. Martinez/Piazza)

PITCHING

Los Angeles Dodgers	IP	H	HR	R	ER	BB	K
R. Martinez W(1–0)	6	6	0	2	2	4	9
Gott	2	0	0	0	0	1	3
Worrell SV(1)	1	2	0	0	0	0	1
Totals	9	8	0	2	2	5	13

Florida Marlins	IP	H	HR	R	ER	BB	K
Armstrong L(0–1)	6.1	6	0	4	4	3	4
McClure	0.1	1	0	0	0	0	0
Lewis	0.1	0	0	0	0	0	0
Aquino	1.2	1	0	0	0	3	1
Hoffman	0.1	0	0	0	0	0	1
Totals	9.0	8	0	4	4	6	6

BK: Lewis (1)
Umpires: Joe West, Charlie Williams, Gary Darling, Frank Pulli
Time of Game: 3:28   Attendance: 42,689

Al Hrabosky
Born: July 21, 1949
Debut: June 16, 1970

Reliever Al Hrabosky wasn't the first sports figure of Hungarian descent to make his mark in the United States. George Halas and Don Shula, maybe two of the greatest NFL coaches of all-time, are both proudly Hungarian in heritage. Larry Csonka, Don Shula, and Lou Groza all excelled on the football gridiron, as did the flamboyant Joe Namath (whose name was originally spelled "Nemeth" when his folks came over on the boat, but they changed it to preserve the Hungarian pronunciation).

On the subject of flamboyance, Hrabosky cultivated both a fine career and a cult following for his on-field histrionics. He was known simply as "The Mad Hungarian." Delighting fans across the country, the California-born lefty would go through an elaborate psyche-up and psyche-out session at the back of the mound, and then even on the rubber, he would snarl and twitch and basically look like he was about to rip out your spleen. To order a batter to get in the box and get ready, he would furiously pound that pitching rubber, his Fu Manchu mustache flaring at both corners. The routine was a source of great amusement and occasional animosity from fans of opposing teams. "My goal when I pitch on the road," said Hrabosky, "is to get a standing boo."

In 1975, Hrabosky won 13 games and saved 22, but the Hrabosky Show took a short hiatus in 1977. His numbers suffered as his "old school" manager, Vern Rapp, insisted on a clean-shaven look and a kinder, gentler act. Hrabosky huffed cross-state to Kansas City where he resurrected both the look and his career. Hrabosky told the Kansas City media that part of his success was due to the Gypsy Rose of Death ring he wore to "ward off the werewolves."

After his playing career sputtered to a halt in Atlanta a few years later, Hrabosky moved back to St. Louis, where he became a broadcaster and philanthropist. His annual charity golf tournament is a huge success, and his insightful commentary on Cardinals telecasts is well-received. And, by the way, off the field, Hrabosky has always been a lot closer to "docile" than "mad." "It's all in the packaging," he says.

Ken Boyer was the manager who called me and told me I was going from Double-A in Arlington, Texas, up to join the big club in St. Louis. Well, not exactly in St. Louis. They had just started an 18-game road trip, so I was asked-to get to San Diego. The date was June 15, payday. I remember that, because I had just gotten my Double-A check and noticed that when I got handed my big league meal money, the meal money was more than my paycheck had been.

I got in when I just kind of mopped up, a 1-2-3 inning. My family was all in Anaheim, so to get to San Diego was no problem for them. My folks went shopping for me; I had told them, "I'm on this big, long road trip and need to be wearing sports coats," so I told them I'd pay them back with my meal money but to please stop and get me some clothes on the way down to San Diego. On that trip, we went from San Diego to Chicago to Pittsburgh, and I remember my second appearance more than my first, because it was at Wrigley, pre-lights, late in the day. I pitched the 16th and 17th innings and got the win. On to Pittsburgh, I got my first and only big league start, and if it wasn't for me, Roberto Clemente wouldn't have had 3,000 hits, I can tell you that! He would have come up just short, but I helped out . . . If it wasn't for me, he would have ended up with 2,998.

Also on June 16, 1970
The Dodgers' Don Sutton wins a battle of four-hitters against the Pirates' Bob Veale, setting the stage for what will be the first of his ten consecutive winning seasons.

BOXSCORE

San Diego Padres 4, St. Louis Cardinals 0

Game Played on Tuesday, June 16, 1970 (Night) at San Diego Stadium

St. Louis	0	0	0	0	0	0	0	0	0	—	0	6	0
San Diego	0	0	0	0	0	0	4	0	x	—	4	10	1

BATTING

St. Louis Cardinals	AB	R	H	RBI	BB	K	PO	A
Brock lf	3	0	0	0	1	0	0	0
Cardenal cf	4	0	0	0	0	1	1	0
Allen 1b	4	0	2	0	0	1	6	0
Torre 3b	4	0	0	0	0	0	0	2
Hague rf	4	0	1	0	0	0	1	0
Simmons c	3	0	0	0	0	2	8	4
Javier 2b	3	0	1	0	0	0	5	1
Kennedy ss	2	0	0	0	0	0	2	4
Ca. Taylor ph	1	0	0	0	0	0	0	0
Maxvill ss	0	0	0	0	0	0	1	0
Carlton p	2	0	1	0	0	1	0	0
Abernathy p	0	0	0	0	0	0	0	0
Beauchamp ph	1	0	1	0	0	0	0	0
Hrabosky p	0	0	0	0	0	0	0	0
Totals	**31**	**0**	**6**	**0**	**1**	**5**	**24**	**11**

FIELDING
DP: 1

San Diego Padres	AB	R	H	RBI	BB	K	PO	A
Campbell 2b	3	1	2	0	1	0	3	6
Slocum 3b	3	0	1	0	0	1	0	2
Ferrara ph	0	0	0	0	1	0	0	0
Arcia pr-3b	0	1	0	0	0	0	0	1
Gaston cf	4	0	2	3	0	1	2	0
Colbert 1b	4	0	0	0	0	2	15	0
Brown rf	4	0	2	0	0	0	0	0
Murrell lf	4	1	1	1	0	1	0	0
Cannizzaro c	3	0	1	0	1	0	5	0
Dean ss	3	1	1	0	0	1	2	5
Corkins p	0	0	0	0	0	0	0	0
Roberts p	2	0	0	0	0	2	0	1
Totals	**30**	**4**	**10**	**4**	**3**	**8**	**27**	**15**

FIELDING
DP: 3
E: Arcia (3)

BATTING
2B: Cannizzaro (7, off Carlton); Gaston (14, off Carlton)
HR: Murrell (8, 7th inning off Carlton, 0 on, 0 out)
SH: Roberts (1, off Carlton)
IBB: Campbell (2, by Carlton)

BASERUNNING
CS: Brown 2 (3, 2nd base by Carlton/Simmons, 2nd base by Hrabosky/Simmons)

PITCHING

St. Louis Cardinals	IP	H	HR	R	ER	BB	K
Carlton L (3–8)	6.2	9	1	4	4	3	8
Abernathy	0.1	0	0	0	0	0	0
Hrabosky	1	1	0	0	0	0	0
Totals	**8**	**10**	**1**	**4**	**4**	**3**	**8**

San Diego Padres	IP	H	HR	R	ER	BB	K
Corkins	1	0	0	0	0	0	0
Roberts W (5–3)	8	6	0	0	0	1	5
Totals	**9**	**6**	**0**	**0**	**0**	**1**	**5**

IBB: Carlton (9, Campbell)
Umpires: Ken Burkhart, Ed Sudol, Lee Weyer, Andy Olsen
Time of Game: 2:01   Attendance: 7012

AUTHOR'S NOTE: Hrabosky later signed a contract with the Braves that would have put him in their broadcast booth at the end of his playing career. Ted Turner bought out the contract, and a few years later, Sutton took the broadcast gig in Atlanta instead of Hrabosky.

Tim Hudson
Born: July 14, 1975
Debut: June 8, 1999

He is listed at six feet but is closer to 5' 10". On the mound, he proves that, like Pedro Martinez, height is one of the greatly overrated traits for a successful big league pitcher. Hudson has spent a lifetime, however, trying to prove he belongs with the big boys. Growing up in Alabama, he was 10 and 12 years younger than his two brothers. In high school, he was barely 150 pounds and thus was never scouted.

Hudson's crew cut finally scraped the bottom of the "You Must Be This Tall To Ride The Ride" line in college. He emerged as one of the best two-way players in Division I history, DH'ing for Auburn when he wasn't dominating on the mound. In his final season for the Tigers, he hit .396 with close to a hundred RBI and, almost incidentally, went 15–2 as the SEC's top pitcher. Still, every big league team passed on Hudson at least five times in the 1997 draft. The A's could have grabbed him early on but spent their time, energy, and money on seven other pitchers before they honed in on "Huddy." West Virginia righty Chris Enochs was Oakland's first-rounder, and two sandwich picks (Eric DuBose and Denny Wagner) quickly followed. Nominal big league success was struck by signing second-rounder Chad Harville, but they missed in the fourth and fifth rounds with Jason Anderson from Radford University and Andy Kimball from Wisconsin-Oshkosh.

With his time at Auburn preparing him well for early big league entry, Hudson made an immediate impact for Oakland. Usually, the learning curve for a pitcher is longer than that of a position player. It's been said that a first-year 20-game winner is like a first-year Super Bowl quarterback. His first full season, he was 20–6, steering the A's into the postseason. He would never again be overlooked.

There were so many rumors during May and June . . . I had a feeling I'd be maybe going up at some point. We were in Vegas playing a Triple-A series, and [AAA manager] Mike Quade told me pretty much as soon as we got there, I'd be going up in a couple days, but just to hang with the team in Vegas 'til then. That was plenty of time to get nervous, sitting around in Vegas!

I had plenty of time to call everyone and tell 'em I'd be going to San Diego, to pitch interleague . . . and that would be the first big league stadium I'd ever be in, the old one in San Diego. Well, except for the one time I went to a Braves game in Atlanta when I was 16. I flew in, and it was exciting to be in a big league locker room, and to get out there. Before the game, warming up, stretching, I wasn't really nervous . . . It was more relief that I had finally been given the chance to get my shot. I told myself, "You're here, now you're gonna stay."

It wasn't a great outing, but I did have a lot of strikeouts. To be honest, I can't even remember many of their players . . . They didn't have Tony Gwynn in the lineup, and that I'll always remember, because that was a big relief. I didn't know them, they didn't know me . . . I didn't even know my own catcher, A. J. Hinch.

Every inning, there was a threat. But every time I needed a big strike-out, I got it. I gave up a home run, opposite field, to the late Mike Darr . . . That was first pitch of an inning. The deeper things went in the few innings I was in there, the more likely I was to come up with a big strikeout or two. Everyone back home seemed to be making a bigger deal of it than me . . . Like I say, not to sound cocky, I just knew there would be plenty more big league starts still to come.

Also on June 8, 1999
Montreal's Dan Smith makes his big league debut and does so by three-hitting the powerful Boston Red Sox in Montreal.

AUTHOR'S NOTE: Hudson and Smith were born eight weeks apart, and while Hudson had only 24 minor league wins at the time of his promotion, the hard-throwing right-handed Smith already had amassed 44. Smith, indeed, had the better of the two debuts. But by the end of the 2004 season, Smith's big league record was 7–12. Hudson's was 92–39.

BOXSCORE

San Diego Padres 5, Oakland Athletics 3												
Game Played on Tuesday, June 8, 1999 (Night) at Qualcomm Stadium												
Oakland	0	1	0	0	0	0	1	1	0	—	3	8	1
San Diego	1	0	1	1	0	0	0	2	x	—	5	11	2

BATTING

Oakland Athletics	AB	R	H	RBI	BB	K	PO	A
Phillips 2b-cf	4	1	0	0	1	2	0	2
Tejada ss	4	0	2	0	1	0	2	1
Giambi 1b	5	0	1	1	0	2	3	1
Saenz 3b	5	1	2	0	0	2	1	0
Stairs rf	4	0	1	1	0	1	0	0
Raines lf	4	0	0	0	0	0	1	0
Christenson cf	2	0	0	0	1	0	0	0
Chavez ph	1	1	1	0	0	0	0	0
Groom p	0	0	0	0	0	0	0	1
Jones p	0	0	0	0	0	0	0	0
Hinch c	2	0	0	0	0	0	11	0
Jaha ph	1	0	0	0	0	0	0	0
Worrell p	0	0	0	0	0	0	0	1
Grieve ph	0	0	0	0	1	0	0	0
Velandia pr-2b	0	0	0	0	0	0	1	0
Hudson p	1	0	1	0	1	0	1	0
Macfarlane c	1	0	0	1	0	0	4	0
Totals	34	3	8	3	5	7	24	6

FIELDING
DP: 1
E: Hinch (4)

BATTING
2B: Saenz (9, off Murray); Chavez (11, off Wall)
SF: Macfarlane (2, off Wall)

San Diego Padres	AB	R	H	RBI	BB	K	PO	A
Jackson ss	3	2	2	0	2	1	1	3
Darr rf	4	1	2	1	0	0	0	0
Matthews ph-rf	0	0	0	0	1	0	0	0
Owens lf	5	0	2	2	0	3	1	1
Myers c	4	0	0	0	0	1	8	0
Leyritz 1b	4	0	1	1	1	2	10	0
Arias 3b	3	1	1	0	0	2	1	2
Boehringer p	0	0	0	0	0	0	0	1
VanderWal ph	0	0	0	0	1	0	0	0
Wall p	0	0	0	0	0	0	0	0
Hoffman p	0	0	0	0	0	0	0	1
Ru. Rivera cf	3	0	0	0	1	3	3	0
Newhan 2b	4	1	3	1	0	0	3	2
Murray p	2	0	0	0	0	2	0	1
Giovanola 3b	1	0	0	0	0	0	0	0
Totals	33	5	11	5	7	15	27	11

FIELDING
DP: 1
E: Jackson (8), Arias (4)

BATTING
2B: Newhan (1, off Hudson); Jackson (11, off Worrell)
HR: Darr (1, 3rd inning off Hudson, 0 on, 0 out)
SH: Giovanola (1, off Groom)
IBB: Jackson (2, by Groom)

BASERUNNING
SB: Jackson 2 (14, 2nd base off Hudson/Hinch; 3rd base off Hudson/Hinch); Owens (7, 2nd base off Hudson/Hinch); Darr (1, 2nd base off Worrell/Macfarlane)

PITCHING

Oakland Athletics	IP	H	HR	R	ER	BB	K
Hudson	5	7	1	3	3	4	11
Worrell	2	2	0	0	0	1	2
Groom L (2–1)	0.1	1	0	2	2	2	0
Jones	0.2	1	0	0	0	0	2
Totals	8.0	11	1	5	5	7	15
San Diego Padres	**IP**	**H**	**HR**	**R**	**ER**	**BB**	**K**
Murray	5.2	5	0	1	1	3	2
Boehringer	1.1	2	0	1	1	1	2
Wall W (4–0)	1	1	0	1	1	1	1
Hoffman SV (11)	1	0	0	0	0	0	2
Totals	9.0	8	0	3	3	5	7

WP: Wall (1)
IBB: Groom (3,Jackson)
Umpires: Sam Holbrook, Dana DeMuth, Charlie Reliford, Jeff Kellogg
Time of Game: 3:09   Attendance: 17,195

Torii Hunter
Born: July 18, 1975
Debut: August 22, 1997

The first thing you notice about Torii Hunter is the unusual first name. "Old Two I's" also has brothers named Taru, Tishique, and Tramar, none of whom were able to get out of the Pine Bluff, Arkansas, ghetto without his assistance. Baseball was his ticket out, and his card was punched his senior year of high school, when the Twins made him their first pick of the 1993 draft. Minnesota had initially sent scouts to Pine Bluff only to watch Hunter's teammate, Basil Shabazz, but instead fell in love with the speedy, charismatic right-hand hitter.

Hunter's defense was immediately noticed in the big leagues as well, with his sprinting, wall-crawling catches become highlight reel staples. High ebb was the 2002 All-Star Game in Milwaukee, when he leaped to rob Barry Bonds of a homer, then saw Bonds carry him off the field like sack of flour. Hunter once literally ran through a wall to rob a minor leaguer of a home run in Double-A. A Gold Glover every year since 2001, the unselfish Hunter handed off his 2003 award to Twins' fielding and baserunning coach Jerry White. As he says in the ubiquitous MLB "I Live For This" commercials, he'd rather rob someone of a home run than hit a home run, although he manages to hit his share of long balls nonetheless. Hunter averaged 27 homers and 91 RBI between 2001 and 2004, with 60 stolen bases during that time.

Immensely popular with the Minnesota fans, he is equally as popular with his Minnesota teammates, for whom he has designed elaborate custom handshakes, each one a vexing combination of finger locks, chest slaps, and fist bumps. He remains among the most likable, unpretentious stars in the sport and has signed to stay with the Twins through 2007.

Baltimore, Maryland . . . Camden Yards. I cabbed it over from the hotel with Matt Lawton. He took care of me. First big league stadium I'd ever been to . . . Sold out . . . 45,000 people . . . First major league game I'd ever seen live, and I'm sitting there in the dugout realizing I could actually be in it at some point. Soon enough, I was, as a pinch runner. TK [manager Tom Kelly] told me to go in there and pinch-run for Terry Steinbach. So I run out of the third base dugout across the field, and Steinbach is standing on the base, and he says, "What are you doing here?" So I kind of swallow and tell him, "I'm pinch-running for you, man." He says, "No you're not," and wouldn't get off the base. I'm like,

"No, man, don't do me like this . . . There are 45,000 people looking at me right now." He says, "No, I'm not leaving," so I'm like, "Oh, man," and turn to start running back into our dugout. Then he calls after me and says, "Hey, I'm just kidding." So now, because I've already started heading back, the joke's on me. And I can hear all these people laughing, "Ahhh, rookie!"

What a day. I had come all the way up from Double-A where Al Newman was my manager . . . He says, "T, you're going to the big leagues." So I laugh and say, "Yeah, man, whatever," and start walking out of his office. I didn't want to hear that. He stopped me, trying to sound serious, and said, "Torii. Really. You're going." He went out and told the rest of the team, and that's when I finally believed him.

I'll always remember my first major league hit because Cal Ripken retrieved the ball for me. That was so special . . . and who knew, but later, when he got his 3,000th hit at the Metrodome, I retrieved that one for him. It rolled right to me, and of course, I put it in my back pocket just to mess with everyone. When I gave it to him about a minute later, I told him, "This is the least I can do. You gave me my number one . . . Least I can do is hand you over your number 3,000."

BOXSCORE

Baltimore Orioles 3, Minnesota Twins 1
Game Played on Friday, August 22, 1997 (Night) at Oriole Park at Camden Yards

Minnesota	0	0	0	0	1	0	0	0	0	—	1	5	1
Baltimore	3	0	0	0	0	0	0	0	x	—	3	5	0

BATTING

Minnesota Twins	AB	R	H	RBI	BB	K	PO	A
Knoblauch 2b	4	0	2	0	0	0	1	2
Walker 3b	4	0	0	0	0	0	1	3
Molitor dh	4	0	0	0	0	1	0	0
Stahoviak 1b	3	0	0	0	1	1	10	0
Steinbach c	4	0	1	0	0	2	4	0
Hunter pr	0	0	0	0	0	0	0	0
Lawton lf	4	1	1	1	0	1	4	0
Coomer rf	3	0	1	0	0	0	2	0
Cordova lf	3	0	0	0	0	2	2	0
Hocking ss	2	0	0	0	1	1	1	3
Tewksbury p	0	0	0	0	0	0	0	0
Swindell p	0	0	0	0	0	0	0	0
Totals	31	1	5	1	2	8	24	8

FIELDING
E: Lawton (5)

BATTING
HR: Lawton (9, 5th inning off Erickson, 0 on, 0 out)

Baltimore Orioles	AB	R	H	RBI	BB	K	PO	A
Anderson cf	3	1	0	0	1	0	1	0
Reboulet 2b	4	0	0	0	0	1	0	2
Surhoff lf	4	1	2	0	0	1	1	0
Berroa rf	4	1	1	2	0	1	0	0
Tarasco rf	0	0	0	0	0	0	0	0
Palmeiro 1b	4	0	1	1	0	0	13	1
Ripken 3b	3	0	1	0	0	0	0	3
Baines dh	3	0	0	0	0	0	0	0
Webster c	2	0	0	0	0	1	9	0
Bordick ss	3	0	0	0	0	0	2	5
Erickson p	0	0	0	0	0	0	1	1
Myers p	0	0	0	0	0	0	0	0
Totals	30	3	5	3	1	3	27	12

FIELDING
DP: 1

BATTING
2B: Berroa (18, off Tewksbury)
HBP: Webster (1, by Tewksbury)

PITCHING

Minnesota Twins	IP	H	HR	R	ER	BB	K
Tewksbury L(4–10)	7	5	0	3	3	1	2
Swindell	1	0	0	0	0	0	1
Totals	8	5	0	3	3	1	3
Baltimore Orioles	**IP**	**H**	**HR**	**R**	**ER**	**BB**	**K**
Erickson W(15–5)	8.1	5	1	1	1	2	8
Myers SV(39)	0.2	0	0	0	0	0	0
Totals	9.0	5	1	1	1	2	8

WP: Erickson (11)
HBP: Tewksbury (1, Webster)
Umpires: Ken Kaiser, Joe Brinkman, Derryl Cousins, Ed Hickox
Time of Game: 2:13   Attendance: 47,785

Also on August 22, 1997
A federal judge rejects President Bill Clinton's request to dismiss the sexual harassment suit of Paula Jones.

AUTHOR'S NOTE: Hunter—an Arkansas native as well—once called on Clinton for a huge favor. After his junior year at Pine Bluff High in 1992, Hunter needed some financial help to attend the Junior Olympics in Korea. He wrote a letter to then-governor Clinton, who wrote back with a $500 check.

Jason Isringhausen
Born: September 7, 1972
Debut: July 17, 1995

For the man known as "Izzy," it was always more of a question of "Will he?" Jason Isringhausen was a highly thought of starter who was supposed to take flight with Paul Wilson and Bill Pulsipher as the Mets' second coming of Ryan, Koosman, and Seaver. Despite a tremendous amount of both hype and hope, none of the three ever made much of a mark at Shea. Isringhausen was alternately hurt and ineffective and was dispatched to the A's during the 1999 season.

Isringhausen's career took flight when he became a closer, first in Oakland, then in St. Louis, once striking out the side on nine pitches. With a knee-buckling curveball and a decent fastball, he averaged 33 saves for the A's in their playoff seasons of 2000 and 2001. Spurning a more lucrative offer from Texas, he signed with the Cardinals in 2002, citing the desire to be closer to his boyhood home of Brighton, Illinois, population 2,300. For St. Louis, he saved 47 games in 2004, helping the Cards win the National League pennant. His three seasons there have featured remarkable stability, holding opposing hitters to batting averages of .199, .200, and .199.

Always a bit of a free spirit, the 6'3" 200-pounder has an impish "Baby Huey" quality about him that has both endeared him to teammates and annoyed various front offices. A onetime alcohol issue was curbed early in his career, and he began his rise towards the big leagues soon after.

Right before the Triple-A All-Star game in Scranton I got the word . . . They let me pitch the first inning and then shut me down . . . I actually got the loss in the game, but I really didn't care. I went from there in Scranton to Chicago for my first start.

Chicago was a great place to debut because it was so close to my home in downstate Illinois . . . There were maybe 70 or 80 people on the pass list there rooting for me, which made it really special. I had never been to Wrigley before, never been to a big league game, I don't think. Not even St. Louis, which was a lot closer to home.

The game went really well—seven innings, two hits, but a no decision. It was a relief. Because the New York media had made such a big deal about it, it was nice to finally get out there get it done. After it was all over, we hit the town, my family and friends and I . . . A beautiful night in Chicago, nothing better.

The next day wasn't nearly as fun . . . Pete Harnisch and a couple of the guys got me and Bill Pulsipher pretty good. They had told us about the rookie ritual of painting the [statue of] the horse downtown there, so we did it, and they had set up some cops to come in and fake-bust us for it the next day. They pulled it off pretty well . . . The cops were really convincing, and Jay Horwitz, our PR guy, was convincing, running around like he was trying to scare up bail money . . . Harnisch was pretty good at stuff like that. They got us.

Also on July 17, 1995
Dave Stewart pitches in his final big league game, getting rocked in a start for the A's at Milwaukee.

AUTHOR'S NOTE: As the agent for A's star Eric Chavez, Stewart was a frequent visitor to A's games when Isringhausen pitched for Oakland.

BOXSCORE

New York Mets 7, Chicago Cubs 2
Game Played on Monday, July 17, 1995 (Night) at Wrigley Field

New York	0	0	0	0	0	1	1	0	5	—	7	11	0
Chicago	0	0	0	2	0	0	0	0	0	—	2	3	4

BATTING

New York Mets	AB	R	H	RBI	BB	K	PO	A
Butler cf	5	1	3	0	1	0	2	0
Alfonzo 2b	4	1	1	1	1	0	1	2
Brogna 1b	4	0	0	0	0	0	12	1
Bonilla 3b	3	1	0	0	2	1	0	4
Orsulak lf	4	1	2	0	0	1	0	0
Stinnett ph	0	0	0	0	0	0	0	0
Spiers ph	1	1	1	1	0	0	0	0
Otero lf	0	0	0	0	0	0	2	0
Hundley c	4	1	2	0	1	1	7	0
Thompson rf	2	0	0	0	1	0	1	0
C. Jones rf	1	1	1	2	0	0	1	0
Vizcaino ss	4	0	1	1	1	1	0	4
Isringhausen p	3	0	0	0	0	0	1	0
Ledesma ph	0	0	0	0	1	0	0	0
DiPoto p	1	0	0	0	0	0	0	0
Totals	**36**	**7**	**11**	**5**	**8**	**4**	**27**	**11**

BATTING
2B: Hundley (7, off Castillo); Orsulak (11, off Castillo); Alfonzo (10, off Castillo)
SH: Brogna (2, off Castillo); C. Jones (2, off Nabholz)
IBB: Vizcaino (2, by Castillo); Bonilla 2 (9, by Nabholz, by Hickerson); Ledesma (1, by Nabholz); Hundley (4, by Perez)

BASERUNNING
SB: Butler (16, 2nd base off Castillo/Pratt); Alfonzo (1, 2nd base off Hickerson/Pratt)

Chicago Cubs	AB	R	H	RBI	BB	K	PO	A
McRae cf	4	0	0	0	0	0	1	0
Dunston ss	1	1	0	0	1	0	1	2
Johnson 2b	2	0	0	0	0	0	1	3
Grace 1b	4	0	1	0	0	2	16	0
Sosa rf	4	1	1	1	0	0	1	0
Zeile 3b	3	0	0	0	1	1	0	3
Gonzalez lf	3	0	1	1	0	1	1	1
Hernandez 2b-ss	3	0	0	0	0	0	1	4
Pratt c	3	0	0	0	0	0	5	1
Castillo p	2	0	0	0	0	2	0	2
Nabholz p	0	0	0	0	0	0	0	1
Bullett ph	1	0	0	0	0	0	0	0
Walker p	0	0	0	0	0	0	0	0
Hickerson p	0	0	0	0	0	0	0	0
Perez p	0	0	0	0	0	0	0	0
Totals	**30**	**2**	**3**	**2**	**2**	**6**	**27**	**17**

FIELDING
DP: 1
E: McRae (1), Zeile 2 (13), Pratt (3)

BATTING
2B: Gonzalez (13, off Isringhausen)

BASERUNNING
SB: Sosa (16, 2nd base off Isringhausen/Hundley)

PITCHING

New York Mets	IP	H	HR	R	ER	BB	K
Isringhausen	7	2	0	2	2	2	6
DiPoto W(2-3)	2	1	0	0	0	0	0
Totals	**9**	**3**	**0**	**2**	**2**	**2**	**6**

Chicago Cubs	IP	H	HR	R	ER	BB	K
Castillo	6.1	6	0	2	1	3	2
Nabholz	1.2	2	0	0	0	2	2
Walker L(1-3)	0	0	0	1	1	1	0
Hickerson	0.1	0	0	1	1	1	0
Perez	0.2	3	0	3	2	1	0
Totals	**9.0**	**11**	**0**	**7**	**5**	**8**	**4**

WP: Isringhausen (1), Perez (2)
IBB: Castillo (3, Vizcaino); Nabholz 2 (3, Bonilla, Ledesma); Hickerson (4, Bonilla); Perez (5, Hundley)
Umpires: Randy Marsh, Brian Gibbons, Charlie Reliford, Jeff Kellogg
Time of Game: 3:10   Attendance: 29,033

Reggie Jackson
Born: May 18, 1946
Debut: June 9, 1967

When Reggie Jackson arrived in New York, he boldly predicted he'd do so well that someone would make a candy bar bearing his name. It happened within three years of his arrival, and as Catfish Hunter once said of the Reggie! bar, "When you unwrap it, it tells you how good it is."

Actually, the human form of Reggie was much more appealing than the candy form. (The Reggie Bar was a pale imitation of a Reese's peanut butter cup, with an unpleasant chalky texture.) Reginald Martinez Jackson proclaimed himself the "straw that stirs the Yankees," and for better of worse, he was, as the Bombers rampaged their way through the late 1970s.

Known as "Mr. October," Jackson had some of his most memorable moments on baseball's biggest stage. His World Series batting average was .357 (as opposed to his career regular season average of .262). In 1977, he single-handedly won Game Six with three home runs on three consecutive swings against three different pitchers. He ended up with a record five homers in the series as the Yanks defeated the Dodgers.

Jackson clobbered 563 home runs in a 21-year career and won the 1973 AL MVP while with Oakland. However, Jackson's braggadocio rubbed many of his Athletics teammates the wrong way. He had anointed himself "Mr. B and B" ("Mr. Bread and Butter") while in Oakland, implying he'd be the one driving in the runs. For what it's worth, he usually was, piling up 1,702 despite a record 2,597 strikeouts.

After time spent in Baltimore, New York, and Anaheim, Jackson came full circle, ending his Hall of Fame career with the A's in 1987.

John McNamara was the one who told me. I was playing Double-A ball in Birmingham, Alabama, and was leading the league in everything. Kansas City came in to play an exhibition game and I was determined to show them what I could do. Turns out they already knew, and thank goodness—I went 0-for-4 with four strikeouts, then after the game, McNamara told me that Alvin Dark had told him he wanted me to come with the team to KC. I had nothing with me. I threw the few things I did have into a duffel bag and got on the team plane. My dad was in town, at the game, and I told him, "Here's where my car's parked, here's the keys. I need you to drive to KC—I'll meet you there!"

I stayed at a hotel in KC that night and [played a doubleheader] the next day. My dad had made it in with the car, and by then I had even gone shopping to get some clothes for myself. Some of the guys, Jim Gosger, Roger Repoz, Catfish Hunter, Danny Cater—I remember they all took the time to make me feel welcome, but I was still real nervous. I faced Orlando Pena and almost beat out a grounder to short for an infield hit [in Game Two]. I was incredibly nervous. My second at bat, though, I got a slider away and put it in the tight center alley for a triple at the old Kansas City ballpark. That made my nerves go away, standing on third base telling myself I had gotten a hit in the big leagues and it was all downhill from there.

After the game, dad and I had a late dinner at the hotel. I had a tuna fish sandwich. Big league tuna fish sandwich. But 30 days later, Alvin Dark sent me out. I was crushed. Embarrassed is a better word. I met the Birmingham team in Evansville, Indiana, and was ashamed. But John McNamara took me aside and told me, "Son, don't look back. You'll pick up where you left off down here and be up there again." September 1, I was, and I never returned to Double-A, or Triple-A for that matter. I never played a day of Triple-A ball. Making it to the big leagues was a nice thing to have done at age 19, and John McNamara was right . . . Just because you don't stick the first time doesn't mean it won't happen for you. I have no regrets.

BOXSCORE

Kansas City Athletics 2, Cleveland Indians 0
(Game 1 of Doubleheader)

Game Played on Friday, June 9, 1967 (Night) at Municipal Stadium

Cleveland	0	0	0	0	0	0	0	0	0	—	0	9	0
Kansas City	0	0	0	0	0	0	2	0	x	—	2	2	0

BATTING

Cleveland Indians	AB	R	H	RBI	BB	K	PO	A
Maye rf	4	0	1	0	0	1	0	0
Hinton cf	4	0	0	0	0	2	4	0
Wagner lf	4	0	2	0	0	0	1	0
Whitfield 1b	4	0	2	0	0	0	9	0
Alvis 3b	3	0	1	0	1	0	1	4
Sims c	4	0	1	0	0	1	7	2
Gonzalez 2b	3	0	0	0	0	0	1	1
Davalillo ph	1	0	0	0	0	0	0	0
Brown ss	3	0	2	0	1	0	1	2
Hargan p	3	0	0	0	0	1	0	0
Horton ph	1	0	0	0	0	0	0	0
Totals	34	0	9	0	2	5	24	9

FIELDING
DP: 1
PB: Sims (5)

BATTING
2B: Whitfield (7, off Dobson)
3B: Brown (2, off Dobson)

Kansas City Athletics	AB	R	H	RBI	BB	K	PO	A
Campaneris ss	4	0	0	0	0	0	3	1
Jackson rf	3	0	0	0	0	1	0	0
Webster 1b	3	0	1	0	0	1	7	1
Monday cf	2	0	0	0	1	1	4	1
Cater 3b	3	1	0	0	0	1	1	1
Green 3b	0	0	0	0	0	0	0	1
Gosger lf	2	1	1	2	1	1	3	0
Donaldson 2b	3	0	0	0	0	1	3	1
Roof c	3	0	0	0	0	2	5	0
Dobson p	3	0	0	0	0	0	1	2
Totals	26	2	2	2	2	8	27	8

FIELDING
DP: 1

BATTING
3B: Webster (2, off Hargan)
HR: Gosger (3, 7th inning off Hargan 1 on, 2 out)

PITCHING

Cleveland Indians	IP	H	HR	R	ER	BB	K
Hargan L(7–5)	8	2	1	2	2	2	8
Kansas City Athletics	**IP**	**H**	**HR**	**R**	**ER**	**BB**	**K**
Dobson W(3–2)	9	9	0	0	0	2	5

Umpires: Nestor Chylak, Cal Drummond, Bill Haller, Jim Honochick
Time of Game: 2:15

Also on June 9, 1967

Celebrity humorist and writer Dorothy Parker is cremated, her ashes ultimately sitting in her lawyer's office for the next 21 years, unclaimed.

AUTHOR'S NOTE: Ms. Parker was renowned for her ability to churn out memorable quotes from her home base in New York. She wrote the original screenplay for *A Star Is Born*, and penned the famous *News Item* anthology. Jackson was always a news item himself and churned out many a memorable quote when *his* home base was New York.

Andruw Jones
Born: April 23, 1977
Debut: August 15, 1996

From the tiny island of Curacao, Andruw Jones blazed a trail to the majors in 1996, going from Single-A ball to Atlanta by mid-August. At the tender age of 19, he starred in the postseason, blasting homers in his first two at bats during Game One of the 1996 World Series, becoming the youngest player ever to homer in the Fall Classic (beating Mickey Mantle, who had been 21). He also became just the second player, after Oakland's Gene Tenace, to homer in his first two Series at bats.

He has known nothing but postseason baseball as a Brave, although he was born during what was probably the franchise's lowest ebb. On April 23, 1977, the Braves began the franchise-record 17-game losing streak that prompted owner Ted Turner to try and manage the team himself.

Jones is usually good for 100 runs scored and 100 RBI and seemed to have put it all together by the age of 23. His 1999 season included a career-best .303 batting average to go with a career-high 36 home runs. But Jones has yet to exceed 36 homers and has yet to bat higher than .277 since then. Although his home run totals have stayed remarkably consistent (36–34–35–36, from 2000 to 2003), he has yet to achieve the Willie Mays-style greatness that had been predicted upon his initial arrival.

The one element of his game that has always stayed spectacular is his defense. He plays the shallowest center field in either league, relying on explosive first-step speed to track balls belted back near the wall. He has won a Gold Glove every year since 1998 and has played in three All-Star Games. Incredibly, he had played in 71 playoff games by the age of 27, and he single-handedly kept the Braves afloat in their 2004 division series against Houston, going 10-for-19. Of the 89 Joneses who have played big league baseball, Andruw may well possess the closest thing to a full, top-of-the-line set of the supposed "five tools." Now it's just a matter of consistently harnessing all that talent.

I got there, and I was just wearing shorts . . . We had been on the road on a hot day in Norfolk, Virginia. Our trainer called me and let me know, "You've got to get to the ballpark to gather your stuff, because you're flying up to Philly to meet the Braves there." I made my flight, but I was still wearing my shorts when I got to the ballpark, and everyone, especially the veterans, they were all laughing at me. "Hey, rookie, we've got rules here," that kind of stuff. It was kind of weird, because I felt bad, but what could I do?

I had to get right in there that day and face Curt Schilling, and all he did was throw me fastballs. With so much gas on them, it was unbelievable. I think I struck out twice and popped out . . . I know I got a hit, but the first things that happened were I struck out, and I made an error in the bottom of the first. Their leadoff guy blooped one into right-center, and I came up firing, but the ball went away and he went all the way to third. One big league inning, I've got an error and a strikeout already. But I knew it would get better . . . and now, I just keep working hard trying to keep going.

We won the game, and we came back, and I was in the middle of that rally . . . I get a hit off the sidearm guy, Toby Borland, and we scored a bunch of runs in the ninth to win. I had something good to tell my family back home when I called them from the hotel that night.

Also on August 15, 1996
Bob Dole claims the Republican presidential nomination at the party's convention, offering himself as the "bridge to a time of tranquility." and describing himself as "the most optimistic man in America."

AUTHOR'S NOTE: Dole was perceived to be "too old" by many, while Jones was perceived to be "too young." Dole lost the election, but Jones helped build a bridge to a time of 13 consecutive division titles for Atlanta. None of the thirteen seasons could be classified as "tranquil."

BOXSCORE

Atlanta Braves 8, Philadelphia Phillies 5
Game Played on Thursday, August 15, 1996 (Day) at Veteran's Stadium

Atlanta	1	2	0	1	0	0	0	4	—	8	14	1
Philadelphia	1	0	0	0	0	1	0	0	3	—	5	13	1

BATTING

Atlanta Braves	AB	R	H	RBI	BB	K	PO	A
Grissom cf	5	3	3	1	0	1	3	0
A. Jones rf	5	1	1	1	0	2	1	0
C. Jones ss	4	1	1	1	1	2	1	1
Belliard ss	0	0	0	0	0	0	0	0
McGriff 1b	5	0	1	2	0	1	10	0
Klesko lf	4	0	1	1	1	2	1	0
Pendleton 3b	5	0	1	0	0	3	0	2
Perez c	4	1	1	0	0	1	8	1
Lemke 2b	4	1	2	1	0	0	2	6
Wade p	3	0	2	1	0	1	0	0
Clontz p	0	0	0	0	0	0	0	0
McMichael p	0	0	0	0	0	0	0	0
Mordecai ph	1	1	1	0	0	0	0	0
Borbon p	0	0	0	0	0	0	0	0
Wohlers p	0	0	0	0	0	0	0	0
Totals	40	8	14	8	2	13	27	10

FIELDING
DP: 2
E: A. Jones (1)

BATTING
2B: Grissom (24, off Schilling); Perez (9, off Schilling); Lemke (12, off Schilling)
HR: Grissom (19, 4th inning off Schilling, 0 on, 2 out)

Philadelphia Phillies	AB	R	H	RBI	BB	K	PO	A
Otero cf	5	1	3	1	0	0	1	0
Morandini 2b	5	0	1	0	0	2	0	4
Rolen 3b	4	0	2	1	1	0	0	0
Zeile 1b	5	0	2	1	0	1	7	1
Santiago c	5	1	2	0	0	1	12	0
Incaviglia lf-rf	2	1	1	0	2	0	2	0
Martinez rf	2	0	0	0	0	1	2	0
Jefferies ph-lf	1	1	1	1	1	0	0	0
Stocker ss	4	0	0	0	0	2	1	3
Schilling p	2	0	0	0	0	1	1	0
Amaro ph	1	0	0	0	0	0	0	0
R. Jordan p	0	0	0	0	0	0	0	0
Borland p	0	0	0	0	0	0	0	0
Parrett p	0	0	0	0	0	0	0	0
Lieberthal ph	1	1	1	1	0	0	0	0
Totals	37	5	13	5	4	9	27	8

FIELDING
DP: 1
E: Santiago (9)
PB: Santiago (7)

BATTING
2B: Otero (8, off Wade); Incaviglia (7, off Borbon); Lieberthal (7, off Borbon)

BASERUNNING
CS: Rolen (1, 2nd base by Wade/Perez)

PITCHING

Atlanta Braves	IP	H	HR	R	ER	BB	K
Wade W(4–0)	5	6	0	1	0	2	6
Clontz	0.2	1	0	1	1	1	0
McMichael	2.1	1	0	0	0	0	1
Borbon	0.1	2	0	3	3	1	0
Wohlers	0.2	3	0	0	0	0	2
Totals	9.0	13	0	5	4	4	9

Philadelphia Phillies	IP	H	HR	R	ER	BB	K
Schilling L(5–6)	7	9	1	4	4	1	12
R. Jordan	1.1	0	0	0	0	0	1
Borland	0	3	0	4	4	1	0
Parrett	0.2	2	0	0	0	0	0
Totals	9.0	14	1	8	8	2	13

Umpires: Tom Hallion, Jerry Crawford, Paul Nauert, Wally Bell
Time of Game: 2:56   Attendance: 28,011

Chipper Jones
Born: April 24, 1972
Debut: September 11, 1993

A charismatic Southerner with an electric bat, Chipper Jones has been the face of the Atlanta Braves since the mid 1990s. As the first overall pick in the 1990 draft, he was burdened with sky-high expectations and, for the most part, has met every challenge, both at the plate and in the field.

Off the field, Jones ran himself into a nightmare when he admitted to fathering a child illegitimately while married, which led to his divorce. He wed the mother of the child in a secret ceremony against his parents' wishes but spoke from his heart when he told the media, "From this day forward, I'm not going to be perfect, and neither is anybody else."

From both sides of the plate, that effortless swing is at the least in the suburbs of perfection, and whenever it goes slightly awry, he has been known to import his personal "swing doctor," his dad, from whom the nickname "Chipper" is derived. (Larry Jones Jr., they say, was a "chip off the old block" of Larry Sr.) In 2004, the Florida native fell just shy of what would have been a ninth consecutive 100-RBI season, burdened by a slow start and injuries to his hand and hamstring. He was NL MVP in 1999, becoming the first-ever player to do all of the following in one season: Drive in 100 runs, walk 100 times, hit 40 homers, steal 20 bases, hit 40 doubles, and keep his average above .300. In that year's September stretch drive, the Mets accused him of stealing signs, which seemed to fire up an already hot hitter—he blasted four home runs in the pivotal late-season series in Atlanta. A career Mets killer, he took the step of naming his newborn son in honor of their home ballpark in 2004—Shea Jones.

Through that 2004 season, Shea's dad (Larry Sr.'s son) has made five trips to the All-Star Game, ten trips to the playoffs, and placed among the National League's top 10 in MVP voting every year, 1996 through '99. He has had as many as 45 home runs in a single season and is perennially among the league leaders in walks. As his manager, Bobby Cox, once said, "He's a powerful hitter with a powerful personality." And a heck of a fit in Atlanta.

Grady Little was my manager at Richmond, so he had the honor, I guess you could say, of telling me the good news. Tony Tarasco, Ramon Caraballo, Mike Kelly, Jerry Willard, and I all got the call. We had just lost a playoff series to Charlotte, the Indians' Triple-A team . . . I'd get my revenge for that loss in the World Series a few years later, I guess, huh? [Laughs.] A few of us got called up, going cross-country to San Diego. First thing I did was pinch-run for Sid Bream, in San Diego, and my lead off first base was about three inches. I mean, I'm a rookie, and the last ting I want to do is cost us a game, so I'm figuring better safe than sorry . . . I would have much rather pinch-hit than pinch-run, I can tell you that. I felt so self-conscious taking that little lead off first, and Archi Cianfrocco was the Padres' first baseman, trying not to laugh at me for taking that little itty-bitty lead. That was the only game we played in San Diego. Three-thousand mile flight West to pinch-run, then 3,000 miles back East. Six-thousand miles to take a three inch lead.

My first at bat was the next day in Atlanta, and my folks were in for that, which was great. We bolted out to a big lead, and I got put in because of that against a guy named Kevin Wickander. First pitch I hit a swinging bunt down the third base line and beat it out for a base hit.

Also on September 11, 1993
The media and public weigh in (mostly favorably) about last night's brand new TV series on FOX, *The X Files.*

AUTHOR'S NOTE: (Vin) Scully he's seen, having played 85 career games against the Dodgers; (Mark) Mulder he's glimpsed now as well, since the lefty was traded from Oakland to St. Louis. Unfortunately for Jones, "The truth [was] out there," when he went through a very public divorce in 1999.

BOXSCORE

Atlanta Braves 13, San Diego Padres 1
Game Played on Saturday, September 11, 1993 (Night) at Jack Murphy Stadium

Atlanta	0	0	0	2	1	0	1	5	4	—	13	15	0
San Diego	0	0	0	0	1	0	0	0	0	—	1	5	2

BATTING

Atlanta Braves	AB	R	H	RBI	BB	K	PO	A
Nixon cf	4	3	0	0	2	1	4	0
Stanton p	0	0	0	0	0	0	0	0
Freeman p	0	0	0	0	0	0	0	0
Blauser ss	5	3	2	0	1	2	1	0
Jones ss	0	0	0	0	0	0	0	0
Gant lf	5	3	3	6	0	2	0	0
Tarasco rf	0	0	0	0	0	0	1	0
McGriff 1b	4	1	2	3	1	0	5	2
Howell p	0	0	0	0	0	0	0	0
Sanders ph-cf	1	0	1	0	0	0	0	0
Justice rf	6	0	1	1	0	0	3	0
Klesko lf	0	0	0	0	0	0	0	0
Pendleton 3b	4	1	0	0	1	2	0	1
Pecota 3b	0	0	0	0	0	0	0	0
Olson c	5	1	3	0	0	0	9	1
Belliard 2b	5	1	3	1	0	1	1	1
Smoltz p	1	0	0	0	1	0	2	1
Bream 1b	1	0	0	1	0	0	1	0
Totals	41	13	15	12	6	9	27	6

BATTING
2B: McGriff (24, off Benes)
HR: McGriff (33, 8th inning off Mauser, 2 on, 1 out); Gant (33, 9th inning off Seanez, 2 on, 2 out)
SH: Smoltz 2 (10, off Benes, off Taylor)
SF: Gant (5, off Benes)
IBB: Pendleton (5, by Benes)

BASERUNNING
SB: Nixon 3 (39, 2nd base off Benes/Higgins, 3rd base off Benes/Higgins, 2nd base off Taylor/Higgins)

San Diego Padres	AB	R	H	RBI	BB	K	PO	A
Brown cf	4	0	1	0	0	0	1	0
Lopez 2b	3	0	0	0	0	1	2	1
Seminara p	0	0	0	0	0	0	0	0
Davis p	0	0	0	0	0	0	0	0
Taylor p	0	0	0	0	0	0	0	0
Mauser p	0	0	0	0	0	0	0	0
Velasquez ph	1	0	0	0	0	1	0	0
Seanez p	0	0	0	0	0	0	0	0
Bean rf	2	0	1	0	1	0	0	0
Staton ph	1	0	0	0	0	1	0	0
Plantier lf	4	0	0	0	0	2	4	0
Bell 3b	4	1	3	1	0	1	0	3
Cianfrocco 1b	4	0	0	0	0	2	6	4
Higgins c	3	0	0	0	0	0	8	0
Shipley ss	3	0	0	0	0	1	2	1
Benes p	1	0	0	0	0	1	1	0
Gardner ph-2b	2	0	0	0	0	1	2	2
Totals	32	1	5	1	1	11	27	11

FIELDING
E: Bell (13), Benes (1)

BATTING
HR: Bell (21, 5th inning off Smoltz, 0 on, 0 out)

BASERUNNING
SB: Bell (25, 2nd base off Smoltz/Olson)

PITCHING

Atlanta Braves	IP	H	HR	R	ER	BB	K
Smoltz W(14–10)	7	3	1	1	1	1	8
Howell	1	1	0	0	0	0	2
Stanton	0.2	1	0	0	0	0	1
Freeman	0.1	0	0	0	0	0	0
Totals	9.0	5	1	1	1	1	11
San Diego Padres	IP	H	HR	R	ER	BB	K
Benes L(15–12)	6	5	0	3	0	3	8
Seminara	0.1	1	0	1	1	0	1
Davis	0.1	1	0	0	0	1	0
Taylor	0.2	2	0	4	4	2	0
Mauser	0.2	1	1	1	1	0	0
Seanez	1	5	1	4	4	0	0
Totals	9.0	15	2	13	10	6	9

IBB: Benes (3, Pendleton).
Umpires: Gerry Davis, Terry Tata, Eric Gregg, Brian Gorman
Time of Game: 3:10   Attendance: 19,824

Al Kaline
Born: December 19, 1934
Debut: June 25, 1953

From a poor childhood in Baltimore, the stately Al Kaline would emerge to be a Detroit Tigers Hall of Famer. As a kid, young Al honed his powerful right arm by throwing rocks at the freight trains that ran through his working-class neighborhood; he would aim for the middle of the "O" on the B&O railroad cars. Years later, that right arm would gun down many a base runner who had the audacity to try him out. In just his fifth big league game, he threw out runners at second, third, and home in successive innings, against the White Sox. It was a harbinger of Gold Gloves to come, ten of them in all.

For all that Kaline accomplished in a 22-year Tigers playing career, he is sometimes recalled nationally as a "great player who fell just short of great milestones." Kaline was never named MVP; never led the league in home runs or in RBI, never had more than 200 hits, and finished with 399 career home runs.

Still, he would not be denied membership to the 3,000-hit club—he made it by seven. Poetically, he got number 3,000 in his hometown during the 1974 season.

His number six was retired by the Tigers and requested by seemingly every Michigan Little Leaguer during the 1960s. His is one of the six statues that stands sentinel over Detroit's new Comerica Park, and, appropriately, the cast iron figure depicts him making a graceful catch, like he used to do in Tiger Stadium's right field, which became known as "Kaline's Corner."

Having debuted as a teenager, he busted out at the age of 20, becoming the youngest player ever to win a batting title (.340 in 1955). Thirteen years later, he was still cranking out production with assembly-line precision, terrorizing the Cardinals in the '68 World Series (11 hits, eight runs batted in). The great Cardinals battery of Gibson and McCarver had been undone by the man who had "alkaline" right there in his autograph.

I had signed my contract right after I graduated from high school in June of '53 . . . My dad and the scout that signed me, we all took a train from Baltimore to Philadelphia, where the big league team was playing. I got there just in time to meet up with the team and take batting practice, outfield practice, and all that, and they had me stay and watch the game from the dugout. Then, seventh inning of the game, our manager, Fred Hutchinson, turns to me and says

"Okay, kid, grab a bat and pinch-hit." He didn't even know my name; he just told me to get in there and hit. I didn't have my own bat, so I borrowed one that was much too heavy. I hit the first pitch from Harry Byrd into center for an out, and it remains the happiest I've ever been to make an out in my life. I replaced Jim Delsing defensively after that, and I guess I was on my way. Of course, I wouldn't have even gotten that at bat if we weren't being blown out!

Everyone in my neighborhood knew that I had signed, but I was just 18 . . . Some were pretty amazed I was going right to the big leagues. I was by far the youngest guy on the team . . . didn't have many people to hang out with. Johnny Pesky took ahold of me though, a veteran guy who basically took me under his wing. He took me out to the ballpark early and would show me how to bunt, because I was a little guy with speed back then . . . I would sit next to him on the bench and he would explain everything to me, piece by piece. On the trains that we rode, city to city, Pesky would have me sit next to him sometimes so we could just talk baseball. How pitchers would pitch and all that. I tried to do the same later in my career for other young guys. I never forgot how nice Johnny Pesky was to an 18-year-old kid.

Also on June 25, 1953
The Singing Cowboy, Gene Autry, records "Here Comes Santa Claus" in Hollywood, but the current chart-topping single is Tony Bennett's "Rags to Riches."

BOXSCORE

Philadelphia A's 5, Detroit Tigers 2

Game Played on Thursday, 6/25/1953 (Night) at Shibe Park

Detroit	0	0	0	0	0	0	0	0	2	—	2
Philadelphia	0	5	0	0	0	0	0	0	x	—	5

Detroit Tigers	AB	R	H	RBI	BB	K	PO	A
H. Kuenn ss	4	0	2	0	0	0	3	3
J. Pesky 2b	5	0	0	0	0	0	1	3
R. Boone 3b	3	0	1	0	1	1	2	0
W. Dropo 1b	4	0	0	0	0	2	5	2
J. Delsing cf	3	0	0	0	0	0	2	0
A. Kaline cf	1	0	0	0	0	0	0	0
B. Nieman rf	4	1	1	0	0	0	4	0
B. Souchock lf	4	0	1	0	0	2	4	0
M. Batts c	4	1	2	0	0	1	2	0
D. Marlowe p	1	0	0	0	0	1	0	0
D. Weik p	1	0	0	0	0	1	1	0
P. Mullin ph	1	0	1	0	0	0	0	0
B. Miller p	0	0	0	0	0	0	0	0
D. Lund ph	1	0	1	2	0	0	0	0
Totals	**36**	**2**	**9**	**2**	**1**	**8**	**24**	**8**

FIELDING
E: B.Souchock 2

BATTING
2B: M.Batts (off H.Byrd)
2-out RBI: D.Lund 2
RBI, scoring position, less than 2 outs: J.Pesky 0–1; R.Boone 0–1; W.Dropo 0–1

BASERUNNING
Team LOB: 9

Philadelphia A's	AB	R	H	RBI	BB	K	PO	A
J. DeMaestri ss	4	1	1	1	0	1	1	2
D. Philley rf	4	1	2	1	0	0	1	0
E. Robinson 1b	2	0	1	1	1	0	5	0
T. Hamilton pr-1b	1	0	0	0	0	0	5	0
G. Zernial lf	4	0	0	0	1	0	1	0
P. Suder 2b	4	0	2	0	0	0	1	2
L. Babe 3b	3	1	0	0	1	0	1	0
E. McGhee cf	3	1	0	0	0	0	4	0
J. Astroth c	3	0	1	0	0	0	9	0
H. Byrd p	3	1	1	1	0	0	0	1
Totals	**31**	**5**	**8**	**4**	**2**	**2**	**27**	**5**

BATTING
2-out RBI: J.DeMaestri; D.Philley; E.Robinson; H.Byrd
RBI, scoring position, less than 2 outs: E.McGhee 0–1; J.Astroth 0–1; H.Byrd 0–1

BASERUNNING
Team LOB: 4

PITCHING

Detroit	IP	H	HR	R	ER	BB	K
D. Marlowe L	1.2	0	5	5	4	1	1
D. Weik	5.1	3	0	0	0	1	1
B. Miller	1.0	0	0	0	0	0	0
Total	**8.0**	**8**	**0**	**5**	**4**	**2**	**2**
Philadelphia	IP	H	HR	R	ER	BB	K
H. Byrd W	9.0	9	0	2	2	1	8

Inherited Runners—Scored: D.Weik 1–1; B.Miller 0–0
HBP: H.Kuenn by H.Byrd
Umpires—HP: Robb, 1B: Summers, 2B: Stevens, 3B: Duffy
Time of Game: 1:53   Attendance: 2,368

AUTHOR'S NOTE: Kaline, too, went from rags to riches, from his humble Baltimore beginnings to the Baseball Hall of Fame. Autry's own rags-to-riches story included ownership of the then-California Angels, who debuted in April 1961 in Kaline's beloved hometown.

Paul Konerko
Born: March 5, 1976
Debut: September 8, 1997

Paul Konerko may be the most unassuming power hitter in baseball. With thinning hair and mild manners, even his goatee fails to make him look even nearly as intimidating as other White Sox sluggers of recent vintage (Belle, Thomas, Bo Jackson, etc.). However, Konerko quietly slugged 41 home runs in 2004, finishing second in the American League. Bouncing back from a subpar 2003, he returned to (and in some respects) exceeded his All-Star form of 2002, when he hit .302 with 104 RBI.

Early in his career, great expectations had been thrust upon him. As the Dodgers' first round pick of the '94 draft, he blistered his way through the minors, including a 1997 PCL MVP season that saw him anointed as *Baseball America*'s minor league player of the year. The Dodgers of the late '90s, however, were looking to win immediately and were loathe to have Konerko continue his development at the big league level. He was passed like a hot potato from the Dodgers to the Reds to the White Sox, being asked to change positions virtually every year.

Settling in as the Sox first baseman, he allowed Frank Thomas to DH, and Chicago began to come together as a threat in the AL Central. Konerko dutifully worked on his swing in-season and attempted to improve his speed in the off-season (each of his first six full seasons in the majors saw him place among his league's top ten in grounding into double plays).

Growing up in Scottsdale, Arizona, Konerko admired the sweet swing of Will Clark from afar, going so far as putting a mirror next to his TV so Clark's swing would appear to be right-handed like his own. Like Clark, Konerko is a natural team leader, happy to engage the media and take the pressure off his teammates whenever he can. He is also a scratch golfer, having once dropped in a hole-in-one in a tournament and, in the process, winning a free trip to Ireland. "I suddenly had a lot more friends after that," he says.

I was a young guy, just 21, and the season had ended at Albuquerque. A big group of us, six or seven, were all asked to head up to L.A. With the year I'd had, I was pretty sure I'd get a look, but you never know. The team was in Arlington, Texas, playing interleague, and I arrived in Texas as a big leaguer, not knowing if I'd play or how much. It turns out that I sat for a week, but that was just fine with me. They had a veteran team and were in a pennant race, so I sure understood them turning to Eddie Murray to pinch-hit instead of me! There were great guys on that team, and I got to see how they behaved in big games, on the field and off. Eric Karros, Mike Piazza, Murray, the guys in the bullpen like Mark Guthrie were all total pros, and they set the tone. I don't think I paid for a cab or a meal that whole month, because the older guys were determined to take care of us young guys. That's a lesson I never forgot. Everyone's a rookie at some point in their life, and now I try to look out for those guys, too.

I got in a game a week after I had gotten called up and got down in the count right away, 0-and-2, then 1-and-2 off Dennis Cook, and I remember saying to myself, "Just don't strike out. Find a way to put it in play." I did, with a line drive [base hit] to right. I knew not to take any borderline pitches, so I was up there swinging!

Also on September 8, 1997
Richie Ashburn broadcasts his final game for the Philadelphia Phillies. The popular Hall of Famer would succumb to a heart attack in his New York hotel room hours after the game.

AUTHOR'S NOTE: Ashburn was a wonderful player who had the misfortune of being overshadowed by Duke Snider, Willie Mays, and Mickey Mantle in his heyday. Konerko's exploits for the White Sox have long been dwarfed by those surrounding him—namely, Frank Thomas and Magglio Ordonez.

BOXSCORE

Florida Marlins 8, Los Angeles Dodgers 4
Game Played on Monday, September 8, 1997 (Night) at Dodger Stadium

Florida	4	0	1	0	0	0	0	3	—	8	9	1
Los Angeles	0	0	1	2	0	0	0	1	0	—	4	15	0

BATTING

Florida Marlins	AB	R	H	RBI	BB	K	PO	A
White cf	4	1	1	0	1	0	2	0
Renteria ss	4	0	1	0	0	2	3	2
Sheffield rf	3	2	2	1	2	0	3	0
Wehner rf	0	0	0	0	0	0	0	0
Bonilla 3b	4	1	0	0	1	1	0	2
Nen p	0	0	0	0	0	0	0	0
Daulton 1b	2	2	1	1	1	0	6	0
Conine 1b	2	1	1	3	0	0	4	0
Alou lf	4	1	1	3	1	0	1	0
Johnson c	4	0	0	0	0	2	5	0
Counsell 2b	4	0	2	0	0	0	3	7
Brown p	2	0	0	0	0	0	0	1
Floyd ph	1	0	0	0	0	0	0	0
Cook p	0	0	0	0	0	0	0	0
Powell p	0	0	0	0	0	0	0	0
Arias 3b	0	0	0	0	0	0	0	0
Totals	34	8	9	8	6	5	27	12

FIELDING
DP: 1
E: Renteria (17)

BATTING
2B: Counsell (7, off Reyes); Alou (20, 1st inning off Nomo, 2 on, 2 out); Daulton (13, 3rd inning off Nomo, 0 on, 0 out); Conine (14, 9th inning off Guthrie, 2 on, 2 out).
HR: Sheffield (18, 1st inning off Nomo, 0 on, 2 out); Alou (20, 1st inning off Nomo, 2 on, 2 out); Daulton (13, 3rd inning off Nomo, 0 on, 0 out); Conine (14, 9th inning off Guthrie, 2 on, 2 out)
SH: Brown (5, off Reyes); Renteria (16, off Guthrie)
IBB: Alou (9, by Reyes); Sheffield (11, by Guthrie).

Los Angeles Dodgers	AB	R	H	RBI	BB	K	PO	A
Young 2b	4	1	2	2	1	0	2	3
Nixon cf	5	0	1	1	0	1	3	0
Piazza c	4	0	1	1	1	0	5	0
Karros 1b	5	0	2	0	0	1	10	1
Zeile 3b	5	0	2	0	0	0	0	4
Kirby rf	3	0	0	0	0	1	2	0
Mondesi ph-rf	2	0	1	0	0	0	0	0
Gagne ss	4	1	2	0	0	0	3	2
Anthony ph	1	0	0	0	0	1	0	0
Butler lf	3	0	1	0	0	0	1	0
Harkey p	0	0	0	0	0	0	0	0
Konerko ph	1	0	1	0	0	0	0	0
Hollandsworth pr	0	1	0	0	0	0	0	0
Guthrie p	0	0	0	0	0	0	0	1
Nomo p	1	0	0	0	0	1	1	0
Guerrero ph	1	1	1	0	0	0	0	0
Reyes p	0	0	0	0	0	0	0	1
Lewis lf	2	0	1	0	0	0	0	0
Totals	41	4	15	4	2	5	27	12

BATTING
2B: Mondesi (37, off Brown)

BASERUNNING
SB: Young (42, 3rd base off Brown/Johnson); Piazza (5, 2nd base off Brown/Johnson)

PITCHING

Florida Marlins	IP	H	HR	R	ER	BB	K
Brown W(13–8)	7	11	0	3	3	2	4
Cook	0	2	0	1	1	0	0
Powell	1	1	0	0	0	0	0
Nen	1	1	0	0	0	0	1
Totals	9.0	15	0	4	4	2	5
Los Angeles Dodgers	**IP**	**H**	**HR**	**R**	**ER**	**BB**	**K**
Nomo L(13–11)	4	5	3	5	5	3	5
Reyes	1.2	2	0	0	0	1	0
Harkey	2.1	1	0	0	0	0	0
Guthrie	1	1	1	3	3	2	0
Totals	9.0	9	4	8	8	6	5

WP: Nen (5)
IBB: Reyes (1, Alou); Guthrie (5, Sheffield).
Umpires: Charlie Reliford, Dana DeMuth, Gary Darling, Jim Quick
Time of Game: 3:11   Attendance: 45,195

Mike Krukow
Born: January 21, 1952
Debut: September 6, 1976

Now part of the popular San Francisco Giants broadcast team, Mike Kru-kow broke in as a Chicago Cub in 1976. He pitched 14 big league seasons for the Cubs, Phillies, and Giants, enjoying his best seasons at Candlestick Park. He was a 20-game winner in 1986, retiring three years later with a career record of 124–117.

His 1987 season was noteworthy for his incredible total of 17 no decisions in his 28 starts. (He went 5–6, with a respectable 3.84 ERA.) In his one post-season start that year, he refused to let his manager come out and get him, gong all nine in a 4–2 win over the Cardinals in the NLCS.

He finished third in the 1986 Cy Young balloting behind Mike Scott and Fernando Valenzuela, completing ten of his team-high 34 starts.

I had driven home from Wichita, taking my time because they'd already called up three other guys, and not me. My wife and I took our sweet time on the road home, Wichita to Los Angeles, and this is before cell phones, of course . . . I get to the driveway and my dad's standing there in the driveway, which is odd. I roll down the window of the car as I pull in the driveway, and he says, "call Saltwell," Salty Saltwell, the Cubs GM. I bop out of the car, make the call, and Salty says, "We want you with the big club, and we want you to leave as soon as you can." Cool. I took the red-eye to Chicago and didn't sleep a wink. I got to the Executive House hotel and try, around seven in the morning, to sleep a little, but no chance. Finally, when the clock turned to nine, I bolted out of bed and said to myself, "Okay. I'm going to the big leagues!" I'd never been to Chicago, let alone Wrigley. I get on the elevator, 15th floor, travel down a couple floors, door opens, and there's Tom Seaver. Tom Seaver's getting on my elevator! And it hits me—the Mets are staying at this hotel, too. He walks in, sees my bag, and says, "first day?" I gulp out something intelligent like, "Yup." And he kind of looks me over and says, "well, don't screw it up."

I go walking out to get a cab, and this is something I'd been dreaming about saying since I was a kid . . . I get in, and I told the cabbie, lady cab driver, "Wrigley Field!" Just as confidently as I could say it. And this lady turns around and says, "Okay, you know how to get there?" I say, "How the f———— do I know?" She had to radio in and winds up dropping me off on the wrong side of the field—the right-field side, and of course the Cubs clubhouse is over on the left-field side. I walk across that parking lot, talked my way in . . . walked in, saw the green of the field, the ivy . . . I go down and start walking across the field, right field to left field, and before I can go in that dugout to head into the clubhouse, I literally had to sit down. Right by the bullpen, I just threw my bag down and sat down because it was so overwhelming. The big leagues! I'm floating on air.

Now it's time to run during batting practice. Bruce Sutter and I are sprinting in the outfielder. The fans are calling after him, but not me. Some guy keeps yelling, though, "Hey number 40! Who are you?" I'm mortified. "Hey, 40, what's your name, man?" Sutter can tell I'm embarrassed, but as we're running, he says, "Here's a line for ya. Next time he asks you what your name is, tell him to go buy a program." So I'm thinking yeah, good, now I'm ready for this guy. And sure enough, thirty seconds later, "Hey, 40, what's your name?" So I look up, fix him with a stare, and yell up, "Go buy a program, meat!" And he yells back, "I did, and you ain't in it!" Sh—.

When I got in the game, I felt like I had nothing, just nothing. But I got in there and retired all six batters I faced. I had always thought to myself, "Please God, let me throw just one pitch in the major leagues, and I'll never ask you for anything ever again." And now here it was. I pitched pretty well. And by the way, I struck out Seaver the next day. Blew his doors away. As he said himself, I couldn't afford to screw it up.

Also on September 6, 1976
While in the on-deck circle, L.A. Dodger Steve Yeager is seriously injured when shards of teammate Bill Russell's broken bat lodge in his throat.

AUTHOR'S NOTE: Yeager would recover and go on to catch ten more years, ending his career on October 5, 1986, the day Krukow won his 20th game of that, his best big league season.

BOXSCORE

New York Mets 7, Chicago Cubs 4
Game Played on Monday, September 6, 1976 (Day) at Wrigley Field

New York	2	2	0	0	3	0	0	0	0	—	7	9	1
Chicago	1	1	0	0	0	2	0	0	0	—	4	9	1

BATTING

New York Mets	AB	R	H	RBI	BB	K	PO	A
Boisclair cf-lf	4	1	1	1	1	0	0	0
Phillips 2b	5	0	1	0	0	0	3	3
B. Baldwin lf	3	2	0	1	1	0	4	0
Brown ph-cf	1	0	0	0	0	0	0	0
Kingman rf	4	2	2	3	0	1	0	0
Kranepool 1b	4	0	1	1	0	0	11	0
Foster 3b	4	0	0	0	0	0	0	9
Stearns c	4	1	2	0	0	0	9	0
Harrelson ss	4	1	1	0	0	1	0	0
Koosman p	4	0	1	1	0	2	0	0
Totals	37	7	9	7	2	4	27	12

FIELDING
DP: 1
E: Boisclair (2)

BATTING
2B: Kingman (12, off Krukow)
HR: Kingman (34, 1st inning off Stone, 1 on, 2 out)

BASERUNNING
SB: Harrelson (8, 2nd base off Stone/Mitterwald)

Chicago Cubs	AB	R	H	RBI	BB	K	PO	A
Monday 1b	5	1	3	3	0	2	8	2
Cardenal lf	5	0	1	0	0	0	2	0
Trillo 2b	4	0	0	0	1	1	0	2
Morales rf	4	0	1	0	1	2	2	0
Mitterwald c	4	0	0	0	0	2	5	0
Sperring 3b	3	2	2	0	1	1	1	2
Kelleher ss	4	1	2	0	0	0	4	2
Wallis cf	3	0	0	0	1	1	3	0
Stone p	0	0	0	0	0	0	1	0
Schultz p	0	0	0	0	0	0	0	0
Madlock ph	0	0	0	1	1	0	0	0
Burris pr	0	0	0	0	0	0	0	0
Krukow p	1	0	0	0	0	0	0	0
P. Reuschel p	0	0	0	0	0	0	0	0
Tyrone ph	1	0	0	0	0	0	0	0
Garman p	0	0	0	0	0	0	0	0
Swisher ph	1	0	0	0	0	0	0	0
Knowles p	0	0	0	0	0	0	1	0
Totals	35	4	9	4	5	9	27	8

FIELDING
E: Kelleher (12)

BATTING
HR: Monday (28, 1st inning off Koosman, 0 on, 0 out)

BASERUNNING
SB: Cardenal (22, 3rd base off Koosman/Stearns)

PITCHING

New York Mets	IP	H	HR	R	ER	BB	K
Koosman W(18–8)	9	9	1	4	4	5	9

Chicago Cubs	IP	H	HR	R	ER	BB	K
Stone L(3–6)	1.1	5	1	4	4	1	0
Schultz	0.2	0	0	0	0	0	0
Krukow	2.1	3	0	3	3	1	0
P. Reuschel	1.2	1	0	0	0	0	2
Garman	2	0	0	0	0	0	2
Knowles	1	0	0	0	0	0	0
Totals	9	9	1	7	7	2	4

Umpires: Art Williams, Tom Gorman, Paul Pryor, John McSherry
Time of Game: 2:31   Attendance: 18,304

Duane Kuiper

Born: June 19, 1950
Debut: September 9, 1974

Slick-fielding Duane Kuiper could handle a bat okay. He was a career .274 hitter with nearly as many walks as strikeouts. However, in a 12-year career spanning 3,379 at bats, the Wisconsin native hit only one home run, a fact recounted in the lead sentence in virtually every bio written about him upon his retirement.

The historic blast came fairly early in his career, on a warm August evening in 1977, when he was the second batter for the Indians against the White Sox's Steve Stone (a Cleveland native). With friends and family watching (part of an intimate Municipal Stadium gathering of around 6,000), Stone served up a belt-high meatball that Kuiper turned on and swatted into the second row of the bleachers.

The affable "Kuip" retired with 917 hits, 796 of which were singles. His ratio of one home run every 3,379 at bats should be a record that stands forever, but then there's Tommy Thevenow. A journeyman who played in the 1920s and '30s, Thevenow had more than 4,000 big league at bats without hitting a ball over a wall as Kuiper did. Thevenow did, however, hit a pair of inside-the-parkers, including one against the Yankees in the 1926 World Series. He went *sans* homer in his final 3,347 at bats, a major league record, and, unlike Kuiper, he never became a popular broadcaster for the San Francisco Giants.

Kuiper has become known for his dramatic calls of Barry Bonds's majestic long balls ("He hits it high, he hits it deep . . ."), and the irony isn't lost on him that if Bonds breaks Hank Aaron's mark for career home runs, number 756 may well be broadcast by a man who hit 755 fewer.

Ken Aspromonte was the Indians manager. He called me in when we got there, and he told me straight out, I wasn't going to play against contenders at all, since the Indians were still in a pennant race. Well, I looked at the schedule and saw pretty much every game was a game that mattered those last few weeks, so I figured I'd just be sitting around. But they got swept by the Orioles in a four-game series, and suddenly they weren't really in the race anymore. Detroit came to town next, and I got in.

First at bat of the game, ball got hit right to me, and I was officially a big leaguer. I faced Jack Brohamer when I got to the plate and hit into a double

100

say "Cool," try and get some sleep, and head to old Stapleton Airport first thing, crack of dawn the next morning. I get there with all my luggage, all set, and there was trouble in Chicago, bad weather. I was diverted to Dallas instead, got rerouted. But there was bad weather there too. So they rerouted me again, up to Detroit. Four hour layover in Detroit, and I finally get to Cincinnati at 6:30 pm, 12 hours after I started. No cell phones then . . . no communication to anyone. My mom and dad had been waiting for me at the airport since one or two in the afternoon. So finally, I get there, my bags haven't made it, no baseball equipment, no nothing. I get whisked away, and there's media there and everything, but the Reds had sent someone to come and get me by escort through all the traffic to the ballpark as quickly as possible. Well, I run through the clubhouse door, and the manager's office is right there, Pete Rose. And it's 6:55, Rose is just leaving his office to head to the field for a 7:05 game, and he sees me and says, "Larkin! What's the hell's the matter with you? Your first day and you're late? You were supposed to be starting today!"

Well, I'm in a panic, not knowing Pete was just kidding with me. It's the last minute, I'm throwing on my uniform, none of my own equipment.

Also on August 13, 1986
Chris Chambliss hits the final home run of his big league career, a walk-off game winner for the Braves.

AUTHOR'S NOTE: Chambliss would go on to be the last of ten different hitting coaches Larkin had in his 19-year Reds career.

BOXSCORE

Cincinnati Reds 8, San Francisco Giants 6
Game Played on Wednesday, August 13, 1986 (Night) at Riverfront Stadium

San Francisco	1	0	4	0	0	0	0	1	0	—	6	10	0
Cincinnati	0	0	0	0	1	3	1	3	x	—	8	11	0

BATTING

San Francisco Giants	AB	R	H	RBI	BB	K	PO	A
Gladden cf	4	1	2	0	1	1	2	0
Thompson 2b	5	1	1	0	0	1	4	5
Youngblood lf	4	1	1	0	1	0	1	0
Clark 1b	3	1	0	1	0	0	9	0
Maldonado rf	3	2	2	5	1	0	3	0
Brenly 3b	4	0	1	0	0	0	0	1
Quinones 3b-ss	0	0	0	0	0	0	0	1
Melvin c	3	0	0	0	1	1	4	1
Uribe ss	4	0	0	0	0	0	0	4
Williams p	0	0	0	0	0	0	0	0
Mulholland p	2	0	1	0	0	1	1	0
Berenguer p	1	0	1	0	0	0	0	0
Robinson p	0	0	0	0	0	0	0	0
Garrelts p	0	0	0	0	0	0	0	0
M. Davis p	0	0	0	0	0	0	0	0
Kutcher 3b	1	0	1	0	0	0	0	0
Totals	**34**	**6**	**10**	**6**	**4**	**4**	**24**	**12**

FIELDING
DP: 1

BATTING
2B: Gladden (14, off Welsh); Brenly (16, off Welsh); Kutcher (7, off Robinson)
HR: Maldonado 2 (10, 3rd inning off Welsh, 3 on, 2 out; 8th inning off Franco, 0 on, 1 out)
SF: Clark (3,off Welsh)

BASERUNNING
SB: Gladden (16, 2nd base off Power/Diaz)
CS: Clark (5, 2nd base by Murphy/Diaz)

Cincinnati Reds	AB	R	H	RBI	BB	K	PO	A
Stillwell ss	4	0	2	3	1	0	1	2
Bell 3b	4	1	1	0	1	0	2	3
Parker rf	4	1	1	0	0	0	5	0
Diaz c	4	1	2	3	0	0	5	2
Davis pr	0	1	0	0	0	0	0	0
Butera c	0	0	0	0	0	0	0	0
Perez 1b	4	0	0	0	0	0	7	1
Esasky lf	4	1	2	0	1	1	1	0
Milner cf	3	1	1	0	1	1	2	0
Oester 2b	2	2	2	1	2	0	4	3
Welsh p	0	0	0	0	0	0	0	1
Murphy p	1	0	0	0	0	0	0	0
Larkin ph	1	0	0	1	0	0	0	0
Power p	0	0	0	0	0	0	0	1
Daniels ph	1	0	0	0	0	1	0	0
Franco p	0	0	0	0	0	0	0	0
Rose ph	1	0	0	0	0	0	0	0
Robinson p	0	0	0	0	0	0	0	1
Totals	**33**	**8**	**11**	**8**	**5**	**3**	**27**	**14**

BATTING
2B: Esasky (13, off Mulholland); Oester (16, off Berenguer)
HR: Diaz (7, 6th inning off Berenguer, 2 on, 0 out)

BASERUNNING
CS: Stillwell (2, 2nd base by Berenguer/Melvin)

PITCHING

San Francisco Giants	IP	H	HR	R	ER	BB	K
Mulholland	5	4	0	3	3	3	0
Berenguer	1.2	4	1	2	2	0	3
Robinson	0.1	1	0	1	1	0	0
Garrelts L(10-8)	0.1	1	0	2	2	2	0
M. Davis	0.1	1	0	0	0	0	0
Williams	0.1	0	0	0	0	0	0
Totals	**8.0**	**11**	**1**	**8**	**8**	**5**	**3**

Cincinnati Reds	IP	H	HR	R	ER	BB	K
Welsh	2.2	6	1	5	5	1	0
Murphy	2.1	1	0	0	0	0	2
Power	2	1	0	0	0	2	2
Franco W(4-4)	1	1	1	1	1	1	0
Robinson SV(9)	1	1	0	0	0	0	0
Totals	**9**	**10**	**2**	**6**	**6**	**4**	**4**

WP: Mulholland (5), Berenguer (3)
Umpires: John McSherry, Greg Bonin, Frank Pulli, Larry Poncino
Time of Game: 2:53   Attendance: 17,162

Pete Rose gave me some shoes to wear, Dave Parker gave me some batting gloves, Buddy Bell came in and loaned me a bat . . . I believe I used Ronny Oester's glove. I was completely patched together, and now I wasn't in the starting lineup because I had gotten there so late. But I did pinch-hit, and I got an RBI on a little groundout to Jose Uribe of the San Francisco Giants. It was against Terry Mulholland.

The Reds had taken care of getting my family in there—my mom, dad, brother, sister. They were all there to see it happen, but I forgot to even look for them until after the game, to be honest. I was so worried about just getting out there in my borrowed equipment and not embarrassing myself.

Courtesy Cincinnati Reds

Tony La Russa
Born: October 4, 1944
Debut: May 10, 1963

Tony La Russa had managed only a year and a half in the minors when the White Sox anointed him to replace Don Kessinger at the tender age of 34. Having graduated with a law degree the previous winter, he became just the fifth lawyer/manager in big league history. The other four are in the Hall of Fame (Monte Ward, Hughie Jennings, Miller Huggins, and Branch Rickey), and La Russa could someday join that quartet. He began by leading the White Sox into the ALCS in 1983, although he was canned a few years later when the Sox stumbled out to a 26–38 start.

The Tampa, Florida, native landed on his feet in Oakland, proving to be a better manager for the A's than he had been a player (he'd washed out with a five-year batting average of .197 for them on his way to a career average of .199; one more hit would have tugged him to .200). He had debuted as an 18-year-old shortstop (something only Robin Yount and Alex Rodriguez would duplicate in coming years) but had retired by the age of 29. It should be noted that many successful managers never did much as big league players, from Sparky Anderson to Earl Weaver to Whitey Herzog. La Russa is a shining example of "Those who can't do, teach."

With the "Bash Brothers" (Jose Canseco and Mark McGwire) leading the way, La Russa's Athletics bombed their way into three consecutive World Series, losing two and winning one. In 1995, he left Oakland for St. Louis and lured some of his Oakland favorites to the Midwest with him, including Dennis Eckersley, whom La Russa had turned into the game's most dominating closer of the time. The Cardinals made the playoffs in '96, regressed in '97, but acquired another La Russa favorite from Oakland—the redheaded ripper, McGwire, who became one of the most popular athletes in St. Louis history. In contention the next several years, the Cardinals finally made it to the World Series on La Russa's watch in '04, only to get dispatched in four games by the Red Sox.

La Russa's managerial style can be described as either "studied" or "anal" depending on one's point of view. He has a remarkable ability to both attract and repel, having been written up for sainthood in George Will's *Men at Work* but having cheesed off everyone from Barry Bonds to Lou Piniella along the way. The bottom line, however, is that for all the caterwauling opposing managers, writers, and broadcasters do about his

BOXSCORE

Minnesota Twins 2, Kansas City Athletics 0
Game Played on Friday, May 10, 1963 (Night) at Metropolitan Stadium

Kansas City	0	0	0	0	0	0	0	0	0	—	0	3	0
Minnesota	0	2	0	0	0	0	0	0	x	—	2	4	0

BATTING

Kansas City Athletics	AB	R	H	RBI	BB	K	PO	A
Causey ss	4	0	0	0	0	1	0	1
Tartabull cf	4	0	0	0	0	0	5	0
Lumpe 2b	4	0	1	0	0	0	0	1
Siebern 1b	3	0	0	0	1	1	5	0
Charles 3b	4	0	0	0	0	1	3	2
Jimenez lf	2	0	1	0	1	0	1	0
Cimoli rf	3	0	0	0	0	0	2	0
Bryan c	3	0	0	0	0	2	8	0
Pena p	2	0	0	0	0	1	0	0
Essegian ph	1	0	1	0	0	0	0	0
La Russa pr	0	0	0	0	0	0	0	0
Wyatt p	0	0	0	0	0	0	0	0
Totals	30	0	3	0	2	6	24	4

BATTING
2B: Lumpe (5, off Pascual); Jimenez (4, off Pascual)

Minnesota Twins	AB	R	H	RBI	BB	K	PO	A
Versalles ss	4	0	2	0	0	0	1	1
Power 1b	4	0	0	0	0	0	10	1
Green cf-lf	4	0	0	0	0	1	3	0
Allison rf	3	0	0	0	0	2	3	0
Battey c	2	0	0	0	1	0	6	1
Hall lf	3	1	1	0	0	1	1	0
Tuttle cf	0	0	0	0	0	0	0	0
Allen 2b	2	1	0	0	1	1	1	5
Ward 3b	3	0	1	2	0	2	1	1
Pascual p	3	0	0	0	0	1	1	1
Totals	28	2	4	2	2	8	27	10

BATTING
2B: Hall (4, off Pena); Ward (1, off Pena)

PITCHING

Kansas City Athletics	IP	H	HR	R	ER	BB	K
Pena L(4–2)	7	3	0	2	2	2	8
Wyatt	1	1	0	0	0	0	0
Totals	8	4	0	2	2	2	8
Minnesota Twins	IP	H	HR	R	ER	BB	K
Pascual W(4–3)	9	3	0	0	0	2	6

Umpires: Eddie Hurley, H. Sam Carrigan, Red Flaherty, Lou DiMuro
Time of Game: 1:59   Attendance: 11,276

penchant for mid-inning pitching changes and "smartest guy in the room" attitude, no active manager has more wins.

As an 18-year-old bonus baby, I got up, but it took a while to get in. Finally, when my parents were vacationing for a week in Kansas City, just on the chance I might get in, I did. I pinch-ran, then a day later I pinch-hit, first against Hank Aguirre. I hit a line drive that Billy Bruton made a running, shoestring catch on. Next at bat was against Steve Barber, who won 20 games that year . . . and I hit a triple to right-center. Eddie Lopat, my manager, may have known that my parents were in town, and who knows, maybe he got me those at bats just because of that. I ended up 11-for-44 that year, and a lot of people thought the A's had done okay with their bonus baby! But I straightened 'em out soon enough. [Laughs.]

Being 18, it was tough being around all those veterans—Gino Cimoli, Jerry Lumpe, guys like that, real established guys . . . But there was one veteran who really went out of his way to befriend me, and he became a lifetime friend, and that's Charlie Lau. He was the backup catcher, and for whatever reason he took a shine to a kid who was in way over his head. He gave me a lot of advice about how to conduct myself. Any questions I had about the game, he answered them. He was coaching with the A's in the '70s when I came back with them as a player, and he left to go to the Kansas City hitting academy, but the last couple years of his life, '82 and '83, I grabbed him back to coach for me in Chicago. Charlie had gone out of his way for me—it was a pleasure for me to return the favor.

Also on May 10, 1963
Decca Recording signs The Rolling Stones on the advice of Beatle George Harrison.

AUTHOR'S NOTE: Harrison's "Isn't it a Pity" may have been La Russa's personal anthem after his Cardinals got bulldozed by Boston in the 2004 World Series.

Mike Lieberthal
Born: January 18, 1972
Debut: June 30, 1994

Mike Lieberthal grew up in an upper-middle-class neighborhood in Southern California, just down the street from major league catcher Steve Yaeger. He would attend dozens of Dodgers games each year and remembers leaning over the railings, trying to get Fernando Valenzuela to autograph his glove or program. A little more than a decade later, Lieberthal would be in a prime position to hobnob with the famous lefty—as his battery mate in Philly.

Lieberthal was drafted third in the nation in 1990 and back then was a scrawny 150 pounds. It took a full seven seasons for him to finally bulk up and start hitting for power, but once he turned on the faucet, it stayed on full-blast. After hitting just 20 home runs total his first six years in the minors, Lieberthal ripped 20 in '97. The 1999 campaign saw him hit 31 homers, which landed him on the National League All-Star team for the first time. Into the mid 00s, he has been nothing if not consistent, with doubles totals of 29, 20, and 31 between 2002 and 2004; his walks totals during that time were 38, 38, and 37.

A terrific all-around athlete, Lieberthal is a devoted football fan and a die-hard Raiders fan from their days at the L.A. Coliseum. When the Raiders played Tampa Bay in Super Bowl XXXVII, there was Lieberthal, just to the left of the goalpost, talking smack along with the rest of Raider Nation every time Warren Sapp came close.

Lieberthal's biggest challenge has been remaining healthy. Through 2004, he has been on the disabled list a half-dozen times, with ACL and MCL trouble popping up more than once. Not too many Phillies first rounders have avoided injury or abject failure. Low ebb may have been the year before Lieberthal's selection, when Philadelphia selected (ahead of Frank Thomas and a host of others) outfielder Jeff Jackson, who topped out at Double-A as a career .215 hitter. Lieberthal, who has hit as high as .313 in a single season, has been the rare first-round jackpot for one of the most star-crossed teams in sports.

I was told in Rochester, New York, where our Triple-A team was playing . . . We had just gotten creamed in a doubleheader, but the good news was, George Culver, our manager, said to get up to Philly, and the coolest part was after this one day in Philly, we left on a West Coast road trip, first stop L.A.,

107

BOXSCORE

Los Angeles Dodgers 4, Philadelphia Phillies 3

Game Played on Thursday, June 30, 1994 (Night) at Dodger Stadium

Philadelphia	0	0	0	2	0	0	0	0	1	—	3	7	0
Los Angeles	0	1	0	0	0	0	0	0	3	—	4	7	0

BATTING

Philadelphia Phillies	AB	R	H	RBI	BB	K	PO	A
Morandini 2b	4	0	1	0	0	1	5	3
Duncan 3b	4	0	1	0	0	1	0	2
Kruk 1b	2	1	0	0	2	2	8	1
Incaviglia lf	4	0	0	0	0	0	0	0
Slocumb p	0	0	0	0	0	0	0	0
Jones p	0	0	0	0	0	0	0	0
Eisenreich cf-rf	4	1	2	2	0	0	1	0
Longmire rf	3	0	1	0	0	0	4	0
Hatcher ph-cf	1	1	1	0	0	0	0	0
Lieberthal c	3	0	1	0	0	0	5	0
Stocker ss	3	0	0	1	0	0	1	2
Munoz p	3	0	0	0	0	0	1	1
Thompson lf	1	0	0	0	0	1	0	0
Totals	32	3	7	3	2	5	25	9

FIELDING

DP: 1

BATTING

HR: Eisenreich (2, 4th inning off Astacio, 1 on, 2 out)
SH: Lieberthal (1, off Seanez); Stocker (3, off Seanez)

Los Angeles Dodgers	AB	R	H	RBI	BB	K	PO	A
Butler cf	5	1	1	0	0	0	3	0
DeShields 2b	5	0	1	3	0	2	1	4
Piazza c	3	0	0	0	1	1	6	0
Wallach 3b	3	0	0	0	1	0	0	2
Rodriguez lf	2	0	1	0	2	0	5	0
Karros 1b	4	0	0	0	0	0	5	0
Mondesi rf	4	1	1	1	0	1	3	0
Bournigal ss	1	0	1	0	2	0	4	1
Treadway ph	1	1	1	0	0	0	0	0
Astacio p	2	0	0	0	0	1	0	0
Gwynn ph	0	0	0	0	1	0	0	0
Valdes p	0	0	0	0	0	0	0	0
Daal p	0	0	0	0	0	0	0	0
Seanez p	0	0	0	0	0	0	0	1
Hansen ph	1	0	1	0	0	0	0	0
Webster pr	0	1	0	0	0	0	0	0
Totals	31	4	7	4	7	5	27	8

BATTING

2B: DeShields (8, off Jones)
HR: Mondesi (13, 2nd inning off Munoz, 0 on, 2 out)

BASERUNNING

SB: Butler (16, 2nd base off Munoz/Lieberthal)

PITCHING

Philadelphia Phillies	IP	H	HR	R	ER	BB	K
Munoz	7	3	1	1	1	6	5
Slocumb	1	0	0	0	0	1	0
Jones L(2–2)	0.1	4	0	3	3	0	0
Totals	8.1	7	1	4	4	7	5
Los Angeles Dodgers	IP	H	HR	R	ER	BB	K
Astacio	7	5	1	2	2	1	4
Valdes	0.2	1	0	0	0	1	0
Daal	0.1	0	0	0	0	0	0
Seanez W(1–1)	1	1	0	1	1	0	1
Totals	9	7	1	3	3	2	5

WP: Seanez (2)
Umpires: Jerry Layne, Paul Runge, Angel Hernandez, Tom Hallion
Time of Game: 2:43   Attendance: 31,295

where I'm from. So my debut was in the stadium I had always gone to as a kid . . . I couldn't have asked for any better.

I called my folks from the pay phone in the visiting clubhouse there in Rochester but had no idea I'd be seeing them soon enough back home . . . I didn't know [the Phillies] schedule at all until my plane touched down in Philly and I bought a newspaper . . . I realized, wow, this is unbelievable! I used to have season tickets, ever since 1978 . . . I had been all over the ballpark, sitting in the yellow section, behind home plate a little to the left. I had seen plenty of that stadium, knew it like the back of my hand, but had never been down to see the clubhouses until that first day as a player there. Steve Sax used to be my favorite player, and I was like, wow, the same tunnel Steve Sax used to come out of, awesome!

My first start, I was 1-for-3 with a line drive hit to left off Pedro Astacio . . . The ball is now in a trophy case in my family room. I must have left 60 passes there at Dodger Stadium for that game: friends, family, you name it.

Milt Thompson was one of the veteran players on the Phillies at the time, and he made it a point to be real outgoing, real kind to the young players.

Also on June 30, 1994
The U.S. Figure Skating Association strips Tonya Harding of the 1994 national championship and bans her from the organization for life for an attack on rival Nancy Kerrigan.

AUTHOR'S NOTE: Lieberthal would suffer a gruesome knee injury, too, just like Kerrigan, but a tad more conventionally—his 2001 season was wiped out when he dove back to first awkwardly on a pickoff attempt in Arizona.

Kenny Lofton
Born: May 31, 1967
Debut: September 14, 1991

With Kenny Lofton's talent, it's difficult to fathom that since the start of the 2001 season, he has played for seven different teams. When the speedy Chicagoan first emerged as a force with the Indians, it appeared he'd be the catalyst of that powerful 1990s Cleveland lineup for as long as his legs could keep him running. It has been said that Lofton was Ichiro "before there was Ichiro," with game-changing defensive skills, baserunning skills, and the ability to slap or bunt the ball to motor his way on base. As Chipper Jones once summed it up, "Every time he comes to bat, he creates chaos." At some point, opponents knew he'd be standing on third base, either by tripling or by bunting his way on and stealing a pair of bases. The "Naughty by Nature" music that accompanied his every Cleveland at bat seemed to sum up Lofton's essence: "Feel me flow, here we go." With Lofton leading the way, the Indians were a postseason staple starting in 1995.

However, just after Lofton peaked in 1996 (.317, 75 steals, 53 extra base hits), he began a vagabond existence, moving from Cleveland to Atlanta, then back to the Tribe for a while, then to the White Sox, Giants, Pirates, Cubs, Yankees, and Phillies.

A six-time All-Star and four-time Gold Glover, he came from humble beginnings in East Chicago, Indiana, surviving the projects with a "me against the world" mentality that would also serve him well professionally. He escaped the ghetto by receiving an athletic scholarship to Arizona, where he excelled on the basketball court. Lofton was the Wildcats' "sixth man," teaming with backcourt mate Steve Kerr to force piles of turnovers and create Final Four excitement. He left campus as the Cats' career leader in steals but began to shift his attention to baseball when the Astros chose him with their 17th pick of the '88 draft. Heading into 1992, he was spun to Cleveland in one of the most lopsided trades of the decade—he and Dave Rhode for Eddie Taubensee and Willie Blair.

Heading into the 2005 season, he ranked 27th all-time with 545 career stolen bases and was a career .297 hitter. He had also been in the playoffs in nine of his twelve full major league seasons.

I was in Tucson, and we had just won the championship down there. Brian Williams, Jeff Juden, and I all got the call . . . and what was awesome is that the Astros were playing in Cincinnati, where I had some family. And the rest

BOXSCORE

Houston Astros 7, Cincinnati Reds 3

Game Played on Saturday, September 14, 1991 (Night) at Riverfront Stadium

										R	H	E
Houston	2	0	0	0	0	0	2	3	—	7	12	1
Cincinnati	0	0	0	3	0	0	0	0	—	3	7	1

BATTING

Houston Astros	AB	R	H	RBI	BB	K	PO	A
Lofton cf	4	3	3	0	1	0	0	0
Finley rf	3	1	0	0	1	1	3	0
Biggio c	4	2	2	1	1	0	9	1
Bagwell 1b	4	0	1	3	0	0	10	0
Caminiti 3b	5	0	2	1	0	1	0	4
Candaele lf	4	0	1	0	0	1	0	0
Mallicoat p	0	0	0	0	0	0	0	0
Schilling p	1	0	0	0	0	0	0	0
Cedeno ss	4	0	2	0	0	1	2	2
Mota 2b	4	0	0	0	0	0	1	0
Portugal p	2	0	0	0	0	1	1	1
Ramirez ph	1	0	0	0	0	0	0	0
Hernandez p	0	0	0	0	0	0	0	0
Gonzalez lf	1	1	1	0	0	0	0	0
Totals	**37**	**7**	**12**	**5**	**3**	**5**	**27**	**10**

FIELDING
DP: 1
E: Cedeno (9)

BATTING
2B: Bagwell (25, off Myers); Cedeno (10, off Myers); Lofton (1, off Dibble)
SH: Finley (8,off Myers)
SF: Bagwell (6, off Power)
IBB: Finley (4, by Dibble)

BASERUNNING
SB: Candaele (9, 2nd base off Dibble/Oliver); Caminiti (4, 2nd base off Power/Oliver)

Cincinnati Reds	AB	R	H	RBI	BB	K	PO	A
Doran lf	4	0	0	0	1	1	3	0
Duncan ss	4	1	2	1	0	0	0	5
Morris 1b	3	1	2	1	1	0	14	1
O'Neill rf	4	1	1	1	0	1	2	0
Sabo 3b	4	0	0	0	0	1	0	3
Quinones 2b	4	0	0	0	0	2	1	5
Hatcher cf	4	0	1	0	0	0	2	0
Oliver c	3	0	1	0	0	0	5	0
Reed ph	1	0	0	0	0	0	0	0
Myers p	3	0	0	0	0	2	0	0
Dibble p	0	0	0	0	0	0	0	0
Power p	0	0	0	0	0	0	0	0
Totals	**34**	**3**	**7**	**3**	**1**	**7**	**27**	**14**

FIELDING
E: Oliver (11)

BATTING
HR: Duncan (11, 4th inning off Portugal, 0 on, 0 out); Morris (14, 4th inning off Portugal, 0 on, 0 out); O'Neill (26, 4th inning off Portugal, 0 on, 0 out).

BASERUNNING
CS: Hatcher (9, Home by Hernandez/Biggio)

PITCHING

Houston Astros	IP	H	HR	R	ER	BB	K
Portugal	6	3	3	3	3	1	4
Hernandez W(1–6)	1.1	3	0	0	0	0	2
Mallicoat	0.1	1	0	0	0	0	1
Schilling SV(7)	1.1	0	0	0	0	0	0
Totals	**9.0**	**7**	**3**	**3**	**3**	**1**	**7**

Cincinnati Reds	IP	H	HR	R	ER	BB	K
Myers	7.1	6	0	3	3	1	4
Dibble L(3–4)	1	5	0	4	4	2	1
Power	0.2	1	0	0	0	0	0
Totals	**9.0**	**12**	**0**	**7**	**7**	**3**	**5**

WP: Dibble (4)
IBB: Dibble (2,Finley)
Umpires: Ed Montague, Dana DeMuth, Bruce Froemming, Greg Bonin
Time of Game: 2:32   Attendance: 25,829

of my family wasn't too far away, in Chicago, so that couldn't have been better. It was a good game for me. I started and went 3-for-4, and I guess it was all downhill from there.

It was a good group of guys . . . Eric Yelding took an interest in me and Gerald Young, guys like that . . . Some of the guys ragged me a little, but for the most part everyone seemed happy to have me there. Ken Caminiti was one of the first guys to come over and shake my hand and tell me to just relax and have fun. That meant a lot, and he was so sincere and serious about it. Of course we had guys who could keep it loose, too, like Mark Portugal and Casey Candaele . . . Casey was something else. But for the most part, I was just real happy that I could contribute right away and that my family could be there to see it happen. I can't say anything bizarre or stupid happened that I remember . . . It was like I was in a daze that whole day anyway. It's a lot for a young guy to digest all at once.

Also on September 14, 1991
The big college football game "out west" features Arizona surviving Stanford and "Touchdown Tommy" Vardell, 28–23. However, Touchdown Tommy's thunder is stolen by a kid from San Diego State named Marshall Faulk, who runs for 388 yards against Pacific.

AUTHOR'S NOTE: Lofton played both baseball and basketball (but not football) for Arizona and later played with Tommy Vardell's high school teammate Brian Giles as a Cleveland Indian. And whatever happened to that Marshall Faulk guy?

Mark Loretta
Born: August 14, 1971
Debut: September 4, 1995

Southern California native Mark Loretta strode onto campus at Northwestern University and within weeks had a place in the cool fraternity and a spot on the baseball team. His emergence as an All-Star caliber National League infielder would fail to come as easily. Loretta began his pro career as a seventh-round pick of the Brewers and in his first full season of minor league ball totaled just one home run between Single-A and Double-A, and, in fact, had only 27 extra-base hits in 430 at bats. However, his instincts and work ethic kept him on course, and by 1997, he emerged as an everyday player in Milwaukee for Phil Garner, a manager who could appreciate a "scrap iron" type like himself. Loretta's versatility was beneficial, and he stayed in the lineup, hopping between all four infield positions and some occasional outfield work as well.

Peddled to the Astros for their stretch run in 2002, Loretta then signed a free agent deal in San Diego and saw his career take off. Given the everyday second base job, he became an All-Star in 2003, hitting .314 and knocking in 72 runs. He proved invaluable the following year, keeping the Padres in the playoff hunt all season with another All-Star performance. Taking advantage of Petco Field's spacious power alleys, he led the team in slugging percentage and placed second in the league with 208 hits, third with a .335 batting average. He smoked 47 doubles and, again using Petco's open spaces, led the league in sac flies with 16.

Sure-handed defensively, he has routinely finished among the top second baseman in fielding percentage. Every baseball observer seems to include the word "smart" in their scouting reports on Loretta. The Padres got smart after his '03 season and locked him up through 2006.

Triple-A, New Orleans, 1995. Last couple days of August, I'm suddenly playing second base, and I had been playing shortstop all year, okay? I thought that was a little fishy, but who am I to question the manager, right? Chris Bando was my manager, and sixth inning of the second game at second base, Chris comes over and asks if I've been wondering why I'm all of a sudden playing a new position. I say, "Yeah, that crossed my mind." And he says, "Well, that's where they're going to play you in the big leagues, and that's where you're going tomorrow. September call-up." I couldn't wait for that game to end so I could run back to my apartment and call home. When I did, there were tears, tears of joy.

From New Orleans, I met the team in Minneapolis, and everyone made the

BOXSCORE

Minnesota Twins 9, Milwaukee Brewers 6
Game Played on Monday, September 4, 1995 (Day) at Hubert H. Humphrey Metrodome

Milwaukee	4	0	0	0	1	0	1	0	0	—	6	8	2
Minnesota	0	3	1	3	0	0	1	1	x	—	9	16	0

BATTING

Milwaukee Brewers	AB	R	H	RBI	BB	K	PO	A
Hamilton cf	4	0	0	0	0	1	0	0
Mieske ph	1	0	0	0	0	0	0	0
Seitzer dh	4	2	2	1	0	0	0	0
Cirillo 3b	3	2	1	1	1	0	0	5
Nilsson rf	3	1	1	0	1	1	2	0
Jaha 1b	4	1	2	4	0	0	11	0
Oliver c	3	0	0	0	1	0	5	0
Hulse lf	4	0	1	0	0	1	1	0
Listach ss	4	0	0	0	0	1	1	3
Vina 2b	3	0	1	0	0	0	4	4
Loretta ph	1	0	0	0	0	1	0	0
Karl p	0	0	0	0	0	0	0	1
Slusarski p	0	0	0	0	0	0	0	0
Dibble p	0	0	0	0	0	0	0	0
Roberson p	0	0	0	0	0	0	0	0
Totals	34	6	8	6	3	5	24	13

FIELDING
DP: 3
E: Listach (3), Roberson (1)

BATTING
2B: Jaha (13, off Trombley); Vina (6, off Trombley); Nilsson (8, off Trombley)
HR: Jaha (16, 1st inning off Trombley, 3 on, 1 out); Cirillo (9, 5th inning off Trombley, 0 on, 1 out); Seitzer (5, 7th inning off Mahomes, 0 on, 1 out)

Minnesota Twins	AB	R	H	RBI	BB	K	PO	A
Knoblauch 2b	4	0	0	0	1	0	1	1
Meares ss	5	1	1	0	0	0	2	9
Puckett rf	5	2	3	3	0	1	3	0
P. Munoz dh	5	1	4	0	0	0	0	0
Cordova lf	2	1	1	0	2	0	3	0
Coomer 1b	3	1	1	2	0	0	9	0
Masteller ph-1b	1	0	0	0	0	0	2	0
Reboulet ph-1b	0	0	0	0	1	0	0	0
Leius 3b	5	1	3	1	0	1	0	1
Walbeck c	3	1	2	1	1	1	5	0
Becker cf	4	1	1	0	0	2	2	0
Trombley p	0	0	0	0	0	0	0	0
Watkins p	0	0	0	0	0	0	0	0
Mahomes p	0	0	0	0	0	0	0	0
Guardado p	0	0	0	0	0	0	0	0
Totals	37	9	16	7	5	5	27	11

FIELDING
DP: 1

BATTING
2B: Coomer (1, off Karl); Becker (12, off Karl); Leius (15, off Slusarski)
3B: Leius (5, off Karl); Meares (4, off Dibble)
HR: Puckett 2 (22, 3rd inning off Karl, 0 on, 1 out, 4th inning off Karl, 1 on, 2 out)
HBP: Cordova (8, by Slusarski)

PITCHING

Milwaukee Brewers	IP	H	HR	R	ER	BB	K
Karl L(5–4)	5	11	2	7	7	3	2
Slusarski	2	4	0	1	1	0	1
Dibble	0.2	1	0	1	1	1	1
Roberson	0.1	0	0	0	0	1	1
Totals	8.0	16	2	9	9	5	5

Minnesota Twins	IP	H	HR	R	ER	BB	K
Trombley W(3–8)	5	6	2	5	5	3	1
Watkins	1.1	1	0	0	0	0	1
Mahomes	1.2	1	1	1	1	0	2
Guardado SV(2)	1	0	0	0	0	0	1
Totals	9	8	3	6	6	3	5

WP: Dibble (8)
HBP: Slusarski (1,Cordova)
Umpires: Ted Hendry, Drew Coble, Durwood Merrill, Chuck Meriwether
Time of Game: 2:57   Attendance: 10,837

trip to see me, from California. Family, Little League coach, you name it. Two games go by, nothing . . . But the third day, Phil Garner got me in as a pinch hitter against Eddie Guardado . . . I fouled a few off but struck out. Boy, I was nervous. I remember the catcher and umpire both asking me if this was my debut, and I could hardly squeak out a "yes." But I was so happy that my folks were there. They saw my first hit a couple days later, against The Gambler, Kenny Rogers . . . Then I hit a home run later that road trip against Jose Lima in Detroit and actually was 2-for-3 total at that point in my big league career. I was feeling pretty good, but then a week went by and I was 2-for-23. Baseball isn't easy when you're first getting your feet wet, that's for sure.

Also on September 4, 1995
Robin Ventura of the White Sox connects for a pair of grand slams vs. Texas, becoming just the eighth player in big league history with two slams in a single game.

AUTHOR'S NOTE: Ventura's own debut was for Chicago on September 12, 1989. On the same day, Loretta arrived in Chicago to begin college at Northwestern. Loretta, then a third basemen, followed the young Ventura's career closely during his time on campus.

Mike Lowell
Born: February 24, 1974
Debut: September 14, 1998

A onetime top prospect with the Yankees, Lowell was dealt to the Marlins for three pitching prospects in 1999, none of whom panned out for New York. Lowell overcame testicular cancer and became a Marlins fan favorite in his hometown of Miami. Lowell had excelled at Coral Gables High School and later at Florida International University, where he earned a degree in finance.

Originally from Puerto Rico, he is fluent in both Spanish and English, which makes him a valuable piece of marketing property for the Marlins. Always a steady, under-the-radar type, he gained national attention with some big late-inning hits in the summer of 2003. He would miss eight weeks of the Marlins' unlikely wild card run with a broken hand, but he came back with a vengeance. When Florida stole away with Game Seven of the NLCS in Chicago, Lowell let out an ear-piercing scream the moment Jeff Conine settled under the final out and was among the first to reach closer Ugueth Urbina for the wild celebration on the mound.

As the Marlins sped towards their World Series victory (accomplished on the field at which Lowell had once debuted, as a Yankee), unsettling talk began that the Marlins wouldn't be able to keep Lowell much longer as he approached free agent status. He would reward his hometown team and fans with a bit of a "hometown discount," signing on through 2007. Originally, the contract was dependant on whether or not the Marlins broke ground on a new, baseball-only stadium, but two weeks after his banner 2004 season (44 doubles, a career-high .293 average), Lowell decided he'd stay no matter what. Marlins fans were relieved that their all-time home run king and all-around good guy would continue to be a Man of Teal.

Stump Merrill was my minor league manager, and it seems like he was pretty happy to give me the good news that my hard work had paid off and I was going up. It was a day game in Yankee Stadium when I finally got in. I had been up for a few days, but Joe Torre told me the day before my official debut to be ready to go the next day, so I called my folks back home and told 'em they should find some way to tune in on TV tomorrow. To play in front of 40 or 50,000 people instead of the five or 10,000 I'd been accustomed to in [AAA] Columbus, that was really neat. Hearing my name announced by Bob Shepherd on the PA was a little different than hearing it by the guy in Columbus.

BOXSCORE

Toronto Blue Jays 5, New York Yankees 3
Game Played on Sunday, September 13, 1998 (Day) at Yankee Stadium

Toronto	1	0	0	0	3	1	0	0	—	5	15	0
New York	1	0	2	0	0	0	0	0	—	3	8	0

BATTING

Toronto Blue Jays	AB	R	H	RBI	BB	K	PO	A
Stewart lf	5	1	1	1	0	1	1	0
Green rf	5	0	2	2	0	2	3	0
Canseco dh	4	0	1	0	0	3	0	0
Delgado 1b	4	0	1	1	1	2	7	0
Cruz cf	4	1	3	1	1	1	3	1
Fernandez 3b	5	0	1	0	0	3	1	1
Fletcher c	3	1	1	0	0	0	5	0
Santiago ph-c	2	0	1	0	0	0	4	1
Grebeck 2b	3	1	2	0	0	0	3	3
Gonzalez ss	4	1	2	0	2	0	0	2
Escobar p	0	0	0	0	0	0	0	0
Sinclair p	0	0	0	0	0	0	0	0
Quantrill p	0	0	0	0	0	0	0	0
Plesac p	0	0	0	0	0	0	0	0
Almanzar p	0	0	0	0	0	0	0	0
Person p	0	0	0	0	0	0	0	0
Totals	39	5	15	5	2	14	27	8

FIELDING
DP: 1

BATTING
2B: Cruz (13, off Cone); Santiago (4, off Stanton)
HR: Stewart (10, 1st inning off Cone, 0 on, 0 out); Cruz (10, 7th inning off Stanton, 0 on, 0 out)
HBP: Grebeck (4, by Cone); Canseco (5, by Nelson)

BASERUNNING
SB: Canseco (29, 2nd base off Cone/Girardi)
CS: Fernandez (7, 2nd base by Cone/Girardi); Canseco (15, 3rd base by Cone/Girardi)

New York Yankees	AB	R	H	RBI	BB	K	PO	A
Knoblauch 2b	3	2	2	0	2	0	2	0
Jeter ss	3	1	1	2	1	1	1	0
O'Neill rf	4	0	1	0	1	0	0	0
Spencer rf	1	0	0	0	0	0	0	0
Williams cf	4	0	0	0	0	2	1	0
Posada dh	3	0	1	0	1	1	0	0
Lowell 3b	4	0	1	0	0	0	1	2
Ledee lf	2	0	0	0	0	1	0	1
Davis ph	1	0	0	0	0	0	0	0
Curtis lf	0	0	0	0	0	0	0	0
Strawberry ph-lf	1	0	0	0	0	1	1	0
Brosius 1b	3	0	1	0	1	1	4	2
Girardi c4	0	1	0	0	1	1	3	2
Cone p	0	0	0	0	0	0	1	2
Lloyd p	0	0	0	0	0	0	0	0
Nelson p	0	0	0	0	0	0	0	0
Stanton p	0	0	0	0	0	0	0	0
Mendoza p	0	0	0	0	0	0	1	0
Totals	33	3	8	3	5	9	27	9

FIELDING
DP: 1

BATTING
3B: Knoblauch (3, off Escobar); Jeter (7, off Escobar)
SF: Jeter (3, off Escobar)

BASERUNNING
SB: O'Neill (15, 2nd base off Escobar/Fletcher); Brosius (11, 3rd base off Plesac/Santiago)

PITCHING

Toronto Blue Jays	IP	H	HR	R	ER	BB	K
Escobar W(6–2)	5.2	5	0	3	3	3	5
Sinclair	0.1	0	0	0	0	0	0
Quantrill	0.2	2	0	0	0	0	1
Plesac	1	1	0	0	0	0	1
Almanzar	0.1	0	0	0	0	0	1
Person SV(4)	1	0	0	0	0	2	1
Totals	9	8	0	3	3	5	9
New York Yankees	**IP**	**H**	**HR**	**R**	**ER**	**BB**	**K**
Cone L(19–6)	5.2	10	1	4	4	2	11
Lloyd	0	1	0	0	0	0	0
Nelson	0	0	0	0	0	0	0
Stanton	1.1	3	1	1	1	0	2
Mendoza	2	1	0	0	0	0	1
Totals	9	15	2	5	5	2	14

WP: Cone (6)
HBP: Cone (15, Grebeck); Nelson (7, Canseco)
Umpires: John Hirschbeck, Rich Garcia, Mike Reilly, Tim McClelland
Time of Game: 3:31   Attendance: 47,471

My first at bat, I had a little bloop single to center, and they put it right up on the scoreboard, "that was Mike Lowell's first major league hit in his first major league at bat," which gave me chills. The crowd cheered real loud, and I remember turning to our first base coach, Jose Cardenal, and saying, "well, if I retire right now, I have a really good batting average." Forty thousand people cheering and Jose Cardenal laughing and knowing I was 1-for-1 in the big leagues made for a pretty good way to start things out.

Also on September 14, 1998
With a pair of long balls, Sammy Sosa catches and then surpasses Roger Maris's long-standing home run record of 61, thereby jumping into a tie with current record holder Mark McGwire, at 62.

AUTHOR'S NOTE: Five months and five weeks later, also at Wrigley, Sosa would punch a dramatic game-tying 9th-inning homer, sending Game One of the '98 NLCS into extra innings. However, Lowell would win it for the Marlins with an 11th-inning blast of his own.

Greg Maddux
Born: April 14, 1966
Debut: September 3, 1986

Greg Maddux has always seemed to have a kind of Clark Kent/Superman dynamic at work. Off the field, he's mild-mannered, wiry, bespectacled, and harmless-looking. On the field, he's an absolute menace, deserving of his nickname, "Mad Dog," as well as his 14 Gold Gloves and four Cy Youngs.

There was no better all-around pitcher in the decade of the 1990s than the unassuming right-hander from Las Vegas. The son of a blackjack dealer, Maddux himself seemed to have a card-counter's edge, always finding whatever hidden advantage he could to tilt the odds in his favor. As his Atlanta pitching coach, Leo Mazzone, liked to say: "Forget about him being the smartest pitcher in the game. He's also smarter than any position player, manager, or coach."

It seemed as though the Cubs had lucked into a franchise pitcher when they selected him second, after Drew Hall, in the 1984 draft. After Maddux won the 1992 Cy Young with 20 wins and a top-three ERA of 2.18, the Cubs refused to meet his contract demands, and he signed as a free agent with the team that would go to the postseason all eleven years he was in uniform.

Pinpoint control would become his legacy. In 1998, you had a better chance of homering off Pedro Martinez than you did drawing a walk off Maddux, who allowed only 14 unintentional bases on balls all season. In 2000, he went to 2–0 on a batter only 11 times in 249 innings. In 2001, he set a National League record by going 72 1/3 innings between walks. He'd come a long way from his first full year in Chicago, when he walked 74 on his way to a record of 6–14 with an ERA of 5.61. "Now," says Luis Gonzalez, "he's Picasso. He paints whatever he wants whenever he wants."

Back with the Cubs in 2004, Maddux duplicated his 2003 season, in which he went 16–11 but for the first time since his initial stay with Chicago missed the postseason. It was his record 17th consecutive year with at least 15 wins, a run that included seasons of 19–2 and 19–4 in the mid-to-late '90s. His 1994 and '95 seasons were perhaps his most remarkable, in that the league ERA was around 4.25 each year while his was around 1.60. His stunning combination of brains and savvy continues to outwit the brawny sluggers of the modern era.

BOXSCORE

Houston Astros 8, Chicago Cubs 7

Game Played on Tuesday, September 2, 1986 (Day) at Wrigley Field

Houston	0	1	0	0	0	2	0	0	1	0	0	0	0	0	3	1	—	8	18	1
Chicago	0	0	1	0	0	0	2	0	1	0	0	0	0	0	3	0	—	7	12	0

Game suspended at the end of the 14th inning with the score HOU 4 CHI 4; completed 9-3-1986.

BATTING

Houston Astros

	AB	R	H	RBI	BB	K	PO	A
Lopes cf	5	1	2	0	0	0	4	0
Kerfeld p	0	0	0	0	0	0	0	0
Andersen p	0	0	0	0	0	0	0	0
Smith p	0	0	0	0	0	0	0	0
Keough p	2	0	0	0	0	1	0	0
Knepper p	0	0	0	0	0	0	0	1
Doran ph-2b	2	0	0	0	0	0	1	1
Pankovits 2b	6	1	1	0	2	0	4	2
Solano p	0	0	0	0	0	0	0	0
Darwin p	1	0	0	0	0	1	0	0
Garner 3b	3	0	1	0	0	0	0	1
Walling ph-3b	5	1	2	1	0	0	1	0
Davis 1b	4	1	2	1	1	1	8	0
Driessen 1b	3	1	2	1	0	0	7	0
Bass rf	8	1	3	1	0	1	3	0
Cruz lf	8	0	1	1	0	1	6	0
Ashby c	5	1	2	1	0	1	10	0
Wine c	3	0	1	0	0	1	4	3
Thon ss	2	0	0	0	1	1	1	4
Reynolds ph-ss	5	0	0	0	0	1	1	4
Ryan p	3	0	0	1	0	1	0	2
Lopez p	0	0	0	0	0	0	0	0
Puhl ph	1	0	0	0	0	0	0	0
Walker cf	0	0	0	0	0	0	1	0
Gainey cf	0	0	0	0	0	0	1	0
Hatcher ph-cf	4	1	1	1	0	1	4	0
Totals	**70**	**8**	**18**	**8**	**4**	**11**	**54**	**18**

FIELDING
E: Pankovits (3)

BATTING
2B: Cruz (16, off Moyer); Lopes (10, off Moyer); Bass (24, off Moyer); Walling (18, off Smith)
HR: Davis (27, 16th inning off Moyer, 0 on, 0 out); Hatcher (4, 18th inning off Maddux, 0 on, 1 out)

BASERUNNING
SB: Lopes (24, 2nd base off Smith/J. Davis)

Chicago Cubs

	AB	R	H	RBI	BB	K	PO	A
Martinez cf	4	0	0	0	0	1	2	0
Smith p	0	0	0	0	0	0	0	0
Dayett rf	5	0	1	0	0	1	0	0
Sandberg 2b	7	1	1	0	1	0	2	8
Mumphrey lf-cf	4	0	1	0	0	1	0	0
Dernier pr-cf	5	2	1	0	0	0	2	0
Moreland rf-1b	6	2	2	3	2	0	11	1
Durham 1b	3	1	1	2	1	1	13	0
Walker pr	0	0	0	0	0	0	0	0
DiPino p	0	0	0	0	0	0	0	0
Sutcliffe ph	0	0	0	0	0	0	0	0
Sanderson pr	0	0	0	0	0	0	0	0
Trillo pr-3b	3	0	0	0	0	1	1	3
J. Davis c	6	0	1	1	1	1	11	0
Maddux pr-p	0	0	0	0	0	0	0	0
Speier 3b	3	1	2	1	2	0	2	2
Hoffman p	0	0	0	0	0	0	0	0
Matthews ph-lf	3	0	1	0	0	1	1	0
Dunston ss	7	0	1	0	1	2	6	8
Moyer p	1	0	0	0	0	1	0	1
Francona ph	1	0	0	0	0	0	0	0
R. Davis p	0	0	0	0	0	0	0	0
Bosley ph-lf	4	0	0	0	2	1	0	0
Trout p	0	0	0	0	0	0	0	0
Cey ph	0	0	0	0	1	0	0	0
Gumpert p	0	0	0	0	0	0	0	0
Martin ph-c	1	0	0	0	0	0	1	0
Totals	**63**	**7**	**12**	**7**	**9**	**12**	**54**	**23**

FIELDING
DP: 2

BATTING
2B: Moreland (25, off Ryan); Dernier (13, off Solano)
HR: Speier (6, 3rd inning off Ryan, 0 on, 0 out); Durham (15, 7th inning off Ryan, 1 on, 1 out); Moreland (9, 17th inning off Solano, 2 on, 0 out)
SH: Sandberg (4, off Smith)
SF: J. Davis (7, off Smith)
HBP: Sutcliffe (1, by Keough)
IBB: Durham (14, by Andersen); Speier 2 (3, by Smith, by Keough); Moreland (10, by Knepper)

BASERUNNING
SB: Speier (2, 2nd base off Ryan/Ashby); Dernier (21, 2nd base off Andersen/Ashby); Walker (1, 2nd base off Smith/Ashby)
CS: Sandberg (9,2nd base by Keough/Wine).

PITCHING

Houston Astros

	IP	H	HR	R	ER	BB	K
Ryan	7	4	2	3	3	1	5
Lopez	1	0	0	0	0	0	1
Kerfeld	0	1	0	1	1	0	0
Andersen	0.1	0	0	0	0	1	1
Smith	0.2	0	0	0	0	0	1
Keough	5	1	0	0	0	3	4
Knepper	2	2	0	0	0	2	0
Solano	0.1	3	1	3	3	1	0
Darwin W(2–1)	1.2	1	0	0	0	0	1
Totals	**18.01**	**2**	**3**	**7**	**7**	**9**	**12**

Chicago Cubs

	IP	H	HR	R	ER	BB	K
Moyer	6	9	1	3	3	2	2
R. Davis	2	1	0	0	0	0	0
Smith	1	2	0	1	1	1	1
DiPino	2	0	0	0	0	1	3
Hoffman	3	1	0	0	0	0	1
Trout	2	1	0	0	0	0	1
Gumpert	1	3	0	3	3	1	1
Maddux L(0–1)	1	1	1	1	1	0	1
Totals	**18**	**18**	**2**	**8**	**8**	**4**	**11**

BK: Moyer (2)
HBP: Keough (2, Sutcliffe)
IBB: Andersen (8, Durham); Smith (3, Speier); Keough (3, Speier); Knepper (12, Moreland)
Umpires: Joe West, John McSherry, Bill Williams, Frank Pulli
Time of Game: 5:14   Attendance: 10,501

I debuted September 3, but, officially, the game was in the book as a game on September 2. They had played 14 innings on September 2, but with no lights at Wrigley, they called it because of darkness, suspending it until the next afternoon. I came in as part of a double switch to pinch-run for Jody Davis. Yep, my big league debut was as a pinch-runner. And when we didn't score in the 17th, there I was pitching instead of running. I got a couple of outs but then gave up a home run into the basket to Billy Hatcher. We lost in 18 innings, and I was the guy that got the loss, after all that.

I had actually arrived a couple days before, just ahead of Rafael Palmeiro. The one wacky thing that happened was that first day, coming from my hotel in downtown Chicago, I had gotten in the cab and we got stuck waiting for the drawbridge. Ten, fifteen minutes, and all I could think of was I was going to be late for my first day in the big leagues. Ten, fifteen minutes felt like an hour. I didn't even know Chicago had a drawbridge, and I had no way of knowing how long it would take before we'd get moving again. Meter's running, you know.

Also on September 3, 1986
The Cubs and Astros use a record 53 players in completing their suspended game from the day before.

AUTHOR'S NOTE: Eighteen years later, the Cubs and Astros would go down to the wire for the 2004 wild card, with the Astros winning out on the season's penultimate day. The Astros' manager, Phil Garner, was also in the 18-inning game, as the Houston third baseman.

Joe Magrane

Born: July 2, 1964
Debut: April 25, 1987

The resident clotheshorse of the Major League broadcasting circuit, Magrane's affinity for fancy threads once made him the victim of a terrific practical joke. One season, his teammates convinced him he'd be involved in a GQ photo spread and told him to dress in his Sunday best and meet a photographer in a public park. For an hour, Magrane sweated his way through his clothes, posing with one forced smile after another only to eventually be told the whole thing was a sham.

He was stylin' for real in his rookie season, however. The 1987 Cardinals reached the World Series, with Magrane's nine wins helping to make it so. He was on the mound in the decisive World Series Game Seven, pitching well but losing to Frank Viola and the Twins, 4–2.

He would reassert himself in 1988, leading the league with a 2.18 ERA and then winning 18 games in '89.

Elbow surgery derailed him by the early '90s, however, and just when he was getting back on his feet, he tumbled off of them, breaking his right heel in 1993. Magrane was trying to remove a wayward playing card from the ceiling of his foyer, left there by a magician he had hired for a New Year's Eve party. He fell from the ladder, cracking a bone. "All for the seven of clubs," he would later sigh.

Magrane's popularity has soared since he became one of the television voices of the Tampa Bay Devil Rays and, as Yankees fan Billy Crystal would say, "He looks mah-velous."

I was in Omaha, Nebraska, and we had just gotten in from Louisville. I got a call from my manager, Mike Jorgensen, and he says, "I just wanted to let you know you're going to be pitching Saturday." I told him, "Yeah, I already knew that." Then he says, "Yeah, but you're going to be doing it at Shea Stadium." And that made my heart skip a beat—the realization of a dream I'd had my entire life. I hung up and dialed my folks, who were elated. We were living in Morehead, Kentucky, 60 miles east of Lexington . . . I think they let everyone in that whole region know . . . and since there weren't a lot of satellite dishes, they had to find a place in Grayson, Kentucky, about 30 miles away, to watch the game.

In Shea Stadium, the bullpens are very close to the crowd . . . There were several Mets fans there, about 15 feet away from me . . . and I quickly came

BOXSCORE

St. Louis Cardinals 3, New York Mets 2

Game Played on Saturday, April 25, 1987 (Day) at Shea Stadium

St. Louis	0	1	0	0	0	2	0	0	—	3	9	1
New York	0	0	0	1	1	0	0	0	—	2	6	1

BATTING

St. Louis Cardinals	AB	R	H	RBI	BB	K	PO	A
Coleman lf	5	0	2	1	0	1	0	0
Smith ss	3	0	0	0	1	0	1	2
Pendleton 3b	3	0	1	0	1	1	2	1
Clark 1b	4	0	0	0	0	1	9	0
McGee cf	4	0	0	0	0	0	2	0
Lindeman rf	4	1	2	0	0	1	3	0
Horton p	0	0	0	0	0	0	0	1
Oquendo 2b	4	1	2	0	0	0	0	3
Pagnozzi c	4	1	2	1	0	0	9	1
Magrane p	2	0	0	0	0	0	0	1
Ford ph	1	0	0	0	0	0	0	0
Dawley p	0	0	0	0	0	0	0	0
Landrum rf	0	0	0	0	1	0	1	0
Total	34	3	9	2	3	4	27	9

FIELDING
DP: 1
E: Magrane (1)

BATTING
2B: Lindeman 2 (7, off Aguilera 2); Pagnozzi (1, off Aguilera)
IBB: Smith (1, by Myers)

BASERUNNING
SB: Coleman (15, 2nd base off Myers/Carter)
CS: Landrum (1, 2nd base by Sisk/Carter)

New York Mets	AB	R	H	RBI	BB	K	PO	A
Wilson cf	3	0	0	0	0	1	3	0
Teufel 2b	4	1	1	0	0	2	1	7
Hernandez 1b	4	0	1	0	0	3	13	0
Carter c	3	0	0	1	0	0	4	1
Strawberry rf	4	0	1	0	0	1	0	0
McReynolds lf	4	1	1	0	0	1	1	0
Johnson 3b	2	0	1	0	1	0	1	2
Santana ss	3	0	0	0	0	1	4	6
Aguilera p	2	0	0	0	0	1	0	3
Myers p	0	0	0	0	0	0	0	0
Leach p	0	0	0	0	0	0	0	0
Mazzilli ph	1	0	1	0	0	0	0	0
Sisk p	0	0	0	0	0	0	0	0
Totals	30	2	6	1	1	10	27	19

FIELDING
DP: 2
E: Wilson (2)

BATTING
SH: Wilson (1, off Horton)
SF: Carter (2, off Magrane)

PITCHING

St. Louis Cardinals	IP	H	HR	R	ER	BB	K
Magrane W(1–0)	6	5	0	2	2	1	7
Dawley	1	0	0	0	0	0	1
Horton SV(4)	2	1	0	0	0	0	2
Totals	9	6	0	2	2	1	10
New York Mets	**IP**	**H**	**HR**	**R**	**ER**	**BB**	**K**
Aguilera L(1–1)	6.1	9	0	3	2	1	1
Myers	0.1	0	0	0	0	1	1
Leach	1.1	0	0	0	0	0	1
Sisk	1	0	0	0	0	1	1
Totals	9	9	0	3	2	3	4

IBB: Myers (1,Smith)
Umpires: John Kibler, Bruce Froemming, Jim Quick, Charlie Williams
Time of Game: 2:39   Attendance: 34,640

to realize as I was warming up, Mets fans apparently have a very poor understanding of human anatomy. Plus, with the New York dialect mixed in, it sure was apparent I wasn't pitching in Louisville or Omaha.

Anyway, right when I was going out there to the bullpen, I put a lot of Icy Hot on my arm and shoulder, what with it being chilly, being the last week in April on the East Coast. I was warming up out there in the bullpen, trying to block out these guys that are yelling at me, and right before I'm ready to head into the dugout, I figured I may as well hit the bathroom. Well, apparently, somehow I had gotten some of that Icy Hot on my hand, and, as a result, in that bullpen bathroom, it got transferred to a place I care a lot more about. So I'm on national TV in my debut, trying to make pitches, trying to stay cool, and I'm on fire down there. And I don't want to make a big deal about it, because I know my folks are back home in Kentucky watching, along with all their friends and my friends.

Also on April 25, 1987
Future lead FOX broadcaster Joe Buck celebrates his 18th birthday by traveling with his dad, Jack, to Shea Stadium. As his dad announces the first four innings on KMOX, young Joe chills in the back of the broadcast booth, chatting with the radio engineer. As the top of the fifth begins, he hears his dad say, ". . . And now, for the fifth inning, my son, the birthday boy, Joe Buck." Scrambling to the microphone in a panic, Joe too makes his big league debut. The first at bat of his Emmy-award winning career would be Magrane grounding out to short.

AUTHOR'S NOTE: Magrane occasionally works as a Saturday Game of the Week analyst for FOX, working the backup game behind Buck and Tim McCarver.

Edgar Martinez
Born: January 2, 1963
Debut: September 12, 1987

In a glorious 18-year career in Seattle, Edgar Martinez had the misfortune of never being the best player on his own team. He was overshadowed at first by Ken Griffey Jr., then later boxed out by Alex Rodriguez and, finally, Ichiro Suzuki, who's so popular the Mariners named a ballpark menu item after him (the Ichi-roll, available down the left field line at Safeco Field; it's got a spicy tuna kick).

Though there was never an Edgar-rilled cheese sandwich or a Mallo-Mar-tinez, there was, by the end of his career, an outpouring of love for this gentlemanly warrior. One standing ovation after another greeted his every at bat during the Mariners' final 2004 home stand. On a postcard-perfect Saturday night, a 90-minute postgame ceremony paid tribute to his 2,247 big league hits. Commissioner Bud Selig announced the creation of the Edgar Martinez Award to honor the league's best DH each subsequent season. City politicians unveiled the street sign for what would now be known as Edgar Martinez Drive, just outside the stadium, and how appropriate to make it a "drive" and not a street or avenue—of those 2,247 hits, teammates surmised 2,000 of 'em were whistling liners.

If, indeed, little things mean a lot, maybe that explains the wonder of Martinez's career: A man who personally weighed his own bats because he doesn't trust the markings from the factory. A man who engaged in daily two-hour leg exercises, not to mention daily 90-minute eye exercises. Batting practice with a weighted donut on his bat, a ritual borrowed from Rickey Henderson. To maintain his hand-eye coordination, he attempted to bunt tennis balls blasted from a machine at 150 mph. An allowance of a mere two days off in between the final out of each season and the first day of rigorous off-season training—and 24 of those 48 hours were spent traveling back from Seattle to Puerto Rico!

Two quotes from famous teammates are especially illuminating. "Edgar understands his swing more than any other hitter in baseball," said Jay Buhner. "It's perfect, but still, he's always trying to get even more out of it." And Alex Rodriguez once said, "He is the most grossly underappreciated player in baseball history."

With the bulk of Martinez's career spent as a designated hitter, Hall of Fame voters may bear out A-Rod's theory. Like the saga of Harold Baines, Edgar Martinez's career is a Cooperstown litmus test. Martinez was a

BOXSCORE

Seattle Mariners 12, Chicago White Sox 2
Game Played on Saturday, September 12, 1987 (Night) at Kingdome

Chicago	1	0	0	0	0	0	1	0	0	—	2	6	0
Seattle	3	3	1	4	0	0	1	0	x	—	12	18	0

BATTING

Chicago White Sox	AB	R	H	RBI	BB	K	PO	A
Guillen ss	2	0	0	0	0	0	2	3
Keedy ss	2	0	0	0	0	0	1	2
Redus lf	3	1	1	0	1	0	2	0
Baines dh	3	0	1	1	1	0	0	0
Calderon rf	4	1	1	1	0	0	2	0
Walker 1b	4	0	1	0	0	0	9	0
Hassey c	4	0	1	0	0	0	2	0
Hill 2b	4	0	0	0	0	0	2	6
Boston cf	3	0	0	0	0	1	4	0
Lyons 3b	3	0	1	0	0	1	0	1
Long p	0	0	0	0	0	0	0	0
Nielsen p	0	0	0	0	0	0	0	0
Winn p	0	0	0	0	0	0	0	0
James p	0	0	0	0	0	0	0	0
Searage p	0	0	0	0	0	0	0	0
Totals	32	2	6	2	2	2	24	12

FIELDING
DP: 4

BATTING
2B: Redus (23, off Bankhead); Baines (19, off Bankhead)
HR: Calderon (24, 7th inning off Bankhead, 0 on, 0 out).

Seattle Mariners	AB	R	H	RBI	BB	K	PO	A
Brantley cf	3	1	1	1	0	0	2	0
Weaver cf	1	0	0	0	0	1	1	0
P. Bradley lf	4	1	2	2	1	1	6	0
Kingery rf	5	2	2	0	0	0	6	0
Davis 1b	4	2	3	3	1	0	6	1
Phelps dh	4	2	3	3	0	0	0	0
Hengel ph-dh	1	0	0	0	0	0	0	0
Presley 3b	3	1	2	0	1	0	1	1
Martinez pr-3b	1	0	0	0	0	0	0	0
Valle c	3	0	1	1	0	0	2	0
Quinones ss	3	0	1	0	0	0	1	1
Diaz ss	1	1	1	0	0	0	1	0
Reynolds 2b	4	2	2	1	0	0	0	2
Bankhead p	0	0	0	0	0	0	1	0
Powell p	0	0	0	0	0	0	0	0
Nunez p	0	0	0	0	0	0	0	0
Totals	37	12	18	11	3	2	27	5

FIELDING
DP: 1

BATTING
2B: P. Bradley (35, off Long); Phelps (12, off Nielsen); Kingery (22, off Nielsen)
3B: Diaz (1, off James)
HR: Davis (23, 1st inning off Long, 1 on, 2 out); Phelps (25, 4th inning off Nielsen, 1 on, 0 out)
SF: Brantley (3, off Nielsen)
HBP: Valle (3, by Winn)

BASERUNNING
SB: Brantley (10, 2nd base off Long/Hassey); Reynolds 3 (52, 2nd base off Long/Hassey, 2nd base off Nielsen/Hassey, 3rd base off Nielsen/Hassey)

PITCHING

Chicago White Sox	IP	H	HR	R	ER	BB	K
Long L(8–8)	1.1	7	1	5	5	0	1
Nielsen	1.2	7	1	6	6	1	0
Winn	3	1	0	0	0	2	0
James	1	2	0	1	1	0	1
Searage	1	1	0	0	0	0	0
Totals	8	18	2	12	12	3	2
Seattle Mariners	**IP**	**H**	**HR**	**R**	**ER**	**BB**	**K**
Bankhead W(9–8)	7	5	1	2	2	0	1
Powell	0.2	1	0	0	0	2	1
Nunez	1.1	0	0	0	0	0	0
Totals	9.0	6	1	2	2	2	2

WP: Nielsen (2)
HBP: Winn (6,Valle)
Umpires: Tim Welke, Larry Young, Joe Brinkman, Mike Reilly
Time of Game: 2:32   Attendance: 10,193

seven-time All-Star, two-time batting champ, and had the unwavering respect of his peers. Will it be enough to get him enshrined?

My first action was as a pinch runner of all things . . . I remember my first at bat more. I hit a fly ball to the left side of the field, way foul, but I was running like it was fair, running hard. The first base coach, Frank Howard, kept yelling, "Edgar! Edgar! Stop! It's foul!" I guess I couldn't hear him.

Mario Diaz and I had just come up from Triple-A Calgary. We had lost in the finals, but we'd had a great year, led all of Triple-A in wins. Bill Plummer, our manager, told me . . . We actually knew right before that last game. We lost. But it was tough to be too sad, because of where I knew I was going the next day.

I was kind of on my own . . . I called my parents and grandparents, and they were very excited, but there was no way they could get from Puerto Rico to Seattle. They never saw me play in the majors until the next year. I worked hard that off-season to make sure I'd be back in Seattle come the spring, so they could make that trip.

Also on September 12, 1987
Vince Coleman reaches triple digits in steals for the third consecutive season as the Cardinals drub the Mets 8–1 at Shea Stadium.

AUTHOR'S NOTE: Edgar Martinez, before his hamstring and knee issues, could actually run a little bit himself. In 1992, he had 14 steals, and he notched a pair of minor league seasons that also produced double-digit totals. However, while Coleman had a three-year total of 326 as his high-water mark, the best Edgar could do over a stretch of three years was 20. His final three years, he had only two. However, his last one was a doozy. It came against the White Sox's Mark Buehrle, who allows, on average, just four stolen bases a year.

Pedro Martinez
Born: October 25, 1971
Debut: September 24, 1992

He has won the Cy Young three times and finished second twice more. Five times he led his league in ERA, and in a couple of those seasons it wasn't even close. (In 1999, when he won the AL pitching Triple Crown, he could have allowed 32 earned runs in an inning of work and still laid claim to the title.) *En Espanol, Pedro Martinez es el primero lanzador de la Republica Dominican.* From the mid '90s through the mid '00s, no other right-hander in baseball put up such staggering numbers.

His ability to pitch at a high level through injuries began in 1997, when he went 17–8 for the Dodgers with a league-best 1.90 ERA, 305 strikeouts, and a major-league-best 13 complete games, all with a strained right thumb. But the Dodgers thought he was too skinny and therefore not durable enough to keep it up, so they peddled him to Montreal (infamously) for Delino DeShields. During his stay with the Expos, Martinez developed a reputation as a headhunter. In his 23 starts in 1994, he was ejected 12 times and participated in three bench-clearing brawls.

Before the 1998 season, he was dealt to the Red Sox to replace the departed Roger Clemens. The Rocket would win the Cy Young that year, but Pedro won Red Sox fans' allegiance, winning 19 and helping the Sox to a wild card berth. In 1999, Martinez stood as the counterpoint to all the batting pyrotechnics, going 23–4 with a 2.07 ERA. In that year's All-Star Game, he struck out five of the six batters he faced and was named the game's MVP. A one-hit, 17-strikeout performance at Yankee Stadium the following month cemented his stature as an all-time Boston great.

He continued to baffle AL hitters, going 59–17 between 2000 and 2003 while turning in an ERA less than half the league average. In the 2003 ALCS, he scrapped with the Yankees, notably tossing popular Yankee bench coach Don Zimmer to the ground in one of the most memorable incidents of that storied rivalry. Following the Red Sox 2004 World Series championship, he bolted via free agency for the Yankees' crosstown rivals at Shea Stadium. Through 2004, he had a major league best winning percentage of .705, and, at 33, insisted his finest work was still in front of him.

His 1999 through 2003 was arguably the most dominant run of pitching in any era. Five consecutive seasons with a sub-2.40 ERA is remarkable no matter when you place it on the baseball timeline. Since 1920, only Pedro had a streak like that—not Koufax, Newhouser, Maddux, or Clemens.

BOXSCORE

Cincinnati Reds 8, Los Angeles Dodgers 4

Game Played on Thursday, September 24, 1992 (Night) at Dodger Stadium

Cincinnati	0	0	0	0	2	0	6	0	0	—	8	15	1
Los Angeles	0	0	1	3	0	0	0	0	0	—	4	9	0

BATTING

Cincinnati Reds	AB	R	H	RBI	BB	K	PO	A
Sanders cf-lf	3	1	0	0	2	0	2	0
Greene 3b	4	1	1	3	0	0	1	2
Larkin ss	5	1	2	1	0	1	3	2
Costo 1b	5	0	2	0	0	1	9	0
Oliver c	2	0	0	0	0	0	3	1
Wilson c	2	1	2	0	1	0	3	0
Berroa lf	2	1	2	0	1	0	1	0
Roberts ph	1	1	1	2	0	0	0	0
Charlton p	1	0	0	0	0	0	0	0
O'Neill rf	4	0	1	1	1	0	1	0
Benavides 2b	2	1	1	1	0	0	1	2
Branson ph-2b	3	0	1	0	0	0	1	2
Ayala p	1	0	0	0	0	0	0	1
Hernandez ph	1	0	1	0	0	0	0	0
Henry p	0	0	0	0	0	0	0	0
Bolton p	0	0	0	0	0	0	0	0
Morris ph	1	0	1	0	0	0	0	0
Hammond pr	0	1	0	0	0	0	0	0
Martinez ph-cf	2	0	0	0	0	0	2	0
Totals	**39**	**8**	**15**	**8**	**5**	**2**	**27**	**10**

FIELDING

DP: 2

E: Oliver (7)

BATTING

2B: Berroa (1, off Ojeda); Morris (21, off McDowell)

3B: Greene (2, off McDowell); Roberts (5, off Gott)

SF: Greene (1, off Ojeda)

Los Angeles Dodgers	AB	R	H	RBI	BB	K	PO	A
Offerman ss	4	1	1	1	1	0	3	3
Butler cf	4	0	2	0	1	0	3	0
Harris 2b	3	0	1	0	0	1	1	3
Sharperson ph-2b	2	0	0	0	0	0	0	1
Karros 1b	3	1	0	0	1	2	9	2
Piazza c	4	0	1	0	0	0	4	0
Webster rf	3	0	1	0	0	0	5	0
Rodriguez lf	2	1	1	1	1	0	2	1
Hernandez ph	1	0	0	0	0	1	0	0
Goodwin lf	0	0	0	0	0	0	0	0
Hansen 3b	2	1	0	0	1	0	0	0
Anderson ph	1	0	1	0	0	0	0	0
Ojeda p	2	0	1	1	0	1	0	0
Kip Gross p	0	0	0	0	0	0	0	0
Scioscia ph	0	0	0	0	0	0	0	0
Young pr	0	0	0	0	0	0	0	0
McDowell p	0	0	0	0	0	0	0	0
Gott p	0	0	0	0	0	0	0	0
Wilson p	0	0	0	0	0	0	0	0
P. Martinez p	0	0	0	0	0	0	0	0
Bournigal ph	1	0	0	0	0	1	0	0
Totals	**32**	**4**	**9**	**3**	**5**	**6**	**27**	**10**

FIELDING

DP: 2

BATTING

2B: Rodriguez (6, off Ayala); Offerman (20, off Ayala)

SH: Webster (7, off Ayala)

HBP: Scioscia (1, by Henry)

IBB: Hansen (2, by Ayala)

BASERUNNING

CS: Butler (19, 2nd base by Ayala/Oliver)

PITCHING

Cincinnati Reds	IP	H	HR	R	ER	BB	K
Ayala	4	6	0	4	3	4	3
Henry	1.1	1	0	0	0	1	1
Bolton W(3–3)	0.2	0	0	0	0	0	0
Charlton SV(26)	3	2	0	0	0	0	2
Totals	**9**	**9**	**0**	**4**	**3**	**5**	**6**

Los Angeles Dodgers	IP	H	HR	R	ER	BB	K
Ojeda	5.2	7	0	2	2	2	1
Kip Gross	0.1	0	0	0	0	0	0
McDowell L(6–10)	0	3	0	4	4	1	0
Gott	0.1	3	0	2	2	1	0
Wilson	0.2	0	0	0	0	0	0
P. Martinez	2	2	0	0	0	1	1
Totals	**9**	**15**	**0**	**8**	**8**	**5**	**2**

WP: Charlton (8), Ojeda (3), Gott (9)

HBP: Henry (1, Scioscia)

IBB: Ayala (2, Hansen)

Umpires: Doug Harvey, Jerry Crawford, Gerry Davis, Charlie Williams

Time of Game: 3:19   Attendance: 18,707

Thirty games out of first place, okay? The Dodgers are thirty games out, and I sit around for thirteen days before I get in to pitch. Thirteen! And I almost didn't get in then! Tommy Lasorda wanted John Candelaria to warm up, but he didn't want to do it. He didn't get up, so I did, while he was arguing with our bullpen coach. And Tommy calls down and says, "Who is that warming up?" And he's told it's Ramon's little brother. I guess he had no choice but to put me in, and I pitched well. Bill Russell kept me in the minor leagues. I pitched for him at Albuquerque, and I pitched well, but he didn't like me. Never gave me a good recommendation to Tommy or anybody. Bill Russell screwed me.

I got in, and I gave up a hit to Barry Larkin but pitched real good otherwise. I wish I had a good memory of my big league debut, but I don't. I hated that whole experience. Hated the Dodgers for how they treated me. They screwed with me, but I got the last laugh, huh?

Also on September 24, 1992
The Mets and Cardinals play thirteen scoreless innings as New York's Bret Saberhagen pitches eight five-hit innings. Eventually, rookie Jeff Kent's three-run homer in the top of the 14th is trumped by the Cardinals' four-run bottom of the inning.

AUTHOR'S NOTE: Martinez saw, up close, the Cardinals' inability to score in "regulation" in the World Series twelve years later. Six weeks after the Series, he would sign with the Mets (who he could only hope had now learned to hold three-run 14th-inning leads).

Don Mattingly
Born: April 20, 1961
Debut: September 8, 1982

Evansville, Indiana, native Don Mattingly had hit plenty in the Yankees minor league system, but there were always concerns about his lack of power and what position suited him best. He languished as a part-timer in 1983 but took off as a regular in 1984, hitting 23 home runs as the Yanks' everyday first baseman. Displaying a remarkable ability to smash base hits with two strikes on him, the lefty won the AL batting title, hitting .343—the highest batting average by a Yankee lefty since Lou Gehrig in 1937.

From 1984 through '89, no player in the big leagues drove in more runs, and only his mustachioed rival Wade Boggs had more hits. In 1985, he was named AL MVP as his home run total ballooned to 35, and he littered the league with a career-best 145 RBI. The following year he set a new franchise standard for doubles (53) while hitting .352, and in '87 he crushed a record six grand slams—the first six of his career. A tear in mid-July saw him homer in a record-tying eight consecutive games, which pretty much ended the concerns about his supposed lack of power.

As it turned out, he was also a slick fielder, retiring with a career fielding percentage of .996, tied for the all-time lead. He was a nine-time Gold Glover—nine times in a stretch of ten years, interrupted only by Mark Mc-Gwire. However, back problems began to slow "Donnie Baseball" in the early '90s, finally forcing his career to end after the Yankees' 1995 postseason series against Seattle. The Yankees imported Tino Martinez from that same Seattle team to replace him, although Martinez refused to wear his customary uniform number 23, citing how proudly and successfully Mattingly had worn it in New York.

Mattingly's Yankee career is best summed up as that of a great player at a poor time in his team's history. He joined the Yankees just after their 1970s dynasty had ended and retired just as their 1990s dynasty was beginning. To think that Clay Bellinger and Homer Bush each appeared in more postseason games than Mattingly is a depressing exercise for Mattingly's many fans. He is now employed as the Yankees hitting coach and remains just as humble and hard-working as he was back in Triple-A, where the onetime 19th-round draft pick was supposed to have maxed out.

I pinch-ran in my big league debut—for Ken Griffey Sr . . . Was I ever that fast? I had come up and sat for a day or two. It was against Baltimore, and I

BOXSCORE

New York Yankees 10, Baltimore Orioles 5
Game Played on Wednesday, September 8, 1982 (Night) at Yankee Stadium

Baltimore	0	0	0	0	0	0	1	1	3	—	5	6	0
New York	1	1	4	0	4	0	0	0	x	—	10	10	2

BATTING

Baltimore Orioles	AB	R	H	RBI	BB	K	PO	A
Bumbry cf	4	0	1	1	0	1	2	0
Rayford c	0	1	0	0	1	0	0	0
Gulliver 3b	3	0	0	0	1	0	2	4
Sakata ph	1	0	0	0	0	1	0	0
Singleton dh	4	1	2	0	1	1	0	0
Murray 1b	4	2	1	3	1	1	9	1
Lowenstein lf	4	0	1	0	0	0	0	0
Roenicke ph	1	0	0	0	0	1	0	0
Ripken ss	3	1	1	1	0	1	1	2
Dwyer rf	3	0	0	0	1	1	4	0
Nolan c	3	0	0	0	0	0	2	0
Shelby cf	1	0	0	0	0	0	2	0
Dauer 2b	2	0	0	0	2	0	1	1
Palmer p	0	0	0	0	0	0	0	0
Grimsley p	0	0	0	0	0	0	0	0
Stanhouse p	0	0	0	0	0	0	1	0
Flinn p	0	0	0	0	0	0	0	0
Totals	**33**	**5**	**6**	**5**	**7**	**7**	**24**	**8**

FIELDING
DP: 1

BATTING
2B: Ripken (29, off Howell); Lowenstein (11, off Howell); Singleton (23, off LaRoche).
HR: Murray (27, 9th inning off LaRoche, 2 on, 2 out).
SF: Ripken (5, off Howell)

New York Yankees	AB	R	H	RBI	BB	K	PO	A
Randolph 2b	4	0	2	1	1	0	3	2
Mumphrey cf	4	2	1	1	1	0	6	0
Griffey rf	5	2	2	3	0	0	2	0
Mattingly lf	0	0	0	0	0	0	0	0
Winfield lf	4	1	1	1	0	1	1	0
Patterson lf-rf	1	0	0	0	0	0	0	0
Gamble dh	2	1	0	0	2	1	0	0
Nettles 3b	4	1	1	1	0	0	0	1
Evans 3b	0	0	0	0	0	0	0	0
Smalley ss	1	2	1	1	2	0	1	0
Robertson ss	1	0	0	0	0	0	0	0
Mayberry 1b	3	0	1	1	0	0	6	1
Wynegar c	2	1	1	1	1	0	7	0
Howell p	0	0	0	0	0	0	0	0
LaRoche p	0	0	0	0	0	0	0	0
Totals	**31**	**10**	**10**	**10**	**7**	**2**	**27**	**4**

FIELDING
E: Nettles 2 (19)

BATTING
2B: Griffey (18, off Grimsley); Nettles (10, off Grimsley)
HR: Mumphrey (6, 1st inning off Palmer, 0 on, 1 out); Smalley (16, 2nd inning off Palmer, 0 on, 2 out); Griffey (12, 3rd inning off Palmer, 2 on, 1 out); Winfield (30, 3rd inning off Grimsley, 0 on, 1 out)
SH: Wynegar (7, off Grimsley)
SF: Mayberry (2, off Grimsley)
IBB: Randolph (3, by Grimsley); Smalley (7, by Grimsley)

PITCHING

Baltimore Orioles	IP	H	HR	R	ER	BB	K
Palmer L(13–4)	2.1	3	3	5	5	2	0
Grimsley	2.1	4	1	5	5	4	1
Stanhouse	2.1	2	0	0	0	1	1
Flinn	1	1	0	0	0	0	0
Totals	**8**	**10**	**4**	**10**	**10**	**7**	**2**

New York Yankees	IP	H	HR	R	ER	BB	K
Howell W(1–1)	8	4	0	2	2	6	5
LaRoche	1	2	1	3	3	1	2
Totals	**9**	**6**	**1**	**5**	**5**	**7**	**7**

WP: Flinn (1), Howell (1)
IBB: Grimsley 2 (5, Randolph, Smalley)
Umpires: Dan Morrison, Dave Phillips, Nick Bremigan, Steve Palermo
Time of Game: 2:53   Attendance: 20,898

think that's why I didn't play right away. They were in that great race with Milwaukee, and with us scheduled to play both the Orioles and the Brewers, the whole integrity-of-the-game thing was in play . . . The young guys sat while the veterans played, even though we weren't in any contention or anything. For me to have gotten in, especially as a pinch runner—that game had to have been a blowout. That whole month of September I only had ten or 12 at bats.

I think I may have played a little first base in that game, but jeez, I can't even remember. It was great just being there, though . . . It was some great down-the-stretch style baseball, and even though I didn't play much, at least I had a real good seat for it.

Also on September 8, 1982
Dave Winfield's 30th home run of the season helps the Yankees end a ten-game Baltimore winning streak; Winfield becomes just the ninth player with 30 home runs in each league.

AUTHOR'S NOTE: Two years later, Mattingly and Winfield would engage in a down-to-the-wire batting title battle, with Mattingly going 4-for-5 in the Yankees' final game to edge his teammate, who went 1-for-4.

Kevin Millar
Born: September 24, 1971
Debut: April 11, 1998

Unlike many of his Red Sox teammates, Kevin Millar was never handed anything and has never taken a moment in the big leagues for granted. Having gone undrafted out of high school, the right-handed hitter battled his way through a small college program (Lamar University), still finding no takers. But he refused to let his baseball dreams die. He tattooed the words "Against all odds" on his left bicep and set out to change some minds. He latched on with the independent St. Paul Saints, the team run by Mike Veeck that's more famous for its nun-masseuses and ball-delivering pigs than for any actual players.

After a summer of solid work in the Northern League, Millar's enthusiasm and work ethic won out, and he landed a free agent contract with the Florida Marlins. He played four seasons in Miami, hitting .306 in 2002 with a team-high 41 doubles. He was about to take his skills overseas, but he got cold feet regarding international travel and the rigors of the Japanese Leagues. After a long, protracted fight, he was able to wiggle out of his contract with Chunichi and sign with the Boston Red Sox for 2003. His ebullience was infectious as he rallied Red Sox Nation with his down-home Texas edict to "cowboy up" in that magical '03 season. The video of his extremely bad karaoke version of "Born in the U.S.A." played at Fenway Park all year to "rally the troops" when necessary. On the field, he drove in a career high 96 runs, leading Boston into the postseason before the team eventually fell in Game Seven of the ALCS to the Yankees.

The following season (having cultivated a bizarre bearded look he characterized as "Amish porn star") he banged out a .297 batting average and cemented his stature as a Red Sox fan favorite, once again helping the Old Towne team into the playoffs and, this time, to their first World Series title since 1918.

Millar was the kind of "grinder" Sox fans could appreciate at first sight. The son of a former army medic, he and his dad grew up playing baseball and Wiffle ball for hours at a time. When Millar was 13, his dad took an entire summer off and installed vapor lights in the family backyard so their father-son Wiffle ball games could continue unabated after dark.

I was in spring training, sent down to the minor league camp, but all of a sudden, I was told to meet the team in Philadelphia. I got on the plane, but it

BOXSCORE

Pittsburgh Pirates 7, Florida Marlins 6
Game Played on Saturday, April 11, 1998 (Day) at Three Rivers Stadium

Florida	2	0	1	0	0	1	1	0	1	0	—	6	8	2
Pittsburgh	2	0	0	0	4	0	0	0	0	1	—	7	11	1

BATTING

Florida Marlins	AB	R	H	RBI	BB	K	PO	A
Floyd lf	5	1	2	0	0	1	2	0
Renteria ss	3	3	1	0	1	0	1	2
Counsell 2b	4	0	0	1	0	0	3	2
Sheffield rf	2	0	0	2	2	0	2	0
Kotsay cf	5	0	1	2	0	0	2	0
Lee 1b	4	1	1	0	1	2	5	1
Powell p	0	0	0	0	0	0	0	1
Johnson c	4	0	1	1	1	1	8	2
Booty 3b	2	0	1	0	0	1	0	1
Eisenreich ph	1	0	0	0	0	1	0	0
Sanchez p	0	0	0	0	0	0	0	0
Cangelosi ph	1	0	0	0	0	1	0	0
Alfonseca p	0	0	0	0	0	0	0	0
Heredia p	0	0	0	0	0	0	1	0
Jackson 1b	1	0	0	0	0	1	1	0
Hernandez p	2	0	0	0	0	1	1	1
Henriquez p	0	0	0	0	0	0	0	0
Millar ph-3b	2	1	1	0	1	0	1	1
Totals	36	6	8	6	6	9	27	11

FIELDING
DP: 1
E: Lee (1), Millar (1)
PB: Johnson (1)

BATTING
2B: Kotsay (3, off Cordova); Johnson (1, off Cordova)
3B: Renteria (1, off Peters)
SH: Counsell (1, off Cordova); Renteria (1, off Loiselle)
SF: Sheffield (1, off Cordova)

BASERUNNING
SB: Renteria (4, 3rd base off Cordova/Kendall)

Pittsburgh Pirates	AB	R	H	RBI	BB	K	PO	A
Womack 2b	3	0	0	0	2	1	1	3
Kendall c	4	1	1	0	1	0	10	0
Martin lf	5	2	1	0	0	1	1	0
Young 1b	5	2	3	4	0	0	10	0
Allensworth cf	4	1	2	0	0	1	4	0
Ward rf	4	0	2	2	1	0	1	0
Garcia 3b	4	0	1	0	1	0	0	4
Collier ss	3	0	0	0	0	2	2	2
Peters p	0	0	0	0	0	0	0	0
Strange ph	0	0	0	0	0	0	0	0
J. Martinez p	0	0	0	0	0	0	0	0
Loiselle p	0	0	0	0	0	0	0	1
Guillen ph	1	1	1	1	0	0	0	0
Cordova p	2	0	0	0	0	1	0	0
Polcovich ss	2	0	0	0	0	2	1	2
Totals	37	7	11	7	5	9	30	12

FIELDING
DP: 1
E: Kendall (2)

BATTING
2B: Young (3, off Hernandez); Ward (1, off Hernandez); Garcia (2, off Alfonseca)
3B: Ward (1, off Hernandez)
HR: Young (1, 1st inning off Hernandez, 1 on, 2 out); Guillen (3, 10th inning off Powell, 0 on, 0 out)
SH: Strange (1, off Alfonseca); Allensworth (2, off Powell)
IBB: Ward (1, by Powell)

BASERUNNING
SB: Womack 2 (4, 2nd base off Sanchez/Johnson, 3rd base off Sanchez/Johnson)

PITCHING

Florida Marlins	IP	H	HR	R	ER	BB	K
Hernandez	4.1	8	1	6	5	2	4
Henriquez	0.2	0	0	0	0	0	1
Sanchez	2	0	0	0	0	1	2
Alfonseca	0.1	1	0	0	0	0	1
Heredia	0.2	0	0	0	0	1	1
Powell L(0–2)	1	2	1	1	1	1	0
Totals	9	11	2	7	6	5	9

Pittsburgh Pirates	IP	H	HR	R	ER	BB	K
Cordova	5.2	5	0	4	3	4	4
Peters	1.1	1	0	1	1	0	1
J. Martinez	1	0	0	0	0	1	1
Loiselle W(1–0)	2	2	0	1	1	1	3
Totals	10	8	0	6	5	6	9

IBB: Powell (1,Ward)
Umpires: Steve Rippley, Gary Darling, Mike Winters, Larry Poncino
Time of Game: 3:05   Attendance: 19,920

---

still didn't seem quite real. I had been in the minors, the independent leagues, I had been through a lot, and I was 26 years old, not a kid anymore. But the main thing to me was the next day, not that day . . . because at two in the afternoon, I was able to go downstairs at the hotel, hail a cab, and tell the guy, "Take me to the Vet [Veteran's Stadium]." I had never been in a cab and said, "Take me to a big league ballpark."

I was on the bench for a while and was actually on-deck to pinch-hit a couple times but never got in until more than a week later—plenty of time to sit around and get nervous. Pinch-hit at bat in Pittsburgh, I finally got to the plate, against Francisco Cordova, who was pretty good then . . . I walked. I remember the game went extra innings, and I got a single of Rich Loiselle, who was closing then . . . I went out and played third base, too, but all I really remember is the walk and the hit.

I called my parents right after [and was] on the phone for hours with friends, too, talking until I was hoarse about basically one official at bat. But after all those years riding buses and all, it was amazing how good it felt to tell everyone I knew that I had gotten a hit in the big leagues. It's something I knew no one could ever take away.

Also on April 11, 1998
There is plenty of buzz about the new anti-impotence drug Viagra, as it appears on the market for the first time this week.

AUTHOR'S NOTE: Millar briefly lobbied for Viagra pitchman Rafael Palmeiro to join the Red Sox as a free agent when it appeared Manny Ramirez was being traded to the Rangers for Alex Rodriguez. Millar figured he'd move to left to replace Ramirez, and Palmeiro could come in and replace him as DH.

Paul Molitor
Born: August 22, 1956
Debut: April 7, 1978

St. Paul, Minnesota, native Paul Molitor carved out a Hall of Fame career in neighboring Wisconsin, spending his first 17 big league seasons as a crowd-pleasing Brewer. Nicknamed "The Ignitor," Molitor totaled 21 major league seasons in all, going to a pair of World Series, including the '82 classic against St. Louis, in which he notched a record five hits in a single game. (Vic Wertz would have also gotten five hits in 1954, had a fellow named Willie Mays not made a famous over-the-shoulder catch on a drive to center.)

The defining stat from Molitor's Milwaukee career: In his 17 years there, the Brewers had only four losing seasons. In the 21 years they've existed without him, they've had not a single *winning* season.

Among his many talents (beyond the home run pop and the .306 career batting average) was the ability to steal a catcher's signs. When Sal Bando played with "Molly," Bando would tell him to try and get on base and steal second as soon as possible, then Bando would take as many pitches as he could, giving Molitor time to decipher and relay the signs from his lead off the bag.

Always an intelligent base stealer as well as base runner, he had a streak of 36 steals without being caught . . . at the age of 39. At age 40, he pounded out 225 hits, a record for a 40-year-old by a cool couple dozen. His 3,000th career base hit was achieved that same season. Appropriately, it was a triple, proving again that the old man still had his legs.

A designated hitter late in his career (he hit .339 as a DH in 1994), Molitor was a kingpin of versatility early in his career, playing every position except pitcher and catcher a minimum of four times. Mostly, he was a third baseman, retiring with 3,319 career hits, eighth on the all-time list.

Molitor was elected to Cooperstown on his first ballot, going in with Dennis Eckersley. (In 1998, the last season for each man, Molitor laid down a game-winning bunt against Eckersley, and Eck had screamed at Molitor all the way off the field and then trashed him in the newspapers. On that day, Molitor celebrated his 42nd birthday, and Eckersley was 43. Two proven winners still kicking, even at the very end.)

Upon his retirement, Molitor took a one-year sabbatical, touring Europe, dabbling in broadcasting, and attending a couple dozen Bruce Spring-

BOXSCORE

Milwaukee Brewers 11, Baltimore Orioles 3

Game Played on Friday, April 7, 1978 (Day) at County Stadium

Baltimore	0	0	0	0	0	0	0	0	3	—	3	9	2
Milwaukee	0	3	1	0	2	0	4	1	x	—	11	9	0

BATTING

Baltimore Orioles	AB	R	H	RBI	BB	K	PO	A
Bumbry cf	4	0	0	0	0	1	1	0
Dauer dh	4	0	0	0	0	0	0	0
Murray 3b	4	1	2	1	0	0	0	2
May 1b	2	1	0	0	2	0	9	0
DeCinces 2b	4	1	3	0	0	0	3	2
Roenicke lf	4	0	2	1	0	0	1	0
Lopez rf	3	0	0	0	1	1	1	0
Dempsey c	3	0	1	1	0	0	8	2
Belanger ss	3	0	1	0	0	0	1	6
Crowley ph	1	0	0	0	0	0	0	0
Flanagan p	0	0	0	0	0	0	0	0
Stoddard p	0	0	0	0	0	0	0	0
T. Martinez p	0	0	0	0	0	0	0	1
Totals	32	3	9	3	3	2	24	13

FIELDING

DP: 1

E: May (1), Belanger (1)

BATTING

HR: Murray (1, 9th inning off Augustine, 0 on, 1 out)

SF: Dempsey (1, off Rodriguez)

Milwaukee Brewers	AB	R	H	RBI	BB	K	PO	A
Molitor ss	5	0	1	1	0	0	2	6
Money 3b	4	1	0	1	1	1	1	2
Bando dh	4	2	1	0	1	2	0	0
Hisle lf	3	2	2	2	0	0	1	0
Lezcano rf	2	2	1	4	2	0	3	0
Cooper 1b	4	0	1	1	0	1	9	0
Thomas cf	4	0	0	0	0	4	4	0
Sakata 2b	4	2	2	0	0	0	5	4
Etchebarren c	3	1	1	2	1	1	2	0
Augustine p	0	0	0	0	0	0	0	0
Rodriguez p	0	0	0	0	0	0	0	0
Totals	33	11	9	11	5	9	27	12

FIELDING

DP: 3

BATTING

2B: Etchebarren (1, off Flanagan); Hisle (1, off Flanagan)

HR: Hisle (1, 5th inning off Stoddard, 1 on, 2 out); Lezcano (1, 7th inning off Stoddard, 3 on, 1 out)

HBP: Hisle (1, by Stoddard)

BASERUNNING

CS: Cooper (1, 2nd base by Stoddard/Dempsey)

PITCHING

Baltimore Orioles	IP	H	HR	R	ER	BB	K
Flanagan L(0–1)	2.2	6	0	4	4	2	2
Stoddard	4.1	2	2	6	3	2	6
T. Martinez	1	1	0	1	1	1	1
Totals	8	9	2	11	8	5	9
Milwaukee Brewers	IP	H	HR	R	ER	BB	K
Augustine W(1–0)	8.1	9	1	3	3	3	2
Rodriguez	0.2	0	0	0	0	0	0
Totals	9.0	9	1	3	3	3	2

WP: Stoddard (1)

HBP: Stoddard (1, Hisle)

Umpires: Jerry Neudecker, George Maloney, Jim McKean, Greg Kosc

Time of Game: 2:18   Attendance: 47,824

steen concerts. He has since recaptured his glory days, so to speak, having dived back in as a coach, first with the Twins, then with Seattle.

Things were pretty straightforward for me. I had the opportunity to start the year for the Brewers as their shortstop in 1978, and the real twist, I guess, is when you wait all that time for your debut, you don't count on waiting through a long rain delay, but we did, and they eventually postponed the game. That was a long 24 hours, waiting for the real debut to be made. An extra day to get all anxious. That long wait the day of the rainout and the long, long wait until the weather cleared the next day, wow, that seemed like it took a month.

In fact, I had only made the team a few days before, called up from Triple-A when Robin Yount got hurt late in spring training. So I went from Triple-A to the majors in a real rush . . . Waiting that extra day was tough. But we got going soon enough, and my parents came down and saw that first game, when I singled in my second at bat against Mike Flanagan. It meant so much to my mom . . . She lived and died with things when I was young, had such a passion for the game, and it was unbelievable to have her there to see that.

Also on April 7, 1978

Ozzie Smith makes his major league debut, as a San Diego Padre.

AUTHOR'S NOTE: Molitor and Smith, two future Hall of Famers, would take the national stage against each other in the 1982 World Series. Molitor outhit the Wizard, 11–5, but the Wizard's Cardinals won the series over the Brewers, four games to three.

Justin Morneau
Born: May 15, 1981
Debut: June 10, 2003

The list of great Canadian baseball players has always been reasonably short. Fergie Jenkins is the clear-cut best-ever Canadian-born pitcher, and Larry Walker is likely the best-ever Canadian-born hitter. Justin Morneau, however, could change that dynamic sometime soon.

The native of New Westminster, British Columbia, gave the 2004 Twins an unlikely duo of left-handed Canadian clubbers back-to-back in the batting order, with Morneau hitting in front of native Manitoban Corey Koskie. Minnesotans warmed to both players but knew that Koskie was likely on his way out after 2004, while Morneau was being hailed as the team's next cornerstone player. Stepping in for the popular Doug Mientkiewicz at first base, Morneau knew he was no match defensively for the man he was replacing. However, he was confident that his moon shot home runs would soon win the fans over, and he was (as many Canadians still say) "right on." In only 280 at bats, he smashed 19 home runs, having already hit 22 in half a year at Triple-A. (Mientkiewicz hit five homers in his 280 Twins at bats that year.)

A onetime hockey player (of course), Morneau was originally drafted as a catcher. As he made the transition to first base in 2000, he became just the third-ever Twins minor leaguer to hit .400, ending his time in the short-season Gulf Coast League at .402. He also set a league record with 58 RBI (in 52 games).

Twins fans are hoping he settles in long-term at first base, much the way Kent Hrbek, another husky lefty, once did. The Twins haven't had a player hit even 30 home runs in a season since Hrbek launched that many in 1987. Incredibly, their last 35-home-run season was from Harmon Killebrew in 1970. The smart money says Morneau will be ending that dry run sometime very soon.

My dad was there to see it, my uncle, my brother, my cousin, five or six people all from British Columbia that found their way to Minneapolis in time . . . I had been in Buffalo myself, where our [Triple-A] Rochester team was playing, and I was in the batting cage, hitting, when Phil Roof, our manager, told me to step out a second, and that I was going up. No cell signal in that place, so I ran outside once I got dressed and cell phoned back, leaving messages all over the place. My mom's a teacher, so she wasn't home . . . It was maybe

BOXSCORE

Colorado Rockies 5, Minnesota Twins 0

Game Played on Tuesday, June 10, 2003 (Night) at Hubert H. Humphrey Metrodome

Colorado	3	1	0	0	0	1	0	0	0	—	5	7	1
Minnesota	0	0	0	0	0	0	0	0	0	—	0	3	0

BATTING

Colorado Rockies	AB	R	H	RBI	BB	K	PO	A
Uribe 2b	4	1	1	0	0	0	0	3
Payton lf	4	1	1	0	0	0	0	0
Helton 1b	4	0	0	0	0	0	10	1
Wilson cf	4	1	1	3	0	1	5	0
Walker rf	3	0	0	0	1	1	0	0
Vaughn dh	4	1	2	1	0	1	0	0
Hernandez ss	4	0	0	0	0	3	2	3
Johnson c	3	1	1	1	0	1	8	0
Norton 3b	3	0	1	0	0	1	1	2
Jennings p	0	0	0	0	0	0	0	0
Fuentes p	0	0	0	0	0	0	1	1
Totals	33	5	7	5	1	8	27	10

FIELDING

DP: 1

E: Uribe (1)

BATTING

2B: Vaughn (2, off Radke)

HR: Wilson (15, 1st inning off Radke, 2 on, 1 out); Johnson (7,2nd inning off Radke, 0 on, 0 out); Vaughn (1, 6th inning off Radke, 0 on, 2 out).

BASERUNNING

CS: Norton (1, 2nd base by Radke/Pierzynski)

Minnesota Twins	AB	R	H	RBI	BB	K	PO	A
Jones lf	4	0	0	0	0	1	2	0
Guzman ss	4	0	0	0	0	1	0	0
Koskie 3b	3	0	0	0	1	0	0	2
Morneau dh	4	0	2	0	0	1	0	0
Hunter cf	4	0	0	0	0	2	5	0
Mientkiewicz 1b	3	0	0	0	1	0	7	1
Kielty rf	4	0	0	0	0	2	1	0
Pierzynski c	3	0	1	0	0	1	8	1
Rivas 2b	1	0	0	0	2	0	3	1
Radke p	0	0	0	0	0	0	1	1
Fiore p	0	0	0	0	0	0	0	0
Nakamura p	0	0	0	0	0	0	0	0
Totals	30	0	3	0	4	8	27	6

FIELDING

PB: Pierzynski (2)

PITCHING

Colorado Rockies	IP	H	HR	R	ER	BB	K
Jennings W(5–5)	7.2	3	0	0	0	4	7
Fuentes	1.1	0	0	0	0	0	1
Totals	9.0	3	0	0	0	4	8

Minnesota Twins	IP	H	HR	R	ER	BB	K
Radke L(5–6)	7	7	3	5	5	1	8
Fiore	1	0	0	0	0	0	0
Nakamura	1	0	0	0	0	0	0
Totals	9	7	3	5	5	1	8

Umpires: Ron Kulpa, Mike Winters, Bruce Froemming, Doug Eddings

Time of Game: 2:12   Attendance: 18,886

one in the afternoon back there . . . and my dad was working at a casino then, so all I could do was leave messages.

My debut was crazy. Fun. It was against the Rockies, and of course that meant facing Larry Walker, who's a hero to all of us Canadian players. And before the game, he sent a bat over to our clubhouse, and he inscribed it—"Welcome to the show, make Canada proud." Signed, Larry Walker. The coolest thing. Then I went out and got a base hit that rolled right to him. DH'ing, batting fourth against Jason Jennings, base hit right away. Seeing my dad in the stands there was pretty awesome, although at one point I looked up and he and my family were trying to get Paul Molitor's autograph. I probably could have gotten it for them later, you know?

Also on June 10, 2003

The St. Louis Cardinals and Boston Red Sox meet for the first time since the 1967 World Series.

AUTHOR'S NOTE: A year later, the two teams would meet again, in the World Series. The Twins came close to meeting the Sox themselves in the ALCS but failed to hold a 5–1 eighth-inning lead against the Yankees in Game Four of the ALDS.

Jamie Moyer
Born: November 18, 1962
Debut: June 16, 1986

Question: How can a pitcher jam a hitter with an 80-mile-per-hour fast-ball? Answer: By setting it up with a 67-mile-per-hour change-up. Jamie Moyer, Master of the Soft, is baseball's Dick Clark, the ageless wonder. Pitching guru Tom House has called him "the standard bearer for dorky little left-handers everywhere." With average talent but superior skill, Moyer's hard work, savvy, and intense preparation made him a first-time All-Star at the age of 40, during a 2003 season in which he went 21–7 with the league's second-best ERA. Released by the Orioles in 1995 and then traded even up for Darren Bragg by Boston two years later, Moyer flourished upon arrival in Seattle, where he went 136–56 in his first seven seasons as a Mariner.

Perhaps baseball's premier overachiever, he has the guts of a burglar, throwing "Bugs Bunny" change-ups to the American League's scariest, brawniest hitters at will. His location is such that his catcher, Dan Wilson, has said, "I could wear a mitt the size of a coffee mug and never have to move it." Relying on his scouting reports and his brain to win games, Moyer keeps a thick, detailed notebook with his thoughts on every batter he's faced in every situation over the last dozen years. Growing up in blue collar Souderton, Pennsylvania, where his folks owned a dry cleaning business, he has channeled his parents' work ethic into his own blueprint for success.

The rare player who hits his peak in his late thirties and early forties, Moyer is living proof of the old Branch Rickey maxim, "Luck is the residue of design." He continues to succeed because he continues to outstudy, outwork, and outfox his opponents.

I was in Triple-A for a month or so, and it was Iowa at Omaha . . . Jim Colborn was my pitching coach, Larry Cox my manager, getaway day. I had showered, eaten, walked out to the bus, and was sitting there on the bus in the parking lot in Omaha when Colborn walked on the bus and with that dry sense of humor says, real stern, "Jamie! Come here!" We go off the bus, he looks me dead in the eye, and says, almost like he's accusing me of something, "So, do you think you're ready to pitch in the big leagues!?" He was real serious. I'm like, "I don't know, do you?" And he says, almost like a concerned parent, "Well, you know, they want you there tomorrow." I kind of laughed it

131

BOXSCORE

Chicago Cubs 7, Philadelphia Phillies 5

Game Played on Monday, June 16, 1986 (Day) at Wrigley Field

Philadelphia	0	0	0	1	1	0	3	0	0	—	5	10	1
Chicago	0	0	0	4	2	1	0	0	x	—	7	10	2

BATTING

Philadelphia Phillies	AB	R	H	RBI	BB	K	PO	A
Roenicke cf	4	1	3	0	1	0	2	0
Schu 3b	4	1	1	0	0	0	2	1
Samuel 2b	4	1	2	1	0	0	1	2
Schmidt 1b	5	1	1	1	0	1	8	1
Carman p	0	0	0	0	0	0	0	0
Hayes lf-1b	3	1	2	1	2	0	1	0
Wilson rf	5	0	1	0	0	1	1	0
Russell c	2	0	0	0	0	1	4	0
Daulton ph-c	1	0	0	0	1	0	2	0
Jeltz ss	3	0	0	1	0	0	2	5
Foley ph-ss	1	0	0	0	0	0	0	0
Carlton p	2	0	0	0	0	0	0	0
Hume p	0	0	0	0	0	0	0	0
Stone ph	1	0	0	0	0	0	0	0
Tekulve p	0	0	0	0	0	0	1	1
G. Gross ph-lf	0	0	0	0	1	0	0	0
Totals	35	5	10	4	5	3	24	10

FIELDING

DP: 2

E: Jeltz (7)

BATTING

2B: Roenicke (6, off Moyer)

SH: Schu (3, off Moyer)

HBP: Samuel (5, by Moyer); Russell (2, by Moyer)

BASERUNNING

SB: Hayes (9, 2nd base off Moyer/Lake); Samuel (17, 2nd base off Moyer/Lake)

Chicago Cubs	AB	R	H	RBI	BB	K	PO	A
Lopes 3b	2	1	0	1	3	0	1	2
Dunston ss	5	0	1	2	0	2	2	6
Sandberg 2b	4	0	2	1	0	0	1	3
Moreland rf	4	2	2	0	0	0	0	0
Matthews lf	4	0	2	0	0	1	0	0
Baller p	0	0	0	0	0	0	0	0
J. Davis c	0	0	0	0	0	0	1	0
Durham 1b	4	1	1	2	0	0	11	0
Mumphrey cf-lf	4	1	2	1	0	0	4	1
Lake c	3	1	0	0	1	1	4	0
Smith p	0	0	0	0	0	0	0	0
Moyer p	2	0	1	0	1	2	0	4
Martinez cf	1	0	0	0	0	0	3	0
Totals	33	7	10	7	5	6	27	16

FIELDING

DP: 3

E: Lopes (4), Durham (2)

BATTING

2B: Mumphrey (6, off Carlton); Dunston (18, off Carlton)

HR: Durham (8, 5th inning off Hume, 1 on, 1 out)

IBB: Lake (1, by Carlton)

BASERUNNING

SB: Lopes (8, 2nd base off Tekulve/Russell); Sandberg (7, 2nd base off Tekulve/Russell)

PITCHING

Philadelphia Phillies	IP	H	HR	R	ER	BB	K
Carlton L(4–8)	3.2	6	0	4	4	4	2
Hume	1.1	3	1	2	2	0	2
Tekulve	2	1	0	1	1	1	1
Carman	1	0	0	0	0	0	1
Totals	8	10	1	7	7	5	6

Chicago Cubs	IP	H	HR	R	ER	BB	K
Moyer W(1–0)	6.1	8	0	5	4	3	2
Baller	1	1	0	0	0	2	0
Smith SV(9)	1.2	1	0	0	0	0	1
Totals	9.0	10	0	5	4	5	3

WP: Baller (2)

BK: Baller (4)

HBP: Moyer 2 (2,Samuel, Russell)

IBB: Carlton (4, Lake)

Umpires: Frank Pulli, Greg Bonin, Bill Williams, John McSherry

Time of Game: 2:56   Attendance: 20,614

off, but he says. "Let's go," and I follow him back into the clubhouse where Larry Cox was waiting for me, and he confirmed it. Wow! I called my parents from the pay phone outside the clubhouse, and they made arrangements to come out along with my college coach, the guy who caught me in high school, a lot of people mobilizing to get from Pennsylvania to Chicago real quick. I bussed back from Omaha to Des Moines with the team, then my roomie, Dave Martinez, and I were off to Chicago . . . He had gotten the same good news I had.

We were told there would be tickets for us at the airport, but at six in the morning, all our belongings with us, no tickets. I called our trainer, who got us straightened out, and we were on our way. The taxi ride to the ballpark—man, we had to tie the trunk closed with a rope with all the stuff we had with us. We get to Wrigley, into the parking lot across from the fire house, and the guard didn't want to let us in. I mean, come on, we've got all our stuff with us! It's an hour 'til game time! We talk our way in, and I get dressed and go out there for the national anthem, sung by Wayne Messmer, who would sing at my wedding years later . . . I'm standing beside Leon Durham, hat in my hand, and Leon starts laughing, that silly

Also on June 16, 1986

Simply Red begins its rise on the pop charts (challenging Madonna) with their hit single "Holding Back the Years."

AUTHOR'S NOTE: "Holding Back the Years" is precisely what Moyer has been doing since his mid '90s renaissance, pitching into his forties for Seattle.

little laugh he had, because he notices the cap in my hand is shaking like a leaf. And he says, "Hey kid, calm down . . . We've all been there at one time."

I was going to pitch the next day, and I'm trying to figure out their rotation, and it dawns on me that I'm going to miss pitching against my hero, Steve Carlton, by a day. Dang it. But after the game, they called me in and said, "Change of plans. [You'll] pitch day after tomorrow," and all I could think was, "Yes! Against Lefty! A dream come true! No way!" I don't think I slept at all the night before that start. Game starts, I give up a double right away, but I settled down and beat my idol. That could have been the end of my career that day, and I would have been happy.

Steve Green Photo Courtesy Chicago Cubs

Mark Mulder

Born: August 5, 1977
Debut: April 18, 2000

Mark Mulder looks like he could be modeling crew-neck shirts or jockey shorts in the Sears catalog. Always impeccably dressed, always perfect in posture, he stood in stark contrast to the Early WWF look his Oakland teammates were cultivating when he first walked into their clubhouse.

If it always appears that Mulder has just walked off the golf course, that's okay with him—he shoots in the low 70s, and while he maintains a handicap of two, he's also managed to maintain a career ERA of less than 4.00.

Mulder is the owner of a plus fastball, but it's not just that he has great stuff—he does, or he wouldn't have been the second pick in the nation (behind Pat Burrell) in 1998. The Athletics, first and foremost, liked his ability to compete, even on days when his best stuff is nowhere to be found.

Rushed quickly to the big leagues, he treaded water his rookie season, going just 9–10, 5.44. Oakland's GM, Billy Beane, was reportedly ready to trade the Michigan Stater straight up for Scott Williamson, something that never quite made it into the book *Moneyball*. Beane's player development people talked him out of doing something so rash, and the rest, as they say, is history.

Mulder's first full season, 2001, produced an American League–leading 21 wins. Strangely, his win totals went down by two each in '02 and '03 while his ERA improved, down to 3.13 in 2003, with a league-best nine complete games. A scary second-half slump derailed his 2004 season, but no one doubts that Mulder will once again be a 20-game winner now that he's in St. Louis. If not, hey, there's always golf.

We were in Salt Lake City when they told me I was going up. I had actually expected to break camp with [the A's] in spring training, but they kept Ron Mahay as the fifth guy instead. I went down, made a start or two, and then they tell me I'm going to Cleveland to pitch against the Indians. And I remember saying, out loud, "Oh, *great*," as sarcastic as could be . . . They had all these great hitters in their lineup then, and all I could think was, "Why Cleveland?"

All my family was in Chicago, everyone. Fifteen or 20 people came down to Cleveland for the game. That pumped me up.

Before the game, Rick Peterson, our pitching coach, headed towards me, and before he could get a word out, Matt Stairs, as only Matt could do, starts yelling, top of his lungs, "Hey! Don't listen to a word [Peterson] says! You just do what got you here! Go out and throw strikes!" And you know what? He was absolutely right. So many times, a guy will get to the big leagues, and the first thing, the pitching coach wants to mess with him. It's true—you got to the big leagues for a reason. Stick with what got you here.

I did okay . . . I wasn't nervous, just anxious. I gave up my first base hit in the first inning, and Manny Ramirez hit a good sinker, down, for a two-run homer right after, but I still thought I had good stuff. Later I gave up a homer to [Travis] Fryman, a fastball that was supposed to be in, but it stayed over the middle, and he hit it out down the left-field line. We were down 4–3 but I wasn't really flustered. We came right back and won the game, and things have been pretty good since then.

Also on April 18, 2000
Anaheim's rookie second baseman Adam Kennedy smashes a grand slam and drives in eight in the Angels' 16–10 win at Toronto.

AUTHOR' NOTE: Four years later, with the Angels and A's jockeying for the AL West title, Mulder was asked to shut down Anaheim as the two teams met on the season's final weekend. He would not have to worry about a Kennedy grand slam, as Kennedy was out with a torn ACL. His replacement at second base that fateful Friday night was light-hitting Alfredo Amezega—who promptly KO'd Mulder and the A's with what else? A grand slam.

BOXSCORE

Oakland Athletics 8, Cleveland Indians 5
Game Played on Tuesday, April 18, 2000 (Night) at Jacobs Field

Oakland	0	0	0	2	1	3	0	0	2	—	8	9	0
Cleveland	2	0	0	0	2	0	0	0	1	—	5	9	1

BATTING

Oakland Athletics	AB	R	H	RBI	BB	K	PO	A
Christenson cf	5	0	2	3	0	0	2	1
Tejada ss	4	2	3	1	1	0	3	7
Ja. Giambi dh	5	1	1	2	0	2	0	0
Saenz 1b	5	1	2	1	0	1	10	0
Stairs rf	4	1	0	1	1	2	1	0
Grieve lf	3	0	0	0	2	2	1	0
Fasano c	4	0	0	0	1	1	6	0
Chavez 3b	3	2	1	0	2	0	2	3
Velandia 2b	2	0	0	0	0	1	1	1
Jaha ph	0	0	0	0	1	0	0	0
Menechino pr-2b	1	1	0	0	0	1	1	0
Mulder p	0	0	0	0	0	0	0	1
Magnante p	0	0	0	0	0	0	0	0
Mathews p	0	0	0	0	0	0	0	0
Isringhausen p	0	0	0	0	0	0	0	0
Totals	36	8	9	8	8	10	27	13

FIELDING
DP: 2

BATTING
2B: Saenz (5, off Nagy); Tejada (1, off Nagy)
3B: Saenz (1, off Nagy)
HR: Ja. Giambi (6, 9th inning off Reed, 1 on, 0 out).
IBB: Chavez (2, by Nagy)

BASERUNNING
SB: Stairs (1, 2nd base off Nagy/Diaz)

Cleveland Indians	AB	R	H	RBI	BB	K	PO	A
Vizquel ss	4	0	0	0	1	1	1	2
Fryman 3b	5	1	2	2	0	0	1	2
R. Alomar 2b	3	1	1	0	1	1	1	3
M. Ramirez rf	4	1	1	2	0	0	1	0
Thome dh	4	1	1	0	0	2	0	0
Sexson 1b	4	0	1	0	0	1	11	1
Justice lf	3	0	1	1	1	0	0	0
A. Ramirez cf	4	0	1	0	0	1	1	0
S. Alomar c	1	0	0	0	0	0	2	0
Diaz c	2	1	1	0	0	0	7	0
Nagy p	0	0	0	0	0	0	0	1
Kamieniecki p	0	0	0	0	0	0	1	1
Reed p	0	0	0	0	0	0	1	0
Martin p	0	0	0	0	0	0	0	0
Totals	34	5	9	5	3	6	27	10

FIELDING
DP: 1
E: Fryman (1)

BATTING
2B: Thome (4, off Isringhausen)
HR: M. Ramirez (4, 1st inning off Mulder, 1 on, 2 out); Fryman (2, 5th inning off Mulder, 1 on, 2 out)
HBP: Diaz (2, by Isringhausen)

PITCHING

Oakland Athletics	IP	H	HR	R	ER	BB	K
Mulder W(1–0)	6	5	2	4	4	3	6
Magnante	1	0	0	0	0	0	0
Mathews	0.2	1	0	0	0	0	0
Isringhausen SV(3)	1.1	3	0	1	1	0	0
Totals	9.0	9	2	5	5	3	6
Cleveland Indians	IP	H	HR	R	ER	BB	K
Nagy L(1–2)	5.2	7	0	6	6	4	6
Kamieniecki	2.1	1	0	0	0	1	3
Reed	0	1	1	2	2	1	0
Martin	1	0	0	0	0	2	1
Totals	9	9	1	8	8	8	10

HBP: Isringhausen (1, Diaz)
IBB: Nagy (1, Chavez)
Umpires: Dale Scott, Gary Cederstrom, Marvin Hudson, Mike Fichter
Time of Game: 3:07   Attendance: 40,551

Bobby Murcer
Born: May 20, 1946
Debut: September 8, 1965

Bobby Murcer was a charismatic player; a good glove man, and a fine hitter who belted 252 career home runs despite playing in a "dead ball" era when he first came up. Averaging 27 homers a season in his first four full years in New York, the native Oklahoman was one of the few bright spots in the Yankees' lean seasons of the early seventies. In 1975, he was traded even-up for Bobby Bonds, the first trade of ball players with six-figure salaries. After two years by the Bay, he moved along to the Cubs and, finally, back to New York, in July of '79.

A close friend of Thurman Munson, Murcer delivered a moving eulogy at Munson's funeral after he tragically crashed his airplane in August, just two weeks after the two had been reunited by the Cubs–Yankees trade. The entire Yankee team attended the funeral, and that same night, Murcer went out and drove in all five Yankee runs in an emotional 5–4 win over Baltimore. Murcer, Lou Piniella, and Munson had been inseparable, spending many nights together at each other's houses.

"Late one night we were sitting around and it was like two o'clock in the morning and I told them I was tired," Murcer told *New York Newsday*. "So I went upstairs and got in bed and I'm lying there 15 minutes, 20 minutes, and Thurman and Lou are still arguing about which one of them would make the best pinch hitter. I have that memory of the two guys sitting in my kitchen, just talking about baseball."

Murcer now talks baseball for a living as one of the Yankee broadcasters for the YES Network. He retired as a five-time All-Star, carving out his best year in 1971, when he finished second in the league in both hitting and runs scored and led the league in total bases.

When they expanded the rosters in September, I had gotten through Single-A ball, and they said I'm going all the way to New York. And not knowing any better at the time, I just figured, shoot, maybe this is the way it works around here. You play one year of minor league ball then they see what you can do in the majors. I went up and spent the last 30 days up there, as a shortstop.

The first game I played in, I was kind of on my own . . . My family was back in Oklahoma, but boy, were they thrilled to find out I was headed to the Yankees, just like Mickey Mantle.

136

My first hit in the big leagues was a home run at RFK Stadium, off a guy named Jim Duckworth. Bobby Richardson was on at second base, and it helped us win the game. It's funny, I guess . . . I remember very little about that first game the week before . . . I think I went 0-for-4 and couldn't tell you if we won or if we lost. But a week later, in Washington, I can tell you all about that one, how I hit my first home run and we beat the Senators 3–1.

BOXSCORE

New York Yankees 6, Washington Senators 5
Game Played on Wednesday, September 8, 1965 (Night) at Yankee Stadium

Washington	0	0	1	0	1	2	0	0	1	—	5	12	0
New York	0	2	0	0	3	0	0	0	1	—	6	9	1

BATTING

Washington Senators	AB	R	H	RBI	BB	K	PO	A
Blasingame 2b	4	0	2	0	1	0	2	4
Hamlin ss	5	0	1	0	0	0	1	1
Kirkland rf	4	1	2	2	0	1	1	0
Held ph	1	0	0	0	0	1	0	0
Kline p	0	0	0	0	0	0	0	0
Howard lf	5	1	1	0	0	2	5	0
Nen 1b	5	0	1	1	0	1	9	1
McMullen 3b	5	1	3	1	0	1	1	2
Brumley c	3	0	0	0	1	0	6	0
Zimmer ph-c	1	0	0	0	0	0	0	0
Lock cf	4	1	2	1	0	1	0	0
Duckworth p	2	0	0	0	0	1	0	0
Cunningham ph	0	1	0	0	1	0	0	0
McCormick p	0	0	0	0	0	0	0	0
King ph-rf	0	0	0	0	1	0	1	0
Totals	39	5	12	5	4	8	26	8

FIELDING
PB: Brumley (6)

BATTING
2B: Nen (5, off Bouton); Lock (12, off Bouton)
HR: Kirkland (14, 5th inning off Bouton, 0 on, 0 out); Lock (16, 6th inning off Bouton, 0 on, 0 out); McMullen (15, 9th inning off Hamilton, 0 on, 2 out)

New York Yankees	AB	R	H	RBI	BB	K	PO	A
Richardson 2b	4	1	1	0	0	0	2	2
Murcer ss	4	0	0	0	1	1	1	4
Tresh lf	4	0	2	0	1	1	3	0
Howard c	4	1	1	1	1	0	8	0
Pepitone 1b	1	0	0	0	0	1	0	0
Barker 1b	3	1	2	3	0	0	7	0
Boyer 3b	3	1	1	0	0	0	0	2
Repoz cf	3	0	0	0	1	0	3	0
Moore rf	2	1	1	2	1	0	2	0
A. Lopez rf	1	0	0	0	0	0	0	0
Bouton p	2	0	0	0	0	2	1	0
Mikkelsen p	1	0	0	0	0	1	0	0
Hamilton p	0	0	0	0	0	0	0	0
White ph	1	1	1	0	0	0	0	0
Totals	33	6	9	6	5	6	27	8

FIELDING
DP: 1
E: Pepitone (4)

BATTING
2B: Boyer (22, off Duckworth); Barker (8, off Kline)
HR: Moore (1, 2nd inning off Duckworth, 1 on, 2 out); Barker (6, 5th inning off Duckworth, 2 on, 2 out)
SH: Boyer (1, off Kline); Richardson (9, off Kline)
IBB: Moore (1, by Duckworth); Tresh (4, by Kline)

BASERUNNING
SB: Tresh (5, 2nd base off Duckworth/Brumley); Richardson (7, 2nd base off Duckworth/Brumley)

PITCHING

Washington Senators	IP	H	HR	R	ER	BB	K
Duckworth	5	6	2	5	5	3	5
McCormick	2	0	0	0	0	1	1
Kline L(7–5)	1.2	3	0	1	1	1	0
Totals	8.2	9	2	6	6	5	6
New York Yankees	IP	H	HR	R	ER	BB	K
Bouton	5	8	2	4	4	3	4
Mikkelsen	2.2	3	0	0	0	1	2
Hamilton W(3–1)	1.1	1	1	1	1	0	2
Totals	9.0	12	3	5	5	4	8

WP: Duckworth (5)
IBB: Duckworth (4, Moore); Kline (13, Tresh)
Umpires: John Rice, Bill Valentine, Bill McKinley, Hank Soar
Time of Game: 2:54   Attendance: 7,156

Also on September 8, 1965
The Athletics' Bert Campaneris plays all nine positions against the Angels, starting at short, then switching his way around the diamond in a 13-inning Angels win. On the mound, he allows one run on two hits and a walk but gets his cousin, Jose Cardenal, on a pop-up.

AUTHOR'S NOTE: Cardenal and Murcer would be teammates with the Cubs in the late seventies, then travel together with the Yankees years later as broadcaster and base coach.

Eddie Murray
Born: February 24, 1956
Debut: April 7, 1977

Eddie Murray's resume bulges with impressive statistics, but with Murray, it was always more about *when* he got the hits than anything else. Assembly-line consistency and RBI production were the hallmarks of his Hall of Fame career, which began when he was a 22-year-old Oriole in 1977.

The L.A. native never had a 35-home-run season, never led the league in any major offensive category, and never won an MVP. He also never had a 125-RBI season, but over a 20-year span, he never had fewer than 75, waiting until his 20th year in major league baseball to finally see the disabled list. He finished his career with just 100 fewer at bats than Ty Cobb and was seventh all-time in runs batted in. (If he had played just another half-season, he could have retired as fifth all-time; he finished just four behind Jimmie Foxx,and just 22 behind Ty Cobb.)

As a member of the exclusive 500 homer/3000 hit fraternity (the third member, behind Aaron and Mays), Murray switch-hit his way into three World Series, including the 1983 title in Baltimore. He and Cal Ripken Jr. became inseparable, Ripken going so far as to single out his friend the night he broke Lou Gehrig's Iron Man record. (In fact, Ripken publicly acknowledged only four people that night: his mom, his dad, his wife, and Eddie Murray.) A year to the day after Ripken's special night in Baltimore, Murray had one of his own, launching his 500th career home run. He remains the only member of the 500-homer club never to have had a 40-homer season.

Murray grew up in a family of twelve children, and for an entire decade, found a surrogate family of Oriole fans, who embraced his quiet professionalism. However, as his relationship with the media deteriorated, so too did his relationship with Baltimore. He was peddled out of town, to the Dodgers, and spent the final seven years of his career bouncing among several organizations, including the Orioles. He led the '96 O's to the AL wild card and a division-series win over Cleveland, one of his former teams. Baltimore lost in the ALCS to the Yankees, with Murray's last at bat as an Oriole resulting in a homer off Andy Pettitte. He retired following the 1997 season with 3,255 base hits. Only recently, as a coach with the Indians, has he begun to drop his guard around the media and speak with the occasional smile. Here's hoping he's smiling during his Hall of Fame speech, coming soon.

We were opening against Texas, in Baltimore, and Bump Wills was making his debut too. I thought I had my first hit and first RBI, but Bump made a stop on a ball I hit up the middle. He got a lot more attention that day than I did because of the fact his dad had played and played so well at the big league level. We lost, and both starting pitchers went ten innings, Blyleven and Palmer. You'd never see that these days, especially not on Opening Day!

I had made the team out of spring training . . . I hit a ball over the wall one day at the old park in Miami, and Earl [Weaver] had it put in the paper the next day that Murray was going to go north with the team. No one ever officially said, "Hey, you made the team." Earl just had it in the papers, and when everyone told me that's what it said, I figured, "Okay, I've made the team." I found out later he and [GM] Hank Peters were feuding about whether I should go to Rochester for another year or whatever, but Earl won out. I kept hitting, and the more I kept doing that, the more Earl was able to convince Hank he was right, that I was ready. I was just an innocent bystander to all that . . . I just kept hitting, one or two hits a game. It was great to have a manager in my corner like that.

The best was going to L.A. to play in May . . . All my family was there to see it the first time we went out to play the Angels, and I remember that scene as much as Opening Day back in Baltimore.

BOXSCORE

Texas Rangers 2, Baltimore Orioles 1

Game Played on Thursday, April 7, 1977 (Day) at Memorial Stadium

Texas	0	0	0	1	0	0	0	0	1	—	2	9	1
Baltimore	0	0	0	0	0	1	0	0	0	—	1	6	0

BATTING

Texas Rangers	AB	R	H	RBI	BB	K	PO	A
Campaneris ss	5	0	1	0	0	1	1	2
Wills 2b	4	0	1	1	1	0	1	0
Washington lf	5	0	2	0	0	0	3	0
May rf	4	0	2	0	0	0	1	0
Hargrove 1b	3	1	1	0	0	0	12	0
Harrah 3b	4	0	1	0	0	0	0	4
Grieve dh	4	0	0	0	0	1	0	0
Sundberg c	3	0	0	1	0	2	8	5
Beniquez cf	2	1	1	0	2	0	4	0
Blyleven p	0	0	0	0	0	0	0	3
Totals	34	2	9	2	3	4	30	14

FIELDING
E: Campaneris (1)

BATTING
2B: Beniquez (1, off Palmer); Washington (1, off Palmer)
SH: Hargrove (1, off Palmer)
SF: Sundberg (1, off Palmer)

BASERUNNING
CS: Campaneris (1, 2nd base by Palmer/Dempsey); Washington (1, 2nd base by Palmer/Dempsey)

Baltimore Orioles	AB	R	H	RBI	BB	K	PO	A
Bumbry cf-lf	5	0	1	0	0	3	2	1
Dauer 2b	5	0	0	0	0	0	2	7
Singleton rf	3	0	0	0	1	0	1	0
Harlow pr-cf	0	0	0	0	0	0	0	0
L. May 1b	4	1	1	0	0	1	12	1
Murray dh	4	0	1	0	0	1	0	0
Kelly lf-rf	4	0	0	0	0	2	1	0
DeCinces 3b	3	0	1	0	1	0	0	5
Dempsey c	3	0	0	1	0	1	7	2
Belanger ss	3	0	2	0	1	0	5	4
Palmer p	0	0	0	0	0	0	0	1
Totals	34	1	6	1	3	8	30	21

BATTING
SF: Dempsey (1, off Blyleven)

BASERUNNING
CS: Belanger (1, 2nd base by Blyleven/Sundberg); DeCinces (1, 2nd base by Blyleven/Sundberg)

PITCHING

Texas Rangers	IP	H	HR	R	ER	BB	K
Blyleven W(1-0)	10	6	0	1	1	3	8
Baltimore Orioles	IP	H	HR	R	ER	BB	K
Palmer L(0-1)	10	9	0	2	2	3	4

WP: Palmer (1)
Umpires: Jerry Neudecker, Art Frantz, Nick Bremigan, Al Clark
Time of Game: 2:34   Attendance: 31,307

Also on April 7, 1977

The Toronto Blue Jays play their first regular season game, in snowy Toronto, beating the White Sox 9–5 as Chicago strands 19 runners.

AUTHOR'S NOTE: The White Sox's inability to hit in the clutch that day is stark, juxtaposed against Murray's debut. There may not have been a better, more consistent RBI man in baseball during Murray's 1980s heyday.

Joe Nathan
Born: November 22, 1974
Debut: April 21, 1999

Native New Yorker Joe Nathan's name has a nice Coney Island ring to it, but this is a guy who actually came close to becoming a Manhattan stockbroker instead of a ballplayer. He was recruited by no Division I colleges and ended up as an undersized shortstop playing for Division III SUNY–Stony Brook. The only reason he was even able to do *that* was that the Stony Brook coach was a onetime college roommate of Nathan's high school coach, who asked that he take a look at the kid as a favor.

Eventually, he became a Giants sixth-round pick, still harboring thoughts of being a big league infielder someday and not a pitcher. The Giants made him stick with pitching, even when he once allowed home runs to four consecutive batters at Triple-A. He emerged in fits and starts once he made it to San Francisco and never dreamed he'd be dealt even-up for All-Star catcher A. J. Pierzynski after the 2003 season. Perhaps the Twins had scouted not just his stuff, but the song to which he entered action. Nathan's jog onto the field wasn't accompanied by throbbing Guns N Roses riffs or screeching Metallica metal; rather, he entered to the soundtrack from a little-known movie called *Rock Star*. The title track is about a talented unknown who, when given a chance, becomes a breakout performer. Hmmm.

In his first year as the Twins stopper, Nathan blew only three saves, knocking down 41 successfully. He enjoyed a ten-week scoreless stretch starting in May and compiled an ERA of 1.62 while holding opposing hitters to a batting average of just .187. With a terrific slider at his disposal, he struck out 89 in 72 innings, allowing a measly three home runs. Not a bad turnaround from a guy who once allowed four home runs to four consecutive batters at Triple-A. And not bad for a onetime Division III shortstop.

I had been in Shreveport, Louisiana, Double-A, and was expecting to start the next day. I happened to check the list and lineup card that was posted by the door when I got to the ballpark and saw my name wasn't anywhere, and just as I'm trying to figure out what that means, [manager] Shane Turner calls me in his office and says, "Let's talk." He was very matter of fact, just said congrats and go get 'em—and that I was starting day after tomorrow.

I get into San Francisco, Shreveport to Dallas to San Francisco, and was told just lie low, stay there, because you're not active yet. That was torture.

Holed up at the Hyatt by the airport, just going crazy thinking about everything . . . But eventually they called me and said, "Okay, you can come on out," so that was a relief . . . It gave me something to do besides go stir crazy. I headed out in the late afternoon and saw some guys I knew, like Rich Aurilia . . . I had only been to 3Com Park once, but it was as a fan, when I had been playing in San Jose and a bunch of us went out to see a day game for the heck of it.

My first start was against the Marlins, and I got to the yard early, really happy that I had been there to kind of scout everything out the night before, watch the hitters up close and all that. I did real well, with seven shutout innings against Florida, and they gave me the game ball, the lineup card . . . Scott Servais was my catcher and he was terrific. Afterwards, my dad, my agent, my uncle, my wife—we all went out for dinner in the city, and then we went to the Blue Light, the really upscale after-dinner place right there on Union [Street] . . . My agent got us in. We had a great view of the city, and it felt like I was literally on top of the world.

BOXSCORE

San Francisco Giants 4, Florida Marlins 0

Game Played on Wednesday, April 21, 1999 (Day) at 3Com Park

Florida	0	0	0	0	0	0	0	0	0	—	0	5	0
San Francisco	1	0	0	3	0	0	0	0	x	—	4	5	0

BATTING

Florida Marlins	AB	R	H	RBI	BB	K	PO	A
Castillo 2b	3	0	1	0	1	1	0	1
Gonzalez ss	4	0	1	0	0	0	0	3
Kotsay rf	4	0	0	0	0	0	3	0
Mantei p	0	0	0	0	0	0	0	0
Lee 1b	4	0	2	0	0	1	10	0
Dunwoody cf	3	0	0	0	1	0	1	0
Wilson lf-rf	4	0	0	0	0	2	2	0
Berg 3b	2	0	1	0	1	0	1	3
Redmond c	3	0	0	0	0	1	7	0
Springer p	1	0	0	0	0	1	0	2
Counsell ph	1	0	0	0	0	0	0	0
Looper p	0	0	0	0	0	0	0	0
Aven ph	1	0	0	0	0	0	0	0
Hyers lf	0	0	0	0	0	0	0	0
Totals	30	0	5	0	3	6	24	9

BATTING

2B: Gonzalez (3, off Johnstone)
3B: Berg (1, off Nathan)

BASERUNNING—

SB: Castillo (5, 2nd base off Nathan/Servais)

San Francisco Giants	AB	R	H	RBI	BB	K	PO	A
Benard cf	4	0	0	0	0	2	4	0
Aurilia ss	4	0	0	0	0	1	1	3
Rios rf	4	2	2	1	0	1	2	1
Kent 2b	3	1	1	0	0	0	2	2
Snow 1b	3	0	0	0	0	2	10	0
Javier lf	3	1	1	1	0	0	1	0
Martinez 3b	3	0	1	2	0	0	0	1
Servais c	2	0	0	0	1	1	7	0
Nathan p	2	0	0	0	0	0	0	3
Santangelo ph	1	0	0	0	0	0	0	0
Johnstone p	0	0	0	0	0	0	0	0
Nen p	0	0	0	0	0	0	0	0
Totals	29	4	5	4	1	7	27	10

FIELDING

DP: 2
PB: Servais (1)

BATTING

2B: Javier (1, off Springer); Martinez (1, off Springer)
HR: Rios (1, 1st inning off Springer, 0 on, 2 out)
IBB: Servais (2, by Springer)

PITCHING

Florida Marlins	IP	H	HR	R	ER	BB	K
Springer L(0–3)	4	5	1	4	4	1	1
Looper	3	0	0	0	0	0	4
Mantei	1	0	0	0	0	0	2
Totals	8	5	1	4	4	1	7

San Francisco Giants	IP	H	HR	R	ER	BB	K
Nathan W(1–0)	7	4	0	0	0	3	4
Johnstone	1	1	0	0	0	0	0
Nen	1	0	0	0	0	0	2
Totals	9	5	0	0	0	3	6

WP: Nathan (1)
IBB: Springer (1,Servais)
Umpires: Charlie Williams, Greg Bonin, Jeff Nelson, Frank Pulli
Time of Game: 2:21   Attendance: 10,249

Also on April 21, 1999

A national day of mourning is declared following the previous day's school massacre at Columbine, in Colorado.

Trot Nixon
Born: April 11, 1974
Debut: September 21, 1996

Everyone has his or her own indelible memories of the events of September 11, 2001. For Trot Nixon, the day was bittersweet, as that same morning he witnessed the birth of his first child. Nixon's entire career has been a mix of good and bad; when healthy, he plays Fenway's challenging right field as beautifully as anyone in the league. However, a series of neck and back injuries have prevented him from becoming the hurricane of a player the Red Sox had forecast he'd become.

The lefty-swinger was born in Durham, North Carolina, the son of a renowned kidney surgeon who was Catfish Hunter's high school catcher. Nixon later attended that same high school as Hunter, which had also produced football stars Sonny Jorgensen and Roman Gabriel. Nixon excelled in the sport himself but turned down a full ride to North Carolina State in order to pursue his career in baseball. He signed as a Red Sox first rounder in 1993.

In spite of the great Red Sox–Yankees rivalry, Nixon asked for uniform number 7, as a tribute to Yankee great Mickey Mantle. Like the Mick, he had a penchant for big home runs when they mattered, namely a tremendous run of big hits in the 2003 playoffs, including a walk-off extra-innings blast against the A's into Fenway's center-field bleachers. Looking like a 1989-vintage Will Clark, Nixon continued to tomahawk balls into both alleys in 2004, but another bout of injuries held him to only 48 games. Through his first 2,500 Red Sox at bats, he had a higher slugging percentage than Sox greats Jim Rice, Vern Stephens, Carl Yastrzemski, Dwight Evans, and Bobby Doerr, among others.

It was in my contract that I'd get called up that September, so I can't say that it was a surprise. I really didn't deserve it . . . I had been in Double-A all year and really didn't have the numbers to suggest I should be in the big leagues yet, but a deal's a deal, I guess. I just sat at my locker and kept real quiet. Kevin Kennedy was the manager, and I don't recall him ever saying one word to me.

When I finally got in a game, it was a heck of a game. I pinch-ran against the Yankees, in there for Wil Cordero. That was nerve-wracking enough, getting out on that field at Yankee Stadium in late September, but then to go play right field—man, I was scared to death. Farm boy from North Carolina standing out there in front of all those bleacher fans! I felt like a deer in the headlights out there.

Eventually, the Yankees won the game 12–11 on a base hit by Jeter, and the place just went nuts. Running off the field, all the way across to our dugout from right field, I was absolutely numb. 12–11. What a game! It was a big loss for us, knocked us from three out to four out in the wild card, I think. Still, after the game, it was rookie dress-up day, so that was kind of odd—and I actually got off easy. They had me dressed up like a caveman. Tony Rodriguez got it the worst. He had to wear a diaper and suck on a pacifier. Rudy Pemberton got to be Superman. He actually looked pretty good.

A week or so later I got in for a start, and that was real memorable . . . Mike Greenwell walked in the clubhouse and asked me if I wanted to play that day, and I said, "Heck yeah!" So he went to Kennedy and asked him to play me instead of him, which I always have appreciated. I went out there and got my first hit at Fenway. Every time I see Mike Greenwell now, spring training or whatever, I always thank him for that.

Also on September 21, 1996
John F. Kennedy Jr. marries Carolyn Bessette in a secret ceremony at Cumberland Island, Georgia.

AUTHOR'S NOTE: Since the 1960 Kennedy–Nixon debates, there have been as many Nixons (Trot and Otis) in uniform for New England's baseball team as Kennedys (Kevin and John), which seems almost sacrilegious in Democrat-dominated Boston.

BOXSCORE

New York Yankees 12, Boston Red Sox 11
Game Played on Saturday, September 21, 1996 (Day) at Yankee Stadium

Boston	0	0	0	1	5	2	3	0	0	0	—	11	14	1
New York	0	0	1	0	3	3	3	1	0	1	—	12	20	0

BATTING

Boston Red Sox	AB	R	H	RBI	BB	K	PO	A
Bragg cf-rf-cf	5	1	2	0	1	1	2	0
Frye 2b	5	1	1	2	1	0	1	2
Vaughn 1b	3	0	0	0	1	1	10	2
Canseco dh	6	1	1	3	0	1	0	0
Greenwell lf	4	2	2	0	0	0	0	0
Tinsley cf	1	0	1	0	0	0	0	0
Cordero ph	0	0	0	0	1	0	0	0
Nixon pr-rf	0	0	0	0	0	0	0	0
Garciaparra ss	5	0	2	2	0	1	2	3
Manto 3b	2	0	0	0	1	1	2	2
O'Leary ph-lf	1	1	0	0	1	0	3	0
Haselman c	5	3	3	3	0	0	7	0
Pemberton rf	3	2	2	1	0	0	0	0
Rodriguez 3b	0	0	0	0	0	1	0	0
Jefferson ph	1	0	0	0	0	0	0	0
Pozo 3b	0	0	0	0	0	0	0	2
Maddux p	0	0	0	0	0	0	2	1
Gunderson p	0	0	0	0	0	0	0	0
Mahomes p	0	0	0	0	0	0	0	0
Eshelman p	0	0	0	0	0	0	0	0
Brandenburg p	0	0	0	0	0	0	0	0
Slocumb p	0	0	0	0	0	0	0	0
Hudson p	0	0	0	0	0	0	0	1
Totals	41	11	14	11	6	6	29	13

FIELDING
DP: 1
E: Vaughn (15)

BATTING
2B: Haselman 2 (12, off Key, off Nelson); Canseco (22, off Key); Bragg (23, off Bones); Greenwell (18, off Pavlas); Pemberton (6, off Nelson)
3B: Garciaparra (3, off Key)
HR: Haselman (6, 6th inning off Bones, 0 on, 0 out)
SH: Garciaparra (1, off Pavlas)
HBP: Vaughn 2 (14, by Key, by Polley); Pemberton (1, by Bones)
IBB: Vaughn (19, by Pavlas); Cordero (4, by Wetteland)

BASERUNNING
SB: Garciaparra (4, 2nd base off Bones/Girardi); Frye (16, 3rd base off Wetteland/Girardi); Nixon (1, 2nd base off Wetteland/Girardi).

New York Yankees	AB	R	H	RBI	BB	K	PO	A
Raines lf	6	3	3	2	1	0	3	0
Boggs 3b	5	3	1	0	2	1	0	1
O'Neill 2b	5	2	4	2	1	1	1	0
R. Rivera pr-rf	0	0	0	0	0	0	0	0
Fielder dh	6	1	1	3	1	1	0	0
Martinez 1b	5	1	1	2	2	1	13	0
B. Williams cf	4	0	3	0	3	1	3	0
Jeter ss	6	0	3	3	1	0	1	4
Girardi c	6	0	2	0	0	1	6	0
Sojo 2b	3	0	0	0	0	1	2	3
Duncan ph-2b	2	1	2	0	0	0	0	0
Fox pr-2b	0	1	0	0	0	0	1	1
Strawberry ph	0	0	0	0	1	0	0	0
Kelly pr-2b	0	0	0	0	0	0	0	1
Key p	0	0	0	0	0	0	0	0
Bones p	0	0	0	0	0	0	0	0
Pavlas p	0	0	0	0	0	0	0	1
Nelson p	0	0	0	0	0	0	0	0
Polley p	0	0	0	0	0	0	0	0
Weathers p	0	0	0	0	0	0	0	0
Lloyd p	0	0	0	0	0	0	0	0
Wetteland p	0	0	0	0	0	0	0	0
Totals	48	12	20	12	12	6	30	12

FIELDING
DP: 2

BATTING
2B: Jeter (24, off Mahomes); B. Williams (25, off Brandenburg)
HR: O'Neill (19, 3rd inning off Maddux, 0 on, 2 out); Raines 2 (8, 5th inning off Maddux, 0 on, 0 out, 6th inning off Mahomes, 0 on, 1 out); Fielder (38, 6th inning off Mahomes, 1 on, 2 out)
SH: R. Rivera (1, off Hudson)
IBB: Strawberry (5, by Slocumb)

BASERUNNING
SB: Raines (10, 2nd base off Slocumb/Haselman)

PITCHING

Boston Red Sox	IP	H	HR	R	ER	BB	K
Maddux	4	7	2	3	2	1	1
Gunderson	0	0	0	1	1	1	0
Mahomes	1.2	4	2	3	3	1	2
Eshelman	0.2	2	0	3	3	4	1
Brandenburg	0.2	2	0	0	0	0	0
Slocumb	2	3	0	1	1	3	2
Hudson L(3–5)	0.2	2	0	1	1	2	0
Totals	9.2	20	4	12	10	12	6
New York Yankees	**IP**	**H**	**HR**	**R**	**ER**	**BB**	**K**
Key	4.2	8	0	6	6	2	2
Bones	0.1	2	1	2	2	0	1
Pavlas	1.1	1	0	1	1	1	0
Nelson	0	2	0	2	2	1	0
Polley	0.2	0	0	0	0	0	0
Weathers	0.2	1	0	0	0	0	2
Lloyd	0.1	0	0	0	0	0	1
Wetteland W(2–3)	2	0	0	0	0	0	0
Totals	10	14	1	11	11	6	6

HBP: Key (2, Vaughn); Bones (10, Pemberton); Polley (3, Vaughn).
IBB: Slocumb (4, Strawberry); Pavlas (2, Vaughn); Wetteland (4, Cordero).
Umpires: Jim Evans, Larry McCoy, Dale Ford, Chuck Meriwether
Time of Game: 4:45   Attendance: 54,599

Joe Nuxhall
Born: July 30, 1928
Debut: June 10, 1944

Joe Nuxhall spent 16 seasons as a big league pitcher, 15 with his hometown Cincinnati Reds. He was a two-time All-Star and led the National League in shutouts in 1955. In journalism, however, all this is known as "burying the lead." Nuxhall will forever be remembered first and foremost for making his big league debut at the age of 15, a record that should stand forever.

He was actually 15 years, 10 months, and 11 days old (if you're scoring at home) when the Reds ushered him onto the mound at Crosley Field to mop up against the Cardinals in a mid-June, wartime blowout. He began his momentous debut in fine fashion, with two quick outs, but ended up allowing two hits, five walks, and making a pair of wild pitches before being relieved.

From there, Nuxhall took a slower, more deliberate path back to the majors, going to the minors for much-needed seasoning. It would be 1952 before he ascended the Crosley mound again, now at the advanced age of 23.

Nuxhall retired in 1967, beginning his second career, as a Reds team broadcaster. His signature signoff, "Rounding third and heading for home," is now displayed in large letters on the Reds' new ballpark.

It all started with my dad. He was a big old right-hander who could throw the ball real hard. It was during the height of World War II, and teams, including the Reds, were looking for guys with some ability. They came to look at my father a couple of times, and he and I were playing in the same league, but on different teams—the old Sunday League in the Cincinnati area. The scouts came and asked where my dad was pitching, and they were told, "On diamond number three," but they looked out there and asked, "Who's that kid out there?" And they were told, "That's Orville Nuxhall's son." I was 14 then, and they wanted me to go to Ogden, Utah, Class-D ball, but I was on the junior high basketball team, having already won two championships, and we decided I really wanted to win a third. So I didn't sign, but after the season, I signed and would go to Crosley Field whenever I had the chance, after my ninth-grade classes were over. This one day, they're playing the Cardinals, [and I'm] enjoying myself sitting in the dugout with the big leaguers, but the Reds are getting killed that day, rockets getting hit all over the place.

144

All of a sudden I hear the manager's voice calling, "Joe!" But I didn't move, thinking it must be some other Joe, certainly not me, he was looking for. So he yells a little louder. And I looked up, and it was me he was looking back at. He told me to go warm up. Then, all of a sudden, I'm in the game. I got the first batter on a groundout to short, had the next batter 0-and-2, wind up walking him. The next batter popped out, so it's two outs, but then, all of a sudden, it hit me what was going on. I was actually in a major league baseball game, and these were the St. Louis Cardinals. And the whole thing came apart from there. But the first big league hit I gave up was to Stan Musial, and I guess there's no shame in that. I was big, remember, for my age, 6' foot 3", 190, so I don't think they knew I was only 15 . . . Maybe they looked in and thought I looked young, but no one really knew I was 15, until it was reported in the papers the next day.

It's funny, I went home after the game (an 18–0 loss), and no one was there. I had to wait for my dad to come home from work, and when he asked me how my day went, boy did I have a story to tell him: "School was fine, and oh, by the way, I faced Stan Musial!"

Also on June 10, 1944
The depleted Reds also break in a 21-year-old left-handed pitcher from Juniata College, Jake Eisenhart.

BOXSCORE

St. Louis Cardinals 18, Cincinnati Reds 0
Game Played on 6/10/1944 at Crosley Field

	1										
St. Louis	1	6	0	1	1	1	1	2	5	—	18
Cincinnati	0	0	0	0	0	0	0	0	0	—	0

St. Louis	AB	R	H	RBI	PO	A
Hopp cf	4	1	2	1	2	0
Bergamo cf	3	2	1	0	0	0
Garms 3b	4	2	1	1	1	1
Musial rf	4	4	3	3	0	0
Sanders 1b	5	2	3	2	5	0
W.Cooper c	6	1	2	3	7	0
Litwhiler lf	6	1	2	3	4	0
Marion ss	5	2	2	0	4	3
Verban 2b	1	0	1	2		
Fallon 2b-ss	4	1	2	1	3	1
M. Cooper p	6	2	2	1	0	0
Totals	48	18	21	17	27	5

FIELDING
DP: (1) Marion-Sanders

BATTING
2B: Hopp, Fallon
Sac: Garms

BASERUNNING
Stolen bases: W. Cooper, Litwhiler
Team LOB: 18

Cincinnati	AB	R	H	RBI	PO	A
Williams 2b	3	0	2	0	2	3
Marshall rf	4	0	0	0	5	0
Walker cf	3	0	0	0	1	0
Clay cf	1	0	0	0	0	0
Tipton lf	3	0	0	0	2	0
Criscola lf	1	0	0	0	0	0
McCormick 1b	4	0	0	0	8	0
Mueller c	0	0	0	0	0	0
Just c-1b	3	0	1	0	2	0
Mesner 3b	3	0	0	0	1	0
Miller ss	3	0	1	0	4	3
Lohrman p	0	0	0	0	0	0
Heusser p	0	0	0	0	0	0
Fausett p	3	0	1	0	2	1
Nuxhall p	0	0	0	0	0	0
Eisenhardt p	0	0	0	0	0	0
Totals	31	0	5	0	27	8

FIELDING
E: Miller, Fausett

BASERUNNING
Team LOB: 6

PITCHING

St. Louis	IP	H	HR	R	ER	BB	K
M.Cooper W	9.0	5	0	0	0	2	2

Cincinnati	IP	H	HR	R	ER	BB	K
Lohrman L	1.1	5	0	?	?	2	0
Heusser*	0	4	0	?	?	0	0
Fausett	6.2	10	0	?	?	6	2
Nuxhall	0.2	2	0	5	5	5	0
Eisenhardt	0.1	0	0	0	0	1	0
Totals	9.0	21	0	18	18	14	2

* pitched to four hitters in the second inning
Wild pitches: Fausett, Nuxhall
Umpires: Goetz, Jorda, and Reardon
Time of Game: 2:23   Attendance: 3,510

AUTHOR'S NOTE: While Nuxhall would become famous for his Reds debut this day, Eisenhart faded into obscurity, never again appearing in a big league game.

Rafael Palmeiro
Born: September 24, 1964
Debut: September 8, 1986

There may never be a superstar more anonymous than Rafael Palmeiro, whose own son once admitted to him that his favorite player is Ken Griffey Jr. He will go to the Hall of Fame having never been the star player on his own team. Coming up with the Cubs in 1986, he was eclipsed by Andre Dawson. In his first go-around with Texas, he was outshone by Ruben Sierra and Jose Canseco. In his first go-around with Baltimore, it was Cal Ripken's team. Back in Texas, both Pudge and Alex Rodriguez were now on board. And finally, back to Baltimore, the Orioles had just gone out and signed Miguel Tejada and Javy Lopez. Spending his entire career in a shadow is something Palmeiro can trace back to college, where he played second banana to Will Clark.

But in 2003, the lefty slugger became the first big league player to hit at least 38 home runs in nine straight seasons. Through 2004, he was 17th all time in slugging percentage, which is astounding when one considers his original scouting report. In fact, the Cubs hung onto Mark Grace, figuring *him* to be the lefty-swinging first baseman who'd develop home run power. Instead, Palmeiro is now headed toward 550 homers and 3,000 hits, a feat accomplished by only Willie Mays and Hank Aaron. Since 1940, the only left-handed hitter to knock in 148 runs in a season besides Palmeiro is Ted Williams—and unfortunately, like Williams, he has put up gaudy numbers without ever having won a World Series. Also like Williams, he shares a dogged dislike of not being in the lineup. During Palmeiro's first five years in Baltimore, he missed only six games.

But for all the glowing comparisons to the likes of Williams, Mays, and Aaron, he is most proud of having passed Mickey Mantle on the home run, RBI, and doubles lists. Palmeiro grew up in Cuba, and Mantle was his dad's favorite player. The elder Palmeiro pushed young Raffy relentlessly to swing as effortlessly and powerfully as The Mick. When the family emigrated to Miami, young Rafael never owned a car, went on a date, or attended a school dance. Jose Palmeiro made it clear: it's your studies and your baseball, no mas. Rafael recalls that after his first nationally televised game (in which he singled three times and was lauded by Tony Kubek as a "budding star"), his dad called him that night and admonished him to "swing like a man" instead of poking singles into left.

146

Palmeiro's 500th home run came on Mother's Day 2003, with his mom watching from a skybox in Arlington, Texas. The only other member of the 500 club to have hit the milestone homer on Mother's Day? Mickey Mantle.

I had been called up at the end of the Double-A season, and [wife] Lynne and I had driven all night to get to Wrigley from Pittsfield, Massachusetts. We got to Chicago around 11 in the morning, and the Cubs were on the road in Cincinnati. I was dog tired from the all-night drive and probably should have gone right to sleep at the hotel, but Greg Maddux was pitching that game in Cincinnati, and I told Lynne I had to stay up and watch it. The Cubs came home after that game, and I was to meet the team at Wrigley the next day. I couldn't find the ballpark. It was real confusing, all those side streets and all, but when I finally figured out where I was headed, it was so amazing to walk into that clubhouse, down those stairs from the concourse. Some of the guys knew who I was—Maddux, and Jamie Moyer, Dave Martinez, guys I had played with in the minors.

Also on September 8, 1986
Hall of Famer Hank Greenberg dies at the age of 75.

AUTHOR'S NOTE: Greenberg played 13 years, compiling 331 homers, 379 doubles, and 1,051 runs scored. Palmeiro's first 13 years produced eerily similar numbers—314 homers, 396 doubles, and 1,061 runs scored. Each man struck out 837 times. In his autobiography, Greenberg wrote, "History labels you incorrectly." Palmeiro, insistent about how misunderstood he is, would concur with that sentiment.

BOXSCORE

Chicago Cubs 7, Philadelphia Phillies 4
Game Played on Monday, September 8, 1986 (Day) at Wrigley Field

Philadelphia	0	0	3	1	0	0	0	0	—	4	10	0
Chicago	3	0	2	0	1	0	0	1	x	—	7	9	1

BATTING

Philadelphia Phillies	AB	R	H	RBI	BB	K	PO	A
Redus lf	5	1	1	1	0	1	1	0
Thompson cf	4	1	2	2	0	1	4	0
Hayes 1b	3	0	0	0	1	0	9	0
Schmidt 3b	4	0	1	0	0	0	1	1
Wilson rf	4	0	1	0	0	0	1	1
Samuel 2b	4	0	1	0	0	0	1	2
Russell c	4	1	1	1	0	3	6	0
Jeltz ss	3	1	2	0	0	0	1	2
G. Gross ph	1	0	1	0	0	0	0	0
Maddux p	0	0	0	0	0	0	0	0
Stone ph	1	0	0	0	0	0	0	0
Hudson p	0	0	0	0	0	0	0	1
Schu ph	1	0	0	0	0	0	0	0
Hume p	0	0	0	0	0	0	0	0
Roenicke ph	1	0	0	0	0	1	0	0
Totals	**35**	**4**	**10**	**4**	**1**	**6**	**24**	**8**

FIELDING
PB: Russell (14)

BATTING
HR: Thompson (5, 3rd inning off Lynch, 1 on, 2 out); Russell (12, 4th inning off Lynch, 0 on, 2 out)
SH: Maddux (2, off Lynch)

BASERUNNING
CS: Redus (6, 2nd base by Lynch/J. Davis)

Chicago Cubs	AB	R	H	RBI	BB	K	PO	A
Martinez cf	4	1	1	0	0	1	3	0
Walker rf-lf	2	1	1	0	2	0	2	0
Sandberg 2b	4	2	2	0	0	0	2	3
Moreland 3b-rf	3	1	2	2	0	0	0	0
Durham 1b	3	2	1	3	1	0	6	1
J. Davis c	4	0	1	0	0	2	7	1
Palmeiro lf	4	0	1	1	0	0	2	0
Smith p	0	0	0	0	0	0	0	0
Dunston ss	4	0	0	0	0	1	5	4
Lynch p	2	0	0	0	0	1	0	0
Sanderson p	1	0	0	0	0	0	0	0
Speier 3b	0	0	0	0	0	0	0	0
Totals	**31**	**7**	**9**	**6**	**3**	**5**	**27**	**9**

FIELDING
DP: 1
E: Moreland (7)
PB: J. Davis (10)

BATTING
HR: Durham (17, 1st inning off Maddux, 2 on, 2 out)
SF: Moreland (11, off Maddux)

BASERUNNING
SB: Walker (4, 2nd base off Maddux/Russell); Durham (8, 2nd base off Hume/Russell)

PITCHING

Philadelphia Phillies	IP	H	HR	R	ER	BB	K
Maddux L(2–6)	3	4	1	5	4	1	1
Hudson	3	3	0	1	1	1	3
Hume	2	2	0	1	1	1	1
Totals	**8**	**9**	**1**	**7**	**6**	**3**	**5**

Chicago Cubs	IP	H	HR	R	ER	BB	K
Lynch W(5–4)	5.1	8	2	4	4	1	1
Sanderson	2.2	1	0	0	0	0	3
Smith SV(26)	1	1	0	0	0	0	2
Totals	**9**	**10**	**2**	**4**	**4**	**1**	**6**

BK: Maddux (2)
Umpires: Bruce Froemming, Bob Davidson, Randy Marsh, Dana DeMuth
Time of Game: 2:32   Attendance: 6,857

Yosh Kawano, the clubhouse guy, had my number, 25, hanging there in my locker. But some of the veterans had seen my glove and shoes, and they got rid of them. Put new shoes and a new glove in there . . . It was my old college glove. The shoes I'd bought right before spring training in minor league camp, so they were pretty tired, too. Stepping out on that field in the new shoes was something I'll never forget. I was in the lineup right away . . . I batted seventh and went 1-for-4, getting my first hit off a reliever named Tom Hume. The Phillies starter was Greg Maddux's brother, Mike. Anyway, Greg and Lynne and I all went out for dinner after. It was a very special day.

Jim Palmer

Born: October 15, 1945
Debut: April 17, 1965

The greatest pitcher in Baltimore history, Jim Palmer spent his entire 19-year career as an Oriole and nearly made it to a 20th year when he attempted a comeback at the age of 45. By then, the tall righty had been derailed by an assortment of arm injuries, but in his prime, he was a world beater, tossing a World Series shutout at the tender age of 20. In a span of nine seasons, he won at least 20 eight times and for his career lost only three of his 15 postseason starts. He remains the only man to have pitched in a World Series in three different decades.

Blessed with the classic ectomorphic "swimmer's build," Palmer won three Cy Young Awards, including one for a 1973 season that saw him go 22–9 with a league-leading ERA of 2.40. He also led the AL in ERA in 1975 and led the circuit in innings pitched four times, while setting the pace in wins three times. With a career record of 268–152, he was swiftly ushered into the Hall of Fame in 1990.

Palmer is remembered in Baltimore not only for his on-field exploits but for his off-field battles with manager Earl Weaver. (Weaver on Palmer's many injuries: "The Chinese tell time by the 'Year of the Horse,' or the 'Year of the Dragon.' I tell time by the 'Year of the Elbow' and the 'Year of the Ulnar Nerve.'")

Palmer's injuries (some of which, according to his manager, were merely imagined) actually conspired to keep him in the Orioles system when he was young. He was regarded as such a high risk physically that the Orioles left him off their protected list in the 1969 expansion draft. Both Kansas City and the Seattle Pilots could have picked him up, but like the Orioles, they figured he wasn't a good gamble to stay healthy. As it turned out, he pitched nearly 4,000 regular-season innings before retiring to the broadcast booth.

Snow flurries in Boston. That's what I remember. Warming up in the bullpen getting ready to relieve my roommate, Robin Roberts, and it was snowing. And there I go, out onto the field at Fenway, to face Tony Conigliaro with the bases loaded. We had gotten four in the first off Bill Monbouquette, but the Red Sox came right back with three against Robin, and it just looked like it was going to be a long, high-scoring game. Well, I'm 19 years old, just up from the Northern League where I had led the league in strikeouts, ERA, wild pitches, and

BOXSCORE

Boston Red Sox 12, Baltimore Orioles 9
Game Played on Saturday, April 17, 1965 (Day) at Fenway Park

Baltimore	5	0	1	0	0	0	1	1	1	—	9	11	1
Boston	2	0	3	0	0	3	0	4	x	—	12	11	0

BATTING

Baltimore Orioles	AB	R	H	RBI	BB	K	PO	A
Blair cf	5	1	2	1	0	0	3	0
Aparicio ss	4	0	0	0	1	0	2	3
Powell lf	4	1	0	0	1	1	3	0
Robinson 3b	5	1	2	2	0	0	1	5
Siebern 1b	5	1	1	0	0	1	7	2
Blefary rf	5	3	3	2	0	0	0	0
Orsino c	4	1	1	1	1	1	3	0
Adair 2b	2	0	0	0	2	0	4	1
Roberts p	2	0	1	2	0	1	1	0
Palmer p	0	0	0	0	0	0	0	0
McNally p	0	0	0	0	0	0	0	0
Hall p	0	0	0	0	0	0	0	0
Haddix p	0	0	0	0	0	0	0	1
Lau ph	1	1	1	1	0	0	0	0
S. Miller p	0	0	0	0	0	0	0	0
Barber p	0	0	0	0	0	0	0	0
Rowe p	0	0	0	0	0	0	0	0
Totals	37	9	11	9	5	4	24	12

FIELDING
DP: 1
E: Robinson (2)

BATTING
2B: Blair (1, off Earley); Blefary (2, off Radatz).
HR: Blair (1, 1st inning off Monbouquette, 0 on, 0 out); Robinson (1, 1st inning off Monbouquette, 1 on, 1 out); Blefary 2 (2, 3rd inning off Heffner, 0 on, 0 out; 9th inning off Radatz, 0 on, 2 out); Lau (1, 8th inning off Radatz, 0 on, 0 out).
SH: McNally (1, off Earley)

Boston Red Sox	AB	R	H	RBI	BB	K	PO	A
Green cf	4	3	2	1	1	0	4	0
Malzone 3b	4	2	3	4	0	0	0	0
Yastrzemski lf	3	1	1	2	2	0	0	0
Conigliaro rf	4	0	0	0	0	2	3	0
Thomas 1b	4	0	1	2	1	0	9	0
Mantilla 2b	4	1	1	1	1	0	4	3
Tillman c	4	0	0	0	1	0	5	1
Petrocelli ss	2	0	0	0	0	0	1	1
Jones ph	1	1	1	1	0	0	0	0
Radatz p	0	1	0	0	1	0	0	0
Monbouquette p	0	0	0	0	0	0	0	0
Heffner p	0	0	0	0	0	0	0	0
Schilling ph	1	1	1	0	0	0	0	0
Earley p	0	0	0	0	1	0	0	2
Bressoud ph-ss	1	2	1	0	1	0	1	3
Totals	32	12	11	12	9	2	27	10

BATTING
2B: Schilling (1, off Roberts)
3B: Green (1, off Roberts)
HR: Yastrzemski (1, 1st inning off Roberts, 0 on, 1 out)
SF: Malzone (1, off Roberts); Conigliaro (1, off Rowe)

PITCHING

Baltimore Orioles	IP	H	HR	R	ER	BB	K
Roberts	2	5	1	5	5	0	0
Palmer	2	1	0	0	0	2	1
McNally	1.1	0	0	2	2	2	1
Hall	0	2	0	1	1	0	0
Haddix	1.2	1	0	0	0	1	0
S. Miller L(0–1)	0	0	0	2	2	2	0
Barber	0	1	0	2	2	2	0
Rowe	1	1	0	0	0	0	0
Totals	8	11	1	12	12	9	2
Boston Red Sox	**IP**	**H**	**HR**	**R**	**ER**	**BB**	**K**
Monbouquette	0.2	3	2	5	5	2	0
Heffner	2.1	3	1	1	1	1	2
Earley	3	1	0	0	0	2	0
Radatz W(1–1)	3	4	2	3	3	0	2
Totals	9	11	5	9	9	5	4

WP: Palmer (1)
Umpires: Red Flaherty, Lou DiMuro, Frank Umont, Eddie Hurley
Time of Game: 3:22   Attendance: 18,018

---

walks. They said, "Go ahead and get up, kid," and with the bases loaded, in I go in the second inning.

Hank Bauer, our manager, greets me on the mound and says, "Okay, this guy's a high fastball hitter," and I'm thinking, "Great, that's what I throw, high fastballs." He says, "Are you nervous?" I say, "Well, maybe a little apprehensive." And Bauer just kind of squints at me and says, "Okay, go get 'em." But then I say, "Wait, what do I do with this ball?" I had brought the one I had been warming up with in the bullpen with me into the game—didn't know any better. I had always been a starter. Hank kind of smiled, and said, "I can take care of that for you, if you take care of this hitter. We'll call it even." So he takes the warm-up ball and leaves me there on the mound. [Conigliaro] swung hard at the first two pitches, then Red Flaherty, the home plate umpire, called him out, strike three. But the funny thing is, everyone makes a big deal out of the fact I never gave up a grand slam in my 3900 innings, or however many it was . . . But with one of those big swings, Tony C. could have ended all that right away in my very first inning. He almost did.

I learned about Fenway right away in that game . . . Felix Mantilla, a

---

Also on April 17, 1965
The big news at the box office is the weekend debut of Elvis Presley's movie *Girl Happy.*

AUTHOR'S NOTE: Palmer's own "box office appeal" is well-documented . . . and you can insert your own line here regarding Palmer's underwear ads and how happy the girls were.

skinny little infielder, got a fastball in, and a little pop fly ends up in the net for a home run. You better pitch to both sides of the plate there; I learned that immediately! After the game, at the Kenmore Hotel, Robin [Roberts] and Dave McNally went out and took the MTA, because the Kingston Trio had a song about it. That's the only reason we rode the darn thing . . . We rode it two stops just to say we had done it. We had a real nice dinner, and Robin picked up the check at the steakhouse . . . I thought that was the greatest thing in the world.

Lance Parrish
Born: June 15, 1956
Debut: September 5, 1977

Any bio of Lance Parrish includes, by federal mandate, the fact that he was a onetime bodyguard for singer Tina Turner. Parrish swears that's a bit of a misnomer: "I worked security detail at a couple of her concerts. It's not like I traveled the country and took bullets for her."

Parrish spent ten years as the catcher for Sparky Anderson's 1980s Tigers and retired as a three-time Gold Glove winner and eight-time All-Star. He was known as "The Big Wheel," which some erroneously assume derives from Tina Turner's lyric about the "Big wheel a-keep on turning." Actually, the nickname comes from a man who is perhaps Tina Turner's polar opposite—Hall of Fame voice of the Yankees, Mel Allen. As host of *This Week in Baseball* during the '80s, Allen once narrated a Tigers highlight and referred to Parrish as "the big wheel in Motown." Teammate and friend Kirk Gibson happened to be in the clubhouse watching the segment on TV and immediately (and loudly) decreed that a new nickname had been born for his buddy.

Parrish maintains that it was always his intention to play his entire career in Detroit, as Whitaker and Trammell would ultimately do, but he let a contract snub sting him deeply enough to divorce himself from then-Tigers owner Jim Campbell. Parrish hit the free agent market in 1987, only to find the onset of collusion. He settled for a cents-on-the-dollar deal with the Phillies and became a walking suitcase from there. The Angels, Mariners, Indians, Pirates, and Blue Jays would hold him in their employ until he hung it up for good in 1995.

The bruising Parrish had been heavily recruited as a football linebacker. He tells of a certain Pac-10 team wooing him by sending their marching band to his high school to play the school fight song for him. He signed to play pro baseball instead, mixing in a marriage that took place in the Virgin Islands with the banquet being held at a local Dairy Queen.

Now a coach with the Tigers, he will forever be remembered by Tiger fans for his seventh-inning home run that helped to seal the final game of the '84 World Series—not to mention for that Tina Turner story.

I was a September call-up, having just finished up in Evansville, Indiana. Les Moss was my manager, and he called me in his office and told me to drive

152

my vehicle to Detroit and check into the Pontchartrain Hotel. My first actual sighting of Tiger Stadium, I didn't realize it was the stadium. I remember thinking, 'huh, look at that big white warehouse.' The next day I go from the hotel to the ballpark and didn't realize that big white warehouse was the stadium! I got in a taxi, and I told the cabbie, 'take me to Tiger Stadium.' He drives a little, and says, 'there it is,' and I say, 'where, behind that warehouse?' He glares at me, and says, 'no, that's it!' I guess I could have figured it out by the light standards, but remember, I was a West Coast kid . . . my recollection of big league stadiums is that they looked like the Big A in Anaheim, or like Dodger Stadium, not like a big white building.

The first game I played in was against Baltimore . . . I grounded out to second base in my first at bat. Next time, I lined to center, and that was it. Next day, though, I started, and I had three hits. I was excited to be in that starting lineup. My first hit, I got a pitch right on the thumbs and blooped it over the pitcher's mound. A seventy-five-foot single, and when I got back to the dugout at the end of the inning, there was the ball, and the guys had put Band-Aids all over it because it was such a weak hit.

Also on September 5, 1977
The Cleveland Indians stage "I Hate the Yankees Hankee Night" and beat the Bronx Bombers in front of 28,184 Hankee-waving fans.

AUTHOR'S NOTE: These days, Parrish is anything but a Yankee-hater since his son David is a catcher in their minor league system. The younger Parrish began his professional career with a view of the Statue of Liberty beyond the outfield wall as one of the first members of the Yankees' Staten Island affiliate.

BOXSCORE

Baltimore Orioles 5, Detroit Tigers 0
(2nd Game of Doubleheader)
Game Played on Monday, September 5, 1977 (Day) at Tiger Stadium

Baltimore	0	4	0	0	0	1	0	0	0	—	5	13	0
Detroit	0	0	0	0	0	0	0	0	0	—	0	8	1

BATTING

Baltimore Orioles	AB	R	H	RBI	BB	K	PO	A
Bumbry cf-lf	5	0	3	0	0	0	5	0
Dauer 2b	5	0	1	0	0	1	3	3
Kelly rf	4	0	0	0	1	1	1	0
Dimmel rf	0	0	0	0	0	0	1	0
Singleton dh	4	0	1	0	1	0	0	0
Murray 1b	4	1	1	0	1	1	10	1
Muser 1b	0	0	0	0	0	0	0	0
Mora lf	4	0	1	0	0	1	2	0
Maddox cf	1	0	0	0	0	0	0	0
DeCinces 3b	3	1	1	0	1	0	0	3
Belanger ss	4	2	3	2	0	0	2	4
Skaggs c	3	1	2	0	1	0	3	0
R. May p	0	0	0	0	0	0	0	0
Totals	37	5	13	5	5	4	27	11

FIELDING
DP: 3

BATTING
2B: Bumbry (22, off Grilli); Singleton (20, off Taylor)
HR: Belanger (2, 6th inning off Grilli, 0 on, 1 out)
IBB: Murray (6, by Taylor)

BASERUNNING
SB: Kelly (23, 2nd base off Grilli/Parrish)
CS: Bumbry 2 (8, 2nd base by Grilli/Parrish, 3rd base by Grilli/Parrish)

Detroit Tigers	AB	R	H	RBI	BB	K	PO	A
LeFlore cf	4	0	2	0	0	1	4	0
Stanley rf	4	0	1	0	0	0	1	0
Staub dh	4	0	2	0	0	0	0	0
Adams 1b	4	0	0	0	0	1	10	1
Parrish c	2	0	0	0	2	0	4	2
Wockenfuss lf	4	0	1	0	0	0	2	0
Rodriguez 3b	4	0	2	0	0	0	1	2
Veryzer ss	3	0	0	0	0	0	2	3
Scrivener 2b	3	0	0	0	0	0	2	5
Grilli p	0	0	0	0	0	0	0	1
Taylor p	0	0	0	0	0	0	1	0
Totals	32	0	8	0	2	2	27	14

FIELDING
DP: 1
E: Rodriguez (6)

BATTING
2B: LeFlore (23, off R. May)

PITCHING

Baltimore Orioles	IP	H	HR	R	ER	BB	K
R. May W(15–12)	9	8	0	0	0	2	2
Detroit Tigers	**IP**	**H**	**HR**	**R**	**ER**	**BB**	**K**
Grilli L(1–2)	8	12	1	5	5	4	4
Taylor	1	1	0	0	0	1	0
Totals	9	13	1	5	5	5	4

IBB: Taylor (2, Murray)
Umpires: Larry McCoy, Dale Ford, Durwood Merrill, Don Denkinger
Time of Game: 2:14   Attendance: 22,062

Tony Pena

Born: June 4, 1957
Debut: September 1, 1980

Tony Pena the manager has proven to be just as tough and glowingly optimistic as Tony Pena the All-Star catcher. From humble beginnings in Monte Cristo, Dominican Republic, he has now begun construction on a new home that will sit on the island's highest point. It is a 9,000-square-foot metaphor for how high his star has risen.

His 18-year playing career began with the Pittsburgh Pirates just after the Bucs' "We Are Family" World Series run of 1979. That summer, Pena had followed the varsity from three hours north, at Double-A Buffalo. Having hit just eight home runs in the Texas League the year before (at a spacious home ballpark in Shreveport), Pena made his Pirates bosses sit up and take notice that summer of '79 by suddenly jolting 34 at Buffalo's old War Memorial Stadium. Suddenly, with those 34 homers and a world of confidence, he was ready to take flight.

He became a five-time All-Star and went to the postseason with four different teams. He hit .409 in the '87 World Series for St. Louis and crushed a game-winning 12th-inning homer for the Indians in the '95 division series. Still, despite all that, he will be most remembered for his unique, if not revolutionary, catching style, crouched low with one leg sticking out.

As the Royals manager in 2003, he steered the team into shocking playoff contention, buoyed by a 16–3 start to the season. Pena, ever Mr. Blue Skies, had T-shirts printed up in both Spanish and English: "Nosotros creemos" and "We Believe." Although the Royals fell a few games short of the Twins, sportswriters across the country named him the American League Manager of the Year, giving him 24 of the 28 first-place votes.

Pena's upbeat, positive nature is most visible when the chips are down. In Toronto, during that near-miss 2003 season, the Royals had blown a seven-run lead and lost to the Blue Jays. Initially, the visiting clubhouse was stone silent. Then Pena entered the room and cranked the radio up to high volume, shouting, "It's just one game, boys! Nobody died! Let's dance a little!" And although no one was brave enough to join him, Pena did the samba down the hall and into his office.

I was in Portland, Oregon, and I was a September call-up . . . Jim Mahoney was our manager. He said, "Hey kid! You're going to the big leagues!" I called my wife and my mom . . . My mom had never really wanted me to go and play baseball . . . She finally said I could, but I had to convince her that baseball was all that was in my heart. She was a wonderful player, too . . . She would pitch to me and my brothers when we were young . . . She had played softball and played it very well. But it took a long time to convince her I needed to go to America, to see if I could make it to the big leagues. So I called her first when I did [make it].

My first at bat was against the Astros' Randy Neimann . . . I struck out. Four pitches. My hands were shaking. But what I remember most is my teammate, Manny Sanguillen. He picked me up, as the driver, from the hotel . . . He personally met me to make sure I got to Three River Stadium okay. I walked into the clubhouse, and the first thing I did was I took the camera out of my bag and started taking pictures of everybody. Willie Stargell, Pops, smiled big for me . . . May he rest in peace.

Also on September 1, 1980
Pena is one of two 23-year-old Dominicans making his debut on this night. The other is Kansas City's Manny Castillo.

AUTHOR'S NOTE: Castillo began his career with a Royals team 20 1/2 games ahead in the AL West at the start of play that evening. Pena, meantime, debuted for a Pirates team that was in a three-way tie for first in the NL East. The Royals would coast into the World Series that autumn, while the Pirates would end up frozen out by the cross-state Phillies. However, while Castillo would eventually total 236 big league games, Pena would play in 2,017, including three dozen in the postseason.

BOXSCORE

Houston Astros 10, Pittsburgh Pirates 4 (1st Game of Doubleheader)
Game Played on Monday, September 1, 1980 (Day) at Three Rivers Stadium

										R	H	E
Houston	5	0	0	0	4	0	1	0	0	—	10	11	1
Pittsburgh	2	1	1	0	0	0	0	0	0	—	4	8	2

BATTING

Houston Astros	AB	R	H	RBI	BB	K	PO	A
Morgan 2b	2	2	1	1	3	0	1	1
Gonzalez ss	1	0	0	0	0	0	0	0
Cabell 3b	4	1	2	1	1	1	0	0
Howe 3b	0	0	0	0	0	0	2	0
Puhl rf	4	1	2	2	1	1	1	0
Loucks rf	0	0	0	0	0	0	0	0
Cruz lf	5	0	0	0	0	0	4	0
Woods lf	0	0	0	0	0	0	0	0
Cedeno cf	2	2	2	1	1	0	1	0
Leonard cf	2	0	0	0	0	0	3	0
Walling 1b	5	1	1	1	0	0	6	0
Ashby c	3	2	1	0	2	0	7	0
Landestoy ss-2b	5	1	2	2	0	0	2	2
Forsch p	1	0	0	0	0	1	0	0
Niemann p	1	0	0	0	0	0	0	0
Heep ph	1	0	0	0	0	0	0	0
Smith p	2	0	0	0	0	1	0	1
Totals	38	10	11	8	8	4	27	4

FIELDING
DP: 1
E: Morgan (5)

BATTING
2B: Puhl (18, off D. Robinson); Landestoy (11, off D. Robinson); Cedeno (28, off Scurry); Cabell (17, off Scurry)
3B: Walling (5, off Mahler)
HR: Morgan (7, 1st inning off D. Robinson, 0 on, 0 out)
IBB: Morgan (5, by Solomon)

BASERUNNING
SB: Cedeno (41, 2nd base off Mahler/Ott)

Pittsburgh Pirates	AB	R	H	RBI	BB	K	PO	A
Moreno cf	3	1	0	0	1	1	3	0
Foli ss	5	0	1	0	0	0	0	2
Madlock 3b	4	2	2	3	0	1	0	3
Parker rf	4	0	2	0	0	0	2	0
Easler lf	4	0	0	0	0	2	2	0
Milner 1b	4	0	0	0	0	1	11	1
Ott c	3	1	2	1	1	0	5	0
Garner 2b	4	0	1	0	0	0	3	2
D. Robinson p	0	0	0	0	0	0	0	0
Scurry p	1	0	0	0	0	0	0	0
Pena ph	1	0	0	0	0	1	0	0
Mahler p	0	0	0	0	0	0	0	0
Solomon p	0	0	0	0	0	0	0	0
Beall ph	1	0	0	0	0	1	0	0
Lee p	0	0	0	0	0	0	1	1
Carbo ph	0	0	0	0	1	0	0	0
Totals	34	4	8	4	3	7	27	9

FIELDING
DP: 1
E: Ott (11), Solomon (3)

BATTING
2B: Parker (25, off Forsch)
HR: Madlock 2 (8, 1st inning off Forsch, 1 on, 1 out; 3rd inning off Forsch, 0 on, 1 out); Ott (7, 2nd inning off Forsch, 0 on, 0 out)
HBP: Moreno (1, by Smith)

BASERUNNING
SB: Moreno (80, 2nd base off Forsch/Ashby)

PITCHING

Houston Astros	IP	H	HR	R	ER	BB	K
Forsch	2.1	5	3	4	4	1	1
Niemann	1.2	1	0	0	0	0	3
Smith W(5–5)	5	2	0	0	0	2	3
Totals	9	8	3	4	4	3	7

Pittsburgh Pirates	IP	H	HR	R	ER	BB	K
D. Robinson L(5–8)	0.2	5	1	5	5	1	0
Scurry	3.1	2	0	0	0	2	3
Mahler	0	1	0	3	3	2	0
Solomon	3	2	0	2	1	3	0
Lee	2	1	0	0	0	0	1
Totals	9	11	1	10	9	8	4

BK: D. Robinson (2)
HBP: Smith (4, Moreno)
IBB: Solomon (4, Morgan)
Umpires: Joe West, Lanny Harris, Paul Pryor, John McSherry
Time of Game: 3:07   Attendance: Unknown

Terry Pendleton
Born: July 16, 1960
Debut: July 18, 1984

Terry Pendleton was supposedly a second baseman, but the switch-hitter was moved to third and responded with three Gold Gloves. He was supposed to be a doubles hitter, but he ended up second on the Cardinals in home runs in 1987, a year after he'd hit just one homer in 578 at bats. He was supposed to be finished after a listless 1990, but he responded with an MVP season for the Braves in '91.

The only thing the classy switch-hitter never got that he was "supposed to" was a World Series ring. He played in five Fall Classics but ended up on the losing end all five times. He pushed St. Louis into the '87 postseason with some dramatic late-season hits, including a crushing ninth-inning homer off the Mets' Roger McDowell.

He added more late-season clutch moments as a Brave in '91. They had been a last-place team the season before, but as the Braves' most significant free agent addition, Pendleton responded by pacing the league in hitting (.319) while smashing 34 doubles, eight triples, and 22 jacks. In the seven-game thriller against Minnesota that fall, he homered twice more while hitting .367.

He followed with a career-best 105 RBI in 1992, winning another Gold Glove, all while providing veteran leadership to a Braves team still a year away from breaking in Chipper Jones and Javy Lopez. When the "new wave" Braves came up, Pendleton was battling neck and back problems, although his "veteran leadership" continued to manifest itself. In a game in which teammate Marvin Freeman failed to retaliate for the opposition's knockdowns, Pendleton walked off the field and into the clubhouse, later explaining to all concerned the "unwritten code" to which his team must learn to adhere.

In 1995, slowed by injuries, he signed on with the Florida Marlins. A year later, he was flipped back to the Braves for a prospect named Roosevelt Brown. Having finished his playing career with the Reds and Royals, he ended up back in Atlanta once more, this time as the team's hitting coach.

I got the good news the day after my 24th birthday. Up to St. Louis from Triple-A. Jim Fregosi called me on the phone about twenty minutes after a game, said, "Are you feeling okay?" And I'm like, "Of course. Why? You just

156

saw me twenty minutes ago. You know I'm healthy." And he says, "I'm just checking because they want you in The Show tomorrow."

Willie McGee and Tommy Herr were both very kind to me when I arrived that next day. I had met them both when they had come through the minors on rehab, and they were both so professional, I never forgot that. They took the time to make me feel welcome when I was joining them in St. Louis, and that solidified everything I'd thought about them before. Lee Thomas was our minor league director, and he met me at the ballpark, telling me to just keep doing what I'd been doing down in Triple-A, that there was no pressure and not to be nervous. I appreciated that, too. I hit sixth and started at third base. They told me I'd be up seven to ten days if I played well, so to just relax . . . But I knew if I played real well, I could stay up there and not be sent back. Force their hand, you know? And that first game was a good start—I played well, and we won in extra innings.

Also on July 18, 1984
Walter Mondale wins the Democratic Party's presidential nomination at the national convention in San Francisco.

AUTHOR'S NOTE: The only state Mondale carried in that fall's election was Minnesota. Minnesota carried a much darker connotation for Pendleton, whose Cardinals lost Game Seven of the '87 World Series there, and whose Braves lost Game Seven of the '91 Series there.

BOXSCORE

St. Louis Cardinals 8, San Francisco Giants 4
Game Played on Wednesday, July 18, 1984 (Night) at Busch Stadium II

San Francisco	0	1	1	0	0	2	0	0	0	0	—	4	15	3
St. Louis	0	0	1	0	0	2	0	0	1	0	4	—	8	13	0

BATTING

San Francisco Giants	AB	R	H	RBI	BB	K	PO	A
Gladden cf	5	1	3	2	0	0	4	0
Trillo 2b	6	0	2	0	0	2	2	2
Baker rf	5	0	2	1	1	0	0	0
Lacey p	0	0	0	0	0	0	0	0
Leonard lf	5	1	2	1	0	2	1	0
Brenly 1b	5	0	1	0	0	1	10	1
Youngblood 3b	4	0	0	0	1	1	0	2
Nicosia c	5	1	3	0	0	0	12	0
Wellman ss	4	1	1	0	1	0	2	4
Hammaker p	1	0	0	0	1	0	0	1
C. Davis ph	0	0	0	0	1	0	0	0
Cornell p	0	0	0	0	0	0	0	0
Thompson ph	1	0	0	0	0	1	0	0
Minton p	0	0	0	0	0	0	1	0
Rabb ph-rf	1	0	1	0	0	0	0	0
Totals	**42**	**4**	**15**	**4**	**5**	**7**	**32**	**10**

FIELDING
E: Leonard (6), Nicosia (2), Minton (1)

BATTING
2B: Leonard (17, off Sutter)
3B: Nicosia 2 (2, off Horton, off Lahti)
HR: Leonard (13, 2nd inning off Horton, 0 on, 0 out)
SH: Gladden (2, off Von Ohlen)
IBB: C. Davis (2, by Lahti)

BASERUNNING
SB: Wellman (8, 2nd base off Lahti/Porter)
CS: Wellman (2, 2nd base by Horton/Porter)

St. Louis Cardinals	AB	R	H	RBI	BB	K	PO	A
L. Smith lf	6	3	4	0	0	0	3	0
Herr 2b	6	1	3	3	0	0	5	5
Landrum lf	2	0	1	0	0	1	0	0
Van Slyke ph-cf	3	1	0	0	1	0	2	1
Hendrick rf	5	1	1	0	1	2	3	0
Green 1b	6	0	0	0	0	2	9	1
Pendleton 3b	5	1	3	1	1	0	1	2
Porter c	4	1	1	4	2	1	9	0
Speier ss	3	0	0	0	0	2	1	2
Jorgensen ph	1	0	0	0	0	0	0	0
Howe ss	0	0	0	0	1	0	0	2
Horton p	1	0	0	0	0	1	0	1
Lahti p	1	0	0	0	0	1	0	0
Allen p	0	0	0	0	0	0	0	0
Braun ph	1	0	0	0	0	0	0	0
Sutter p	0	0	0	0	0	0	0	0
Salas ph	1	0	0	0	0	0	0	0
Citarella p	0	0	0	0	0	0	0	0
Brummer ph	1	0	0	0	0	1	0	0
Von Ohlen p	0	0	0	0	0	0	0	1
Totals	**46**	**8**	**13**	**8**	**6**	**11**	**33**	**15**

FIELDING
DP: 3

BATTING
2B: L. Smith 2 (15, off Hammaker, off Cornell); Herr 2 (14, off Cornell, off Lacey)
HR: Porter (9,11th inning off Lacey, 3 on, 2 out)
IBB: Porter (9, by Cornell); Hendrick (1, by Minton); Howe (1, by Minton)

BASERUNNING
SB: L. Smith 2 (24, 2nd base off Cornell/Nicosia, 2nd base off Minton/Nicosia)

PITCHING

San Francisco Giants	IP	H	HR	R	ER	BB	K
Hammaker	5	3	0	1	0	0	7
Cornell	2	4	0	2	2	2	2
Minton	3	3	0	1	1	4	2
Lacey L(0–1)	0.2	3	1	4	4	0	0
Totals	**10.21**	**3**	**1**	**8**	**7**	**6**	**11**

St. Louis Cardinals	IP	H	HR	R	ER	BB	K
Horton	4.1	8	1	2	2	2	3
Lahti	1	2	0	2	2	2	1
Allen	1.2	1	0	0	0	0	0
Sutter	2	2	0	0	0	1	2
Citarella	1	0	0	0	0	0	1
Von Ohlen W(1–0)	1	2	0	0	0	0	0
Totals	**11**	**15**	**1**	**4**	**4**	**5**	**7**

BK: Hammaker (2)
IBB: Cornell (6, Porter); Minton 2 (8, Hendrick, Howe); Lahti (8, C. Davis)
Time of Game: 3:38   Attendance: 18,492

Tony Perez
Born: May 14, 1942
Debut: July 26, 1964

Hall of Famer Tony Perez was a vital cog in Cincinnati's "Big Red Machine" of the 1970s. In fact, his 379 career home runs and seven RBI titles probably should have put him in Cooperstown many years before he was finally inducted, in 2000. Reds manager Sparky Anderson always said, "With a runner at second base, there was no one you'd rather see at the plate than Perez." Dave Bristol, perhaps Perez's favorite manager, once said, "If a game goes long enough, Perez will find a way to win it for you."

After Perez piled up triple-digit RBI totals year after year for the Reds, Cincy fans were stunned when president/GM Bob Howsam dealt the popular slugger to Montreal following the '76 championship season. Howsam later lamented the trade as the worst he ever made. After three years in Montreal, Perez logged three years in Boston, one in Philadelphia, then had a three-year curtain call with the Reds in the mid '80s.

Now a member of the Florida Marlins front office, Perez totaled 23 major league seasons, amassing seven All-Star appearances and one All-Star Game MVP Award, when he won the '67 contest with a 15th-inning homer in Anaheim.

The Cuban-born Perez played in five World Series, including four with the Reds. His sixth-inning two-run homer off Bill Lee was critical in propelling his team past Boston in 1975's Game Seven. Perez stayed productive well into his forties, hitting a grand slam off former Phillies teammate John Denny the day before he turned 43. In his 23 big league seasons, he never spent a day on the disabled list.

An immensely proud man, Perez closed his Hall of Fame induction speech with these words of wisdom: "To all the present and future players, please, respect and honor the uniform you wear. Respect your fans and, more important, respect the game of baseball, our national great pastime." Perez's contributions to "our national great pastime" have been tremendous.

What I remember is that I was at Triple-A with the San Diego Padres, who were the farm team for the Reds back then. We were playing in Oklahoma City, and I got the call from the manager, Dave Bristol, who called [me] in my hotel room. He said he needed to hang up so the Reds traveling secretary could call me. So I sat there staring at the phone until it rang again a few minutes later. The traveling secretary called and arranged for me to go to Cincinnati.

I took a cab right to the ballpark and there was a doubleheader, and I played right away, both games. I had traveled all night from Oklahoma, but it didn't matter. I hit a few balls well, but I went 0-for-8. My very first swing, a line drive right to the shortstop, and it would be like that for both games, pretty much.

I had known most of the guys from spring training, which made me feel welcome. Fred Hutchinson was the manager, and he was very supportive. It wasn't easy to call home with the news that I had made it. My family was all back in Cuba, and back then, 1964, it was very difficult to find a way to get through and call to home. I had to send a telegram. That's how they found out that one of the family had made it all the way to the major leagues—a telegram I sent from a hotel in Cincinnati.

Also on July 26, 1964
Hall of Fame induction weekend in Cooperstown ushers in Red Faber, Luke Appling, Burleigh Grimes, Heinie Manush, and Miller Huggins.

AUTHOR'S NOTE: The Cincinnati-born Huggins once said, as Yankees manager, "A manager has his cards dealt for him, and he must play them." Perez, as the Reds' 1993 manager, was dealt a brutal hand. He was kept on the job only a few weeks before owner Marge Schott canned him in favor of Davey Johnson. Outraged Reds players called for a strike, which they never did carry out.

BOXSCORE

Cincinnati Reds 7, Pittsburgh Pirates 2

Game Played on Sunday, 7/26/1964, Game 1 of Doubleheader (Day) at Crosley Field

Pittsburgh	0	2	0	0	0	0	0	0	0	—	2
Cincinnati	1	0	0	0	2	0	0	4	x	—	7

Pittsburgh Pirates	AB	R	H	RBI	BB	K	PO	A
B. Bailey 3b	4	0	1	0	0	0	0	2
B. Virdon cf	4	0	0	0	0	1	3	1
R. Clemente rf	4	0	1	0	0	1	2	0
J. Lynch lf	4	1	1	1	0	1	0	0
W. Stargell 1b	4	1	2	1	0	0	9	0
S. Burgess c	4	0	2	0	0	0	7	0
O. McFarlane pr-c	0	0	0	0	0	0	1	0
B. Mazeroski 2b	4	0	1	0	0	1	1	2
D. Schofield ss	4	0	0	0	0	2	1	2
J. Gibbon p	2	0	1	0	0	0	0	2
D. Schwall p	0	0	0	0	0	0	0	0
G. Freese ph	1	0	0	0	0	0	0	0
R. Face p	0	0	0	0	0	0	0	0
F. Bork p	0	0	0	0	0	0	0	1
D. Clendenon ph	1	0	0	0	0	1	0	0
Totals	**36**	**2**	**9**	**2**	**0**	**7**	**24**	**10**

FIELDING
E: B.Bailey (fumble); S.Burgess (throw)
PB: S. Burgess
Outfield assist: B. Virdon (D. Johnson at 1B)
DP: (2). D. Schofield-B. Mazeroski-W. Stargell; B. Virdon-W. Stargell

BATTING
2B: B. Bailey (off J. Jay); J. Gibbon (off J. Jay); B. Mazeroski (off J. Jay)
HR: J. Lynch (2nd inning off J. Jay, 0 on, 0 out); W. Stargell (2nd inning off J. Jay, 0 on, 0 out)
RBI, scoring position, less than 2 outs: B. Virdon 0–2; R. Clemente 0–1; D. Schofield 0–1

BASERUNNING
Team LOB: 8

Cincinnati Reds	AB	R	H	RBI	BB	K	PO	A
P. Rose 2b	4	1	1	1	0	1	1	4
C. Ruiz ph-2b	1	0	0	0	0	0	0	0
T. Harper cf	2	1	0	0	1	1	1	0
V. Pinson ph-cf	2	0	0	0	0	1	0	0
F. Robinson rf-lf	4	1	1	0	0	0	2	0
D. Johnson lf-1b	3	1	2	1	1	0	1	0
T. Perez 1b	2	0	0	0	1	1	10	0
M. Keough rf	1	1	1	0	0	0	1	0
D. Pavletich c	3	1	1	0	1	0	7	0
L. Cardenas ss	4	1	2	4	0	0	3	2
S. Boros 3b	3	0	2	0	1	1	1	2
J. Jay p	3	0	0	0	0	2	0	1
S. Ellis p	1	0	0	0	0	0	0	0
Totals	**33**	**7**	**10**	**6**	**5**	**7**	**27**	**9**

FIELDING
E: L. Cardenas (fumble)
DP: (1). T. Perez, unassisted

BATTING
2B: S. Boros (off F.Bork)
HR: P. Rose (1st inning off J. Gibbon, 0 on, 0 out); L. Cardenas (8th inning off R. Face, 3 on, 0 out)
RBI, scoring position, less than 2 outs: C. Ruiz 0–1; D. Johnson 1–1; D. Pavletich 0–2; L. Cardenas 2–2; J. Jay 0–2; S. Ellis 0–1
GIDP: D. Pavletich

BASERUNNING
SB: T. Harper (double SB, HP off J. Gibbon/S. Burgess); F. Robinson (double SB, 2nd base off J. Gibbon/S. Burgess)
Team LOB: 7

PITCHING Pittsburgh	IP	H	HR	R	ER	BB	K
J. Gibbon L*	4.0	6	1	3	3	4	3
D. Schwall	2.0	0	0	0	0	0	3
R. Face +	1.0	3	1	4	4	1	0
F. Bork	1.0	1	0	0	0	0	1
Total	**8.0**	**10**	**2**	**7**	**7**	**5**	**7**
Cincinnati	**IP**	**H**	**HR**	**R**	**ER**	**BB**	**K**
J. Jay W	7.2	9	2	2	2	0	6
S. Ellis S	1.1	0	0	0	0	0	1
Total	**9.0**	**9**	**2**	**2**	**2**	**0**	**7**

* Pitched to 3 batters in 5th
+ Pitched to 4 batters in 8th
Inherited Runners—Scored: D. Schwall 1–0; R. Face 0–0; F. Bork 0–0; S. Ellis 2–0
HBP: B. Bailey by J. Jay
WP: J. Jay
Umpires: Unknown
Time of Game: 2:31   Attendance: Unknown

Lou Piniella
Born: August 28, 1943
Debut: September 4, 1964

In accepting the Devil Rays managing job, "Sweet" Lou Piniella was going home to Tampa-St. Pete (good) but taking over a team that had generated all the excitement of a wet tennis ball (not good). After a fifth consecutive last-place finish in the franchise's five-year history, Piniella was hailed as the team's saving grace. Sadly, the team finished last again in 2003. Before 2004 began, the combative Piniella "guaranteed," Joe Namath style, that the run of futility was at its end. The '04 D-Rays started the year losing 28 of 38, and things looked a shade beyond grim. Then, somehow, Tampa Bay ripped off a 12-game winning steak in June and would indeed finish . . . second-to-last. Mission accomplished, and with only two ejections.

According to SABR's Doug Pappas, Piniella has been kicked out of a game (as a player and manager) 70 times, one more than his friend and fellow Tampa native, Tony La Russa. It's a stunner, but the famously demonstrative Piniella has actually been ejected 32 fewer times than Atlanta's Bobby Cox. In fact, Piniella once went nearly four years (September '78 to July '82) without being asked to leave a game. For the record, Larry Barnett has gotten to give Piniella the thumb more than any other umpire—four times in a stretch of five seasons, including the memorable meltdown in Cleveland (August '98), when Lou kicked his hat around Jacobs Field like a soccer ball. Barnett said afterwards it was the best blowup he'd seen live since Earl Weaver dramatically ripped up a rule book on the pitcher's mound.

In his playing days, Piniella was a live wire, too, memorably igniting a brawl in a Yankees–Red Sox showdown at Fenway. The collision at home plate with Carlton Fisk led to a nasty fight in which Bill Lee shredded his shoulder grappling with Graig Nettles and Mickey Rivers. At the plate, Piniella once hit .330 for the Yankees, and although he always had low walk totals, he had the low strikeout total to match.

After being named Manager of the Year in both 1995 and 2001, Piniella is now looking to pull off a miracle at Tropicana Field. *Third* place, anyone?

I was well-traveled for a young guy . . . The Orioles brought me up at the age of 20, all the way from Aberdeen, South Dakota. They had a hell of a team there, with Eddie Watt, Mark Belanger, and Cal Ripken as our manager. Senior, that is. Junior was probably four years old back then. I went from being an

Aberdeen Pheasant to being a Baltimore Oriole, which was quite a jump, of course, but I wasn't really supposed to play that much. But the general manager, Mr. McPhail, told me, "We're going to send you to Aberdeen for two or three weeks, let you be around that team a little, and I know that's a step back for you since you played a higher classification last year. But if you do that for me, we'll bring you up to Baltimore when Aberdeen is done." Who could resist that?

My first at bat was against the Angels. I pinch-hit for a Hall of Famer, Robin Roberts, in the Coliseum. They had a right-handed pitcher on the mound, and I grounded out to the shortstop on a 3–2 pitch. Robin Roberts comes up to me, strides up to me, and says, "Young man! I could have done *that*!" And that was my only at bat ever for Hank Bauer. My next big league at bat was in 1969. I had five full years to think about that ground out.

Also on September 4, 1964
Gilligan's Island makes its television debut on CBS. The "Three Hour Tour" would eventually shift from Friday night programming to Saturday, ahead of *The Jackie Gleason Show* and behind the forgettable *Mr. Broadway*.

AUTHOR'S NOTE: Piniella's tour as George Steinbrenner's personal Mr. Broadway lasted three years, rather than three hours. He served a three-year stewardship soon after in Cincinnati, followed by a ten-year run in Seattle. Piniella's Seattle experience was occasionally compared to that of the Skipper from the aforementioned sitcom: Piniella would have his mid-to-late-90s Mariner teams in position to win (get off the island), only to see Little Buddy (the bullpen) mess it all up at the last minute. The Skipper used to vent his frustration by whacking Gilligan with his sailor's hat; Piniella took out *his* frustration on Seattle's pitching coaches.

BOXSCORE

Los Angeles Angels 7, Baltimore Orioles 1
Game Played on Friday, 9/4/1964 (Night) at Dodger Stadium

Baltimore	0	0	0	0	0	0	0	0	1	—	1
Los Angeles	0	0	3	0	2	0	2	0	x	—	7

Baltimore	AB	R	H	RBI	BB	K	PO	A
R. Snyder lf	5	0	0	0	0	0	0	0
L. Aparicio ss	4	0	2	0	0	0	5	4
N. Siebern 1b	3	0	0	0	1	0	7	0
B. Robinson 3b	3	0	0	0	1	0	0	1
S. Bowens rf	4	0	0	0	0	1	1	0
C. Lau c	3	1	2	0	1	0	5	0
J. Brandt cf	4	0	1	0	0	0	4	0
J. Adair 2b	4	0	0	1	0	1	2	2
R. Roberts p	0	0	0	0	1	0	0	1
L. Piniella ph	1	0	0	0	0	0	0	0
C. Estrada p	0	0	0	0	0	0	0	0
D. Vineyard p	0	0	0	0	0	0	0	0
J. Orsino ph	1	0	1	0	0	0	0	0
B. Saverine pr	0	0	0	0	0	0	0	0
S. Jones p	0	0	0	0	0	0	0	0
B. Johnson ph	1	0	0	0	0	0	0	0
Totals	**33**	**1**	**6**	**1**	**4**	**2**	**24**	**8**

FIELDING
DP: (1). L. Aparicio-J. Adair-N. Siebern

BATTING
2B: L. Aparicio (off F. Newman); C. Lau (off F. Newman)
RBI, scoring position, less than 2 outs: N. Siebern 0–3; J. Adair 1–1
GIDP: R. Snyder; B. Robinson

BASERUNNING
Team LOB: 9

Los Angeles	AB	R	H	RBI	BB	K	PO	A
P. Schaal 3b	5	1	1	0	0	1	0	4
J. Fregosi ss	4	1	2	1	0	0	4	7
W. Smith lf	3	2	1	1	1	0	0	0
J. Adcock 1b	4	2	3	4	0	0	9	0
V. Power 1b	0	0	0	0	0	0	4	1
L. Clinton rf	4	0	1	1	0	0	3	0
B. Rodgers c	3	0	0	0	1	1	2	0
R. Reichardt cf	4	0	0	0	0	1	3	0
B. Knoop 2b	4	0	2	0	0	0	2	4
F. Newman p	3	1	1	0	1	0	0	1
Totals	**34**	**7**	**11**	**7**	**3**	**3**	**27**	**17**

FIELDING
E: W. Smith (fumble); F. Newman (fumble)
DP: (2) B. Knoop-J. Fregosi-J. Adcock; J. Fregosi-V. Power

BATTING
2B: J. Fregosi (off R. Roberts); L. Clinton (off R. Roberts)
HR: W. Smith (5th inning off C. Estrada, 0 on, 0 out); J. Adcock 2 (5th inning off C. Estrada, 0 on, 0 out; 7th inning off S. Jones, 1 on, 1 out)
2-out RBI: J. Adcock; L. Clinton
RBI, scoring position, less than 2 outs: J. Fregosi 1–1; W. Smith 0–2
GIDP: P. Schaal

BASERUNNING
Team LOB: 6

PITCHING

Baltimore	IP	H	HR	R	ER	BB	K
R. Roberts L	3.0	6	0	3	3	1	2
C. Estrada	2.0	3	2	2	2	0	1
D. Vineyard	1.0	0	0	0	0	1	0
S. Jones	2.0	2	1	2	2	1	0
Total	**8.0**	**11**	**3**	**7**	**7**	**3**	**3**

Los Angeles	IP	H	HR	R	ER	BB	K
F. Newman W	9.0	6	0	1	1	4	2

Inherited Runners—Scored: C. Estrada 0–0; D. Vineyard 0–0; S. Jones 0–0
IBB: B. Robinson by F. Newman; B. Rodgers by R. Roberts
Umpires: HP: Red Flaherty, 1B: Bill Haller, 2B: Eddie Hurley, 3B: Sam Carrigan
Time of Game: 2:01   Attendance: 9,737

Jorge Posada
Born: August 17, 1971
Debut: September 4, 1995

It took a few years before Jorge Posada really got going as a member of the Yankees' winning fabric, but once he got going, he began a run that put him among the elite catchers in both leagues. During Posada's first three big league seasons, he was labeled as a streaky hitter who had a tough time calling a game and managing a veteran pitching staff. Joe Girardi, with inferior skills, was the Yankees catcher of choice, lauded for his composure and ability to bring out the best in everyone around him. When Girardi left for his hometown Chicago Cubs in 1999, it was time for Posada to sink or swim, and he glided beautifully through sometimes turbulent waters.

The '99 season saw Posada shore up his defense while blasting 28 home runs and driving in 86 runs. He made his first All-Star team a year later and had some big hits the following year as the Yankees made it a run of four trips to the Fall Classic in a span of five seasons. His solo homer was the only run of the Division Series' Game Three against Oakland. The 2002 season saw him explode for 40 doubles, the highest total for a catcher since Pudge Rodriguez in 1996. He followed with what became his high-water season in 2003, when he placed third in MVP voting, hitting 30 home runs and collecting 101 RBI. He followed it up with a stellar 2004 (81 RBI, fourth in the league in on-base percentage), joining fellow Puerto Ricans Javy Lopez and Rodriguez as the class of American League backstops.

Having begun his pro career as a second baseman, Posada wasn't moved to catcher until his third minor league season. His ability to speak both English and Spanish served him well as he moved through the ranks. Off the field, he has helped raise awareness of birth defects. His son, Jorge Jr., was diagnosed with craniosynostosis when he was an infant and had to undergo five major surgeries to correct the condition. The Jorge Posada Foundation has been providing financial support to families whose children are similarly afflicted.

I was a September call-up in 1995, right around the time Cal Ripken was going to break Lou Gehrig's record . . . Stump Merrill, my Triple-A manager, told me the good news, and I called my parents back home right away. I remember getting in at two in the afternoon to New York, grabbing a cab and going right to the stadium. I didn't play right away, but the first time I saw my name on the lineup card, that was real exciting.

I'll always remember Don Mattingly making it a point to congratulate me, first for getting there, then for getting a start, then for getting my first hit . . . He made it a point to come shake my hand, and to me, he was what the Yankees were all about. That was his last year, too, so I feel privileged to have had the chance to get to know him that year. Now he's my hitting coach, and he's still got that same interest in me, on the field, and off the field.

I had been in spring training with the guys that past March, and when Jeter and Ruben Rivera and I had been sent out to Columbus, we all knew we'd be up with the big leaguers again soon enough. We had that confidence, but we knew we had a little more work to do with Stump [Merrill] down at Triple-A. We just went to Columbus and worked hard, and sure enough, we all got [to New York].

Also on September 4, 1995
Posada is one of three future All-Stars to debut on this night, joining Mark Loretta and Mike Sweeney.

AUTHOR'S NOTE: Posada and Sweeney, each picked in the later rounds of the 1991 draft, were both All-Star catchers in the Single-A Carolina League (Posada in '93, Sweeney in '95).

BOXSCORE

New York Yankees 13, Seattle Mariners 3

Game Played on Monday, September 4, 1995 (Day) at Yankee Stadium

Seattle	2	0	0	0	0	0	0	1	0	—	3	9	2
New York	3	4	2	1	0	0	0	3	x	—	13	19	0

BATTING

Seattle Mariners	AB	R	H	RBI	BB	K	PO	A
Coleman lf	2	0	0	0	0	1	0	0
Diaz lf	3	0	0	0	0	0	0	0
Sojo ss	2	1	2	0	0	0	0	0
Rodriguez ss	2	0	0	0	0	1	3	2
Griffey cf	3	0	1	0	0	0	1	0
Amaral cf	1	0	0	0	0	0	2	0
E. Martinez dh	3	1	1	2	0	1	0	0
Strange ph-dh	1	1	1	0	0	0	0	0
Buhner rf	2	0	0	0	0	0	0	0
Newson rf	1	0	1	1	1	0	1	0
Blowers 3b	4	0	0	0	0	3	1	1
T. Martinez 1b	1	0	1	0	0	0	4	0
Pirkl ph-1b	3	0	1	0	0	0	6	1
Widger c	4	0	0	0	0	1	5	1
Fermin 2b	4	0	1	0	0	0	0	4
Torres p	0	0	0	0	0	0	0	0
Ayala p	0	0	0	0	0	0	0	0
Mecir p	0	0	0	0	0	0	0	0
Davison p	0	0	0	0	0	0	0	1
Totals	36	3	9	3	1	7	24	10

FIELDING
DP: 1
E: Diaz (2), Griffey (1)

BATTING
2B: Sojo (13, off Pettitte); Strange (8, off Pettitte)
HR: E. Martinez (27, 1st inning off Pettitte, 1 on, 2 out)

New York Yankees	AB	R	H	RBI	BB	K	PO	A
Boggs 3b	5	3	3	1	1	0	0	1
Davis 3b	0	0	0	0	0	0	1	0
B. Williams cf	6	3	3	4	0	1	2	0
O'Neill rf	5	2	3	3	1	1	0	0
R. Rivera pr-lf	0	0	0	0	0	0	0	0
Sierra dh	5	2	2	1	1	1	0	0
James lf-1b	5	0	3	1	0	0	1	1
Mattingly 1b	5	0	1	0	0	1	7	0
G. Williams rf	0	0	0	0	0	0	0	0
Leyritz c	4	0	1	1	1	0	7	0
Posada c	0	0	0	0	0	0	1	0
Fernandez ss	4	1	2	0	1	1	4	3
Jeter ss	0	0	0	0	0	0	0	0
Velarde 2b	4	2	1	0	1	1	3	2
Pettitte p	0	0	0	0	0	0	0	1
Ausanio p	0	0	0	0	0	0	1	0
Totals	43	13	19	11	6	6	27	8

BATTING
2B: O'Neill (25, off Torres); James (6, off Ayala); Boggs (18, off Ayala)
3B: B. Williams (8, off Ayala); Fernandez (2, off Mecir)
HR: B. Williams (16, 8th inning off Davison, 2 on, 2 out)
IBB: Leyritz (2, by Ayala)

PITCHING

Seattle Mariners	IP	H	HR	R	ER	BB	K
Torres L(3–8)	1	7	0	6	6	2	2
Ayala	1	3	0	3	3	2	1
Mecir	3.2	4	0	1	0	1	2
Davison	2.1	5	1	3	3	1	1
Totals	8.0	19	1	13	12	6	6
New York Yankees	**IP**	**H**	**HR**	**R**	**ER**	**BB**	**K**
Pettitte W(8–8)	8	8	1	3	3	1	6
Ausanio	1	1	0	0	0	0	1
Totals	9	9	1	3	3	1	7

WP: Ayala (3)
IBB: Ayala (4, Leyritz)
Umpires: Dale Scott, Jim McKean, Vic Voltaggio, Jim Joyce
Time of Game: 3:00   Attendance: 24,885

Mark Prior
Born: September 7, 1980
Debut: May 22, 2002

Being anointed a "savior" is never an easy load to carry, especially when it's for a team that hasn't won a World Series since the presidency of William Howard Taft. Cub fans were pretty sure they had something special when Mark Prior became the second player chosen in the 2001 draft and said all the right things about looking forward to pitching at Wrigley Field. The former Golden Spikes winner (college player of the year) cruised through some minor league seasoning and, with plenty of fanfare, arrived in late May 2002 to begin his attempt at rescuing the star-crossed franchise.

His rookie season opened eyes across the nation. Although he won only six of his 19 starts (six losses, seven no decisions), he struck out 147 batters in 117 innings. He was also a success at the plate, batting .250 with each of his first four hits landing as doubles.

His 2003 was even better. He finished third in the Cy Young balloting and went 18–6, including 10–1 down the stretch. A baserunning mishap landed him on the disabled list in July, but he responded with NL Pitcher of the Month honors in both August and September. His October was shaping up tremendously as well. A complete game two-hitter in the NLDS helped the Cubs survive the Braves, and he dealt the Marlins a 12–3 loss in Game Two of the NLCS, only to be done in by the infamous Steve Bartman eighth inning of Game Six.

Prior's 2004 season was beset by injury, and the Cubs missed the postseason entirely after many had forecast a world championship.

The tall right-hander somehow continues to mix extreme confidence with extreme modesty. Pitching guru Tom House worked with Prior when the Californian was just 15 years old and proclaimed after several sessions that his pupil would win a Cy Young Award within the next ten years. Said House in a *USA Today* interview years later: "Mark Prior is the poster child for sports science. He brings together the foundation of genetics, biomechanics, nutrition, the mental and emotional aspects—he is simply the complete package." The son of a football-playing father and a tennis star mother, the ultra-athletic Prior was later given the nickname "Calfzilla" by his minor league teammates, for his hyper-developed calf muscles. "It looks like he's got a couple of surfboards sewn in there," said one impressed teammate. If he's healthy, the pressure's on Prior to help the Cubs ride the wave and finally break their decades-long curse.

The first hit I gave up was to Chad Hermansen, right back to my forehead, first batter of the game. Welcome to the big leagues! I got out of the way just in time. It was a real nice night, a clear night with one of those orange-purple skies overhead at sunset, just perfect. I got a real boost after I got out of that first inning because the guys went out and scored two quick runs. That took a lot of pressure off, and I ended up relaxing and I ended up with, I think, ten strikeouts.

I got in trouble in the second, but a double play got me out of it, and again, that 2–0 lead was huge because I kept thinking, "Okay, if I give up one here, no big deal because we're still in the lead." If it had been nothing-nothing, I don't know how that would have gone. Joe Girardi was my catcher, and he was great, said "Just trust your stuff, and whatever I call, you throw." I trusted him entirely.

My parents, a bunch of buddies all came in, and I got home about midnight, having said hello and thanks for coming to all of them afterwards . . . Day game the next day, quick turn around. But it was a big relief to have that first one out of the way and know that it had gone pretty well.

Also on May 22, 2002
The Tigers' Jeff Weaver settles for a one-hitter vs. Cleveland when Chris Magruder doubles over a leaping Bobby Higginson in the game's eighth inning.

AUTHOR'S NOTE: Weaver's younger brother, Jered, spent his college career at Long Beach State being compared to Prior. Many suspected he'd ask for Mark Prior money in the '04 draft, but Weaver's advocates kept insisting he was worth it because of his Mark Prior stuff.

BOXSCORE

Chicago Cubs 7, Pittsburgh Pirates 4
Game Played on Wednesday, May 22, 2002 (Night) at Wrigley Field

												R	H	E
Pittsburgh	0	1	0	0	0	1	1	1	0	—		4	7	1
Chicago	2	0	1	0	2	0	0	2	x	—		7	9	0

BATTING

Pittsburgh Pirates	AB	R	H	RBI	BB	K	PO	A
Hermansen cf	4	0	1	0	1	2	3	0
J. Wilson ss	4	0	0	0	0	1	1	4
Giles lf	4	1	3	1	0	1	0	0
Ramirez 3b	4	0	0	0	0	3	0	1
Benjamin pr-3b	0	1	0	0	0	0	1	0
Mackowiak rf	2	1	0	0	1	2	3	0
C. Wilson ph-rf	1	0	0	0	0	0	0	1
Kendall c	3	0	1	1	0	0	3	0
Young 1b	2	1	0	0	2	0	10	0
Reese 2b	4	0	1	1	0	0	3	3
D. Williams p	2	0	0	0	0	2	0	4
Villone p	0	0	0	0	0	0	0	0
Brown ph	1	0	1	1	0	0	0	0
Fetters p	0	0	0	0	0	0	0	0
Sauerbeck p	0	0	0	0	0	0	0	0
Nunez ph	1	0	0	0	0	0	0	0
Totals	32	4	7	4	4	11	24	13

FIELDING
E: Young (4)

BATTING
HR: Giles (9,6th inning off Prior, 0 on, 0 out)
SH: J. Wilson (4,off Prior)
HBP: Kendall (1,by Prior)

BASERUNNING
SB: Giles (5, 2nd base off Prior/Girardi); Brown (7, 2nd base off Mahomes/Girardi)

Chicago Cubs	AB	R	H	RBI	BB	K	PO	A
Patterson cf	4	0	0	0	0	1	2	0
Girardi c	5	1	2	1	0	0	10	0
Sosa rf	2	3	1	1	2	0	2	0
McGriff 1b	4	1	2	2	0	0	10	0
Alou lf	3	0	2	1	1	0	0	0
Alfonseca p	0	0	0	0	0	0	0	0
Mueller 3b	3	0	0	1	0	0	0	4
Hill 2b	4	0	0	0	0	1	2	1
Ojeda ss	2	1	1	0	1	0	0	6
Prior p	2	0	0	0	0	1	0	0
Stynes ph	1	0	0	0	0	0	0	0
Mahomes p	0	0	0	0	0	0	0	1
Fassero p	0	0	0	0	0	0	0	0
Lewis lf	1	1	1	1	0	0	0	0
Totals	31	7	9	7	4	3	27	12

FIELDING
DP: 1

BATTING
2B: McGriff (7, off D. Williams); Ojeda (2, off D. Williams); Lewis (2, off Sauerbeck); Girardi (3, off Sauerbeck)
3B: Alou (1, off D. Williams)
HR: Sosa (17, 3rd inning off D. Williams, 0 on, 1 out)
SH: Ojeda (4, off D. Williams)
SF: Mueller (3, off Villone)
HBP: Patterson (3, by Villone)
IBB: Sosa (8, by D. Williams)

BASERUNNING
SB: Hill (1, 2nd base off D. Williams/Kendall)

PITCHING

Pittsburgh Pirates	IP	H	HR	R	ER	BB	K
D. Williams L(2–5)	4.1	7	1	5	5	2	2
Villone	1.2	0	0	0	0	0	0
Fetters	1	0	0	0	0	1	0
Sauerbeck	1	2	0	2	2	1	1
Totals	8	9	1	7	7	4	3

Chicago Cubs	IP	H	HR	R	ER	BB	K
Prior W(1–0)	6	4	1	2	2	2	10
Mahomes	1	1	0	1	1	1	1
Fassero	0.1	1	0	1	1	0	0
Alfonseca SV(7)	1.2	1	0	0	0	1	0
Totals	9.0	7	1	4	4	4	11

WP: D. Williams (2)
HBP: Villone (2, Patterson); Prior (1, Kendall)
IBB: D. Williams (2, Sosa)
Umpires: Tim Welke, Gary Cederstrom, Brian O'Nora, Alfonso Marquez
Time of Game: 2:49   Attendance: 40,138

Albert Pujols
Born: January 16, 1980
Debut: April 2, 2001

The injury-riddled status of the powerful Mark McGwire left a huge void for the Cardinals heading into 2001. Fans began to wonder, who would ever replace the big first baseman's production and popularity once the big redhead broke down completely? Enter a 21-year-old 13th-round draft pick who had played the previous season in Peoria, Illinois, three rungs down the ladder from The Show.

His name was Albert Pujols, and a skeptical fan base was almost instantly won over when the Dominican-born pure hitter ripped his way through spring training. Having gone to high school and junior college in Kansas City, Pujols spoke serviceable English and charmed his way into the fans' hearts before he had even made the team.

Once the season got going, Pujols unleashed one of the best rookie seasons in National League history. With 37 homers, 47 doubles, and 130 RBI, he tossed aside long-standing rookie records as though they were made out of balsa wood. He hit .329, remarkable for a rookie with no Triple-A experience. In addition, he played at least three dozen games at four different positions (first base, third base, left field, and right field), with all the movement failing to affect his fireworks show at the plate.

Far from a one-year wonder, Pujols seemed to improve in at least one category every year during his first four seasons. With an almost maniacal devotion to his craft, the studious Pujols became the first player ever to start his career with four straight 30-homer, 100-RBI seasons.

He has emerged as a rock of consistency, quite willing to put the entire team on his broad shoulders. In a city that appreciates hard work, St. Louis fans thrilled to hitting coach Mitchell Page's description of their newfound hero: "Albert's game day preparation essentially starts the moment he wakes up. He is the hardest worker in the entire organization." Which plays not just in Peoria but across the whole landscape of Cardinal devotees.

My family called me. They knew before I did! We were finishing playing spring training by playing two games up in Seattle. And I guess it was being reported back in St. Louis and Kansas City that I was going to make the team. So my phone rang in my hotel room around 7:00 a.m., woke me up, and it was my parents. They said, "Yeah, it's all over the news, you're going to open in the big leagues," but I told them, "Until I hear it from the manager, I won't get too excited." Later, Tony La Russa made it official. Bobby Bonilla wasn't going to be able to play right away because he was hurt, and that's what opened up the spot for them to take me. I gave myself permission to be excited then.

I'd had a really good spring, and there was a lot of talk about how well I was doing, so it wasn't a complete surprise, but wow, it was still unbelievable. There I was in Colorado for Opening Day. It wasn't like "Oh, man, I'm in the big leagues," because I always thought I could achieve that. It was just very special to be there for the Opening Day ceremonies. I will always remember the F-16 planes that went overhead during the anthem. They came up overhead, and it was so loud and so inspiring. They didn't have that [at] Opening Day in Peoria the year before, I can tell you that!

I'll remember my first hit, always—up the middle, off Mike Hampton, and I still have the ball. We lost the first three games of the year, but then we went to Arizona and swept them, and we ended up having a good year. So did I.

Also on April 2, 2001
The town of Edgar Springs, Missouri, is named the population center of the U.S. It marks the point where the U.S. would balance if its population of 281 million were equally distributed.

AUTHOR'S NOTE: Edgar Springs, near the Mark Twain National Forest, is also virtually a midpoint between St. Louis and Kansas City, the place where Pujols now plays and the place where he attended high school and college. The affection for Pujols is, as they say, "equally distributed."

BOXSCORE

Colorado Rockies 8, St. Louis Cardinals 0
Game Played on Monday, April 2, 2001 (Day) at Coors Field

St. Louis	0	0	0	0	0	0	0	0	0	—	0	5	0
Colorado	2	0	1	1	2	0	0	2	x	—	8	15	0

BATTING

St. Louis Cardinals	AB	R	H	RBI	BB	K	PO	A
Vina 2b	3	0	0	0	0	0	4	3
Renteria ss	4	0	1	0	0	0	4	1
Edmonds cf	3	0	1	0	1	0	1	0
McGwire 1b	3	0	0	0	1	1	6	1
Mabry pr	0	0	0	0	0	0	0	0
Polanco 3b	3	0	1	0	0	0	2	3
Sutton ph	1	0	0	0	0	0	0	0
Pujols lf	3	0	1	0	0	0	5	0
Matheny c	3	0	1	0	0	0	1	3
Tabaka p	0	0	0	0	0	0	0	0
James p	0	0	0	0	0	0	0	0
Drew rf	2	0	0	0	1	0	0	0
Kile p	2	0	0	0	0	2	0	0
Matthews p	0	0	0	0	0	0	0	0
Marrero ph-c	1	0	0	0	0	1	1	0
Totals	**28**	**0**	**5**	**0**	**3**	**5**	**24**	**11**

FIELDING
DP: 1

BATTING
2B: Matheny (1, off Hampton); Edmonds (1, off Hampton)
HBP: Vina (1, by Hampton)
IBB: Drew (1, by Hampton)

BASERUNNING
CS: Pujols (1, 2nd base by Hampton/Mayne)

Colorado Rockies	AB	R	H	RBI	BB	K	PO	A
Pierre cf	4	2	2	0	0	1	0	0
Little ph-cf	1	0	0	0	0	0	0	0
T. Walker 2b	4	2	3	3	1	0	0	2
L. Walker rf	5	1	2	2	0	1	2	1
Helton 1b	2	2	1	0	2	0	12	0
Norton pr-1b	0	0	0	0	0	0	2	0
Cirillo 3b	5	1	3	1	0	1	0	4
Hollandsworth lf	3	0	0	0	1	0	1	0
Perez ss	4	0	2	1	0	0	4	5
Mayne c	3	0	2	1	0	0	6	1
Hampton p	3	0	0	0	0	0	0	4
Jimenez p	0	0	0	0	0	0	0	0
Totals	**34**	**8**	**15**	**8**	**4**	**3**	**27**	**17**

FIELDING
DP: 3

BATTING
2B: Cirillo (1, off Kile); T. Walker (1, off Kile)
3B: Pierre (1, off Kile)
HR: T. Walker (1, 1st inning off Kile, 1 on, 0 out); L. Walker (1, 8th inning off James, 1 on, 2 out)
SH: Hampton (1, off Kile)
SF: Mayne (1, off Kile)
HBP: Helton (1, by Kile)

PITCHING

St. Louis Cardinals	IP	H	HR	R	ER	BB	K
Kile L(0–1)	5	11	1	6	6	3	0
Matthews	2	1	0	0	0	1	2
Tabaka	0.2	0	0	0	0	0	0
James	0.1	3	1	2	2	0	1
Totals	**8.0**	**15**	**2**	**8**	**8**	**4**	**3**

Colorado Rockies	IP	H	HR	R	ER	BB	K
Hampton W(1–0)	8.1	5	0	0	0	3	5
Jimenez	0.2	0	0	0	0	0	0
Totals	**9.0**	**5**	**0**	**0**	**0**	**3**	**5**

HBP: Kile (1, Helton); Hampton (1, Vina)
IBB: Hampton (1, Drew)
Umpires: Bruce Froemming, Greg Bonin, Jerry Meals, Phil Cuzzi
Time of Game: 2:43   Attendance: 48,113

Manny Ramirez
Born: May 30, 1972
Debut: September 2, 1993

Many Ramirez was once written up in *Sports Illustrated* as being "tougher to read than Sanskrit." The outfielder suggests he isn't moody at all, just painfully shy. Indeed, if he goes out clubbing with his teammates after a game, he asks for a corner table, back where it's dark. Because of his talent, it is sometimes expected Ramirez should commandeer the spotlight and/or act with dignity and grace. As it stands, Ramirez has no interest in outward appearance, or being the Latino Joe DiMaggio—he'd really just like to be left alone to do his thing.

Few modern players can be so consistently penciled in for a 40 homer/ 130 RBI season. In some years, Ramirez has blown by those numbers. He hoarded 165 RBI for the '99 Indians, becoming the only player with more than 160 since 1938. In 2003, he led the Red Sox to within a game of the World Series, hitting .325, one point off the league lead. Having won the 2002 batting title at .349, he told his teammate, Bill Mueller, "I'll sit down so you can win it this year. I already have mine from last year."

Such a selfless offer seemed inconsistent with other more infamous "Man-Ram" episodes. In August of that year, he was branded as selfish for refusing to pinch-hit in a game against the Yankees, claiming a sore throat. Later that evening, he was discovered hanging out at a local pub with his friend Enrique Wilson, a member of the hated opposition. In September, he moped his way out of the batter's box in Tampa Bay, taking an immediate turn into the dugout rather than run out a soft ground ball. In October, after crushing an ALDS-deciding home run off Barry Zito, he stood in the batter's box for a full three seconds before starting a painfully slow trot around the bases. But for all of the bluster about Ramirez's supposed apathy and lack of grace, he is also one of the game's hardest workers. A daily routine of a hundred swings against the Indians' "curveball machine" helped him become one of the game's most lethal breaking-ball hitters.

His high school coach in New York City swears that Ramirez was always a good kid who simply couldn't sit still and sometimes couldn't remember to show up. Indeed, at George Washington High, of the four team pictures taken while Ramirez was in school, he appears in only one. (Years earlier, the same high school, located in a high crime neighborhood, produced another foreign-born legend—a fellow named Henry Kissinger.

Ramirez has needed Kissinger-style diplomacy at times in his career to explain his way out of sticky, self-inflicted situations.)

For all of the stories about Ramirez's runaway attention deficit disorder (e.g., the time he left behind his paycheck, stuffed in a pair of brand new cowboy boots, in his Arlington, Texas, locker), the bottom line continues to be his on-field production. His 2004 season featured 43 homers and 130 runs batted in, not to mention the trophy for World Series MVP. *That* one he took home with him.

Anyone that says they don't have butterflies that first day is lying to you. I had to fly from Richmond, Virginia, to Minnesota, and I could feel the butterflies in my stomach every minute. On the way to the stadium, more butterflies. In the clubhouse, butterflies, and when I saw I'd be playing, I could hardly breathe, man . . . But I also felt blessed. Blessed to be in the big leagues already at 21 years old, and knowing that after that game at Minnesota, I'd be playing at Yankee Stadium, where I basically grew up, you know? All my friends, my family live not too far from there.

First I had to get through that game in Minnesota . . . They had me

Also on September 2, 1993
The United States and Russia formally end decades of competition in space by agreeing to a joint venture to build a space station.

AUTHOR'S NOTE: Although Ramirez has long been accused of being a "space cadet," it is unlikely either country's government will recruit him to fix any o-rings.

BOXSCORE

Cleveland Indians 4, Minnesota Twins 3
Game Played on Thursday, September 2, 1993 (Night) at Hubert H. Humphrey Metrodome

Cleveland	0	1	1	0	0	0	2	0	—	4	8	0
Minnesota	0	0	1	0	0	1	0	0	1	—	3	9	0

BATTING

Cleveland Indians	AB	R	H	RBI	BB	K	PO	A
Lofton cf	4	2	2	0	0	0	4	0
Kirby rf	4	1	3	2	0	0	1	0
Baerga 2b	4	0	1	0	0	4	3	
Belle lf	3	1	0	0	1	1	0	0
Sorrento 1b	4	0	1	0	0	2	11	0
Ramirez dh	4	0	0	0	0	0	0	0
Thome 3b	2	0	0	1	1	1	1	3
Espinoza 3b	0	0	0	0	0	0	0	1
Fermin ss	4	0	1	0	0	0	0	2
Alomar c	3	0	0	0	0	1	5	1
Grimsley p	0	0	0	0	0	0	0	0
Kramer p	0	0	0	0	0	0	0	1
Plunk p	0	0	0	0	0	0	0	0
DiPoto p	0	0	0	0	0	0	0	0
Totals	32	4	8	4	2	5	27	11

FIELDING
DP: 2
PB: Alomar (3)

BATTING
2B: Fermin (14, off Tapani); Lofton (25, off Tapani); Kirby (16, off Tapani)
SF: Thome (2, off Tapani)

BASERUNNING
SB: Lofton (56, 2nd base off Tapani/Harper); Alomar (3, 2nd base off Tapani/Harper)
CS: Kirby (5, 2nd base by Tapani/Harper)

Minnesota Twins	AB	R	H	RBI	BB	K	PO	A
Knoblauch 2b	4	2	2	0	1	0	5	3
McCarty 1b	5	0	2	0	0	1	8	3
Puckett dh	4	0	2	0	1	1	0	0
Winfield rf	5	0	1	1	0	0	2	0
Harper c	3	0	0	0	2	1	4	1
Hale 3b	3	1	1	1	1	0	0	3
Mack cf	4	0	0	0	0	2	2	0
Munoz lf	2	0	1	0	2	1	3	0
Meares ss	4	0	0	0	0	0	0	2
Tapani p	0	0	0	0	0	0	3	0
Willis p	0	0	0	0	0	0	0	0
Totals	34	3	9	2	7	6	27	12

FIELDING
DP: 2
PB: Harper (17)

BATTING
2B: Winfield (21, off DiPoto)
HR: Hale (3, 6th inning off Grimsley, 0 on, 1 out).
IBB: Munoz (2, by Grimsley); Harper (8, by Kramer).

BASERUNNING
SB: Knoblauch 2 (23, 2nd base off Grimsley/Alomar; 3rd base off Grimsley/Alomar); Hale (2, 2nd base off Grimsley/Alomar)
CS: Knoblauch (8, 2nd base by Grimsley/Alomar)

PITCHING

Cleveland Indians	IP	H	HR	R	ER	BB	K
Grimsley	6	6	1	2	2	5	3
Kramer W(7–3)	1	2	0	0	0	1	0
Plunk	1	0	0	0	0	0	1
DiPoto SV(5)	1	1	0	1	1	1	2
Totals	9	9	1	3	3	7	6

Minnesota Twins	IP	H	HR	R	ER	BB	K
Tapani L(7–14)	7	8	0	4	4	1	5
Willis	2	0	0	0	0	1	0
Totals	9	8	0	4	4	2	5

WP: Grimsley (1)
IBB: Grimsley (1, Munoz); Kramer (5, Harper)
Umpires: Larry Young, Chuck Meriwether, Rich Garcia, Dale Ford
Time of Game: 2:49   Attendance: 14,189

in as the designated hitter, and I remember Glenallen Hill talking to me right before the game, telling me just to relax and enjoy it. I told him I'd try. I ended up 0-for-4, but I knew I'd have success once we got to New York. I thought about it all the way there on the plane. First at bat there, I thought I hit a home run, but it was high off the wall for a double. I almost hit one out my second at bat, but it got caught at the wall. Next two at bats though, no doubt. Two home runs, and my family was going crazy. I could hear them in the stands. I think everyone could. I came close to four home runs in my first game at Yankee Stadium, and that's what I'll always remember.

Courtesy Boston Red Sox

Willie Randolph
Born: July 6, 1954
Debut: July 29, 1975

Willie Randolph was probably never the best or most popular New York Yankee, but in his 13 years in pinstripes, he ended up second in stolen bases, seventh in at bats and runs, eighth in games played, and tenth in hits at the time of his departure. The South Carolina native suffered through an injury-marred season in 1988 and was not re-signed by New York. Instead, he signed a free-agent contract with the Dodgers and spent time with the A's and Brewers before rounding out his playing career with the Mets.

As the Mets' new manager for 2005, he was expected to be a stabilizing force in a tumultuous environment, much the way he had been across town as a player for all those years. Randolph immediately became the Yanks' starting second baseman as soon as he was dealt there from the Pirates in 1976, and he stayed in that role through 32 double-play partners at short. During Randolph's first six seasons with the Yankees, they won five division championships and four AL pennants. Randolph played on World Series–winning teams in '77 and '78.

During 1980, when the Yankees won 103 games, Randolph led the AL in walks with 119, the most by a Yankee since Mickey Mantle in 1962. He was also second in the league in on-base percentage (.429) and appeared in the third of his six All-Star Games.

My manager at Charleston was Johnny Lipon, a legendary guy . . . He called me and told me I was going up, and it's not like I doubted him, but it didn't make sense as to why until I found out Rennie Stennett had twisted his ankle. He had been playing really well that year, so I figured it had to be an injury of some sort, and I was right.

All of a sudden, I was playing next to Willie Stargell in the big leagues. Richie Zisk, Manny Sanguillen, all these great players, and there I am with them. It was really humbling. It's funny because Tommy Underwood was the pitcher I got my first major league hit off of . . . I had played against him in the minor leagues and remembered what he threw, so that was bit of a break. It wasn't like I was facing someone I hadn't faced before. I took a fastball and smacked it right up the middle.

We were playing the Phillies, and their first baseman was Richie Allen. I get that base hit, and he walks over to me, and he just looks bigger than life. Big

BOXSCORE

Philadelphia Phillies 5, Pittsburgh Pirates 1

Game Played on Tuesday, July 29, 1975 (Night) at Three Rivers Stadium

Philadelphia	0	0	0	4	0	0	0	1	0	—	5	11	0
Pittsburgh	0	0	0	1	0	0	0	0	0	—	1	4	1

BATTING

Philadelphia Phillies	AB	R	H	RBI	BB	K	PO	A
Cash 2b	5	0	0	0	0	0	2	2
Bowa ss	5	0	4	1	0	0	0	6
Schmidt 3b	3	0	1	0	1	1	1	1
Luzinski lf	5	0	0	0	0	1	2	0
Allen 1b	3	1	0	0	1	1	10	0
Johnstone rf	4	2	2	0	0	0	2	0
Anderson rf-cf	0	0	0	0	0	0	1	0
Maddox cf	3	1	3	1	1	0	3	0
Brown rf	0	0	0	0	0	0	0	0
Oates c	4	0	0	1	0	1	6	0
Underwood p	3	1	1	2	0	1	0	0
Totals	35	5	11	5	3	5	27	9

BATTING

2B: Underwood (1, off Ellis)

SH: Underwood (6, off Tekulve); Schmidt (6, off Tekulve)

BASERUNNING

SB: Maddox (14, 2nd base off Ellis/Sanguillen); Bowa (17, 2nd base off Ellis/Sanguillen); Johnstone (6, 2nd base off Ellis/Sanguillen)

Pittsburgh Pirates	AB	R	H	RBI	BB	K	PO	A
Randolph 2b	4	0	1	0	0	0	3	4
Sanguillen c	4	0	0	0	0	0	5	0
Oliver cf	3	1	2	0	1	0	3	0
Stargell 1b	4	0	0	0	0	1	13	0
Zisk lf	4	0	0	1	0	0	1	0
Parker rf	3	0	0	0	2	0	1	0
Howe 3b	3	0	0	0	0	1	0	4
Taveras ss	2	0	0	0	0	1	1	3
Stennett ph	1	0	0	0	0	0	0	0
Mendoza ss	0	0	0	0	0	0	0	0
Ellis p	1	0	0	0	0	0	0	0
Tekulve p	1	0	0	0	0	1	1	2
Robinson ph	1	0	1	0	0	0	0	0
Demery p	0	0	0	0	0	0	0	1
Totals	31	1	4	1	1	6	27	14

FIELDING

DP: 2

E: Randolph (1)

BATTING

2B: Oliver (21,off Underwood)

PITCHING

Philadelphia Phillies	IP	H	HR	R	ER	BB	K
Underwood W(11–7)	9	4	0	1	1	1	6

Pittsburgh Pirates	IP	H	HR	R	ER	BB	K
Ellis L(7–7)	3.2	7	0	4	4	3	0
Tekulve	4.1	4	0	1	1	0	4
Demery	1	0	0	0	0	0	1
Totals	9	11	0	5	5	3	5

Umpires: Satch Davidson, Frank Pulli, Tom Gorman, Lee Weyer

Time of Game: 2:29   Attendance: 33,340

man, broad, in great shape, he looked like the black Paul Bunyan. I remember saying, "Hi, Mr. Allen." And he says, "Nice going, kid. Here's some advice for you—don't ever let anyone play your position but you. Play your position every day. Never take a day off." That was about the soundest piece of advice I had ever gotten, and it stood the test of time . . . It still is a great piece of advice, and he gave it to me while I was standing there shaking on the Astroturf, standing next to him. This is a guy who I had emulated, imitated, was one of my favorites growing up playing stickball with my brothers. And there's the real Richie Allen telling me, to my face, play every day. I couldn't believe he was even talking to me. I stammered and said something like, "Thank you, sir." What a huge, massive strong man. What a great day.

Also on July 29, 1975

"Love Will Keep Us Together" remains the most-played single on Top 40 radio across the country, followed by "Please Mister Please" and "The Hustle."

AUTHOR'S NOTE: Forget both the Captain and Tennille. "Hustle" defined Randolph's playing days, and "Please Mister Please" could have been his anthem as he tried for several years to land that elusive big league managing job.

Jerry Remy
Born: November 8, 1952
Debut: April 7, 1975

Jerry Remy is the most famous son of Fall River, Massachusetts. The most famous daughter of that town is murderess Lizzie Borden, but that's neither here nor there. The affable "Rem Dawg" had a ten-year career as the scrappy second baseman for the Angels and then for his hometown Red Sox.

Listed at 5'9" but in reality an inch shorter, he debuted as one of several diminutive infielders in an Angels–Royals game, Opening Night, 1975. Kansas City featured the 5'9" Cookie Rojas and the 5'4" Freddie Patek. Remy's Colombian-born double-play partner, Orlando Ramirez, was the giant of the group at 5'10".

Remy jokes about his ability to remember the exact details of every one of his big league homers, since he hit only seven, with none coming in his final 2,323 at bats. Of his seven victims, however, five were twenty-game winners: Fergie Jenkins, Jack Morris, Mike Norris, Jim Perry, and Catfish Hunter. At 5'9", predictably, Remy survived with his brain, heart, and legs, not necessarily in that order. He stole at least 30 bases in each of his first four big league seasons and came close to finishing his career with more walks than strikeouts.

Remy is now the popular color commentator on BoSox television broadcasts, and the proof of Red Sox Nation's adoration is on display via the nightly signage at Fenway Park. In between each half inning, a mosaic of poster board dots the ballpark grandstand, held aloft by those hoping to get noticed by the cameramen. "Remy's #1," "Hiya, Jerry," "Somerset Loves Remy," and a pastiche of other salutations are just as visible as Pesky Pole and the Green Monster itself.

For a legion of fans who'd been longing for a champion, they were always quick to champion one of their own, the Rem Dawg, as a true state treasure.

I found out I was going to make the team about ten days before we broke camp . . . Our [Angels] manager, Dick Williams, told me, so I had plenty of time to call my family and tell them the good news. They couldn't all afford to fly in, so just my dad came out to Anaheim. He saw me start, batting seventh on Opening Night. I got a single to left off Steve Busby in my first at bat. And on

BOXSCORE

California Angels 3, Kansas City Royals 2
Game Played on Monday, April 7, 1975 (Night) at Anaheim Stadium

Kansas City	0	1	0	0	0	1	0	0	—	2	3	0
California	0	1	0	0	0	0	0	2	—	3	7	1

BATTING

Kansas City Royals	AB	R	H	RBI	BB	K	PO	A
Patek ss	2	0	0	0	2	2	2	2
Otis cf	3	0	0	0	0	0	1	0
Mayberry 1b	4	1	1	1	0	1	13	0
McRae lf-rf-lf	4	0	0	0	0	3	1	0
Killebrew dh	4	0	0	0	0	4	0	0
Brett 3b	3	1	1	0	1	1	0	2
Pinson rf	3	0	0	0	0	0	0	0
Cowens lf-rf	0	0	0	0	0	0	2	0
Rojas 2b	3	0	1	1	0	1	0	2
Healy c	3	0	0	0	0	0	6	0
Busby p	0	0	0	0	0	0	0	6
Mingori p	0	0	0	0	0	0	0	0
Bird p	0	0	0	0	0	0	0	0
Totals	29	2	3	2	3	12	25	12

FIELDING
DP: 1

BATTING
HR: Mayberry (1, 6th inning off Ryan, 0 on, 1 out)
HBP: Otis (1, by Ryan)

BASERUNNING
SB: Otis (1, 2nd base off Ryan/Rodriguez); Brett (1, 2nd base off Ryan/Rodriguez); Patek 2 (2, 2nd base off Ryan/Rodriguez 2)
CS: Rojas (1, 2nd base by Ryan/Rodriguez)

California Angels	AB	R	H	RBI	BB	K	PO	A
Nettles cf	3	1	1	0	1	1	4	0
Rivers lf	4	0	1	0	0	0	0	0
Harper dh	4	0	1	1	0	0	0	0
Bochte 1b	3	0	0	1	0	0	5	1
Lahoud rf	3	1	1	0	0	2	2	0
Chalk 3b	2	0	1	0	1	0	0	1
Rodriguez c	3	0	0	0	0	2	13	0
Remy 2b	3	0	1	1	0	0	1	1
Ramirez ss	2	0	0	0	0	1	2	3
Meoli ph	1	1	1	0	0	0	0	0
Ryan p	0	0	0	0	0	0	0	1
Totals	28	3	7	3	2	6	27	7

FIELDING
E: Rodriguez (1)

BATTING
2B: Chalk (1, off Busby)
SF: Bochte (1, off Bird)

BASERUNNING
CS: Nettles (1, 2nd base by Busby/Healy)

PITCHING

Kansas City Royals	IP	H	HR	R	ER	BB	K
Busby	8	5	0	2	2	1	6
Mingori L(0–1)	0	1	0	1	1	1	0
Bird	0.1	1	0	0	0	0	0
Totals	8.1	7	0	3	3	2	6
California Angels	IP	H	HR	R	ER	BB	K
Ryan W(1–0)	9	3	1	2	2	3	12

WP: Mingori (1)
HBP: Ryan (1, Otis)
Umpires: Russ Goetz, Merlyn Anthony, George Maloney, Bill Deegan
Time of Game: 2:34   Attendance: 24,105

the very next pitch, the old fake-to-third, throw-to-first, he picks me off. How many times do we say as announcers, "That play never works!" Well, it worked on me in the freaking second inning of my first game. My legs are still shaking from getting my first base hit, driving in the first run of the season, no less, and I get back to the dugout, Dick Williams, calls me over. I think he's going to congratulate me on the base hit. Instead, he says, "If you ever get picked off again, you're back in Salt Lake City."

We had gone over Busby's pickoff move in meetings that afternoon . . . Sure enough, he gets me, and now, I laugh my ass off every time I see that play tried out when I'm broadcasting a game. I always go back to, "Hey, I fell for that, and I did in front of my dad and 30,000 other people!"

AUTHOR'S NOTE: Royals' great George Brett played in that same game and, in fact, would steal a base under Remy's tag that evening. Brett, an Orange County native, would later achieve his 3,000th hit at that same stadium, and he too would get picked off on the very next pitch. Brett remains the only player in the 3,000 Club to have gotten picked off immediately after making the club.

Also on April 7, 1975
The *Sports Illustrated* dated April 7, 1975, features another single-digit infielder, from the other L.A.-area team. "Steve Garvey: Proud to Be a Dodger Hero," reads the headline in *SI*'s Opening Day issue.

AUTHOR'S NOTE: Three years, three months, and three days later, Garvey would be the hero of the '78 All-Star Game in San Diego, the only Midsummer Classic to which Remy was invited. As the AL's third-string second baseman, he never did get in the game.

Cal Ripken Jr.
Born: August 24, 1960
Debut: August 10, 1981

For Cal Ripken Jr., it was always a question of "Why?" Insatiable in his desire to learn every nuance of the game, he had a stern but sensitive headmaster in his father, Cal Sr. From his earliest memories, Jr. was on the field with his dad, a manager in the Orioles minor league system, and young Cal would pepper the players with questions about how to become a better player. He went on to become one of the best of all-time, playing in a record 2,632 consecutive games before ending "The Streak" on his own terms.

It's been said, originally by Bill Veeck, that baseball is an "island of surety" in an ever-changing world, and from May 1982 until September 2000, Ripken's presence in the lineup was the surest of sure things. During The Streak, nearly 4,000 players came and went off the disabled list. At one point, Ripken played in 8,243 *innings* in a row. And to put The Streak in perhaps its best perspective, consider that heading into 2005, 2,632 consecutive games was longer than the next 22 active streaks combined.

The consecutive games streak defined Ripken's career, although he bristled at the notion that it was either selfish or detrimental to the ball club. The fates seemed to bristle as well. When *Baltimore Sun* columnist Ken Rosenthal wrote a column suggesting Ripken end The Streak in 1996, that same night, Ripken fouled a ball back into the Camden Yards press box— and broke Rosenthal's laptop computer.

The Maryland native blazed a trail for bigger shortstops. He had broken in as a third baseman before Earl Weaver bucked conventional wisdom by moving the 6'4" Ripken closer to the middle of the diamond. He won a pair Gold Gloves, a pair of MVP awards, and went to the All-Star Game 19 times, winning the home run derby in Toronto and, memorably, homering in his final All-Star Game at bat in Seattle. With a constant flair for the dramatic, he also homered in the games in which he tied and broke Lou Gehrig's supposedly unbreakable Iron Man record. He ended his career with more than 3,000 hits, more than 400 home runs, and with 3,001 games played—the extra small turn of the odometer appropriately showing how he always did "just that little bit more."

In the end, though, he will always be remembered first and foremost for the Iron Man Streak. Early on, Ripken was told by his good friend Eddie Murray, "Even if you feel rotten and know you're staring at an 0-for-4,

BOXSCORE

Baltimore Orioles 3, Kansas City Royals 2
Game Played on Monday, August 10, 1981 (Night) at Memorial Stadium

Kansas City	0	0	0	2	0	0	0	0	0	0	0	0	—	2 9 0
Baltimore	2	0	0	0	0	0	0	0	0	0	0	1	—	3 4 0

BATTING

Kansas City Royals	AB	R	H	RBI	BB	K	PO	A
Wilson lf	6	0	2	0	0	0	5	0
McRae dh	5	0	2	0	1	0	0	0
G. Brett 3b	4	0	0	0	2	1	0	5
Aikens 1b	5	1	0	0	0	1	16	1
Otis cf	5	1	1	2	0	0	4	0
Motley rf	5	0	1	0	0	0	2	0
White 2b	5	0	1	0	0	0	3	2
Wathan c	5	0	2	0	0	0	2	1
Washington ss	3	0	0	0	2	1	0	6
Leonard p	0	0	0	0	0	0	0	0
Jones p	0	0	0	0	0	0	1	0
Quisenberry p	0	0	0	0	0	0	0	1
Martin p	0	0	0	0	0	0	0	0
Totals	43	2	9	2	5	3	33	16

BATTING
HR: Otis (4, 4th inning off D. Martinez, 1 on, 2 out)

BASERUNNING
SB: Wilson (9, 2nd base off D. Martinez/Dempsey)
CS: Washington (7, 2nd base by D. Martinez/Dempsey)

Baltimore Orioles	AB	R	H	RBI	BB	K	PO	A
Bumbry cf	4	0	0	0	1	0	4	0
Dauer 2b	4	0	0	0	0	0	2	2
Singleton rf	4	1	2	1	1	0	9	0
Ripken pr	0	1	0	0	0	0	0	0
Murray 1b	4	1	1	1	1	0	7	2
Crowley dh	2	0	0	0	0	0	0	0
Ayala ph-dh	0	0	0	0	1	0	0	0
Lowenstein ph-dh	2	0	1	1	0	0	0	0
Roenicke lf	4	0	0	0	0	1	5	0
DeCinces 3b	4	0	0	0	0	0	2	3
Dempsey c	4	0	0	0	0	0	3	0
Belanger ss	3	0	0	0	0	0	3	1
Graham ph	1	0	0	0	1	0	0	0
Sakata ss	0	0	0	0	0	0	0	0
D. Martinez p	0	0	0	0	0	0	0	3
Stewart p	0	0	0	0	0	0	1	0
T. Martinez p	0	0	0	0	0	0	0	0
Totals	36	3	4	3	4	2	36	11

BATTING
2B: Singleton (11, off Martin)
HR: Singleton (10, 1st inning off Leonard, 0 on, 2 out); Murray (9, 1st inning off Leonard, 0 on, 2 out)
SH: Dauer (3, off Quisenberry)
IBB: Singleton (4, by Quisenberry); Murray (4, by Martin)

PITCHING

Kansas City Royals	IP	H	HR	R	ER	BB	K
Leonard	5	2	2	2	2	0	1
Jones	3	0	0	0	0	2	0
Quisenberry	3	0	0	0	0	1	1
Martin L(2–4)	0	2	0	1	1	1	0
Totals	11	4	2	3	3	4	2
Baltimore Orioles	**IP**	**H**	**HR**	**R**	**ER**	**BB**	**K**
D. Martinez	7	6	1	2	2	3	2
Stewart	4.2	3	0	0	0	2	0
T. Martinez W(3–2)	0.1	0	0	0	0	0	1
Totals	12.0	9	1	2	2	5	3

IBB: Quisenberry (6, Singleton); Martin (6, Murray)
Umpires: Dave Phillips, Dallas Parks, Larry McCoy, Durwood Merrill
Time of Game: 3:18   Attendance: 19,850

play anyway, because the opposing manager doesn't know how you're feeling. Seeing you in that lineup will make his day tougher." Eddie Murray, by the way, says he learned that pearl of wisdom from Cal Ripken, Sr.

The strike had just been settled, and I had been highlighted a couple times on *This Week in Baseball*, because they were paying a lot of attention to what was going on in the minors. When they announced that big league rosters would expand by two players immediately following the strike, I had a sense that maybe I'd get my chance. Sure enough, we were in Syracuse, and after the game, Doc Edwards pulled me into his office and told me I was going up. Excitement just shoots through you when that happens . . . You can't sleep the whole night. I know I didn't. I drove back from Syracuse to Rochester, packed, and drove the six hours from Rochester to Baltimore— the fastest six hours you'll ever have, trying to get there in five.

We had a couple practice days, then the games started again, and I made my debut as a pinch runner for Ken Singleton. Earl Weaver had

Also on August 10, 1981
Pete Rose breaks Stan Musial's National League hit record with number 3,631. Musial, in attendance, congratulates Rose from his box seat.

AUTHOR'S NOTE: Ripken was to Baltimoreans what Rose was to Cincinnatians—a hometown hero who played the game hard, played every day, and could do no wrong. Nationally, Ripken's name is still synonymous with greatness. Rose's name is mud.

alerted me: "Get your legs loose and ready." I felt like I was going out on a stage. I had been on that field many, many times as a kid because of my dad, but this felt entirely different. Running out there with my helmet on, Singy says, mock surprised, "You're running for *me*?" But he runs off the field, laughing, and immediately Frank White and the Royals put a pickoff play on trying to catch me napping. Frank White says, "Just checking, kid." John Lowenstein hit a bullet into the corner, and I scored easily to win the game in the 12th inning. I went home to my mom and dad's house in Aberdeen. So many times I had played a winning baseball game and gone home to that house . . . It's just this time, it was a big league game, not a Little League or high school game.

Frank Robinson
Born: August 31, 1935
Debut: April 17, 1956

Hall of Famer Frank Robinson is the only man to win Most Valuable Player Awards in both leagues. Additionally, he was the MVP of the '71 All-Star Game and '66 World Series, helping the Orioles to their first title in his first year with the team. The right-handed slugger had been dismissed by the Reds, having been called "an old 30 [years old]." Proving the Cincinnati brass wrong, he went on to hammer 273 more home runs on his way to a total of 586 (including one clear out of Baltimore's Memorial Stadium).

In fact, Robinson's first year in Baltimore may have been his best, a Triple Crown season of .316/49/122. He was the heart of three more pennant winners in Baltimore, providing veteran leadership and showing a knack for "doing whatever it takes," including wiping out second basemen and shortstops on potential double plays. His all-out style almost obscured his gaudy numbers—12 All-Star appearances, 10,006 at bats, close to 3,000 hits, and even 204 stolen bases. Four times he led his league in slugging percentage and twice in on base percentage.

Breaking the managerial color barrier, Robinson debuted as Indians manager in 1975 and proved he still had plenty left to offer as a player. Inserting himself as a pinch hitter on Opening Day, he clocked the game-winning home run. In his subsequent managerial stints in San Francisco and Baltimore, Robinson often rubbed his players the wrong way with biting honesty and his penchant of expecting others to perform at the level he had. Moving to the Orioles front office in 1991, he harbored thoughts of becoming a general manager but ultimately left Baltimore, joining the commissioner's office as the sport's "discipline czar" and also working games as a commentator for FOX. He returned to the manager's office at the request of MLB in 2003, running the lame duck Expos their final two years in Montreal before moving with them to Washington, DC.

I'm never one to be gushy or emotional anyway, but I can honestly say I felt comfortable that first day. Opening Day in Cincinnati, as big as it gets, but I felt very comfortable. A little nervous before my first at bat, sure, but I knew I belonged. I hit a long one to center off [Vinegar Bend] Mizell my first time up, ended up 2-for-3 and even got intentionally walked!

It had been a long time proving myself in the minors, and proving that I was over my arm injury. Actually, I was far from being over it, but [manager] Birdie Tebbets told me the last day of spring training that year, "If you can just get it in to the cutoff man, that'll do fine."

Don Hoak hit a home run for us that first game, but Musial won it for St. Louis with one of his own. After the game, the writers gathered around my locker, and the first question was, "Did you see the difference between minor league and major league pitching?" And I had said, "No, not really. They have better control up here, but that's really about it, no big difference at all." Then I went 0-for-my-next-23.

That whole first week I was worried more about my defense than my hitting . . . and I'll always remember the kindness of one of our players, Hal Jeffcoat. He volunteered to hit me fly balls fifteen minutes every day so I could get better on my routes and build my arm back to where it needed to be. His kindness, and one of our coaches, Reggie Otero, made it a lot easier those first several days. A young guy needs to have someone in his corner when he first comes up, and I was thankful that I found that.

BOXSCORE

St. Louis Cardinals 4, Cincinnati Reds 2
Game Played on 4/17/1956

St. Louis	1	0	0	1	0	0	0	0	2	—	4
Cincinnati	0	1	0	1	0	0	0	0	0	—	2

St. Louis	AB	R	H	RBI	PO	A
Moon 1b	4	1	2	1	9	3
Schoendienst 2b	5	1	2	0	1	1
Musial rf	5	1	1	3	2	0
Sauer lf	4	0	0	0	0	0
Boyer 3b	3	0	2	0	0	0
Virdon cf	4	0	1	0	3	0
Sarni c	4	1	3	0	7	0
Grammas ss	4	0	0	0	2	3
Mizell p	4	0	1	0	3	3
Kinder p	0	0	0	0	0	0
Totals	37	4	12	4	27	10

FIELDING
DP: (1) Grammas-Moon

BATTING
2B: Moon, Sarni 2
HR: Musial

BASERUNNING
SB: Boyer
Team LOB: 9

Cincinnati	AB	R	H	RBI	PO	A
Temple 2b	4	0	1	0	1	4
Burgess c	5	0	1	0	4	1
Harmon pr	0	0	0	0	0	0
Kluszewski 1b	5	0	1	0	12	0
Post rf	5	0	1	0	3	0
Bell cf	4	0	1	0	0	0
Jablonski 3b	4	2	3	1	0	0
Robinson lf	3	0	2	0	3	0
McMillan ss	4	0	2	1	4	5
Nuxhall p	3	0	0	0	0	2
Crowe ph	1	0	0	0	0	0
Totals	38	2	12	2	27	12

FIELDING
DP: (1) Temple-Kluszewski

BATTING
2B: Kluszewski, Jablonski, Robinson, McMillan
HR: Jablonski (off Mizell)

BASERUNNING
Team LOB: 11

PITCHING

St. Louis	IP	H	HR	R	ER	BB	K
Mizell W (1–0)	8.2	12	1	2	2	2	5
Kinder S	0.1	0	0	0	0	0	1
Total	9.0	11	1	2	2	2	6
Cincinnati	IP	H	HR	R	ER	BB	K
Nuxhall L (0–1)	9.0	12	1	4	4	3	3

Umpires: Pinelli, Goggess, Gorman, and Dixon
Time of Game: 2:31   Attendance: 32,095

Also on April 17, 1956
Luis Aparicio, Whitey Herzog, Charlie Neal, and Don Drysdale also make their big league debuts.

AUTHOR'S NOTE: Robinson clinched the 1966 World Series for Baltimore, homering off Drysdale for Game Four's only run.

Alex Rodriguez
Born: July 27, 1975
Debut: June 9, 1994

His arrival in Gotham seemed fated. Where else should the most prized athlete in the game ply his craft? Spending three years in multimillion-dollar exile in dusty Arlington, Texas, the 2003 MVP pined for playing the big stage. Great artwork should hang in great museums, and A-Rod's personal Louvre had long been the storied House that Ruth Built. After a near nuclear winter of denials, speculation, and angst for all concerned, he was granted the trade that cemented the Yankees' standing as a bona fide juggernaut.

First, it had appeared Alex was headed to Boston, but the Red Sox history of incredible heartbreak continued as the deal fell apart and Rangers' management anointed A-Rod team captain. It was a captaincy with the shelf life of Britney Spears's marriage. After the Rangers had proclaimed, "It'll be a snowy day in Dallas when we trade Alex Rodriguez," incredibly, it snowed four inches Valentine's Day morning. By nightfall, A-Rod was in pinstripes, and Red Sox fans were on their roofs.

The owner of 323 home runs before his 28th birthday, the thoughtful New York-born, Miami-raised Rodriguez is destined for a spot 200 miles west of Yankee Stadium—Cooperstown. His insatiable desire to master the game's every nuance has made admirers of many players. He handles the media with the same ease he does a smash to the hole. He donates large sums of money to the Miami Boys Club, where he was virtually raised, and he reads the selected works of Gabriel Garcia Marquez. He is, in short, a renaissance man with a 50-home-run bat.

However, the shine was off the stone during the 2004 postseason, when he karate-chopped the Red Sox's Bronson Arroyo in Game Six of the ALCS. Meantime, Yankee fans bemoaned his failure to deliver the "big hit" when it mattered, and the rest, as they say, is history. Having nearly been traded to the Sox some eight months prior, instead A-Rod watched from his couch when Boston won its first World Series in 86 years.

His introduction to the big leagues came at the tender age of 18, a year after he was selected first overall in the '93 draft. It came at, of all places, Fenway Park.

I got the word the Mariners wanted me in Boston to check me out before the All-Star Break. Ken Griffey [Jr.] was the first guy to greet me when I got into the clubhouse. He had been the big deal as an 18-year-old a few years before me, and it meant a lot that he came over first. [Manager] Lou Piniella came over, and we talked, and he told me I'd be in the lineup that night, batting ninth. I would have been happy to bat tenth or 11th! When the game finally started, all I wanted was to have a ball hit to me, so I could get it over with. First inning, twenty pitches by our guy [Dave Fleming], but I never touched the ball. I knew I wouldn't hit 'til maybe the second or third . . . I just wanted to do *something*!

I had so much nervous energy, I probably burned off five pounds just walking around back and forth in the dugout. It was a huge crowd, a Fenway crowd. And there was just so much electricity, I couldn't fight it. Oh, and while all I wanted was a chance to field the ball at short? I had one ball hit to me all night. Their shortstop [John Valentin] turned an unassisted triple play. At least I wasn't the one who hit into it!

The next day I went 2-for-4, and then, my third day up, I got buzzed by The Rocket. Right up at my head, which of course, he would do again in the playoffs a few years later. It was an amazing way to get things going . . . Fenway, man.

Also on July 8, 1994
The Pittsburgh Pirates unveil their statue commemorating baseball star and philanthropist Roberto Clemente, outside Three Rivers Stadium. The accompanying plaque reads, in part: "He is . . . an example for many generations of people to admire, perhaps even emulate, as an athlete, humanitarian, father and a man."
The biographical movie of Ty Cobb's career, *Cobb*, is released over the weekend to critical acclaim.

AUTHOR'S NOTE: No player has ever been as universally admired as Clemente, none as universally despised as Cobb. A-Rod falls somewhere in between.

BOXSCORE

Boston Red Sox 4, Seattle Mariners 3
Game Played on Friday, July 8, 1994 (Night) Fenway Park

Seattle	0	0	1	0	1	0	0	0	1	—	3	8	1
Boston	0	0	0	0	0	4	0	0	x	—	4	9	1

BATTING

Seattle Mariners	AB	R	H	RBI	BB	K	PO	A
Turang lf	4	0	0	0	0	0	1	0
Fermin 2b	3	1	2	1	1	0	2	4
Griffey cf	4	0	3	1	0	0	2	0
E. Martinez 3b	3	0	0	0	1	1	1	0
Blowers 1b	4	1	2	1	0	0	7	0
Mitchell rf	3	0	0	0	1	0	2	0
Newfield dh	4	0	1	0	0	0	0	0
Haselman c	3	1	0	0	0	0	9	1
Jefferson ph	1	0	0	0	0	0	0	0
Rodriguez ss	3	0	0	0	0	0	0	3
Fleming p	0	0	0	0	0	0	0	2
Risley p	0	0	0	0	0	0	0	0
Gossage p	0	0	0	0	0	0	0	0
Totals	32	3	8	3	3	1	24	10

FIELDING
DP: 1
E: E. Martinez (7)

BATTING
3B: Griffey (4, off Nabholz)
HR: Blowers (7,9th inning off Nabholz, 0 on, 0 out)

BASERUNNING
CS: Fermin (3, 3rd base by Nabholz/Rowland)

Boston Red Sox	AB	R	H	RBI	BB	K	PO	A
Fletcher 2b	4	0	2	0	0	0	4	2
Naehring 1b	4	0	0	0	0	1	11	0
Valentin ss	3	1	2	1	1	0	3	5
Dawson dh	4	1	1	0	0	1	0	0
Brunansky lf	3	1	1	2	1	1	1	0
Chamberlain rf	4	0	1	0	0	3	3	0
Cooper 3b	4	0	0	0	0	1	1	6
Rowland c	3	1	1	1	0	0	1	1
Tinsley cf	3	0	1	0	0	0	3	0
Nabholz p	0	0	0	0	0	0	0	0
Ryan p	0	0	0	0	0	0	0	0
Totals	32	4	9	4	2	7	27	14

FIELDING
DP: 1. TP: 1
E: Valentin (7)

BATTING
2B: Dawson (17, off Fleming)
HR: Valentin (6, 6th inning off Fleming, 0 on, 0 out); Brunansky (6,6th inning off Risley, 1 on, 0 out); Rowland (5, 6th inning off Risley, 0 on, 2 out)

BASERUNNING
CS: Fletcher (1, 2nd base by Fleming/Haselman)

PITCHING

Seattle Mariners	IP	H	HR	R	ER	BB	K
Fleming	5	6	1	2	2	4
Risley L(6–5)	2	3	2	2	2	0	1
Gossage	1	0	0	0	0	0	2
Totals	8	9	3	4	4	2	7
Boston Red Sox	IP	H	HR	R	ER	BB	K
Nabholz W(1–2)	8	8	1	3	2	3	1
Ryan SV(7)	1	0	0	0	0	0	0
Totals	9	8	1	3	2	3	1

Umpires: Jim Joyce, Ed Hickox, Matthew Winans, Jim McKean
Time of Game: 2:51   Attendance: 33,355

Ivan Rodriguez
Born: November 30, 1971
Debut: June 20, 1991

Nicknamed "Pudge" by a minor league coach, Ivan Rodriguez emerged as a Gold Glove–caliber catcher for the Rangers at the tender age of 19. He monopolized the award every year from 1992 to 2001, and, by the age of 32, he had ten All-Star appearances to go with those ten Gold Gloves.

Pudge grew up poor on a country road in Puerto Rico, but he later compensated for his modest upbringing with one of the most immodest homes in South Florida—nine bedrooms, 12 bathrooms, and plenty of parking spaces for his Hummers, Bentleys and Mercedes (the plurals are not typographical errors). Out back, on his private waterway, there is a high-speed cigarette boat and a 118-foot yacht, and don't forget the solid bronze life-size statue of . . . himself. Singer Ricky Martin lives across the street, Enrique Iglesias is around the corner, and Jennifer Lopez is just a few doors down.

As a Texas Ranger, he was the 1999 AL MVP, putting up numbers no catcher ever had before. Before that season, no big league catcher had ever claimed a 20-homer, 20-stolen-base season; Rodriguez had it taken care of by the middle of August.

Most All-Star catchers are specialists of some sort. Mike Piazza is known for his bat, Charles Johnson for his arm, Brad Ausmus for his glove. Rodriguez, however, has run the table. After 12 popular seasons in Texas, he found only one team willing to give him what he felt he was worth for 2003, the Florida Marlins, who play not far from that life-size bronze statue in his backyard. The Marlins were picked by *Sports Illustrated* as the 18th-best team in baseball in its preseason issue, but they would win the World Series, with Rodriguez named MVP of the NLCS.

For Pudge's trouble, the Marlins failed to offer him what he was seeking in a 2004 contract. He shocked fans across the country by signing with the 119-loss Tigers, vowing to turn down-on-its-luck Detroit into a contender. The Tigers didn't exactly run away with the AL Central in 2004, but they did improve by a full 30 wins. Pudge was given a great deal of the credit.

I was supposed to get married in between games of a doubleheader in Tulsa that day . . . Maribel and I were all set with everything. We were going to have the ceremony in between home plate and the pitcher's mound. But the day before, my manager, Bobby Jones, says, "Sorry, but they need you with the Rangers in Chicago. You're getting called up." So we arranged to go to the courthouse in Tulsa the next morning, and then she flew with me to Chicago to watch me play against the White Sox.

The team in Tulsa was very helpful getting us all set at the courthouse . . . It took twenty, twenty-five minutes, that was it. It was very different than what we had planned, but it worked out fine. We ran to make our flight to Chicago, and it was all very rushed. I was very, very tired after that game . . . Not much of a honeymoon. We went on to Anaheim and Oakland then, so it was kind of an extended honeymoon, I guess—three cities, three hotels. It was all very exciting.

That first game went very well. We won, and I singled in two runs in the ninth. I also caught a couple guys stealing, Joey Cora in the middle of the game, then somebody else [Warren Newsom] later. Kevin Brown pitched for us, and people told me later I did a good job catching all his sinkers. I don't know about that. I just did what came naturally.

Also on June 20, 1991
Newspapers in South Florida report that the recently approved expansion franchise in Miami will be known as the Florida Marlins, subject to formal approval at the July 5 owners meetings. Dave Dombrowski's name first surfaces as a potential general manager candidate.

AUTHOR'S NOTE: Pudge and his family would eventually settle in Miami, and, years later, he would realize his dream of a World Series title as a key member of those Florida Marlins. When the Fish cut him loose after that magical '03 season, he was signed to a lucrative contact in Detroit . . . by Dombrowski, now the Tigers GM.

BOXSCORE

Texas Rangers 7, Chicago White Sox 3
Game Played on Thursday, June 20, 1991 (Night) at Comiskey Park II

Texas	0	1	0	0	0	0	1	0	5	—	7	8	0
Chicago	0	0	0	0	0	0	3	0	0	—	3	9	0

BATTING

Texas Rangers	AB	R	H	RBI	BB	K	PO	A
Downing dh	5	0	0	0	0	1	0	0
Palmeiro 1b	3	1	0	0	1	0	9	0
Sierra rf	3	1	1	2	1	1	1	0
Franco 2b	3	2	2	1	1	0	5	6
Reimer lf	3	0	0	0	0	2	0	0
Pettis cf	0	0	0	0	1	0	2	0
Gonzalez cf-lf	4	2	3	2	0	0	4	0
Buechele 3b	4	1	1	0	0	2	0	4
Diaz ss	4	0	0	0	0	1	1	2
Rodriguez c	4	0	1	2	0	1	4	2
Brown p	0	0	0	0	0	0	1	0
Jeffcoat p	0	0	0	0	0	0	0	1
Totals	33	7	8	7	4	8	27	15

FIELDING
DP: 2

BATTING
2B: Buechele (9, off Perez)
HR: Gonzalez (8, 7th inning off McDowell, 0 on, 2 out); Sierra (11, 9th inning off Thigpen, 1 on, 0 out); Franco (8, 9th inning off Thigpen, 0 on, 0 out)

BASERUNNING
SB: Gonzalez (4, 2nd base off McDowell/Fisk); Franco (12, 2nd base off McDowell/Fisk)
CS: Sierra (4, 2nd base by McDowell/Fisk); Pettis (8, 2nd base by Perez/Fisk)

Chicago White Sox	AB	R	H	RBI	BB	K	PO	A
Johnson cf	4	0	1	2	1	0	3	0
Ventura 3b-1b	5	0	0	1	1	1	2	0
Thomas dh	4	0	1	0	1	0	0	0
Merullo 1b	3	0	1	1	1	1	6	1
Guillen ss	0	0	0	0	0	0	0	0
Fisk c	4	0	1	0	0	1	8	2
Pasqua rf	1	0	0	0	2	0	2	0
Sosa pr-rf	1	1	0	0	0	0	1	0
Newson lf	4	1	2	0	0	0	2	0
Grebeck ss-3b	3	0	0	0	0	1	1	3
Cora 2b	2	1	2	0	0	0	2	1
McDowell p	0	0	0	0	0	0	1	1
Thigpen p	0	0	0	0	0	0	0	0
Perez p	0	0	0	0	0	0	0	0
Totals	31	3	9	3	5	4	27	10

BATTING
SH: Grebeck (2, off Brown)
HBP: Cora 2 (3, by Brown 2)
IBB: Thomas (8, by Brown)

BASERUNNING
CS: Cora (3, 2nd base by Brown/Rodriguez); Newson (1, 2nd base by Jeffcoat/Rodriguez)

PITCHING

Texas Rangers	IP	H	HR	R	ER	BB	K
Brown	6.2	7	0	3	3	4	4
Jeffcoat W(3–1)	2.1	2	0	0	0	1	0
Totals	9.0	9	0	3	3	5	4

Chicago White Sox	IP	H	HR	R	ER	BB	K
McDowell	8	3	1	2	2	2	8
Thigpen L(3–2)	0	2	2	3	3	2	0
Perez	1	3	0	2	2	0	0
Totals	9	8	3	7	7	4	8

HBP: Brown 2 (6, Cora 2)
IBB: Brown (2,Thomas)
Umpires: Don Denkinger, Larry McCoy, Durwood Merrill, Tim McClelland
Time of Game: 2:58   Attendance: 32,869

Scott Rolen

Born: April 4, 1975
Debut: August 1, 1996

An ill fit for Philadelphia, Scott Rolen nonetheless won a Gold Glove there at the tender age of 23, and no greater authority than Mike Schmidt proclaimed him "the best third baseman I've ever seen." Born near Evansville, Indiana (Don Mattingly's hometown), the right-handed slugger drove in 386 runs in his first four seasons—more than Alex Rodriguez and Manny Ramirez had logged in their first four years. His Midwest sensibilities pulled him to the Cardinals, the team he had rooted for as a kid.

The Gold Gloves kept on coming as Rolen deftly played his position. Teammate John Mabry described him as a "big panther, tackling ground balls," but few panthers can leap to their feet and throw four-seam strikes across the diamond. At the plate, he averaged 103 RBI between '01 and '03, then streaked to a total of 124 the following year, hitting a career-best .314. He had a bizarre postseason that fall in which he went 0-for-12 in the division series and 0-for-15 in the World Series, but he went 9-for-29 with three huge home runs in the NLCS.

Rolen finished fourth in the MVP balloting in 2004, his best finish for a major award since winning Rookie of the Year in 1997. He had qualified for rookie status by the slimmest of margins. One more at bat the summer before, and he would have exhausted his eligibility for the following year, but he was hit in the hand by the Cubs' Steve Trachsel and finished his season three weeks early. His '98 season featured 120 runs scored, 110 RBI, and a flirtation with a .300 average.

It is not easy being both a .300 hitter and an egghead simultaneously, but with Midwestern good manners and an earthy pleasantness, Rolen pulls it off. When Rolen was reading Ayn Rand on a team flight in the late 90s, a teammate once grabbed the book out of his hand and tore out the final ten pages. *Atlas Shrugged*, Gregg Jeffries grabbed. Actually, Rolen has said he most closely identifies with the protagonist in *The Fountainhead*, Howard Roarke. "He was his own man," explains Rolen, "capable of making his own tough decisions." In 2002, Scott Rolen became Howard Roarke, walking away from the Phillies and becoming public enemy number one, knowing that he belonged somewhere else.

I was overwhelmed. Game's starting, and there's Ozzie Smith getting in the batter's box—one of my favorite players, having grown up as a Cardinals fan. That put it all in perspective, that Ozzie Smith might try and bunt on me!

184

My debut was a doubleheader. It was a race to see if my parents could get there in time, because they decided to drive from Florida. Twenty-hour drive with a quick stop to rest. They arrived around the fifth inning of the first game, and I remember seeing them coming in. I was in the field, and I saw my dad making his way to his seat. He had a big smile on his face, which is probably, to this day, the best, most emotional moment I've had on a baseball field. No one in the park knew it but me, but to see Mom and Dad, especially Dad, with that big smile—it was all I could do not to wave at them, right there. Dad missed my first at bat, but he saw my second, against Donovan Osborne.

My first hit was a double, and suddenly, as I'm standing there on second base, there's Ozzie Smith coming over patting me on the back, saying, "Congratulations, kid." I was speechless.

Also on August 1, 1996
Reds third baseman Chris Sabo begins serving a seven-game suspension for using a corked bat.

AUTHOR'S NOTE: "Sabo" and "Sosa" became four-letter s-words thanks to corked bats during this era. Rolen gives the impression that he never even would have allowed anyone to peek at his spelling tests in third grade.

BOXSCORE

Philadelphia Phillies 2, St. Louis Cardinals 1 (1st game of Doubleheader)

Game Played on Thursday, August 1, 1996 (Night) at Veteran's Stadium

												R	H	E
St. Louis	0	0	1	0	0	0	0	0	0	—		1	7	1
Philadelphia	0	0	0	0	2	0	0	0	x	—		2	10	0

BATTING

St. Louis Cardinals	AB	R	H	RBI	BB	K	PO	A
Smith ss	4	1	1	0	0	0	1	4
Lankford cf	4	0	1	1	0	0	4	0
McGee rf	4	0	1	0	0	0	1	0
Sweeney lf	4	0	1	0	0	0	1	0
Mejia pr	0	0	0	0	0	0	0	0
Gaetti 3b	4	0	1	0	0	1	0	2
Mabry 1b	4	0	0	0	0	0	9	1
Pagnozzi c	3	0	1	0	0	0	4	0
Alicea 2b	3	0	1	0	0	0	3	3
Osborne p	2	0	0	0	0	1	1	1
Gant ph	1	0	0	0	0	1	0	0
Bailey p	0	0	0	0	0	0	0	0
Totals	33	1	7	1	0	3	24	11

FIELDING
DP: 2
E: Alicea (22)
PB: Pagnozzi (3)

BATTING
2B: Lankford (23, off Springer)

BASERUNNING
CS: Mejia (3, 2nd base by Ryan/Santiago)

Philadelphia Phillies	AB	R	H	RBI	BB	K	PO	A
Otero cf	4	1	1	0	1	0	6	0
Doster 2b	4	0	2	1	0	1	0	1
Ryan p	0	0	0	0	0	0	0	1
Jefferies lf	4	0	1	1	0	1	5	0
Zeile 1b	4	0	2	0	0	0	7	0
Santiago c	4	0	1	0	0	0	3	1
Rolen 3b	4	0	1	0	0	0	1	1
Martinez rf	4	0	1	0	0	0	1	0
Stocker ss	2	1	1	0	2	0	4	1
Springer p	2	0	0	0	0	2	0	0
Morandini 2b	0	0	0	0	0	0	0	2
Totals	32	2	10	2	3	4	27	6

FIELDING
PB: Santiago (5)

BATTING—
2B: Rolen (1, off Osborne); Doster (5, off Osborne); Stocker (4, off Bailey)
SH: Springer (2, off Osborne)
HBP: Morandini (5, by Bailey)
IBB: Stocker (7, by Osborne)

PITCHING

St. Louis Cardinals	IP	H	HR	R	ER	BB	K
Osborne L(9–7)	6	8	0	2	2	2	2
Bailey	2	2	0	0	0	1	2
Totals	8	10	0	2	2	3	4
Philadelphia Phillies	**IP**	**H**	**HR**	**R**	**ER**	**BB**	**K**
Springer W(3–9)	7	6	0	1	1	0	2
Ryan SV(5)	2	1	0	0	0	0	1
Totals	9	7	0	1	1	0	3

WP: Osborne (4)
HBP: Bailey (1, Morandini)
IBB: Osborne (4, Stocker)
Umpires: Steve Rippley, Mark Hirschbeck, Charlie Williams, Bruce Dreckman
Time of Game: 2:38   Attendance: 22,934

Juan Samuel
Born: December 9, 1960
Debut: August 24, 1983

He was Alfonso Soriano before there was an Alfonso Soriano. A free-swinging, happy-go-lucky Dominican second baseman, Samuel was a trifle challenged defensively but burst onto the scene with a World Series–bound team. Like Soriano, he could hit for average despite high strikeout totals, and like Soriano, he could really wheel around the bases. Samuel's energy helped spark the otherwise-veteran '83 Phillies to the NL East title.

In Samuel's first full big league season (1984), he stole 72 bases and set a record for right-handed hitters with 701 regular season at bats. The huge pile of ABs was due in part to an apparent allergy to walks; he managed only 28, while striking out a league-high (and rookie record) 168 times.

Samuel became the only player to reach double figures in doubles, triples, and homers in each of his first four full big league seasons, and he kept doing enough offensively to stay in an everyday lineup until 1991. His last seven seasons, however, he was a part-time player, for the Royals, Tigers, Dodgers, Reds, and Blue Jays.

He is now a coach for Detroit and the father of three children, including a son named Samuel. That's right: Samuel Samuel. "So nice, we named him twice," Dad says. Thankfully, Doug Mientkiewicz passed on the opportunity to name his child similarly.

I was in the minor leagues, playing for the Portland Beavers, and I had just had a great game the night before, with two home runs. So I'm standing there taking ground balls in Salt Lake City, and our manager, John Felske, comes up to me and says, "'You're not playing." And I stare at him, and I say, "[You've] got to be kidding. Of course I'm playing. I hit two home runs for you yesterday." And he insists, "No you're not playing. It's because you have to catch a flight to San Francisco." I ask him what's in San Francisco, and he says, "That's where the Phillies are playing right now." And so all I could say was, "Uh, uh, uh." He says, "Go! Get packed!" But I told him, "First I've got to go back to Portland to get all my money out of the bank." Because I was sure that once I was called up, I'd never be coming back. Joe Morgan had been struggling, at the end of his career, and I'm thinking, "Maybe they're releasing him, letting me play. I'll never see Portland, Oregon, again, so I gotta go get out my money." He says, "No, we can go get it for you." And I insist, "No, I gotta get it myself," so they got me a flight while I was changing out of my uniform back into my street clothes.

I went to Portland that night, then to San Francisco the next morning. Paul Owens was the manager for the Phillies, and I went right into his office, and he says, "Okay, kid, you're not going play right away, but you'll be in tomorrow. You'll play against lefties, Joe Morgan will play against righties. Don't change anything. Just do what you always do." Which sounded easy, but then I walked out of his office and saw some of my teammates, like Pete Rose, Mike Schmidt, Steve Carlton, and I'm like, "Whoa! I'm going to be playing with these guys?"

Well, sure enough, next day, there's my name on the lineup card, leading off. I punched out against Mark Davis, but next at bat, a triple, and I scored on a throwing error—all the way around the bases, one trip! It was wonderful to call back home to the Dominican after the game and tell everyone that I had done that. Turns out, San Francisco was the site of the All-Star Game the following year, too, and I was proud to make that phone call, too . . . It's a long way from the Dominican to the Major League All-Star Game.

Also on August 24, 1983

On Cal Ripken Jr.'s 23rd birthday, the Orioles are pressed into an emergency tenth-inning situation, whereby utility infielder Lenn Sakata has to go in as catcher. Three straight Toronto batters reach base, and each takes a long lead, with no respect for Sakata's throwing arm. Each of the three are promptly picked off by Tippy Martinez. Sakata then wins the game with a homer in the bottom of the inning.

AUTHOR'S NOTE: Samuel would later play three seasons for the Blue Jays but only get picked off once.

BOXSCORE

San Francisco Giants 5, Philadelphia Phillies 3

Game Played on Wednesday, August 24, 1983 (Day) at Candlestick Park

											R	H	E
Philadelphia	0	0	1	1	0	1	0	0	0	—	3	8	0
San Francisco	1	0	0	2	0	0	0	0	2	—	5	9	3

BATTING

Philadelphia Phillies	AB	R	H	RBI	BB	K	PO	A
Samuel 2b	4	1	1	0	1	1	6	2
Lefebvre rf	3	0	1	1	1	1	2	0
Matthews lf	5	0	0	0	0	0	2	0
Schmidt 3b	4	0	2	0	1	1	0	3
Perez 1b	4	0	0	0	1	1	2	0
Diaz c	4	0	0	0	0	1	11	1
Dernier cf	3	1	1	0	0	0	0	0
Morgan ph	1	0	0	0	0	0	0	0
G. Gross cf	0	0	0	0	0	0	1	0
DeJesus ss	3	1	2	0	1	0	1	1
Carlton p	3	0	1	0	0	1	0	2
Totals	**34**	**3**	**8**	**1**	**5**	**6**	**25**	**9**

FIELDING

DP: 2

BATTING

2B: Lefebvre (12, off Martin)
3B: Samuel (1, off M. Davis)
SH: Carlton (5, off Martin)
HBP: Lefebvre (2, M. Davis)
IBB: Samuel (1, by M. Davis)

San Francisco Giants	AB	R	H	RBI	BB	K	PO	A
LeMaster ss	4	1	0	0	1	2	1	4
Youngblood 3b	4	2	3	2	1	0	1	2
Clark rf	2	0	1	0	2	0	0	0
Leonard lf	4	0	1	1	0	2	3	0
C. Davis cf	3	0	0	0	1	2	4	0
Nicosia c	3	1	1	0	0	0	9	0
Brenly 1b	3	1	1	2	1	2	6	0
Wellman 2b	4	0	2	0	0	1	2	1
M. Davis p	1	0	0	0	0	0	0	0
Martin p	1	0	0	0	0	1	1	1
O'Malley ph	1	0	0	0	0	0	0	0
Totals	**30**	**5**	**9**	**5**	**6**	**10**	**27**	**9**

FIELDING

DP: 1
E: C. Davis 2 (7), Nicosia (2)

BATTING

HR: Brenly (7, 4th inning off Carlton, 1 on, 1 out); Youngblood (11, 9th inning off Carlton, 1 on, 1 out)
SH: M. Davis (6, off Carlton); Nicosia (3, off Carlton)
IBB: Brenly (4, by Carlton)

PITCHING

Philadelphia Phillies	IP	H	HR	R	ER	BB	K
Carlton L(12–13)	8.1	9	2	5	5	6	10
SanFrancisco Giants	**IP**	**H**	**HR**	**R**	**ER**	**BB**	**K**
M. Davis	5.2	6	0	3	2	4	4
Martin W(2–4)	3.1	2	0	0	0	1	2
Totals	**9.0**	**8**	**0**	**3**	**2**	**5**	**6**

WP: M. Davis (4)
HBP: M. Davis (2, Lefebvre)
IBB: Carlton (8, Brenly); M. Davis (3, Samuel)
Umpires: Doug Harvey, Frank Pulli, Jerry Crawford, Eric Gregg
Time of Game: 2:33   Attendance: 14,317

Ron Santo
Born: February 25, 1940
Debut: June 26, 1960

Perhaps no player better epitomizes blind devotion to his organization than the Cubs' Ron Santo. As a high school star in Seattle, he had his pick of signing with literally any team in either league, but he told his family, "I just have a good feeling about the Cubs."

As their everyday third baseman in the 1960s and early 1970s, the popular right-handed hitter played an often-spectacular third base and blasted an average of 28 home runs over a 12-year period, this during an era that saw power totals at a collective low tide. As every modern Cub fan knows, he is a five-time Gold Glover and a nine-time All-Star. He led the National League in walks four times and in triples during a 1964 season that saw him hit a career-best .313.

He somehow played a 15-year big league career keeping his diabetic condition a secret, but he is now a very vocal advocate for the Juvenile Diabetes Foundation, raising millions each year for research. Complications from the disease have robbed Santo of both of his legs below the knee, but he continues to win his health battles, at least enough to keep rooting for the Cubbies as the team's radio color commentator.

His supporters have adamantly clamored for his inclusion in the Baseball Hall of Fame, citing his career 342 home runs in an era dominated by pitchers. His career .277 batting average was ten points higher than Hall of Famers Mike Schmidt and Brooks Robinson. Apologists often cite the fact that he lacked postseason exposure, having never made the playoffs. However, his Cub teammates, Billy Williams and Ernie Banks, are both in, both having suffered the same home-in-October fate as Santo.

John Holland was the Cubs GM, and he had told me when I was the last cut of spring training that he'd be calling me soon. Well, two or three months is certainly sooner than September, so I was thrilled when my phone rang in my apartment in Houston, 7:30 A.M. on a Saturday, and it was John finally making that call. Problem was, it was right in the middle of one of those brutal Houston thunderstorms. I had my wife drive me to the airport, and the water was up past our wheels, and she wanted to turn back but I told her, "No, ya gotta keep driving! I'm going to join the Cubs today!"

I get to Pittsburgh, where the Cubs are playing, late Saturday night, after a lot of flight delays, so it was Sunday when I got to Forbes Field. I walk up to the clubhouse guy, and he shows me where to dress, gives me my uniform, and no sooner does that happen than Lou Boudreau, the manager, comes over and says, "You're in there, playing third and batting sixth." Smokey Burgess was catching, Bob Friend was pitching, for the Pirates . . . I came up in the second inning. Forty thousand people there, and my knees started shaking. I mean, really shaking. And Smokey Burgess says, "Are you nervous, kid?" I jump back and say, "No!'" I get a curveball and I back off, taking it all the way, and Smokey Burgess fires it back to the mound and tells me, "*That's* a big league curveball." I figure, man, I'll show him. And I get back in there and rip a single. I ended up with four hits and five RBI, and we won a double-header.

I was off and going, although they were a last place team that year. And the next. And not much better for a while. But I never regretted signing and staying with the Cubs. I've always said that if it was a choice between never winning a World Series with the Cubs and winning one for someone else, I'd have chosen my 14 years with the Cubs.

Also on June 26, 1960
The Ed Sullivan Show is headlined by the Ames Brothers, the Gene Krupa Orchestra, and opera singer Rise Stevens, who performs "Climb Every Mountain."

AUTHOR'S NOTE: "Ain't no mountain high enough" to deter the eternally optimistic Santo, who has beaten diabetes and the amputation of both legs as he continues to broadcast Cubs baseball.

BOXSCORE

Chicago Cubs 7, Pittsburgh Pirates 6
Game Played on Sunday, 6/26/1960, Game 1 of Doubleheader (Day) at Forbes Field

Chicago	0	0	0	0	6	0	0	0	1	—	7
Pittsburgh	1	0	0	1	0	0	0	0	4	—	6

Chicago	AB	R	H	RBI	BB	K	PO	A
R. Ashburn lf	4	2	3	1	1	0	2	0
D. Murphy cf	5	1	1	1	0	0	0	0
E. Banks ss	4	1	1	1	1	1	1	2
E. Bouchee 1b	4	0	1	1	0	0	3	0
G. Altman rf	3	1	0	0	1	0	0	0
R. Santo 3b	4	0	2	3	0	0	0	0
J. Kindall 2b	4	1	2	0	0	0	0	0
J. Hegan c	4	1	2	0	0	2	7	0
M. Freeman p	4	0	1	0	0	2	0	0
D. Elston p	0	0	0	0	0	0	0	0
Totals	36	7	13	7	3	5	13	2

FIELDING
DP: (1). E. Banks-E. Bouchee

BATTING
2B: D. Murphy (off B.Friend); R. Santo (off B. Friend); E. Banks (off J. Umbricht)
2-out RBI: E. Banks; R. Santo 3
RBI, scoring position, less than 2 outs: R. Ashburn 1–1; D. Murphy 1–4; E. Bouchee 1–3; M. Freeman 0–1
SF: E. Bouchee
GIDP: D. Murphy; G. Altman

BASERUNNING
SB: R. Ashburn (2nd base off J. Umbricht/H. Smith)
CS: J. Kindall (3rd base by J. Umbricht/H. Smith)
Team LOB: 6

Pittsburgh	AB	R	H	RBI	BB	K	PO	A
B. Virdon cf	3	1	2	0	2	0	1	0
D. Groat ss	5	0	1	0	0	1	2	2
B. Skinner lf	3	0	0	1	0	0	0	0
R. Nelson 1b	4	1	1	0	0	0	3	0
G. Cimoli rf	3	1	1	0	1	2	0	0
H. Smith c	4	1	1	2	0	1	5	1
D. Hoak 3b	4	1	1	0	0	2	0	1
B. Mazeroski 2b	3	0	0	0	1	0	0	1
B. Friend p	1	0	0	0	0	0	0	0
B. Daniels p	1	0	0	0	0	0	0	0
D. Schofield ph	1	0	0	0	0	1	0	0
J. Umbricht p	0	0	0	0	0	0	0	0
S. Burgess ph	1	1	1	2	0	0	0	0
Totals	33	6	8	5	4	7	11	5

FIELDING
E: H. Smith
DP: (2). D. Hoak-D. Groat-R. Nelson; B. Mazeroski-D. Groat-R. Nelson

BATTING
2B: R. Nelson (off M. Freeman); H. Smith (off M. Freeman)
3B: B. Virdon (off D. Elston)
HR: S. Burgess (9th inning off M. Freeman, 1 on, 2 out)
2-out RBI: S. Burgess 2
RBI, scoring position, less than 2 outs: D. Groat 0–1; B. Skinner 1–1; G. Cimoli 0–1; H. Smith 1–1; B. Mazeroski 0–1
SF: B. Skinner

BASERUNNING
SB: R. Nelson (3rd base off M. Freeman/J. Hegan)
Team LOB: 5

PITCHING

Chicago	IP	H	HR	R	ER	BB	K
M. Freeman W	8.2	7	1	6	6	4	7
D. Elston S	0.1	1	0	0	0	0	
Total	9.0	8	1	6	6	4	7
Pittsburgh	IP	H	HR	R	ER	BB	K
B. Friend L	4.2	10	0	6	6	2	3
B. Daniels	2.1	0	0	0	0	0	1
J. Umbricht	2.0	3	0	1	1	1	1
Total	9.0	13	0	7	7	3	5

Inherited Runners—Scored: D. Elston 0–0; B. Daniels 1–0; J. Umbricht 0–0
IBB: E. Banks by B. Friend; G. Altman by B. Friend
WP: M. Freeman
Umpires: HP: Smith, 1B: Sudol, 2B: Boggess, 3B: Gorman
Time of Game: 2:58   Attendance: Unknown

Curt Schilling
Born: November 14, 1966
Debut: September 7, 1988

The saga of Curtis Montague Schilling had its humble beginnings in the Red Sox minor league system. A second-round draft pick in 1986, he was summarily dealt to Baltimore with Brady Anderson for Mike Boddicker during the Sox's quest for the 1988 division title. For years, as he bounced from Baltimore to Houston to Philadelphia, Schilling was the poster child for underachievement. His poor work habits and out-all-night lifestyle took away from his on-field performance, a fact noted by none other than his idol, Roger Clemens.

At a wintertime workout session, Clemens pulled young Schilling aside, and after tearing into him for the better part of an hour, a new commitment to excellence was spawned. Less than ten years later, teacher and pupil met head-to-head in the finale of the 2001 World Series, with Schilling outdueling his mentor through seven before allowing a home run to Alfonso Soriano. The Diamondbacks rallied to win, capping a standout season for the Arizona-raised right-hander in which he went 22–6 with league-high totals in innings and starts. He followed with 23 wins in '02, at one point going 165 batters between walks. In 2003, he moved back to Boston, where it had all begun—and he was now anything but out-of-control, as his major league–best strikeouts-to-walks ratio would attest.

After an injury-plagued '03, Schilling bounced back with 21 wins in 2004, finishing second to Johan Santana for the AL Cy Young. His best work was still to come, as he pitched courageously with a torn ankle tendon in the ALCS. With his tendon sutured together (and leaking blood onto what became, literally, a Red Sock) he went on to steer Boston to its first World Series in 86 years, ending lifetimes worth of misery in New England.

Never shy about speaking his mind, he has used his passion for good (he is a tireless advocate for ALS research, and he and his wife, Shonda, were named to Barbara Walters's list of "Most Fascinating People of 2004") but also has stirred talk show passions (e.g., calling Deion Sanders a "glorified flag football player"), occasionally calling said talk shows from his car. There may not be a more quotable player in baseball, and few have ever come as far as the powerful right-hander.

I left Double-A the final day of the season and hopped all the way to Baltimore. Gregg Olson had known when he signed his contract, he was guaranteed to go up, but I sure had nothing like that. Our manager at Charlotte, Greg Biagini, called me into his office and told me I had a phone call. It was Doug Melvin, the farm director. He says, "Congrats on a nice year, Curt. Would you like to come up here and join us for the final month?" Uh, yeah, I'll do that. So next day Gregg and I flew to Seattle. I hadn't slept. I had been at a pay phone for hours calling home, calling everywhere . . . My dad had passed away nine months before, and I was sorry he didn't get to hear that news straight from me, but I called everyone else I knew, all my Little League coaches, my college coaches, everyone. It was just the one day in Seattle, enough time for Eddie Murray to buy Gregg and me a beer, which I thought was awful nice of him. I learned on the flight home I'd be pitching against the Red Sox when we got home.

I stayed at the Cross Keys Inn, down the street from Memorial Stadium, and the Sox were staying at the hotel too. They tried to get me drunk the night before I pitched. Greenwell, Boggs, Stanley buying me beers, and I'm thinking, "Cool! These guys want to hang out with me!" I never sus-

---

Also on September 7, 1988
Vice President George Bush Sr. startles an American Legion audience in Louisville by referring to September 7 as "Pearl Harbor Day," which is actually December 7.

AUTHOR'S NOTE: Schilling, a military and war buff, knows virtually every detail about Pearl Harbor. In 2004, he actively supported George W. Bush, making campaign speeches and appearances just two days after the World Series ended.

BOXSCORE

Baltimore Orioles 4, Boston Red Sox 3
Game Played on Wednesday, September 7, 1988 (Night) at Memorial Stadium

Boston	0	0	0	1	2	0	0	0	0	—	3	7	0
Baltimore	0	1	0	0	0	0	1	0	2	—	4	8	1

BATTING

Boston Red Sox	AB	R	H	RBI	BB	K	PO	A
Boggs 3b	3	1	1	0	2	0	0	3
Barrett 2b	4	0	1	0	1	0	4	4
Evans rf	3	0	1	2	1	0	1	0
Greenwell lf	3	0	0	0	1	0	3	0
Burks cf	4	1	1	1	0	0	1	0
Benzinger 1b	4	0	1	0	0	1	11	0
Parrish dh	4	0	0	0	0	0	0	0
Reed ss	2	1	0	0	1	0	1	5
Gedman c	4	0	2	0	0	1	5	1
Hurst p	0	0	0	0	0	0	0	0
Smith p	0	0	0	0	0	0	0	0
Stanley p	0	0	0	0	0	0	0	0
Totals	31	3	7	3	6	2	26	13

FIELDING
DP: 1

BATTING
2B: Gedman (11, off Schilling); Evans (30, off Schilling)
3B: Benzinger (1, off Aase)
HR: Burks (16, 4th inning off Schilling, 0 on, 2 out)
HBP: Reed (2, by Schilling)
IBB: Greenwell (17, by Schilling)

BASERUNNING—
SB: Evans (5, 2nd base off Schilling/Tettleton)

Baltimore Orioles	AB	R	H	RBI	BB	K	PO	A
Stanicek lf	3	0	0	0	2	0	3	0
B.Ripken 2b	5	0	2	1	0	0	3	4
C.Ripken ss	5	0	1	1	0	1	1	2
Murray dh	4	0	0	0	0	1	0	0
Tettleton c	2	1	0	0	2	1	2	0
Davis rf	3	1	2	0	0	0	2	0
Orsulak ph-rf	1	0	0	0	0	0	0	0
Gerhart cf	1	0	0	1	1	0	3	0
Anderson ph	1	0	0	0	0	1	0	0
Traber 1b	4	0	2	1	0	0	9	0
Schu pr	0	1	0	0	0	0	0	0
Gonzales 3b	3	0	1	0	0	1	3	4
Sheets ph	0	1	0	0	1	0	0	0
Schilling p	0	0	0	0	0	0	0	0
Aase p	0	0	0	0	0	0	1	1
Thurmond p	0	0	0	0	0	0	0	0
Totals	32	4	8	4	6	5	27	11

FIELDING
DP: 3
E: Traber (5)

BATTING
2B: Davis (1, off Hurst); Gonzales (6, off Hurst)
SF: Gerhart (2, off Hurst)

PITCHING

Boston Red Sox	IP	H	HR	R	ER	BB	K
Hurst	7.1	5	0	2	2	3	3
Smith	1.0	2	0	1	1	1	2
Stanley L(6–3)	0.1	1	0	1	1	2	0
Totals	8.2	8	0	4	4	6	5
Baltimore Orioles	**IP**	**H**	**HR**	**R**	**ER**	**BB**	**K**
Schilling	7.0	6	1	3	3	5	2
Aase	1.0	1	0	0	0	0	0
Thurmond W(1–6)	1.0	0	0	0	0	1	0
Totals	9.0	7	1	3	3	6	2

HBP: Schilling (1, Reed)
IBB: Schilling (1, Greenwell)
Umpires: Steve Palermo, Larry Young, Dan Morrison, Dave Phillips
Time of Game: 3:02 Attendance: 35,569

pected they were just trying to get me drunk so they could destroy me the next day.

The game was kind of surreal. Packed house. I get out there to start the game, and Wade Boggs is digging in the batter's box with a smirk, and I'm like, "Oh, sh—." Steve Palermo, who's now a wonderful friend, was the home plate umpire, and before I could throw that first pitch, Steve ran the ball out to me there on the mound, and said, "Okay, kid, just throw that first one close, we'll get the game going, you'll be all right." I got Marty Barrett, I struck out Todd Benzinger, Ellis Burks homered off me, I remember it all . . . We came back and won in the ninth. My mom and sister and I went out to eat and celebrate after . . . We had beaten a team in a pennant race, and I had done okay.

Jason Schmidt
Born: January 29, 1973
Debut: April 28, 1995

For years, big right-hander Jason Schmidt had teased with the promise of a "breakout season." It came in 2003, when he steamrolled to a 17–5 record for the Giants, leading the league in ERA and lowest batting average allowed. Despite season-long elbow issues and the death of his mother (with whom he'd always been quite close), he finished runner-up in the Cy Young balloting, going 8–1 down the stretch and leading the Giants to the postseason. He pitched, seemingly, on heart alone in the Division Series against eventual World Series champ Florida. With a throbbing elbow that awaited much-needed surgery, Schmidt pitched a complete-game, three-hit shutout for the Giants' only win in the best-of-five series.

His best start of that 2003 season—and maybe of his career—came in May, a one-hit masterpiece that was completely overshadowed by the other events of the day, a perfect game by Randy Johnson. In 2004, Schmidt again bid for a Cy Young with a strong first half but faded down the stretch after a groin injury. He and the Giants were nosed out of the playoffs by the Dodgers and Astros on the season's final weekend.

Nicknamed "Sweet Pea" because of his supposed resemblance to the Popeye cartoon character, he possesses a rare combination of power and finesse. As an eighth-round draft pick of the Braves in 1995, he learned from Greg Maddux in his first years in Atlanta, rooming with the veteran for a couple months and picking his brain while raiding his fridge. Blessed with a much more ferocious fastball than Maddux ever had, he is also blessed (or is it cursed?) with a playful sense of humor that encompasses everything from joy buzzers to whoopie cushions.

He has fashioned spectacular strikeout-to-walks ratios as he's turned from his late 20s to early 30s, topping out at 208 of the former and just 46 of the latter in '03. He raised his strikeout total to 251 in 2004 and was second best in the league, allowing an average of just 6.6 hits per nine innings. An All-Star in both the '03 and '04 seasons, he has quietly gone a stellar 55–21 since being dealt to the Giants from Pittsburgh.

Facing the first guy, I felt like I was 15 years old. I was shaking. It was Opening Night at Dodger Stadium, and the place was just electric, as you can imagine.

I came in for Steve Avery, in relief. I walked Delino DeShields, and I was

193

BOXSCORE

Los Angeles Dodgers 9, Atlanta Braves 1
Game Played on Friday, April 28, 1995 (Night) at Dodger Stadium

Atlanta	0	0	0	0	1	0	0	0	0	—	1	4	1
Los Angeles	1	0	0	2	2	0	4	0	x	—	9	9	1

BATTING

Atlanta Braves	AB	R	H	RBI	BB	K	PO	A
Grissom cf	2	0	0	0	1	0	1	0
Blauser ss	4	0	0	0	0	3	0	2
Jones 3b	3	0	0	1	1	0	1	0
McGriff 1b	3	0	0	0	1	0	6	0
Justice rf	4	0	1	0	0	1	3	0
Klesko lf	4	0	1	0	0	0	0	0
O'Brien c	1	1	0	0	3	0	10	1
Lemke 2b	4	0	1	0	0	0	2	2
Avery p	1	0	0	0	0	1	0	1
Clark p	0	0	0	0	0	0	0	1
Smith ph	1	0	1	0	0	0	0	0
Schmidt p	0	0	0	0	0	0	0	0
Oliva ph	1	0	0	0	0	1	0	0
Borbon p	0	0	0	0	0	0	0	1
Wohlers p	0	0	0	0	0	0	0	0
Bedrosian p	0	0	0	0	0	0	0	0
Kelly ph	1	0	0	0	0	1	0	0
Totals	**29**	**1**	**4**	**1**	**6**	**7**	**24**	**8**

FIELDING
DP: 1
E: O'Brien (1)

BATTING
2B: Klesko (1, off Astacio)
HBP: Grissom (1, by Astacio)

Los Angeles Dodgers	AB	R	H	RBI	BB	K	PO	A
DeShields 2b	3	2	1	0	2	1	0	2
Murphy p	0	0	0	0	0	0	0	0
Worrell p	0	0	0	0	0	0	0	1
Offerman ss	3	2	0	0	2	2	1	3
Mondesi cf	4	2	2	1	0	0	3	0
Karros 1b	4	2	2	1	1	0	11	0
Ashley lf	3	1	2	5	0	1	0	0
Hollandsworth lf	1	0	0	0	0	0	1	0
H. Rodriguez rf	3	0	0	0	1	2	3	0
R. Williams pr-rf	0	0	0	0	0	0	1	0
Ingram 3b	3	0	2	1	0	0	0	1
Hansen ph-3b	0	0	0	0	1	0	0	0
Hernandez c	3	0	0	0	1	2	6	1
Astacio p	2	0	0	0	0	0	0	1
Daal p	0	0	0	0	0	0	0	0
Hansell p	0	0	0	0	0	0	0	0
Webster ph	1	0	0	0	0	0	0	0
Osuna p	0	0	0	0	0	0	0	0
Treadway ph-2b	1	0	0	0	0	0	1	1
Totals	**31**	**9**	**9**	**8**	**8**	**8**	**27**	**10**

FIELDING
DP: 2
E: Hernandez (1)

BATTING
2B: DeShields (2, off Avery); Mondesi (3, off Avery); Ashley (1, off Avery)
HR: Ashley (1, 7th inning off Wohlers, 2 on, 0 out)
SF: Ashley (1, off Schmidt)
HBP: Mondesi (1, by Borbon)

BASERUNNING
SB: DeShields 2 (2, 3rd base off Avery/O'Brien; 2nd base off Schmidt/O'Brien); Karros (1, 2nd base off Avery/O'Brien); Mondesi (1, 3rd base off Avery/O'Brien)

PITCHING

Atlanta Braves	IP	H	HR	R	ER	BB	K
Avery (0–1)	3.1	5	0	3	3	1	5
Clark	0.2	0	0	0	0	1	0
Schmidt	1	1	0	2	2	2	1
Borbon	1	2	0	3	3	1	0
Wohlers	1	1	1	1	1	3	2
Bedrosian	1	0	0	0	0	0	0
Totals	**8**	**9**	**1**	**9**	**9**	**8**	**8**

Los Angeles Dodgers	IP	H	HR	R	ER	BB	K
Astacio	4.2	2	0	1	1	5	5
Daal (1–0)	0.2	1	0	0	0	0	0
Hansell	0.2	1	0	0	0	0	0
Osuna	1	0	0	0	0	0	0
Murphy	1	0	0	0	0	0	0
Worrell	1	0	0	0	0	1	1
Totals	**9**	**4**	**0**	**1**	**1**	**6**	**7**

HBP: Borbon (1, Mondesi); Astacio (1, Grissom)
Umpires: Gus Rodriguez, Jeff Jenkins, Bill Rosenberry, Wade Ford
Time of Game: 3:08   Attendance: 51,181

really worried about balking him to second because my hands were shaking so bad. My legs, too. He stole second base and it was almost a relief, because at least I didn't have to worry about it anymore. Afterwards, I was getting calls from back home, and everyone said the same thing—"Hey, they had a close-up of you on TBS, and they were pointing out how your hands were shaking." Believe me, I knew they were. I got out of the inning . . . Actually, somehow I struck out Henry Rodriguez on three pitches to finally get off the mound and get off the field. The only word I can use to describe how I felt was "relieved."

I walked into the dugout and I told [pitching coach] Leo [Mazzone], "I really don't think I can pitch at this level." I was dead serious. I said, "I am so scared out there," and I remember guys were laughing in the dugout when I said it, but I was serious. When I first walked onto that field, even before the game, it was incredible to me how nice the grass was—how clean, how perfect. It was pretty obvious this wasn't the minor leagues anymore. It took a few more games before I felt like I was in control . . . I still felt completely overwhelmed for that whole first week or two.

Also on April 28, 1995
The Giants play their first game at home since Candlestick Park has been renamed 3Com Stadium, later changed to 3Com Park and finally (hopefully) to Monster Park.

AUTHOR'S NOTE: By the time Schmidt arrived in San Francisco (from Pittsburgh), the Giants had moved out of the blustery stadium on Candlestick Point and were playing at beautiful SBC Park on Third and King.

Mike Scioscia
Born: November 27, 1958
Debut: April 20, 1980

As a player, Mike Scioscia was known for being a line-drive hitter who made great contact and excelled at the hit and run. As a manager, his Anaheim team adopted those same traits, winning the World Series in 2002. That entire year, the steady mid-forties skipper preached the virtues of focus, invoking the phrase "one day at a time" so often he may as well have worn Schneider's tool belt from the old sitcom by the same name. The Philadelphia native was named Manager of the Year, having taken a team that had won only 75 games the year before and turned it into a championship club. The fact that he led an L.A.-area team other than the Dodgers to a title made many Dodger fans bristle, as L.A. had let him walk away from their organization to manage the hated Angels only a season before.

In his playing days, he was known as "The Rock." When he broke the Dodgers' team record for games caught, Orel Hershiser presented him with a granite slab in the shape of home plate, inscribed, "From the Bulldog, to the Rock." Hershiser says he'll always remember Scioscia lying down in the trainer's room after games, ice packs on every part of his body except his stomach, on which would invariably be a large box of pizza. ("He's the only guy I ever knew who could catch 140 games a year and still gain 10 pounds," said his battery mate.)

Scioscia may have been the best in the business at blocking the plate. He tagged out 134 runners in his ten-year career. (Said onetime teammate Tim Belcher: "He's like a tree stump with a never-ending root system.") When wielding a bat, it wasn't so much how many hits he got as it was the *timeliness* of them. In 1988, he bombed one of the Dodgers' biggest-ever home runs, a two-run, two-out, ninth-inning shot off Doc Gooden in Game Four of the NLCS. The onetime first-round draft pick caught a pair of no-hitters and started the 1990 All-Star Game. Rotator cuff problems finished him as a Dodger by 1992, and aborted comebacks with San Diego and Texas finally led to his retirement in 1994. He ended his career with 4,373 at bats, all of them as a Dodger.

I was one of the last cuts, the spring of 1980 . . . I started in the minors, and at the end of the season, I dislocated a ring finger and had still been rehabbing from that early in '81. I came up from Tucson, where our Triple-A team was playing, and they actually had to catch Derrel Thomas for a day with Joe Ferguson on the DL and me not yet eligible to come off and be activated. I'm-

BOXSCORE

Los Angeles Dodgers 4, Houston Astros 2
Game Played on Sunday, April 20, 1980 (Day) at Dodger Stadium

Houston	0	0	0	0	0	0	2	0	0	—	2 7 1
Los Angeles	1	0	1	0	0	0	0	2	x	—	4 5 0

BATTING

Houston Astros	AB	R	H	RBI	BB	K	PO	A
Landestoy 2b	3	0	1	0	0	0	3	2
Morgan ph-2b	1	0	0	1	0	1	1	1
Reynolds ss	4	0	1	0	0	0	1	5
Puhl cf	4	0	0	0	0	0	4	0
Cruz lf	4	0	0	0	0	1	4	0
Walling 1b	2	0	1	0	2	0	8	1
Cabell 3b	4	1	1	0	0	0	0	3
Leonard rf	3	1	1	1	1	0	0	0
Pujols c	3	0	1	0	0	1	3	0
Niekro p	3	0	1	0	0	0	0	1
Howe ph	1	0	0	0	0	0	0	0
Totals	32	2	7	2	3	3	24	13

FIELDING
DP: 1
E: Cruz (1)

BATTING
2B: Landestoy (1, off Sutcliffe); Cabell (2, off Sutcliffe)
SF: Morgan (2, off Reuss)
HBP: Pujols (1, by Sutcliffe)

BASERUNNING
SB: Walling (1, 2nd base off Sutcliffe/Scioscia)

Los Angeles Dodgers	AB	R	H	RBI	BB	K	PO	A
Lopes 2b	3	1	1	0	0	0	1	2
Law cf	2	1	1	2	1	0	4	0
Baker lf	3	0	0	0	1	1	2	0
Garvey 1b	3	0	2	0	1	0	12	0
Cey 3b	3	0	0	1	0	1	2	4
Monday rf	3	0	0	0	0	0	1	0
Russell ss	3	0	0	0	0	1	0	1
Scioscia c	3	1	1	0	0	0	5	0
Sutcliffe p	1	0	0	0	0	0	0	0
Reuss p	1	1	0	0	0	0	0	0
Totals	25	4	5	3	3	3	27	7

FIELDING
DP: 1

BATTING
2B: Scioscia (1,off Niekro).
3B: Lopes (1,off Niekro).
SH: Sutcliffe (1, off Niekro); Lopes (1, off Niekro).
SF: Law (1, off Niekro); Cey (1, off Niekro)
HBP: Monday (1, by Niekro)
IBB: Baker (1, by Niekro); Garvey (1, by Niekro)

BASERUNNING
SB: Law 2 (5, 2nd base off Niekro/Pujols; 3rd base off Niekro/Pujols); Baker (1, 2nd base off Niekro/Pujols)

PITCHING

Houston Astros	IP	H	HR	R	ER	BB	K
Niekro L(1–1)	8	5	0	4	2	3	3
Los Angeles Dodgers	IP	H	HR	R	ER	BB	K
Sutcliffe	6.1	5	0	2	2	3	1
Reuss W(2–0)	2.2	2	0	0	0	0	2
Totals	9.0	7	0	2	2	3	3

WP: Niekro (2)
BK: Sutcliffe (2)
HBP: Niekro (1, Monday); Sutcliffe (1, Pujols)
IBB: Niekro 2 (2, Baker, Garvey)
Umpires: Jerry Crawford, Lanny Harris, Harry Wendelstedt, Frank Pulli
Time of Game: 2:27   Attendance: 39,442

sitting there watching that, going nuts. J. R. Richard was pitching for Houston, shortly before he had his stroke . . . I remember sitting there in the dugout going, "Wow! This is unbelievable!" The next day, Sunday, I got in there catching Rick Sutcliffe, who had just won a Rookie of the Year Award, and the next day I caught Don Sutton! It was against the Astros, a heck of a team then . . . My first at bat was against Joe Niekro, and I hung in there and got a double. I had never hit against a knuckleballer before. I scored on a passed ball; I always had that great speed, right? [Laughs.]

The Dodger organization is special regarding the pitcher/catcher relationship. They really nurture it, right from spring training, so even as a young kid, 21 years old, having hung out with and learned from Sutcliffe and Sutton and Burt Hooton and Doug Rau, Rick Rhoden—by the process, by osmosis, you pick things up and your level of confidence is elevated. Sutton, the first time I caught him in the bullpen in spring training, he said, "Hey, good job, I like your target." That kind of stuff really means a lot. To put down a sign and have Don Sutton nod like he believes in you, that's great for a young catcher. You feel you belong.

Also on April 20, 1980
Final preparations are made for tomorrow's Boston Marathon, where Rosie Ruiz would be the first woman to cross the finish line; she was later disqualified as a fraud when officials discovered she had jumped into the race about a mile from the finish.

AUTHOR'S NOTE: That's probably the only way Scioscia could ever win a race himself. As Tommy Lasorda once quipped, "If Scioscia was racing his pregnant wife, he'd finish third."

Ken Singleton
Born: June 10, 1947
Debut: June 24, 1970

The Mets expected greatness from switch-hitting Ken Singleton, the number three pick in the 1967 draft, but they flipped him a few years later to Montreal in exchange for Rusty Staub. After three seasons at Jarry Park, he was dealt back to the U.S., where he settled in during the Orioles 1970s glory years, playing right field at Baltimore's Memorial Stadium.

When the Orioles steamrolled into the '79 World Series, it was due in part to Singleton's huge 35-homer, 111-RBI season that saw him finish just behind the Angels' Don Baylor for AL MVP. He had another fine season in 1980 (.304 batting average, 104 RBI), then began 1981 like an inferno.

About to turn 34, Singleton roared to a .472 April batting average, going ten-for-ten at one point, the streak beginning and ending with home runs. His torrid season was interrupted by the players' strike, but there ended up being good that came from that as well. It was during the strike that Singleton began dabbling in TV work. Upon his retirement, he settled into the Expos' broadcast booth, then moved to the Yankees, where his announcing has merited rave reviews. "I loved Montreal as a city," he says, "but what's nice about New York is not having to speak French!"

A second Singleton could soon be playing in Canada. Ken's son, Justin, is a highly thought of prospect in the Blue Jays system. "To announce one of my son's games at Yankee Stadium, that would be incredible," he says.

If Justin is a shred as successful as his dad, he'll have to be ecstatic. Ken Singleton retired with 246 home runs, more than 1,000 RBI, and three trips to the All-Star Game.

I found out after playing at a Triple-A game in Columbus. We had lost, 2–1, and I had hit a home run for our only run. Our manager, Chuck Hiller, was berating us for having played such a poor game. At the end of his tirade, he looks at me and says, "By the way, tomorrow you're going to Chicago." And it took a moment for it to register, because I'm like, "Chicago? What's in Chicago? Oh! The Mets are in Chicago! I'm being called up to the Mets!" I was having a good year, leading the International League in batting average and home runs, one off the RBI lead for the Triple Crown.

I got back to the hotel that night in Columbus and called my parents, but they already knew. News travels fast in New York. On to Chicago, and I remember walking down the tunnel at Wrigley Field for the first time and seeing

BOXSCORE

New York Mets 6, Chicago Cubs 1 (2nd Game of Doubleheader)
Game Played on Wednesday, June 24, 1970 (Day) at Wrigley Field

New York	0	3	0	0	0	0	2	1	0	—	6	10	0
Chicago	1	0	0	0	0	0	0	0	0	—	1	2	0

BATTING

New York Mets	AB	R	H	RBI	BB	K	PO	A
Agee cf	5	0	1	1	0	1	2	0
Harrelson ss	4	0	0	1	0	0	2	1
Singleton lf	4	0	0	0	0	2	4	0
Shamsky 1b	3	2	2	0	1	0	10	1
Marshall rf	4	1	1	0	0	0	2	0
Boswell 2b	4	1	1	1	0	1	1	5
Garrett 3b	3	2	2	2	1	0	0	3
Dyer c	4	0	1	1	0	1	4	0
Ryan p	3	0	2	0	0	1	2	1
McGraw p	1	0	0	0	0	0	0	0
Totals	**35**	**6**	**10**	**6**	**2**	**6**	**27**	**11**

BATTING
2B: Garrett (5, off Rodriguez)
SF: Harrelson (3, off Rodriguez)

BASERUNNING
SB: Boswell (5, 2nd base off Reynolds/Martin)

Chicago Cubs	AB	R	H	RBI	BB	K	PO	A
Kessinger ss	3	1	1	0	0	0	1	3
Beckert 2b	4	0	0	0	0	0	1	6
Williams lf	4	0	0	1	0	1	2	0
Smith 1b	3	0	0	0	0	2	13	0
Hickman ph	1	0	0	0	0	1	0	0
Callison rf	3	0	0	0	0	0	2	0
Popovich 3b	3	0	0	0	0	0	1	1
James cf	3	0	0	0	0	0	1	0
Martin c	1	0	0	0	1	0	6	0
Banks ph	1	0	1	0	0	0	0	0
Hall pr	0	0	0	0	0	0	0	0
Rudolph c	0	0	0	0	0	0	0	0
Reynolds p	1	0	0	0	1	0	0	1
Rodriguez p	0	0	0	0	0	0	0	0
Gagliano ph	1	0	0	0	0	0	0	0
Gura p	0	0	0	0	0	0	0	0
Totals	**28**	**1**	**2**	**1**	**2**	**4**	**27**	**11**

FIELDING
DP: 1

BATTING
SH: Kessinger (3, off Ryan)

BASERUNNING
SB: Kessinger (3, 2nd base off Ryan/Dyer)

PITCHING

New York Mets	IP	H	HR	R	ER	BB	K
Ryan W(5–5)	7	1	0	1	1	2	2
McGraw SV(6)	2	1	0	0	0	0	2
Totals	**9**	**2**	**0**	**1**	**1**	**2**	**4**

Chicago Cubs	IP	H	HR	R	ER	BB	K
Reynolds L(0–2)	6	7	0	5	5	2	5
Rodriguez	2	3	0	1	1	0	1
Gura	1	0	0	0	0	0	0
Totals	**9**	**10**	**0**	**6**	**6**	**2**	**6**

Umpires: Ed Sudol, Lee Weyer, Andy Olsen, Ken Burkhart
Time of Game: 2:32   Attendance: 35,071

the big, manual scoreboard there in center. Of course, I had seen it on TV many times, but it looked like it was as tall as the Empire State Building up close. And I remember thinking, "Wow, I really am in the big leagues." Big crowd, Mets coming off the World Series the year before, and at the start of play that day, these were the two first place teams in the NL East, one a game or so in front of the other, so the atmosphere was electric, even though the scoreboard wasn't!

I took an 0-for-4, but at the end of the game, Jack Brickhouse interviewed me, because he knew I had family living in Chicago, including my grandmother. I thought that was a really nice touch. 0-for-4, but he wanted my grandmother to see me on TV.

Also on June 24, 1970
An eventful day for Ohio-based teams, as the Reds play their last game at Crosley Field, while the Indians compete in a doubleheader in New York. In that doubleheader, Bobby Murcer slams four consecutive home runs for the Yanks (one in the opener, three in the nightcap).

AUTHOR'S NOTE: Thirty years later, Singleton and Murcer would become part of the popular Yankees broadcast team, sharing a booth and, frequently, rides to and from Manhattan.

John Smoltz
Born: May 15, 1967
Debut: July 23, 1988

Right-hander John Smoltz has authored a very cool story: Chapter One, dominating starter. Chapter Two, career-threatening elbow surgery. Chapter Three, dominating closer. Chapter Four, back to the starting rotation. And, as an epilogue, perhaps a shot at the Hall of Fame.

As the only Braves pitcher who was around for each of their 13 consecutive division titles, Smoltz was originally acquired from Detroit in a prospect-for-veteran deal for Doyle Alexander. Smoltz was initially crushed to leave his beloved Tigers organization—he had grown up in Lansing, Michigan, 90 minutes from Tiger Stadium. His dad had played the accordion at the Tigers' team party following their 1968 World Series title, and his grandfather had worked at the stadium itself, first on the grounds crew, then in the press room, serving soup to the Voice of the Tigers, Ernie Harwell.

As a Braves starter, he had his most memorable season in 1996, when he went 24–8 (including 14 straight wins at one point) with a sub-three ERA and 276 strikeouts. He became the fourth consecutive Brave to win a Cy Young and followed with two more terrific seasons, winning 15 games in '97 and going 17–3 in '98. Sidetracked by injuries, he eventually moved to the bullpen, knocking down a then National League–record 55 saves in his first year as a closer.

Smoltz has always been known as a "big game" pitcher in both of his roles. As a starter, he routinely got the call for playoff openers over Greg Maddux and Tom Glavine, and he pitched heroically in Game Five of the '96 World Series, losing 1–0 to Andy Pettitte. Through 2004, he has appeared in six All-Star Games and has logged nearly 200 postseason innings, with a career ERA of 2.70. Through all his success, he has remained remarkably charitable and humble, with a penchant for good-natured G-rated mischief. His teammates once took to calling him "Marmaduke" after the big, friendly cartoon dog who was occasionally in trouble but always pure of heart.

Someone got hurt, I can't remember who, but Jim Beauchamp, our manager at Richmond, called me over after I had pitched five no-hit innings, and I thought, "This is weird, them wanting to talk to me right now," but when Jim said I was out at 75 pitches because they wanted me in the big leagues, I figured, "Oh, okay, that's pretty good too!"

BOXSCORE

Atlanta Braves 6, New York Mets 1
Game Played on Saturday, July 23, 1988 (Day) at Shea Stadium

Atlanta	2	0	0	0	0	0	1	0	3	—	6	10	0
New York	1	0	0	0	0	0	0	0	0	—	1	4	0

BATTING

Atlanta Braves	AB	R	H	RBI	BB	K	PO	A
Gant 2b	5	1	1	0	0	1	3	2
Sutter p	0	0	0	0	0	0	0	0
Thomas ss	5	1	1	0	0	0	4	1
Perry 1b	4	1	1	1	0	0	4	1
Murphy rf	4	2	3	1	0	0	1	0
Morrison 3b	3	1	2	2	0	0	2	1
Roenicke lf	4	0	1	1	0	0	3	0
Benedict c	4	0	0	0	0	0	4	0
Royster cf	3	0	1	0	1	0	5	0
Smoltz p	2	0	0	0	0	0	1	0
Runge ph-2b	0	0	0	1	1	0	0	0
Totals	**34**	**6**	**10**	**6**	**2**	**1**	**27**	**5**

FIELDING
DP: 2

BATTING
2B: Morrison (1, off Ojeda)
3B: Murphy (4, off Ojeda)
SH: Smoltz (1, off Ojeda)
SF: Morrison (2, off Ojeda)
IBB: Royster (1, by Myers)

BASERUNNING
CS: Morrison (1, 2nd base by Ojeda/Carter)

New York Mets	AB	R	H	RBI	BB	K	PO	A
Dykstra cf	3	1	1	0	0	0	5	0
Nunez p	0	0	0	0	0	0	0	0
Myers p	0	0	0	0	0	0	0	0
Backman 2b	4	0	1	0	0	0	3	3
Magadan 1b-3b	3	0	1	1	1	0	12	1
Strawberry rf	4	0	0	0	0	2	3	0
Johnson 3b-ss	4	0	0	0	0	1	0	1
Carter c-1b	3	0	0	0	1	0	1	2
Mazzilli lf	2	0	1	0	0	0	2	0
Elster ss	2	0	0	0	0	0	0	8
Sasser ph-c	1	0	0	0	0	0	1	0
Ojeda p	2	0	0	0	0	0	0	1
Wilson ph-cf	1	0	0	0	0	0	0	0
Totals	**29**	**1**	**4**	**1**	**2**	**3**	**27**	**16**

BATTING
2B: Magadan (8, off Smoltz); Backman (4, off Smoltz)
HBP: Dykstra (1, by Smoltz); Mazzilli (1, by Smoltz)

BASERUNNING
SB: Dykstra (21, 2nd base off Smoltz/Benedict)

PITCHING

Atlanta Braves	IP	H	HR	R	ER	BB	K
Smoltz W(1–0)	8	4	0	1	1	1	2
Sutter	1	0	0	0	0	1	1
Totals	**9**	**4**	**0**	**1**	**1**	**2**	**3**
New York Mets	**IP**	**H**	**HR**	**R**	**ER**	**BB**	**K**
Ojeda L(7–8)	8	6	0	3	3	0	0
Nunez	0	4	0	3	3	0	0
Myers	1	0	0	0	0	2	1
Totals	**9**	**10**	**0**	**6**	**6**	**2**	**1**

WP: Ojeda (3), Nunez (1)
HBP: Smoltz 2 (2, Dykstra, Mazzilli)
IBB: Myers (1, Royster)
Umpires: John Kibler, Jim Quick, Dave Pallone, Bill Hohn
Time of Game: 2:30   Attendance: 43,637

I went to New York to meet the team, and I had a day or so to get acclimated, but it was tough getting ready to face a team like the Mets, because they were just ridiculously powerful back then . . . That's the year they got upset by the Dodgers in the LCS, but man, they were tough. I was warming up in the bullpen, and the place was just packed. It was Tom Seaver Night, honoring one of the all-time greats, and there were probably 50,000 people there. Ceremonies before the game, and I'm just trying to warm up and block it all out of my mind. My first batter was Lenny Dykstra—a 1-and-2 pitch, I hit him on the toe. Dykstra was always tough on me . . . He broke up a no-hitter in the ninth inning a couple years later, too. Anyway, he scored in that inning, but I was already ahead by a couple runs because the guys had gotten me two in the top of the first inning. My first strikeout was Darryl Strawberry, and that gave me a real shot of confidence to have done that. I gave up only two hits all game, and I had a nice rhythm with my catcher, Bruce Benedict. He was a pretty funny guy and did a good job just keeping me loose.

Also on July 23, 1988
Massachusetts Governor Michael Dukakis hits the campaign trail, having accepted the Democratic presidential nomination at the party's convention in Atlanta, declaring, "This election isn't about ideology; it's about competence."

AUTHOR'S NOTE: Fifteen years later, when the Braves switched Smoltz from star starter to star closer, they essentially told him the same thing—"It isn't about ideology; it's about competence."

My whole family pretty much came in, and after the game, we went out to some small but real nice Italian restaurant and they cleared out a whole area for us, table for eleven. Great meal, great day, everything was just magical to believe.

One thing I'll never forget—and I won't say who said it, but it was in the paper, and I saw it and it stuck with me—one of the Mets said after I beat 'em, "If this guy Smoltz was any good, he'd have been called up a long time ago." Basically, [he was saying] it wasn't me or my talent that beat them, that they had just had an off day. That motivated me. I never forgot it.

Alfonso Soriano
Born: January 7, 1976
Debut: September 14, 1999

There are many Dominican success stories in baseball, but Alfonso Soriano's may be among the most interesting of all. He was one of the many *Macorisanos* to dream of playing in the big leagues, as fellow San Pedro de Macoris natives Sammy Sosa, George Bell, Tony Fernandez, et al had already done. None of those players detoured first to Japan in order to get noticed, but at age 17, having participated in the Hiroshima Carp's "campo de beisbol," Soriano agreed to go overseas to refine his game and play professionally right away. By the time Soriano was 20, the Japanese League team was looking for a long term commitment, but he was looking for a Major League team to sign with instead. After some sometimes tense legal wrangling, Soriano's agent sprung him from his contract, and he began a series of tryouts with the Diamondbacks, Brewers, Indians, Cubs, Rockies, Dodgers, Mets, and, of course, the Yankees.

The Indians were most impressed, offering him a contract on the spot, but eventually (as usual) Mr. Steinbrenner's money won out, as the Yankees won his services with an offer of four years and three million dollars. Indians GM John Hart was crestfallen but later, as Rangers GM, he landed the player he'd wanted (in the Alex Rodriguez deal of 2004).

In between his time in Japan and North Texas, Soriano spent a productive four seasons in pinstripes. Using one of the biggest bats this side of Julio Franco (33 inches, 35 ounces), he came tantalizingly close to a 40-homer, 40-steal season in 2002, ending up at 39 and 42 and finishing third in the MVP balloting. (No second baseman had ever gone 30/30, let alone 40/40. Soriano stayed stuck on 39 home runs for his final 51 at bats of the regular season.)

Blessed with a wiry but explosive body, he had become the only rookie besides Tommy Agee to debut with a 15-homer, 40-steal season. Batting ninth, he managed 18 home runs and 73 RBI, prompting Roger Clemens to nickname him "Señor Peligroso" ("Mister Dangerous"). Soriano lived up to the nickname when he homered off Clemens in the 2004 All-Star Game in Houston on his way to being named the game's Most Valuable Player.

He is still prone to low walk and high strikeout totals but continues to hit for average. He is among a handful of players (Sammy Sosa, Mo Vaughn, Bobby Bonds) to strike out as many as 150 times in a season and still hit .300. The three-time All-Star has been among the AL's top three in total bases twice and has clubbed as many as 51 doubles in a single season.

I walked into Yankee Stadium and there were all those superstars in the clubhouse. I was so shy, just went over into the corner . . . Some of the players came into the corner and tried to say hello, but I was so shy. Mariano Rivera and Bernie Williams kept after me to talk to them, and I finally did, but I was a little scared, you know? They had been nice to me in spring training, but this was different. This was Yankee Stadium!

I played against Toronto and all I was was a pinch runner, and I played third base at first because Scott Brosius was hurt. I didn't do that much at first, but a couple weeks later against Tampa Bay I hit a home run to win the game. That's when I felt like I was really a Yankee, all those fans cheering for me, and my teammates congratulating me at home plate. A walk-off home run, and I called my mom back in the Dominican right away. My mom is the most important person to me . . . She wasn't always happy when I went away to try and be a big league ballplayer, but I told her it would work out, and I was very proud to call her and tell her that I was doing well.

Also on September 14, 1999
Hurricane Floyd clobbers the Bahamas before heading toward the southeastern United States. The hurricane forces the evacuation of 800,000 in South Carolina and 500,000 in Georgia.

AUTHOR'S NOTE: Soriano's family dodged hurricanes themselves in the Dominican, especially in 1998, when Hurricane Georges ravaged his neighborhood.

BOXSCORE

New York Yankees 10, Toronto Blue Jays 6
Game Played on Tuesday, September 14, 1999 (Night) at Skydome

										R	H	E
New York	0	0	1	0	0	0	5	4	—	10	9	2
Toronto	0	0	2	0	0	2	2	0	0	—	6	11	2

BATTING

New York Yankees	AB	R	H	RBI	BB	K	PO	A
Knoblauch 2b	4	2	1	0	1	2	1	1
Jeter ss	3	2	1	1	2	0	2	1
O'Neill rf	5	2	1	4	0	0	2	0
Williams cf	5	1	2	4	0	0	2	0
Strawberry dh	4	0	1	0	0	3	0	0
Soriano pr-dh	1	0	0	0	0	0	0	0
Martinez 1b	3	0	0	0	1	0	4	0
Posada c	4	1	2	0	0	1	13	1
Ledee lf	4	1	1	0	0	1	0	0
Sojo 3b	2	0	0	1	0	0	2	0
Davis ph	1	0	0	0	0	0	0	0
Bellinger 3b	1	1	0	0	0	0	0	0
Cone p	0	0	0	0	0	0	0	1
Watson p	0	0	0	0	0	0	0	0
Mendoza p	0	0	0	0	0	0	0	0
Rivera p	0	0	0	0	0	0	0	0
Totals	37	10	9	10	4	7	27	4

FIELDING
DP: 1
E: O'Neill (7), Cone (1)

BATTING
2B: Ledee (12, off Halladay); Williams (23, off Halladay); Strawberry (3, off Koch)
HR: Williams (23, 8th inning off Koch, 3 on, 2 out); O'Neill (16, 9th inning off Spoljaric, 3 on, 1 out)
IBB: Martinez (6, by Koch)

Toronto Blue Jays	AB	R	H	RBI	BB	K	PO	A
Bush 2b	4	0	0	0	1	1	0	3
Segui dh	5	2	2	0	0	2	0	0
Green rf	4	2	2	2	1	1	3	0
Delgado 1b	5	0	1	0	0	3	11	1
Fernandez 3b	5	1	2	1	0	2	0	1
Fletcher c	4	1	2	3	0	0	6	1
Batista ss	4	0	1	0	0	2	3	6
Brumfield lf	4	0	0	0	0	2	3	0
V. Wells cf	3	0	1	0	0	2	1	0
Greene ph	1	0	0	0	0	0	0	0
Cruz cf	0	0	0	0	0	0	0	0
Halladay p	0	0	0	0	0	0	0	0
Lloyd p	0	0	0	0	0	0	0	0
Koch p	0	0	0	0	0	0	0	0
Spoljaric p	0	0	0	0	0	0	0	0
Totals	39	6	11	6	2	15	27	12

FIELDING
DP: 1
E: Fernandez (16), Fletcher (2)
PB: Fletcher (9)

BATTING
2B: Segui (25, off Cone)
HR: Green (39, 3rd inning off Cone, 1 on, 2 out); Fletcher (17,6th inning off Cone, 1 on, 1 out)

BASERUNNING
CS: Bush (6, 2nd base by Cone/Posada)

PITCHING

New York Yankees	IP	H	HR	R	ER	BB	K
Cone	6	6	2	4	4	2	10
Watson	0.2	4	0	2	2	0	1
Mendoza W(7–8)	1.1	0	0	0	0	0	2
Rivera	1	1	0	0	0	0	2
Totals	9	11	2	6	6	2	15
Toronto Blue Jays	IP	H	HR	R	ER	BB	K
Halladay	7.2	5	0	4	2	2	6
Lloyd	0	0	0	1	0	0	0
Koch L(0–4)	0.2	3	1	4	3	2	1
Spoljaric	0.2	1	1	1	1	0	0
Totals	9.0	9	2	10	5	4	7

WP: Cone (6)
IBB: Koch (5, Martinez)
Umpires: Lazaro Diaz, Jim McKean, Mike Reilly, Chuck Meriwether
Time of Game: 3:13 Attendance: 29,140

Sammy Sosa
Born: November 12, 1968
Debut: June 16, 1989

It had the makings of a rags-to-riches-to-rags story, along the lines of Navin Johnson in Steve Martin's movie *The Jerk*. Sammy Sosa came from incredibly humble beginnings, shining shoes in the Dominican Republic to help his family scrape by while playing on the most ramshackle, rock-strewn fields of San Pedro de Macoris. After underachieving as a young player in Texas and with the White Sox, he hit his stride on Chicago's North Side, matching Mark McGwire homer for homer during the magical summer of '98. He broke Roger Maris's longstanding home run mark of 61 three times, including a year when he had almost as many homers (63) as his team had wins (67 in '99). History lesson: "Chicago" is a Potawatomi Indian word meaning "anything powerful or great." It seemed that the likable, powerful Sosa was a Cinderella-slipper perfect fit. In 1998, he was the National League MVP, and as his teammate Mark Grace said, "I don't think MVP is enough to describe it." In leading the Cubs to the postseason, he walloped 66 homers, 158 RBI, and the most total bases (416) since 1948.

However, things began to unravel in 2002. Sosa began to bristle at suggestions he was using steroids, angrily snapping at *Sports Illustrated*'s Rick Reilly, who asked if he'd consent to being tested. In 2003, trying to come back from an infected toe, he struggled in his first week off the disabled list, then was caught using a corked bat in a seemingly meaningless game against Tampa Bay. Sosa offered an excuse deemed by most to be implausible, and slowly but surely, the Cubs fan base that had cheered so mightily for him began to turn on him.

An underwhelming 2004 season (which included a four-week DL stint caused by a violent sneeze) was magnified by his teammates' inability to hit much themselves. For years, Sosa had carried the Cubs, but now, when he needed some help, they failed to carry him. The season ended with the Cubs choking away a wild card birth with a series of ugly losses to the sub .500 Mets and Reds. On top of it all, Sosa bailed on his team that final Sunday, leaving Wrigley Field without permission. For many, that was the final straw.

Sosa now sees himself as the Russell Crowe character in the movie *Gladiator*, rather than Navin Johnson—a great warrior stripped of his standing who must rebound to reclaim his might and his dignity. He's attempting to do just that in Baltimore.

Tommy Thompson, my manager in the minors, told me that Pete Incaviglia had gotten hurt and they wanted me in the major leagues. None of my friends on the team believed me when I told them. Juan Gonzalez, he says, "No, that can't be right." I had a big smile that gave me away. It was the truth. I couldn't believe it.

I batted leadoff. Rickey Henderson was the other leadoff hitter in that game. See, back then I was fast, too. [Laughs.] I faced Andy Hawkins and got two hits, one right away in the first inning. Oh my goodness, I'm standing at first base at Yankee Stadium. I'm 19 years old, and I'm standing there next to Steve Balboni at first base at Yankee Stadium. It was like a dream.

It was a very happy day back in the Dominican. When I called home to tell my family what had happened, there were a lot of tears, a lot of joy. I didn't know how long I'd be up, but I knew to enjoy every minute of it.

Also on June 16, 1989

The controversy surrounding Pete Rose's alleged gambling continues to swirl as Rose begins to make noise about initiating a lawsuit against MLB and commissioner Bart Giamatti. He and his lawyers do so three days later. Rose contends Giamatti cannot fairly judge him and demands a jury trial.

AUTHOR'S NOTE: Rose's apologists were out in full force in Cincinnati at this time, much the way Sosa's apologists would rally behind him during "Corkgate."

BOXSCORE

New York Yankees 8, Texas Rangers 3 (1st Game of Doubleheader)

Game Played on Friday, June 16, 1989 (Day) at Yankee Stadium

Texas	0	0	0	0	0	2	0	0	1	—	3	7	1
New York	0	1	0	0	1	4	0	2	x	—	8	12	3

BATTING

Texas Rangers	AB	R	H	RBI	BB	K	PO	A
Sosa cf	4	1	2	0	0	0	2	0
Fletcher ss	4	1	0	0	0	1	3	2
Palmeiro 1b	3	0	1	1	0	0	9	0
Sierra rf	4	1	2	0	0	0	2	1
Franco 2b	4	0	0	0	0	1	1	4
Petralli dh	3	0	0	0	0	0	0	0
Bell ph-dh	1	0	0	1	0	0	0	0
Leach lf	3	0	1	0	0	0	1	0
Kunkel ph	1	0	0	0	0	0	0	0
Buechele 3b	4	0	1	0	0	0	0	0
Sundberg c	3	0	0	0	0	0	6	1
Witt p	0	0	0	0	0	0	0	1
Rogers p	0	0	0	0	0	0	0	0
Mielke p	0	0	0	0	0	0	0	0
Guante p	0	0	0	0	0	0	0	0
Totals	34	3	7	2	0	2	24	9

FIELDING
E: Sosa (1)

BATTING
2B: Palmeiro (17, off Hawkins); Sosa (1, off Hawkins); Sierra (20, off Hawkins)
SF: Palmeiro (2, off Hawkins)

BASERUNNING
CS: Sosa (1, 2nd base by Hawkins/Slaught)

New York Yankees	AB	R	H	RBI	BB	K	PO	A
Henderson lf	2	3	1	1	3	0	3	0
Sax 2b	5	2	3	2	0	0	3	1
Mattingly dh-1b	2	0	0	3	0	1	0	0
Balboni 1b	4	0	1	0	0	1	4	0
Phelps ph	1	0	1	2	0	0	0	0
Guetterman p	0	0	0	0	0	0	0	0
Hall rf	2	1	1	1	1	0	4	0
Kelly ph-cf	2	0	2	1	0	0	0	0
Pagliarulo 3b	3	1	1	0	0	0	1	0
Brookens ph-3b	2	0	0	0	1	0	0	0
Barfield cf-rf	4	1	1	0	1	2	7	0
Slaught c	4	0	1	1	0	0	1	2
Espinoza ss	4	0	0	0	0	0	3	3
Hawkins p	0	0	0	0	0	0	0	0
Totals	35	8	12	8	8	4	27	6

FIELDING
DP: 2
E: Barfield (4), Espinoza 2 (8)

BATTING
2B: Barfield (6, off Witt); Henderson (13, off Witt)
3B: Sax (2, off Witt)
HR: Hall (4, 2nd inning off Witt, 0 on, 1 out)
IBB: Mattingly 2 (4, by Witt, by Guante)

BASERUNNING
CS: Henderson (8, 2nd base by Witt/Sundberg)

PITCHING

Texas Rangers	IP	H	HR	R	ER	BB	K
Witt L(5–7)	5.2	7	1	6	6	5	2
Rogers	0	2	0	0	0	1	0
Mielke	1.1	0	0	0	0	0	0
Guante	1	3	0	2	2	2	2
Totals	8	12	1	8	8	8	4

New York Yankees	IP	H	HR	R	ER	BB	K
Hawkins W(7–7)	8	7	0	3	0	0	2
Guetterman	1	0	0	0	0	0	0
Totals	9	7	0	3	0	0	2

IBB: Witt (2, Mattingly); Guante (5, Mattingly)
Umpires: Rich Garcia, Dale Scott, Larry McCoy, Mike Reilly
Time of Game: 3:00   Attendance: 28,372

Steve Stone
Born: July 14, 1947
Debut: August 8, 1971

The diminutive (5'10") Steve Stone had what his friends called a "Joe Hardy" Cy Young season in 1980. That is, he sold his soul in exchange for one great year. With a record of 25–7 that summer, Stone won the Cy Young Award (although, unceremoniously, they shipped Steve Carlton's NL award to him, and Stone's AL award to Carlton). However, in the rest of an otherwise undistinguished big league career, he was just 84–93 during ten years with the Orioles, Giants, White Sox, and Cubs.

Stone began a 22-year run as one of the Cubs TV voices after getting hurt in the summer of '81, on the recommendation of the legendary Harry Caray. Caray and Stone teamed up for 15 years on WGN, Stone cast as the erudite Felix Unger to Caray's slovenly Oscar Madison.

Stone was the "voice of reason," effectively countering Caray's outlandishness. When Caray would mistakenly report that a player had a sore tooth treated with a "shot of cocaine," it was Stone who would chime in with, "I believe that's Novocaine, Harry." Stone's Cubs broadcast career ended in 2004 after some ugly run-ins with manager Dusty Baker and various players, who accused him of being too negative. Stone insisted the offended parties look in the mirror before pointing fingers.

When he first came up with the Giants, Stone drew comparisons to Sandy Koufax for his hard fastball, big curve, and Jewish faith. Although the Ohio native never approached Koufax's heights, he's proud to say that he and Koufax are the only two Jewish Cy Young winners in history.

I had a great spring down in Arizona, and the Giants told me I'd be their number three starter to open the season behind Gaylord Perry and Juan Marichal. Plenty of butterflies from that alone, right? Well, we opened in San Diego, and I remember looking out and seeing Willie Mays behind me in center, Willie McCovey at first, Bobby Bonds in right, and thinking, "This is the neatest thing."

The Padres led off with Dave Campbell, now of ESPN fame, then a journeyman infielder. I got him to 3-and-2 and I throw him a slider, and he singles to center field. Then Larry Stahl comes up, and I figure I'm going to trick him with a first-pitch straight change. And Larry Stahl hit it out of the ballpark. Two hitters, two hits, two runs, and I have an ERA of infinity. I knew at that point things only could get better. I had faced that team all spring in Yuma and never

206

really had a problem, but here it was, games that counted, and I had an infinite ERA.

My catcher was Dick Dietz, who they called "The Mule." I think he may have come out to try and settle me down. I didn't see our pitching coach, Larry Jaster, until later. Keep in mind, back then, we didn't have pitching coaches in the minors. The very first pitching coach I ever had was when I got to the big leagues. When Jaster came out, first thing he did was stick his finger through one of my belt loops. I thought that was really odd. Then the veterans told me later, he does that so you're forced to look at him and pay attention to what he's saying. I would have liked to have known that beforehand, because I looked at him like, "What exactly are you doing?"

My first strikeout was Nate Colbert, but I only lasted a few innings and didn't really have anyone to call afterwards, since my family was all back in Ohio, and there was the three-hour time difference from California. Alone in my misery, until my friends and family came to see me pitch in my fourth start, in Pittsburgh. That one was a complete game win.

Also on April 8, 1971
The Astros' Jesus Alou takes over the early-season NL lead in hits, singling twice against the Cubs.

AUTHOR'S NOTE: Alou's nephew, Moises, would launch the first offensive against Stone and broadcast partner Chip Caray some 33 years later. Alou complained about Stone's negativity and was quickly followed by a tirade from Kent Mercker. Both Caray and Stone grew tired of the Cubs players' badgering and resigned following the 2004 season.

BOXSCORE

San Diego Padres 7, San Francisco Giants 6
Game Played on Thursday, April 8, 1971 (Night) at San Diego Stadium

San Francisco	1	0	0	0	0	0	5	0	0	—	6	10	0
San Diego	3	0	0	1	0	0	0	0	3	—	7	13	2

BATTING

San Francisco Giants	AB	R	H	RBI	BB	K	PO	A
Bonds rf	4	2	2	0	1	2	0	0
Speier ss	4	1	1	0	1	0	3	4
Mays cf	5	1	2	5	0	2	3	0
McCovey 1b	4	1	2	0	1	0	9	0
Henderson lf	3	0	1	0	1	1	1	0
Dietz c	4	0	0	0	0	2	5	0
Gallagher 3b	4	0	1	1	1	1	0	1
Lanier 2b	4	0	0	0	0	0	5	4
Foster ph	1	0	0	0	0	1	0	0
Heise 2b	0	0	0	0	0	0	0	0
Stone p	1	0	0	0	0	1	0	0
J. Johnson p	0	0	0	0	0	0	0	2
Rosario ph	1	1	1	0	0	0	0	0
McMahon p	2	0	0	0	0	1	0	0
Totals	37	6	10	6	6	11	26	11

FIELDING
DP: 2

BATTING
2B: Bonds (1, off Arlin)
HR: Mays (3, 7th inning off Kelley, 3 on, 1 out)
SH: Dietz (1, off Ross)
HBP: Henderson (1, by Arlin)
IBB: Gallagher (1, by Ross)

San Diego Padres	AB	R	H	RBI	BB	K	PO	A
Campbell 2b	4	2	2	0	1	0	0	2
Stahl lf	5	2	2	3	0	0	1	0
Gaston cf	5	0	3	1	0	1	2	0
Colbert 1b	4	1	1	1	0	3	7	0
Brown rf	4	0	1	1	0	0	2	0
Spiezio 3b	3	0	1	0	1	0	2	1
Cannizzaro c	3	1	1	0	1	0	12	0
Dean ss	2	0	0	0	0	0	0	3
Mason ph	1	1	1	0	0	0	0	0
Arlin p	3	0	1	1	0	0	1	0
Kelley p	0	0	0	0	0	0	0	0
Ross p	0	0	0	0	0	0	0	0
Ferrara ph	1	0	0	0	0	1	0	0
Totals	35	7	13	7	3	5	27	6

FIELDING
E: Gaston (1), Dean (1)

BATTING
2B: Brown (1, off Stone); Cannizzaro (1, off Stone)
HR: Stahl (1, 1st inning off Stone, 1 on, 0 out)
SH: Dean (1, off J. Johnson)
SF: Colbert (1, off McMahon)

PITCHING

San Francisco Giants	IP	H	HR	R	ER	BB	K
Stone	3	6	1	4	4	2	1
J. Johnson	3	2	0	0	0	1	1
McMahon L(0–1)	2.2	5	0	3	3	0	3
Totals	8.2	13	1	7	7	3	5

San Diego Padres	IP	H	HR	R	ER	BB	K
Arlin	6.1	4	0	4	4	4	7
Kelley	0	2	1	2	2	1	0
Ross W(1–0)	2.2	4	0	0	0	1	4
Totals	9.0	10	1	6	6	6	11

WP: Ross (1)
HBP: Arlin (1, Henderson)
IBB: Ross (1, Gallagher)
Umpires: Doug Harvey, Jerry Dale, Tom Gorman, Chris Pelekoudas
Time of Game: 3:05   Attendance: 6,199

Rick Sutcliffe
Born: June 21, 1956
Debut: September 29, 1976

After winning a Rookie of the Year Award, Rick Sutcliffe seemed to be on his way to a terminally mediocre career, with the Dodgers and Indians, but things began to come together for him in 1983, when he led the American League with a 2.96 ERA and won 14 for a middling Cleveland team. He would be slingshot into national prominence a year later, when the Indians dealt him in mid-June to the Cubs. Upon joining Chicago, he reeled off a 16–1 record, helping the Cubs into their first postseason since 1945. He was rewarded with the Cy Young and would later make a pair of All-Star appearances as well.

The affable "Sut" has accumulated a who's who list of actor friends including Bill Murray and Mark Harmon, whose bachelor party he hosted in spring training 1988. Sutcliffe paid for Mark and his buddies to be decked out in full Cubs gear, even getting them on the field where he was going to hit fly balls. The catch was, Sutcliffe arranged for the groundskeeper to turn the sprinklers on full blast, drenching the whole group. Harmon and his friends got back at Rick before the 1989 All Star Game. They rented the billboard across from Wrigley Field and posted this message: Welcome to the 1989 All Star Game. For information, call (Rick's home phone number). To make it worse, they used Sutcliffe's high school senior picture. "Which wasn't me at my studliest," Sutcliffe allowed.

I was at Dodger Stadium, and with four days left in the regular season, Walt Alston picks that day to announce his retirement. He's going to go upstairs with Walter O'Malley, and Tommy Lasorda's going to manage the last four games. So they have this press conference to announce that Walter's turning it over to Tommy, and I'm standing in the back of the room listening. And it comes out that Walt Alston said, "Tommy, you're making the lineup these last four games, it's all you. The only thing is, I want the kid to start." I watched the game that night, went home, went to sleep, picked up the paper the next day, read the paper, and it said, "Sutcliffe is starting tonight." So that' s when I realized, "Damn, man, I guess the kid is me! I guess I've got a nickname!"

I remember warming up for that first start in the Dodger Stadium bullpen, in that tunnel, where if you're throwing 85 it sounds like you're throwing 95 because of the acoustics. Everything's perfect, warming up. Then I get on the mound, and all of a sudden I hear this voice. At Dodger games, so many

208

people bring their radios, you stand on that mound, you can hear Vin Scully's play-by-play. That's freaky enough, but there I am about ready to face the first hitter, and I hear Vin say, "You know what's going through the kid's mind right now." Well, I had just learned that morning that I was the kid, that I was pitching. I really didn't have anything on my mind, until Scully says, "He knows he's on the mound that has been home to Drysdale, Koufax, and, just last night, one of his heroes, Don Sutton." So I looked down at that mound, and I thought, "Damn, he's right!" Next thing you know, I throw that last warm-up pitch, and Steve Yeager throws a missile down to Davey Lopes, who throws it to Russell, who throws it Cey, who throws it to me, and I'm like, "Wow, The Penguin! Damn, Ron Cey, The Penguin, just threw me the ball!" Then all of a sudden, somebody touched me, and I jumped. I turned around and it was [Steve] Garvey! He says, "Good luck, kid," and I'm like, "Okay, thanks, Garv." I look in, Yaeger puts down a fastball, and I throw it right down the middle—but I found out later the radar gun said it was at 62 miles an hour. Yeager comes out, says, "You all right?" And I'm like, "I guess so." Fortunately, the next one was in there at 91, and I pitched five shutout innings and got the win.

BOXSCORE

Los Angeles Dodgers 1, Houston Astros 0

Game Played on Wednesday, September 29, 1976 (Night) at Dodger Stadium

Houston	0	0	0	0	0	0	0	0	0	—	0	3	0
Los Angeles	0	0	0	0	0	0	1	0	x	—	1	3	2

BATTING

Houston Astros	AB	R	H	RBI	BB	K	PO	A
Taveras ss	4	0	0	0	0	1	3	4
Cabell 3b	3	0	0	0	1	0	0	0
Cedeno cf	3	0	1	0	1	0	3	0
Johnson 1b	3	0	0	0	1	1	10	0
Howe 2b	3	0	1	0	0	1	1	3
Watson ph	1	0	0	0	0	1	0	0
Gross rf	3	0	1	0	0	1	2	0
Javier lf	3	0	0	0	0	1	2	0
Herrmann c	3	0	0	0	0	1	3	0
Sambito p	1	0	0	0	1	0	0	4
Roberts ph	1	0	0	0	0	0	0	0
Forsch p	0	0	0	0	0	0	0	0
Totals	**28**	**0**	**3**	**0**	**4**	**7**	**24**	**11**

FIELDING
DP: 1

BASERUNNING
SB: Cedeno (55, 2nd base off Hough/Yeager)
CS: Cedeno (15, 2nd base by Sutcliffe/Yeager)

Los Angeles Dodgers	AB	R	H	RBI	BB	K	PO	A
Lopes 2b	3	0	0	0	0	1	3	4
Russell ss	2	0	1	0	0	0	0	0
Auerbach ss	1	0	0	0	0	0	0	2
Buckner lf	3	1	1	0	0	0	2	0
Cey 3b	2	0	0	0	1	0	1	1
Garvey 1b	3	0	1	1	0	0	9	0
Lacy rf	3	0	0	0	0	0	5	0
Burke cf	3	0	0	0	0	0	1	0
Yeager c	3	0	0	0	0	0	6	3
Sutcliffe p	1	0	0	0	0	1	0	0
Wall p	1	0	0	0	0	0	0	0
Goodson ph	1	0	0	0	0	1	0	0
Hough p	0	0	0	0	0	0	0	0
Totals	**26**	**1**	**3**	**1**	**1**	**3**	**27**	**10**

FIELDING
DP: 2
E: Russell (28), Yeager (9)

PITCHING

Houston Astros	IP	H	HR	R	ER	BB	K
Sambito L(3–2)	7	3	0	1	1	1	2
Forsch	1	0	0	0	0	0	1
Totals	**8**	**3**	**0**	**1**	**1**	**1**	**3**
Los Angeles Dodgers	**IP**	**H**	**HR**	**R**	**ER**	**BB**	**K**
Sutcliffe	5	2	0	0	0	1	3
Wall W(2–2)	3	1	0	0	0	2	2
Hough SV(18)	1	0	0	0	0	1	2
Totals	**9**	**3**	**0**	**0**	**0**	**4**	**7**

Umpires: Doug Harvey, Bob Engel, Jerry Dale, Paul Runge
Time of Game: 1:52   Attendance: 11,600

Also on September 29, 1976
Tommy Lasorda is named to succeed Walter Alston as the team's manager for 1977.

AUTHOR'S NOTE: Sutcliffe would not only pitch under Lasorda for parts of five years as a Dodger, he would pitch for him in the 1989 All-Star Game as well, allowing two runs in a 5–3 AL win.

Don Sutton
Born: April 2, 1945
Debut: April 14, 1966

He never did win a Cy Young Award, but then again, neither did Nolan Ryan. Don Sutton simply pitched consistently (and at times, brilliantly) for 22 seasons, never spending a day on the disabled list. As a 21-year-old rookie, he struck out 209 in 1966, helping the Dodgers reach the World Series. By the end of his Dodgers career, he had become the franchise's career leader in wins, strikeouts, and shutouts.

He never pitched a no-hitter, but he pitched five one-hitters and nine two-hitters on his way to a career mark of 324–256 with a 3.26 ERA. He came within one strikeout of 22 consecutive seasons with triple-digit totals; in his final big league season, he stalled at 99. The four-time All-Star pitched a total of eight All-Star innings without allowing a run. (He started and won the '77 All-Star Game, being named MVP for his efforts.) In 1982, he outdueled Jim Palmer on the season's final day, pushing the Brewers past the Orioles and (eventually) into the World Series.

He won 20 games in a season only once, led his league in ERA only once, but in his time with the Dodgers, Astros, Brewers, A's, and Angels, he struck out 3,574 hitters and went on to gain election to Cooperstown in 1998.

Known for a killer curve, he was accused towards the end of his career of doctoring baseballs. When he was thrown out of a game in 1978, he threatened both the umpire who accused him and the National League with lawsuits. In the end, he was merely warned instead of fined or suspended. He now dispenses his insight on TBS, covering the Atlanta Braves, a team (like those 1960s Dodgers he broke in with) that's been all about pitching.

This is going to sound immodest, and I'm sure people will take me to task for this, but I actually remember thinking about why it took so long for me to get there. I had just turned 21 when I made my debut, so believe me, I know that's not old, but it was my personality. I never played Little League to have fun. I played it because I knew it was a step along the way to get me to where I wanted to be—the major leagues. Pony League, Colt League, high school—there were guys that just wanted to play a little then goof off and go to the beach. Not me. It was all a means to an end. I knew when I was 12 I was going to pitch in the big leagues. So when I went out there against Houston in April of '66, the best way I can describe it is that I was completely prepared and at peace. Like a final exam you've got all year to study for. The day finally comes, and you know you're ready.

Yes, I was excited, but I wasn't nervous or scared for one minute. I came out up 2–1 in the eighth, but Rusty Staub hit Ron Perranoski's first pitch into the back of the bullpen with a couple men on, and I got the loss. Dream come true, yes. Scared, no. Koufax, Drysdale, Osteen, and me— that was our starting rotation, and none of us missed any starts. Walter Alston's managing was outstanding, and his personality was like an extension of my father's. He was the perfect guy for me. John Roseboro was my catcher, and he said, that day, "Stick with me, kid, and we'll be all right." I knew that to be the case. Lefty Phillips was the pitching coach. He said, "Same thing you've been doing your whole life, kid." And I knew he was right. I had felt at home in spring training, getting to pitch every fourth day while Koufax and Drysdale were holding out, not liking their contracts. I knew I was getting a chance to shine on the stage for Walter Alston that entire month of March, and I was ready for real come April.

Also on April 14, 1966
Greg Maddux is born.

AUTHOR'S NOTE: Sutton went on to describe many of Maddux's wins during the Mad Dog's Hall of Fame run as an Atlanta starter. Maddux enters 2005 within range of Sutton's 324 career victories.

BOXSCORE

Houston Astros 4, Los Angeles Dodgers 2
Game Played on Thursday, 4/14/1966 (Night) at Dodger Stadium

Houston	1	0	0	0	0	0	0	3	0	—	4
Los Angeles	0	1	0	1	0	0	0	0	0	—	2

Houston	AB	R	H	RBI	BB	K	PO	A
L.Maye lf	5	1	1	0	0	0	0	0
S.Jackson ss	3	1	0	0	1	0	5	5
J.Wynn cf	3	1	2	2	0	1	3	0
J.Morgan 2b	3	0	2	0	0	1	2	5
R.Staub rf	4	1	1	2	0	1	1	0
B.Aspromonte 3b	4	0	0	0	0	2	0	2
J.Gentile 1b	4	0	1	0	0	1	12	1
J.Bateman c	3	0	1	0	0	1	2	0
N.Colbert pr	0	0	0	0	0	0	0	0
R.Brand c	1	0	1	0	0	0	2	0
B.Bruce p	2	0	0	0	0	2	0	0
C.Sembera p	1	0	0	0	0	0	1	0
Totals	33	4	9	4	1	9	27	13

FIELDING
DP: (3). J.Morgan-S.Jackson-J.Gentile; S.Jackson-J.Gentile [2]

BATTING
2B: J.Wynn (off D.Sutton)
HR: R.Staub (8th inning off R.Perranoski, 1 on, 1 out)
RBI, scoring position, less than 2 outs: L.Maye 0–1; J.Wynn 1–1; R.Staub 1–3; B.Aspromonte 0–1; C.Sembera 0–1
S: S.Jackson; J.Morgan; B.Bruce
SF: J.Wynn

BASERUNNING
SB: J.Morgan (2nd base off D.Sutton/J.Roseboro)
Team LOB: 7

Los Angeles	AB	R	H	RBI	BB	K	PO	A
M.Wills ss	4	0	0	0	0	0	0	0
W.Parker 1b	3	0	1	0	1	1	6	2
W.Davis cf	4	0	2	0	0	0	4	0
R.Fairly rf	3	0	0	1	1	0	1	0
J.Lefebvre 3b	4	2	2	2	0	0	0	3
L.Johnson lf	4	0	2	0	0	0	2	0
J.Roseboro c	4	0	1	0	0	0	9	0
N.Oliver 2b	3	0	0	0	0	2	2	0
D.Griffith ph	1	0	0	0	0	0	0	0
D.Sutton p	3	0	2	0	0	0	2	0
R.Perranoski p	0	0	0	0	0	0	1	0
T.Davis ph	1	0	0	0	0	1	0	0
Totals	34	2	10	2	2	4	27	5

FIELDING
E: (3). L.Johnson; M.Wills (fumble); W.Davis

BATTING
2B: W.Davis (off B.Bruce)
HR: J.Lefebvre 2 (2nd inning off B.Bruce, 0 on, 1 out; 4th inning off B.Bruce, 0 on, 0 out)
RBI, scoring position, less than 2 outs: W.Davis 0–1; R.Fairly 0–1; J.Lefebvre 0–1; N.Oliver 0–1
GIDP: R.Fairly; J.Roseboro

BASERUNNING
SB: M.Wills (2nd base off B.Bruce/J.Bateman)
Team LOB: 7

PITCHING

Houston	IP	H	HR	R	ER	BB	K
B.Bruce W	7.1	10	2	2	2	2	3
C.Sembera S	1.2	0	0	0	0	0	1
Total	9.0	10	2	2	2	2	3

Los Angeles	IP	H	HR	R	ER	BB	K
D.Sutton L*	7.0	7	0	3	2	1	7
R.Perranoski	2.0	2	1	1	1	0	2
Total	9.0	9	1	4	3	1	9

* Pitched to 2 batters in 8th
Inherited Runners—Scored: C.Sembera 2–0; R.Perranoski 1–1
Umpires: HP: Stan Landes, 1B: Mel Steiner, 2B: Al Barlick, 3B: Augie Donatelli
Time of Game: 2:33   Attendance: 18,550

Mark Teixeira
Born: April 11, 1980
Debut: April 1, 2003

As a high school phenom in Maryland, Mark Teixeira had scouts across the country salivating for his services. The switch-hitter was both graceful and powerful, and although he was drafted in the first round by the Red Sox his senior year, he opted for college and an All-American career at Georgia Tech, where his .409 career average is a school record. After three seasons of dominating ACC play, he was drafted fifth overall by the Rangers, and after just 321 minor league at bats, he was ready to open the '03 season in Arlington.

Rangers manager Buck Showalter was taken with what he called Teixeira's "condor-like" wing span and the ease with which he played his adopted position of first base. His rookie season produced 26 home runs, second most by a switch-hitting rookie in MLB history. The following year, he stroked 38, driving in 112 despite a slow (and injury-marred) April and May.

Easygoing and thoughtful, he has been said to be a ringer for actor Jason Biggs of *American Pie* fame. The son of a naval officer (who also played a little ball, including Little League with Bucky Dent), "Tex" grew up a huge fan of the Orioles' Eddie Murray, going so far as learning to switch-hit because, he said, "That's how Eddie did it." In August of 2004, Teixeira accomplished something Murray never did; he hit for the cycle, driving in seven runs in the process.

His last name (pronounced "tuh-SHARE-ah") keeps getting mangled by those who don't yet have him on their fantasy league teams, but his bat ensures he'll be a popular pick for years to come. An avowed Neil Diamond fan (perhaps the only one in baseball), he is also the owner of a savvy business mind, with Academic All-American among the items on his off-field resume.

I wasn't in the lineup Opening Day 2003, but when I checked the lineup card, Jerry Narron told me not to worry, I'd be in there the next day, so just enjoy Opening Night from the bench and soak it all in. I did that and watched us beat the Angels in Anaheim on national TV, the defending World Series champs. The next day was an off-day, so I had plenty of time to just think about things and get nervous. The day of my first game, I had breakfast and went right to the ballpark, first one there by a mile. The anticipation was incredible. This is what I had worked for ever since I was a little kid.

I really don't remember anything in between then and my first at bat, my

212

nerves were running so fast. I remember thinking that hitting sixth, maybe I could lead off the second inning, no one on, no one out, no pressure. But no, we had a rally going right away against Mickey Callaway, who's now my teammate. Bases loaded, two out, and I come for my first big league at bat with my wife, my parents, and sister watching from the stands and 50,000 Angels fans banging those Thunder Stix together, making all that noise in the first inning. Man, it was loud. I had a good at bat, a few fouls, but I finally grounded out. Later on, I walked though, and I remember trotting down there to first, saying to myself, "Okay, I've made it. On base in the big leagues," And it wasn't easy, because I went something like 0-for-my-first-16 at bats.

We got crushed that night, 10–0, but afterwards, I remember going out to that Mexican restaurant near our hotel in Anaheim, El Torito. I had fajitas and a cold beer, and I remember feeling very relieved that I had my first game, and I didn't embarrass myself too badly.

Also on April 1, 2003
Boston debuts its controversial new "closer by committee" bullpen, blowing an 8–6 lead in Tampa Bay in the eighth inning before finally winning in 16.

AUTHOR'S NOTE: Teixeira was originally drafted by the Red Sox out of Georgia Tech, but after a contentious negotiation, he and his family stormed away from the table. Boston could have had three-fifths of its infield from Tech had Teixeira signed his contract, with Nomar Garciaparra and Jason Varitek already in the fold.

BOXSCORE

Anaheim Angels 10, Texas Rangers 0
Game Played on Tuesday, April 1, 2003 (Night) at Edison International Stadium

Texas	0	0	0	0	0	0	0	0	—	0	5	0
Anaheim	2	1	3	1	0	2	0	1	x	—	10	13	0

BATTING

Texas Rangers	AB	R	H	RBI	BB	K	PO	A
Glanville cf	4	0	1	0	0	1	3	0
Everett lf	3	0	1	0	0	1	3	0
Clark lf	1	0	0	0	0	0	0	0
Rodriguez ss	4	0	1	0	0	1	1	4
Gonzalez rf	2	0	0	0	1	0	3	0
Greene ph	1	0	0	0	0	0	0	0
Palmeiro 1b	2	0	0	0	1	0	4	0
Lamb 1b	1	0	0	0	0	0	1	0
Teixeira dh	3	0	0	0	1	1	0	0
Blalock 3b	4	0	1	0	0	0	2	1
Young 2b	4	0	0	0	0	0	5	3
Kreuter c	3	0	1	0	0	1	2	0
Park p	0	0	0	0	0	0	0	0
Nitkowski p	0	0	0	0	0	0	0	0
Powell p	0	0	0	0	0	0	0	0
Re. Garcia p	0	0	0	0	0	0	0	0
Yan p	0	0	0	0	0	0	0	0
Totals	32	0	5	0	3	5	24	8

FIELDING
DP: 2

BATTING
2B: Everett (1, off Callaway); Kreuter (1, off Callaway)

Anaheim Angels	AB	R	H	RBI	BB	K	PO	A
Eckstein ss	4	0	0	0	1	0	0	2
Erstad cf	3	3	3	1	1	0	1	0
Owens ph-rf	1	0	0	0	0	0	2	0
Salmon rf	3	1	1	0	1	0	0	0
Ramirez cf	1	0	0	0	0	0	1	0
Anderson lf	4	3	4	2	1	0	2	0
Fullmer dh	3	1	2	4	0	0	0	0
Wooten ph-dh	1	0	0	0	0	1	0	0
Glaus 3b	5	0	0	0	0	0	0	2
Spiezio 1b	2	0	1	0	2	0	12	1
Gil ph-1b	1	0	0	0	0	1	0	0
B. Molina c	4	1	1	0	0	0	5	0
Kennedy 2b	3	1	1	1	0	1	3	8
Callaway p	0	0	0	0	0	0	1	0
Shields p	0	0	0	0	0	0	0	0
Weber p	0	0	0	0	0	0	0	0
Totals	35	10	13	8	6	3	27	13

BATTING
2B: Salmon (1, off Park); B. Molina (1, off Park); Anderson (1, off Yan)
HR: Fullmer (1, 3rd inning off Park, 1 on, 0 out)
SF: Fullmer (1, off Nitkowski)
HBP: Kennedy (1, by Park)

BASERUNNING
SB: Kennedy (1, 2nd base off Nitkowski/Kreuter); Erstad (1, 2nd base off Nitkowski/Kreuter)

PITCHING

Texas Rangers	IP	H	HR	R	ER	BB	K
Park L(0–1)	2.2	6	1	6	6	3	0
Nitkowski	2.2	6	0	3	3	2	0
Powell	0.2	0	0	0	0	1	0
Re. Garcia	1	0	0	0	0	0	1
Yan	1	1	0	1	1	0	2
Totals	8	13	1	10	10	6	3

Anaheim Angels	IP	H	HR	R	ER	BB	K
Callaway W(1–0)	6	4	0	0	0	2	4
Shields	2	0	0	0	0	0	1
Weber	1	1	0	0	0	1	0
Totals	9	5	0	0	0	3	5

WP: Powell (1), Yan 2 (2).
HBP: Park (1, Kennedy)
Umpires: Mike Winters, Doug Eddings, Ron Kulpa, Bruce Froemming
Time of Game: 2:48   Attendance: 43,267

Jim Thome
Born: August 27, 1970
Debut: September 4, 1991

If Woody from the TV show *Cheers* had been a ballplayer, he would have been Jim Thome. While Woody Boyd supposedly hailed from tiny Hanover, Indiana, Thome really is from tiny Limestone, Illinois, just outside Peoria. Both have the same likable hayseed quality, and both the fictional character and the real Thome are down to earth and moral above all else.

Thome began his career as a third baseman, but with the Indians' acquisition of Matt Williams, he was shifted cross-diamond to first, where he turned himself into a serviceable defensive player. It has always been said of Thome by his family that the best way to get him to do something is to tell him he can't succeed. Tell him he can't play first base, he'll vacuum up practice grounders until he's got it down. Tell him he can't hit lefties, and he'll work on it until he can.

He became a fan favorite during the time the Indians routinely sold out Jacobs Field in the mid-to-late '90s, walloping home runs with his uppercut swing born out of a most unlikely stance. "It came from watching the movie *The Natural*," Thome has said. He and hitting coach Charlie Manuel were watching the Robert Redford flick together, and Manuel pointed out that the Redford character was extending his bat out in front of him, shoulder high, as a mechanism to get set to uncoil. Manuel suggested Thome adopt the Redford habit as his own, and he suddenly transformed into a pull-hitting long-ball machine as opposed to an opposite field doubles guy.

Thome became known for racking up plenty of walks and plenty of strikeouts, as well as for the way he wore his socks, pulled up high on his bulging calves. When the Indians failed to sign him to a contract extension after the 2002 season, he was courted by the Phillies, a franchise starved for a marquee player.

Thome ratcheted 47 home runs his first year in Philly, which was the last year of old Veteran's Stadium. He followed with 42 in 2004, giving him a total of 190 over a four-year period. Thome has also amassed a minimum of 105 RBI every year since 1999. As his general manager Ed Wade said upon Thome's signing, "You can't measure the credibility he brings or the buzz he creates. Fans can think to themselves, 'I might see something I'll remember for years if I watch this guy play.'"

I was in Colorado Springs, 1991. Charlie Manuel, one of my all-time favorites, gave me the good news, and what a happy, exciting time. I called my parents and told 'em I was going to Minnesota to meet the Indians there, and they said they'd be there too. My brothers and sisters were there, too.

I got out to the Metrodome, and it was like, wow. I was 20, turning 21. And I'm going to play at the Metrodome! I saw Kirby Puckett during that first batting practice, and around the cage, he actually walked by and said hello to me. He made it a point to say welcome, and I'll always remember that. When I got in, I got two hits and gave my parents the ball from that first one. I can remember, plain as day, the scene outside our clubhouse after, telling them that Kirby Puckett said hello to me, and the look on my brothers' faces that I had actually played in a big league game. But you know, I can't for the life of me remember if we won or lost the game. Let me think here. [Long pause.] Gosh, I remember it was David West, the big lefty, who I got my first hit off of. I remember making a pretty good play at third base on a ground ball. Jeez, I can't remember at all if we won or lost, though. That's embarrassing.

Also on September 4, 1991
Baseball's Committee on Statistical Rulings states, with the backing of commissioner Fay Vincent, that the qualification (asterisk) on Roger Maris's record 61 home runs will be removed.

AUTHOR'S NOTE: If a corn-fed, powerful left-handed East Coast slugger is ever going to pass Maris's mark, the smart money's on Thome.

BOXSCORE

Cleveland Indians 8, Minnesota Twins 4

Game Played on Wednesday, September 4, 1991 (Night) at Hubert H. Humphrey Metrodome

Cleveland	0	0	4	1	2	0	0	1	0	—	8	12	0
Minnesota	3	0	0	0	0	0	0	0	1	—	4	10	1

BATTING

Cleveland Indians	AB	R	H	RBI	BB	K	PO	A
Cole cf	5	1	4	1	0	0	1	0
James dh	5	1	0	0	0	1	0	0
Baerga 2b	4	2	1	1	0	1	4	5
Belle lf	5	1	2	5	0	2	1	0
Whiten rf	0	0	0	0	0	0	0	0
Gonzalez rf	3	1	1	0	1	1	4	0
Martinez 1b	4	0	1	0	0	2	8	0
Aldrete 1b	0	0	0	0	0	0	3	0
Thome 3b	4	1	2	1	0	1	2	4
Fermin ss	3	0	1	0	1	0	2	4
Skinner c	4	1	0	0	0	0	2	0
Blair p	0	0	0	0	0	0	0	0
Olin p	0	0	0	0	0	0	0	0
Hillegas p	0	0	0	0	0	0	0	0
Totals	**37**	**8**	**12**	**8**	**2**	**8**	**27**	**13**

FIELDING
DP: 3

BATTING
2B: Belle (22, off West); Cole (11, off Guthrie)
HR: Belle (25, 5th inning off Willis, 1 on, 0 out)
HBP: Baerga (4, by West)

BASERUNNING
SB: Gonzalez (2, 2nd base off Leach/Harper)
CS: Cole (13, 2nd base by Anderson/Harper)

Minnesota Twins	AB	R	H	RBI	BB	K	PO	A
Gladden lf	5	0	2	0	0	0	1	0
Knoblauch 2b	4	1	1	0	0	0	2	1
Puckett cf	4	1	2	0	0	0	2	0
Hrbek 1b	4	1	1	3	0	0	7	2
Davis dh	4	1	2	0	0	0	0	0
Harper c	4	0	1	0	0	1	9	0
Mack rf	2	0	0	0	2	0	3	0
Pagliarulo 3b	4	0	1	0	0	0	0	4
Gagne ss	2	0	0	0	0	0	2	1
Sorrento ph	1	0	0	0	0	0	0	0
Newman ss	0	0	0	0	0	0	0	1
Larkin ph	0	0	0	0	1	0	0	0
West p	0	0	0	0	0	0	0	0
Edens p	0	0	0	0	0	0	1	0
Willis p	0	0	0	0	0	0	0	0
Anderson p	0	0	0	0	0	0	0	1
Leach p	0	0	0	0	0	0	0	0
Guthrie p	0	0	0	0	0	0	0	0
Totals	**34**	**4**	**10**	**3**	**3**	**1**	**27**	**10**

FIELDING
DP: 2
E: Gagne (9)

BATTING
2B: Puckett (24, off Blair)
HR: Hrbek (16, 1st inning off Blair, 2 on, 1 out)

PITCHING

Cleveland Indians	IP	H	HR	R	ER	BB	K
Blair W(2–2)	8	8	1	3	3	1	1
Olin	0	2	0	1	1	1	0
Hillegas SV(7)	1	0	0	0	0	1	0
Totals	**9**	**10**	**1**	**4**	**4**	**3**	**1**

Minnesota Twins	IP	H	HR	R	ER	BB	K
West L(4–4)	2.1	2	0	4	3	2	2
Edens	1.2	2	0	1	1	0	0
Willis	1	2	1	2	2	0	2
Anderson	2	2	0	0	0	0	1
Leach	1	3	0	1	1	0	0
Guthrie	1	1	0	0	0	0	3
Totals	**9**	**12**	**1**	**8**	**7**	**2**	**8**

HBP: West (1, Baerga)
Umpires: Rocky Roe, Rick Reed, Joe Brinkman, Derryl Cousins
Time of Game: 2:55   Attendance: 19,760

Joe Torre
Born: July 18, 1940
Debut: September 25, 1960

He was an All-Star every year from 1963 through '67 and again from 1970 through '73. He led the National League in both batting average and RBI in 1971, winning the MVP. However, everything Joe Torre accomplished as a player pales against what he's accomplished as manager of the New York Yankees. Hall of Famers Miller Huggins, Joe McCarthy, and Casey Stengel notwithstanding, he has been the most successful manager of the sport's most successful franchise. Torre's Yankees played 16 playoff series between 1996 and 2001, losing only twice (to Cleveland in '97 and to Arizona in '01). Between those two failures, the Yanks were undefeated in 11 consecutive postseason series.

Torre's managerial career began with a couple of false starts. He washed out as boss of the Braves, Mets, and Cardinals. When George Steinbrenner anointed him to succeed the popular Buck Showalter in 1996, the New York tabloids unilaterally bashed the decision. (One headline described him as "Clueless Joe.") However, all of Torre's players have pretty much arrived at the same conclusion—that he is a calming force in what can only be described as a chaotic environment.

Torre is the first native New Yorker to manage the team and seemed to take a measure of territorial pride in having been at the helm for the Yanks' first World Series win since 1978. He had played and managed in close to 4,300 games before experiencing a championship, having originally signed with the Milwaukee Braves. Actually, he had originally been scouted by the Giants, but having been offered a bonus of only $10,000, he decided to hold out for the ten grand plus a car, which caused the Giants to walk away from the table. So he signed with the Braves for $20,000, bought the car himself, and had enough left over to pay off the mortgage on his mother's house.

His playing days saw him play catcher, first base, and third base, and he played all three very well. His career-high batting average came during his 1971 MVP season, when, as his teammate Bob Gibson said, "He batted .363 without a leg hit in sight." Indeed, his lack of speed accounted for one seemingly unbreakable big league record—he once grounded into four double plays in a single game.

My season had ended at C-ball, Eau Claire, Wisconsin. I stopped in Milwaukee because I was going to wait for my brother to get done with his season so we could go on home together. I was just planning on hanging around. But I decided to head over to the Braves offices, since I was there anyway, and they told me, "Since you're here, we're going to put you on the roster for the rest of the season." John McHale, the general manager, told me I'd get the prorated major league minimum of $6,000 a year for, what, two weeks or so. But back then, that just sounded great.

When I finally got in a game, it was a Saturday afternoon at County Stadium. Ninth inning, sitting on the bench, and my manager, Charlie Dressen, says, "Torre, get a bat!" My legs started shaking. I mean, really, I could feel each leg start to shake, first one, then the other. I was going to pinch-hit for Warren Spahn. Against the Pirates and Harvey Haddix. Second pitch, a ground ball single up the middle. I somehow run to first base, and I'm standing there, and I realize that my legs are still shaking. It was quite a feat to have had that at bat and been able to run at all, because I was an absolute mess. Lee Maye came in immediately to pinch-run for me.

Now, in those days, rookies felt like what they were—rookies. These days, these kids come in like they belong here right away. Which is fine, I guess, but there really is a difference there.

Also on September 25, 1960
Red Sox owner Tom Yawkey formally announces the impending retirement of Ted Williams. That night, Casey Stengel's Yankees beat the Red Sox for their 35th American League pennant, 4–3.

AUTHOR'S NOTE: Torre's Yankees would beat the Red Sox four games to three for the AL pennant in 2003; the Red Sox turned the tables the following season.

BOXSCORE

Milwaukee Braves 4, Pittsburgh Pirates 2 (10)

Game of Sunday, 9/25/1960 (Day) at County Stadium

Pittsburgh	0	0	0	0	1	0	1	0	0	0	—	2
Milwaukee	0	0	0	0	0	0	0	2	0	2	—	4

Pittsburgh	AB	R	H	RBI	BB	K	PO	A
G.Cimoli cf	4	0	0	0	0	1	2	0
B.Skinner lf	4	0	1	0	0	0	3	0
R.Clemente rf	4	1	2	0	0	0	1	0
D.Stuart 1b	4	0	0	0	0	1	14	2
H.Smith c	4	0	1	1	0	0	6	0
D.Hoak 3b	4	0	0	0	0	1	0	2
B.Mazeroski 2b	4	1	1	1	0	1	1	3
D.Schofield ss	4	0	1	0	0	0	1	7
H.Haddix p	3	0	0	0	0	0	1	3
R.Face p	0	0	0	0	0	0	0	0
Totals	35	2	6	2	0	4	29	17

FIELDING
E: D.Schofield (fumble); H.Smith (dropped throw)
DP: (1). D.Schofield-B.Mazeroski-D.Stuart

BATTING
2B: H.Smith (off W.Spahn); B.Skinner (off R.Piche)
HR: B.Mazeroski (5th inning off W.Spahn, 0 on, 2 out)
2-out RBI: B.Mazeroski
RBI, scoring position, less than 2 outs: D.Stuart 0–1; D.Hoak 0–1

BASERUNNING
SB: R.Clemente (2nd base off R.Piche/D.Crandall)
Team LOB: 3

Milwaukee	AB	R	H	RBI	BB	K	PO	A
B.Bruton cf	5	1	1	0	0	1	4	0
D.Crandall c	3	1	1	1	1	0	5	0
E.Mathews 3b	4	1	1	2	1	2	0	4
H.Aaron rf	4	0	0	0	0	1	1	1
A.Dark lf	4	0	1	0	0	0	3	0
J.Adcock 1b	4	0	0	0	0	1	15	2
F.Mantilla ss	3	0	2	0	1	0	1	3
C.Cottier 2b	2	0	0	0	0	0	0	3
M.Roach ph-2b	2	0	0	0	0	0	0	1
W.Spahn p	2	0	0	0	0	1	0	0
J.Torre ph	1	0	1	0	0	0	0	0
L.Maye pr	0	1	0	0	0	0	0	0
R.Piche p	1	0	0	0	0	0	1	0
Totals	35	4	7	3	3	5	30	14

FIELDING
Outfield assist: H.Aaron (B.Skinner at HP)

BATTING
2B: A.Dark (off H.Haddix); D.Crandall (off H.Haddix)
HR: E.Mathews (10th inning off R.Face, 1 on, 2 out)
2-out RBI: E.Mathews 2
RBI, scoring position, less than 2 outs: D.Crandall 1–2; E.Mathews 0–1; H.Aaron 0–1; J.Adcock 0–1
SF: D.Crandall
GDP: M.Roach

BASERUNNING
Team LOB: 6

PITCHING

Pittsburgh	IP	H	HR	R	ER	BB	K
H.Haddix	7.1	6	0	2	1	1	4
R.Face L, BS	2.1	1	1	2	2	2	1
Total	10.0	7	1	4	3	3	5

Milwaukee	IP	H	HR	R	ER	BB	K
W.Spahn	8.0	4	1	2	2	0	2
R.Piche W	2.0	2	0	0	0	0	2
Total	10.0	6	1	2	2	0	4

Inherited Runners—Scored: R.Face 2–1; R.Piche 0–0
WP: H.Haddix
Umpires: HP: Tom Gorman, 1B: Vinnie Smith, 2B: Ed Sudol, 3B: Dusty Boggess
Time of Game: 2:14 Attendance: 38,109

Alan Trammell
Born: February 21, 1958
Debut: September 9, 1977

Alan Trammell grew up in San Diego, one of the first "real" fans of the expansion Padres when he was 11. He had idolized Willie Mays of the Giants and the Pirates' Roberto Clemente. When the Pirates first came to Jack Murphy Stadium, Trammell and his friends once snuck in early to watch Clemente take batting practice. On a dare, he tiptoed into the visiting dugout when the guard wasn't looking and swung one of Clemente's bats.

Years later, another native San Diegan was asked if he believed Alan Trammell belonged in the Baseball Hall of Fame—and Ted Williams said, "Yes. Yes, I certainly do."

Voters disagreed with the Splendid Splinter's endorsement, but 185 career home runs used to be an astronomical total for a shortstop, and Trammell's career fielding percentage is higher than every shortstop currently enshrined. An MVP would have helped his candidacy, and Tiger fans will tell you he was robbed in '87. Sure, the Blue Jays' George Bell had the better RBI season and blasted 47 homers, but Trammell hit .343 that year and beat Bell's Jays when it mattered most, head-to-head late in the season.

Trammell and the Tigers were ousted in the ALCS that year, but they won it all in '84, racing out to a 35–5 start and never needing to check the rearview mirror. The Tigers crushed Trammell's hometown Padres in a five-game mismatch. Some 19 years later, however, that 35–5 start would be nothing but a distant memory. As the Tigers rookie manager in 2003, Trammell watched in horror as the wretched ball club checked in not at 35–5, but at 35–103, on the way to 43–119. Still, Trammell made sure his young club never quit on him. With the record of 120 losses seemingly unavoidable, the Tigers somehow had their best stretch of the year in the season's final week. They won five of their last six and kept themselves a game ahead of the '62 Mets.

"My goal now is to make sure this organization never gets embarrassed like that again," Trammell said. "These fans deserve—and this city deserves—a winner."

I was scared to death. I mean, absolutely scared to death. At least I was hitting ninth, off Reggie Cleveland, and that took the edge off a little. I had some time to think about everything, to try and get my feet wet since I didn't bat 'til the third inning. I got a single, and that took a lot of the pressure off. I put one right in front of Fred Lynn in center.

When I got the call, it was after winning the Double-A championship down in Montgomery, Alabama. Eddie Brinkman, what a guy, was the manager there, a former shortstop himself. What I took most from him is that he always talked about what it was like in the big leagues, what to expect, what would happen. I found out later he didn't give those talks to everyone, just the guys he thought would make it.

I finished up in Montgomery on a Wednesday, flew to Baltimore, and didn't play on Thursday but found there was a doubleheader scheduled in Boston for Friday and was told I'd play in one of those games. I called my mom, and she could hardly believe it. She didn't see me play that debut game, but because I got two hits, [manager] Ralph Houk called me over afterwards and said, "You're

---

Also on September 9, 1977

Trammell's double play partner for the next 18 years makes his debut alongside him at Fenway. Lou Whitaker trumps Trammell's two hits with three of his own, although not a single ball was hit his way all game at second base. Trammell handled only one ground ball, off the bat of the Sox's Butch Hobson.

AUTHOR'S NOTE: Whitaker and Trammell set a record, playing the most games as a double-play combo. The number of games played may have gone down sour for Fenway faithful were it not for the Sox's recent championship, with 1918; it's ironic that a streak of that length would start in Boston.

BOXSCORE

Boston Red Sox 8, Detroit Tigers 6 (2nd Game of Doubleheader)
Game Played on Friday, September 9, 1977 (Night) at Fenway Park

Detroit	0	0	3	2	0	0	1	0	0	—	6	16	0
Boston	2	3	0	0	1	1	0	1	x	—	8	9	1

BATTING

Detroit Tigers	AB	R	H	RBI	BB	K	PO	A
LeFlore cf	4	1	2	1	1	1	1	0
Whitaker 2b	5	1	3	1	0	2	0	0
Staub dh	5	0	1	1	0	0	0	0
Kemp lf	5	0	1	1	0	1	4	0
Thompson 1b	5	1	2	1	0	0	3	1
Oglivie rf	5	0	1	0	0	2	2	0
Parrish c	5	1	2	0	0	2	12	1
Rodriguez 3b	4	1	2	1	0	1	0	1
Trammell ss	3	1	2	0	0	1	1	1
Molinaro ph	1	0	0	0	1	0	0	0
Scrivener ss	0	0	0	0	0	0	0	0
Grilli p	0	0	0	0	0	0	0	0
Ruhle p	0	0	0	0	0	0	1	0
Hiller p	0	0	0	0	0	0	0	0
Totals	42	6	16	6	1	11	24	4

BATTING
2B: Whitaker (1, off Cleveland); LeFlore (25, off Willoughby)
3B: Rodriguez (1, off Willoughby)
HR: Thompson (27, 7th inning off Campbell, 0 on, 1 out)

BASERUNNING
SB: Whitaker (1, 2nd base off Cleveland/Montgomery); LeFlore (33, 2nd base off Campbell/Montgomery)

Boston Red Sox	AB	R	H	RBI	BB	K	PO	A
Burleson ss	5	1	3	2	0	0	2	0
Doyle 2b	4	1	0	0	1	2	2	4
Lynn cf	4	2	2	2	0	1	5	0
Yastrzemski lf	4	0	1	1	0	1	1	0
Rice dh	2	0	0	1	1	1	0	0
Carbo rf	4	0	1	2	0	2	1	0
Miller rf	0	0	0	0	0	0	0	0
Scott 1b	4	1	1	0	0	3	4	0
Hobson 3b	3	1	0	0	1	1	0	2
Montgomery c	2	1	1	0	1	1	9	0
Dillard pr	0	1	0	0	0	0	0	0
Fisk c	0	0	0	0	0	1	1	0
Cleveland p	0	0	0	0	0	0	1	0
Willoughby p	0	0	0	0	0	0	0	0
Wise p	0	0	0	0	0	0	0	0
Campbell p	0	0	0	0	0	0	0	0
Totals	32	8	9	8	4	12	27	6

FIELDING
DP: 1
E: Cleveland (3)

BATTING
2B: Burleson (34, off Grilli); Lynn (25, off Ruhle)
3B: Lynn (5, off Grilli)
SF: Rice (4, off Ruhle)
HBP: Montgomery (1, by Grilli)

PITCHING

Detroit Tigers	IP	H	HR	R	ER	BB	K
Grilli	1.2	4	0	5	5	3	1
Ruhle L(3–5)	3.1	1	0	1	1	0	3
Hiller	3	4	0	2	2	1	8
Totals	8	9	0	8	8	4	12

Boston Red Sox	IP	H	HR	R	ER	BB	K
Cleveland	2.1	5	0	3	3	1	2
Willoughby	1	3	0	2	2	0	2
Wise W(11–5)	2.1	4	0	0	0	0	1
Campbell SV(26)	3.1	4	1	1	1	0	6
Totals	9.0	16	1	6	6	1	11

WP: Grilli (3), Ruhle (3)
HBP: Grilli (3, Montgomery)
Umpires: Vic Voltaggio, Marty Springstead, Larry Barnett, Jim Evans
Time of Game: 3:03   Attendance: 34,581

back in there tomorrow," and that one was the Game of the Week on national TV. So that one she saw. She saw me playing against a darn good team. I could hardly believe I was sharing a field with those guys. Jim Rice, Fred Lynn, Yaz, George Scott, Carlton Fisk. Butch Hobson hitting eight or ninth in the order, for goodness sake! We lost that first game, but it's one of the few times—maybe the only time—I can say it almost didn't matter. To be in the big leagues at age 19, that was pretty special.

Courtesy Detroit Tigers

Omar Vizquel
Born: April 24, 1967
Debut: April 3, 1989

When he first began his big league career, Vizquel was dubbed "Omar the Out Maker" by Seattle fans. Indeed, Omar Vizquel's career began slowly, as he hit only .220, .247, and .230 in his first three seasons.

However, as he continued to dazzle with his defense, his hitting gradually improved, and by the mid '90s, he was thought of as one of the game's elite all-around shortstops. By 1999, he was at .333, helping the Indians stay in power in the AL Central.

There was never any question about his glove. Vizquel cultivated his super-soft Gold Glove hands growing up in Venezuela, chasing bad-hop grounders on rock-strewn infields and firing balls off brick walls from close range to sharpen an already gifted set of reflexes. He won nine Gold Gloves, bridging the gap between Cal Ripken Jr. in 1992 and Alex Rodriguez in 2002. As a minor league manager, Doc Edwards, once said of him, "He's a hundred-RBI player. He'll drive in 50 and save you 50."

Through hours of work in the batting cage, Vizquel sharpened his offense to the point that he actually drove in as many as 72 runs (in 2002, when he also hit a career-best 14 home runs). His boundless energy reminded some observers of another shortstop who was initially "all glove, no hit"—Hall of Famer Ozzie Smith. Like Smith, Vizquel can use both the stolen base and the bunt as a weapon. From 1997 to '99, Vizquel was an incredible 45-for-45 when attempting to lay down a sacrifice.

Two things he does better than Smith are drawing and painting. A renowned artist, he has lent both his name and his artwork to the salsa business, where Clevelanders have been lapping up official Omar Vizquel–brand salsa for the last several years. Vizquel signed a lucrative free agent contract with the Giants heading into 2005, ending an 11-year association with Cleveland, his adopted hometown.

Proud of his Venezuelan heritage, he has put himself in the company of his heroes Luis Aparicio and Chico Carrasquel in career fielding percentage. With 2,100 career base hits and 57 games of postseason experience, he has also landed squarely as one of Northern Ohio's all-time favorite athletes.

I hadn't thought much about making the team out of spring training. They had Rey Quinones and Mario Diaz, so I assumed I was going to Triple-A. But Quinones was holding out for more money, and Diaz got hurt, so the day be-

221

BOXSCORE

Oakland Athletics 3, Seattle Mariners 2
Game Played on Monday, April 3, 1989 (Night) at Oakland-Alameda County Coliseum

Seattle	0	0	0	0	1	1	0	0	0	—	2	5	1
Oakland	1	0	2	0	0	0	0	0	x	—	3	6	1

BATTING

Seattle Mariners	AB	R	H	RBI	BB	K	PO	A
Reynolds 2b	4	0	0	0	0	1	2	2
Griffey cf	3	1	1	0	1	0	5	0
Davis 1b	4	0	0	0	0	1	13	0
Coles rf	4	0	1	1	0	2	1	0
Leonard dh	4	1	1	0	0	1	0	0
Briley lf	3	0	0	0	1	1	1	0
Valle c	4	0	1	0	0	0	2	1
Martinez 3b	3	0	1	1	0	0	0	5
Vizquel ss	3	0	0	0	0	0	0	5
Langston p	0	0	0	0	0	0	0	0
Totals	32	2	5	2	2	6	24	13

FIELDING
DP: 1
E: Vizquel (1)

BATTING
2B: Griffey (1, off Stewart)

Oakland Athletics	AB	R	H	RBI	BB	K	PO	A
Phillips lf	4	1	1	0	0	0	3	0
D. Henderson cf	3	0	1	0	0	0	5	0
Lansford 3b	4	1	1	0	0	0	1	1
McGwire 1b	3	1	2	3	0	0	3	0
Steinbach c	2	0	0	0	1	0	6	0
Parker dh	3	0	0	0	0	0	0	0
Hubbard 2b	3	0	0	0	0	0	2	2
Javier rf	3	0	1	0	0	2	6	0
Weiss ss	3	0	0	0	0	0	1	2
Stewart p	0	0	0	0	0	0	0	0
Nelson p	0	0	0	0	0	0	0	0
Honeycutt p	0	0	0	0	0	0	0	0
Eckersley p	0	0	0	0	0	0	0	0
Totals	28	3	6	3	1	2	27	5

FIELDING
DP: 1
E: Hubbard (1)

BATTING
2B: Phillips (1, off Langston)
HR: McGwire (1, 3rd inning off Langston, 1 on, 1 out)
SF: McGwire (1, off Langston)
HBP: D. Henderson (1, by Langston)

BASERUNNING
SB: Javier (1, 2nd base off Langston/Valle)

PITCHING

Seattle Mariners	IP	H	HR	R	ER	BB	K
Langston L(0–1)	8	6	1	3	3	1	2
Oakland Athletics	**IP**	**H**	**HR**	**R**	**ER**	**BB**	**K**
Stewart W(1–0)	5.1	4	0	2	1	2	2
Nelson	1.2	1	0	0	0	0	2
Honeycutt	0.2	0	0	0	0	0	1
Eckersley SV(1)	1.1	0	0	0	0	0	1
Totals	9.0	5	0	2	1	2	6

HBP: Langston (1, D. Henderson)
Umpires: Al Clark, Rick Reed, Mark Johnson, Dale Scott
Time of Game: 2:19   Attendance: 46,163

fore spring training ended, Jim Lefebvre, our manager, called me in his office and told me I was going to go to the big leagues right now, and that I'd be starting Opening Day in Oakland. The A's were a championship team then, with all those big guys—Parker, Canseco, McGwire. Canseco hit me an easy ground ball late in the game, but I threw it away for an error, and then McGwire came up next and hit a home run off Mark Langston. Dave Parker hit me in the face with a ground ball, too, but I made the play on that one. That was the first ball ever hit to me in the big leagues, and it hit me in the face. We lost, 3–2, and I went 0-for-3. A very exciting game, but my error was the difference, unfortunately, especially for Langston, because he pitched a hell of a game.

I remember the pre-game stuff from Opening Day very well—Opening Night, actually, since it was Oakland. The national anthem was awesome, gave me chills. An elephant threw out the first pitch. No kidding! You know, the A's have an elephant for a mascot, and they sent this elephant out there near the pitcher's mound, and he threw the ball with his trunk. They had a high wire act and fireworks. It was like a big carnival, and I was in it. That wasn't going to be happening at Calgary!

Also on April 3, 1989
Cleanup continues in Alaska after the *Exxon Valdez*'s massive oil spill the week before.

AUTHOR'S NOTE: Vizquel is a noted fan of marine life. His home features a large, in-the-wall saltwater fish tank, with (as he describes it) "exotic, brilliantly colored fish." He says he keeps the tank completely free of oil.

Billy Wagner
Born: July 25, 1971
Debut: September 13, 1995

Billy Wagner hurdled his humble beginnings and has proven that indeed, you can't judge a book by its cover. Wagner stands an unimposing 5'10" and has finally muscled up to 195 pounds, but many scouts had long dismissed the six-and-under as being all but six feet under. The Astros were happy to discover that good arms sometimes dangle off of small bodies.

Wagner was born and raised in the southwest part of the state, in a town of 300 people. Wagner has described Tannersville as "a general store and then plenty of hunting and fishing." Living in the rural Blue Ridge Mountains, Wagner grew up without other kids his age, meaning no kids with whom to play catch. Wagner developed his bionic left arm by throwing rocks across a field, as far as he could heave them, then walking down to retrieve the rocks, throwing them back, and repeating the exercise until dark. In high school, geography wasn't the only thing keeping him from being scouted; it was the fact that he stood 5'3", 135 pounds. However, by his sophomore year at tiny Ferrum College, he'd grown seven inches and added 40 pounds, not to mention a dozen miles an hour to his fastball.

Once in the majors, he astounded hitters with a fastball that consistently hit triple digits on the radar gun. In 2003, 135 of his pitches were clocked at at least 100 mph. No one else in baseball threw as many as twelve.

After three All-Star Game appearances as an Astro, he signed with the Phillies and kept piling up ninth inning strikeouts. Through 2004, he had averaged 12.2 K's per nine innings pitched, the best ratio in major league history. (In '99, he struck out nearly half the batters he faced, 124 of 260.) Wagner backs up his major league heat with a major league mouth, which at times gets him in trouble with management. However, Philly fans appreciate "tell it like it is" candor, even if it's delivered with a twang.

When I was coming up, I was in Tucson. We had just finished the playoffs, but we waited a day, then flew up to New York, a couple of us. Rick Sweet, our manager, told me that night before the game. We lost, but the whole time, I knew there was good news for me, anyway. It was tough to be too upset. I get to Shea Stadium, and I had never really worn a suit before, but I had bought one at JCPenney the day before. I walk in the clubhouse, and there's Jeff Bagwell, Derek Bell, Pat Borders, and Mike Simms, big old boys, and they're wrestling. Wrestling! And I'm like, "Wow, I better leave these guys alone."

223

BOXSCORE

New York Mets 10, Houston Astros 5

Game Played on Wednesday, September 13, 1995 (Night) at Shea Stadium

Houston	0	1	3	0	0	0	0	1	0	—	5	10	4
New York	1	3	0	0	2	1	1	2	x	—	10	14	0

BATTING

Houston Astros	AB	R	H	RBI	BB	K	PO	A
Cangelosi lf	5	0	2	0	0	1	1	0
Biggio 2b	4	1	1	1	0	1	3	1
Bagwell 1b	4	2	2	2	0	0	5	1
May rf	4	1	1	0	0	0	3	0
Magadan 3b	4	0	2	0	0	0	0	2
Eusebio c	4	0	0	1	0	0	6	0
Hunter cf	4	0	1	1	0	0	4	0
Gutierrez ss	4	0	1	0	0	1	2	2
Hampton p	1	1	0	0	1	1	0	3
Dougherty p	0	0	0	0	0	0	0	0
Wagner p	0	0	0	0	0	0	0	0
Thompson ph	1	0	0	0	0	0	0	0
Kile p	0	0	0	0	0	0	0	0
Brumley ph	1	0	0	0	0	1	0	0
Totals	36	5	10	5	1	5	24	9

FIELDING
E: Cangelosi 2 (4), Bagwell (7), Hunter (7)

BATTING
2B: May (11, off B. Jones); Magadan 2 (20, off B. Jones 2)
3B: Cangelosi (1, off B. Jones)
HR: Bagwell (18, 3rd inning off B. Jones, 1 on, 1 out)

BASERUNNING
SB: Hunter (18, 2nd base off B. Jones/Stinnett)

New York Mets	AB	R	H	RBI	BB	K	PO	A
Buford lf	5	2	2	3	0	1	2	0
Vizcaino ss	5	0	1	0	0	0	1	8
Everett rf	5	2	3	1	0	0	0	0
Kent 2b	5	1	2	2	0	0	3	5
Brogna 1b	4	1	1	0	1	0	15	0
Thompson cf	4	2	1	0	1	1	1	0
Bogar 3b	4	1	2	0	0	0	0	2
Stinnett c	3	1	2	2	1	1	5	0
B.Jones p	3	0	0	0	0	3	0	0
Henry p	0	0	0	0	0	0	0	0
Totals	38	10	14	8	3	6	27	15

FIELDING
DP: 1

BATTING
2B: Bogar (6, off Hampton); Brogna (23, off Hampton)
HR: Buford 2 (4, 1st inning off Hampton, 0 on, 0 out; 2nd inning off Hampton, 1 on, 2 out); Everett (12, 6th inning off Dougherty, 0 on, 2 out); Kent (18, 8th inning off Kile, 1 on, 1 out)
SH: B. Jones (18, off Hampton)

PITCHING

Houston Astros	IP	H	HR	R	ER	BB	K
Hampton L(9–7)	4.2	9	2	6	5	2	1
Dougherty	1.0	2	1	1	1	0	2
Wagner	0.1	0	0	0	0	0	0
Kile	2.0	3	1	3	2	1	3
Totals	8.0	14	4	10	8	3	6
New York Mets	IP	H	HR	R	ER	BB	K
B.Jones W(9–8)	8.0	10	1	5	5	1	4
Henry	1.0	0	0	0	0	0	1
Totals	9.0	10	1	5	5	1	5

Umpires: Charlie Williams, John McSherry, Ed Montague, Greg Bonin
Time of Game: 2:29   Attendance: 13,165

I got in a game the second day in New York, and I faced one batter—Rico Brogna. I threw 95 miles an hour, got him out, and that was my whole season up there that year. I had run in, completely numb. Jeff Kent's on base. Biggio and Bagwell are over there. And it hit me right then—I'm actually in a big league game.

I got sent back to start the next year at Triple-A, and I'll tell you about the second time I got called up, 'cause I remember that even more. I had just pitched seven innings and pitched well, but they took me out. I was pissed and throwing a fit. Here I am throwing 95 miles per hour and our manager, Tim Tolman, says, "You're done." He knew why, but he didn't tell me. I stewed all night and then saw him the next day in the hotel lobby, and he says, "You know why I took you out?' And I said, "No, dammit, you should have left me in." He says, "Well, I felt that was plenty, because tomorrow you're going to join the big club in New York." And I'm like, "What? Why didn't you tell me last night?" And he says, "It was more fun watching you squirm."

Also on September 13, 1995
The Drew Carey Show debuts on ABC.

AUTHOR'S NOTE: Like Carey, Billy Wagner may be a little unrefined, but there's no doubting his ability, perseverance, or his appeal.

Tim Wakefield
Born: August 2, 1966
Debut: July 31, 1992

Some people get to regale audiences with some sort of Lazarus Act tale, but very few get to trot out *two*. Tim Wakefield began his pro baseball career as a first- and third baseman, a Pirates eighth-round pick in '88. After a year of flailing at curveballs and change-ups, he was moved to the pitcher's mound, and his outlook immediately improved. He developed a wicked knuckleball, and the kid who was once a nonprospect was suddenly blazing a trail to the big leagues.

He arrived in July 1992 and ripped off 14 wins in his first 15 decisions, almost single-handedly steering the Pirates into the postseason against Atlanta. He won twice more in the postseason and, were it not for Francisco Cabrera singling home two runs in the ninth inning of Game Seven, he would have been named NLCS MVP. Braves visiting clubhouse personnel reported the trophy, along with a bottle of champagne, was in his locker. Both items had to be quickly removed as soon as Sid Bream slid under Mike LaValliere's tag with the series-winning run.

Soon after that magical '92 season, however, the knuckleball magic disappeared. He was dispatched back to Triple-A, and after he was pounded for a .324 batting average there, the Pirates released him.

Enter Lazarus Act II. Having signed with the Red Sox to play at Triple-A Pawtucket, he arrived at spring training to find the Sox sharing their minor league complex with the Silver Bullets women's team, which was about to head out on its barnstorming tour. He quickly found the coaches of the team, Joe and Phil Niekro, who had knuckleballed their way to a combined total of 539 big league wins themselves. A couple days' of knuckleball fixer-up from the masters, and Wakefield was reborn. He is now the longest-tenured member of the Boston Red Sox, having won 114 regular season games and taken the ball in some huge postseason situations. The Sox's 2004 World Series win vaporized the memories of the home run he allowed to end the '03 ALCS.

Marc Bombard was my manager at Buffalo, and he said "You need to get to Chicago, where the team is. You're going to work out with them for a day, then head back to Pittsburgh where you're starting on Friday against the Cardinals."

BOXSCORE

Pittsburgh Pirates 3, St. Louis Cardinals 2

Game Played on Friday, July 31, 1992 (Night) at Three Rivers Stadium

St. Louis	0	0	0	0	2	0	0	0	0	—	2	6	0
Pittsburgh	2	0	1	0	0	0	0	0	x	—	3	5	1

BATTING

St. Louis Cardinals	AB	R	H	RBI	BB	K	PO	A
Gilkey lf	3	0	0	1	1	0	3	0
O. Smith ss	4	0	0	0	1	2	0	1
Lankford cf	4	0	2	1	0	1	2	0
Jose rf	3	0	0	0	1	1	4	0
Galarraga 1b	3	0	2	0	1	0	7	1
Zeile 3b	4	0	1	0	0	2	1	3
Alicea 2b	4	0	0	0	0	3	1	2
Pagnozzi c	4	1	0	0	0	1	6	0
DeLeon p	2	1	1	0	0	0	0	0
Thompson ph	0	0	0	0	1	0	0	0
Osborne p	0	0	0	0	0	0	0	0
Perry ph	1	0	0	0	0	0	0	0
Totals	**32**	**2**	**6**	**2**	**5**	**10**	**24**	**7**

BATTING

2B: Lankford 2 (27, off Wakefield 2)

SF: Gilkey (2, off Wakefield)

BASERUNNING

CS: Zeile (10, 2nd base by Wakefield/Slaught)

Pittsburgh Pirates	AB	R	H	RBI	BB	K	PO	A
A. Cole rf	4	1	2	0	0	2	2	0
Bell ss	3	1	1	1	0	2	1	0
Van Slyke cf	3	0	0	0	0	0	3	0
Bonds lf	3	1	1	2	0	0	2	0
Merced 1b	3	0	0	0	0	0	5	0
King 3b	3	0	1	0	0	0	3	1
Slaught c	3	0	0	0	0	1	9	2
Lind 2b	3	0	0	0	0	0	1	0
Wakefield p	3	0	0	0	0	1	0	1
Totals	**28**	**3**	**5**	**3**	**0**	**6**	**27**	**4**

FIELDING

DP: 1

E: King (5)

BATTING

2B: King (8, off DeLeon)

HR: Bonds (20, 1st inning off DeLeon, 1 on, 2 out); Bell (5, 3rd inning off DeLeon, 0 on, 1 out)

SH: Bell (10, off DeLeon)

PITCHING

St. Louis Cardinals	IP	H	HR	R	ER	BB	K
DeLeon L(2–7)	5	5	2	3	3	0	4
Osborne	3	0	0	0	0	0	2
Totals	**8**	**5**	**2**	**3**	**3**	**0**	**6**
Pittsburgh Pirates	**IP**	**H**	**HR**	**R**	**ER**	**BB**	**K**
Wakefield W(1–0)	9	6	0	2	0	5	10

WP: Wakefield 3 (3)

Umpires: Doug Harvey, Jerry Crawford, Charlie Williams, Gerry Davis

Time of Game: 2:17   Attendance: 20,299

I had never been on a big league charter, so that was one of many awesome things, heading back to Pittsburgh—this after walking into the clubhouse at Wrigley and seeing Bonds in one corner, Van Slyke in another. I had never been to big league spring training with the Pirates, so I had never really seen those guys up close and never met them. What helped me catch my breath was that Orlando Merced was there, and I knew him from minor league camp. Steve Cooke and Paul Wagner were there too, so at least there were a couple people who recognized me and came over to say hello.

Back in Pittsburgh, the start couldn't have gone better. A complete game, and we won, 3–2. Don Slaught did a real good job catching the knuckler, and I had a bunch of strikeouts. I think I got Ozzie Smith more than once, so that was cool. My family came up on their own—my mom, my dad, my aunt, my uncle. My mom was the most emotional of the group, just elated that she was seeing her son pitch in the big leagues. She and my dad both worked real hard when I was growing up, and they knew I'd worked real hard myself to get to where I wanted to be, so it was gratifying to share that with them. It couldn't have been a better night.

Also on July 31, 1992

Summer Sanders becomes the first American athlete to win four medals at the Barcelona Olympics as she takes the gold in the women's 200-meter butterfly.

AUTHOR'S NOTE: Female athletes would, unwittingly, have an effect on Wakefield's own pro career. Had the Niekros not been coaching the Silver Bullets women's baseball team in Ft. Myers in February of '95, they wouldn't have bumped into Wakefield and helped him spruce up that knuckler.

Larry Walker
Born: December 1, 1966
Debut: August 16, 1989

He is a onetime MVP and a seven-time Gold Glover, but more importantly to Larry Walker, he is a *three*-time batting champ. The number three
pretty much lords over Walker's existence, a superstition that borders on
obsessive-compulsive. Three swings in the on-deck circle. If he taps dirt
out of his spikes, he takes three whacks with his bat to get it done. Wakeup
calls are, whenever possible, at 33 after the hour. Food is microwaved in the
clubhouse in increments of 33. After the game, Walker must stand under
showerhead number three in the clubhouse, and if it is occupied, he'll simply stand there and wait.

Wearing number (surprise!) 33, he became the most popular Colorado
Rockie in the franchise's short history, the first player in close to 70 years
to hit .360 or better three consecutive seasons. Even adjusting for the zero
gravity advantage of Coors Field, Walker put up tremendous numbers, all
while carrying himself with a complete lack of pretense. He usually arrives
at ballparks in baggy shorts and untucked shirts. His Colorado teammates
referred to him, lovingly, as "Dirt Bag," and when asked by reporters to
name his best talent, he proudly announced that he could belch the alpha-
bet both forwards and backwards.

Having begun his career as a hockey-player-turned-outfielder for the
Expos, the big lefty was initially a work in progress. His first minor league
season featured a moment in Utica when he cut across the field, third to
first, without touching second after a teammate had made a long out, not
knowing it's against the rules. But with a rifle arm and a line drive swing,
he was in the big leagues soon enough, thrilling Expos fans with the fact
that an actual *Canadian* was making All-Star Games. However, when Montreal began stripping its team for parts after the 1994 strike, Walker signed
a free agent contract with the Rockies, where he won the MVP a few years
later. His 1997 season featured a .366 average with 49 home runs, not to
mention something Ted Williams, Frank Robinson, Mickey Mantle, and
Willie Mays had never done—collect 400 total bases in a single season.

His quiet leadership was packed off to St. Louis during the summer of
2004, as the Cardinals geared up for their first World Series appearance
since the 1980s. In the mold of Mark McGwire in '97, Will Clark in 2000,
and Scott Rolen in 2002, Walker became an instantly popular midseason
veteran addition to Busch Stadium. He played well in thepostseason,

BOXSCORE

Montreal Expos 4, San Francisco Giants 2
Game Played on Wednesday, August 16, 1989 (Night) at Stade Olympique

San Francisco	0	0	0	1	0	0	1	0	0	—	2 7 1
Montreal	0	0	0	0	0	0	1	3	x	—	4 4 0

BATTING

San Francisco Giants	AB	R	H	RBI	BB	K	PO	A
Butler cf	3	0	1	0	1	1	3	0
Thompson 2b	4	0	1	0	0	0	2	3
Clark 1b	3	0	1	0	1	1	8	0
Mitchell lf	4	1	2	1	0	0	5	0
Williams 3b	4	0	0	0	0	3	0	2
Bedrosian p	0	0	0	0	0	0	0	0
Knepper p	0	0	0	0	0	0	0	0
Maldonado rf	2	1	1	1	1	1	1	0
Sheridan ph	1	0	0	0	0	0	0	0
Manwaring c	2	0	0	0	1	1	4	0
Riles ph	1	0	0	0	0	0	0	0
Uribe ss	3	0	1	0	0	0	1	3
Kennedy ph	1	0	0	0	0	0	0	0
LaCoss p	2	0	0	0	1	1	0	0
Lefferts p	0	0	0	0	0	0	0	0
Oberkfell 3b	0	0	0	0	0	0	0	0
Totals	30	2	7	2	5	8	24	8

FIELDING
DP: 1
E: Maldonado (4)
PB: Manwaring (7)

BATTING
HR: Mitchell (38, 4th inning off Langston,, 0 on, 0 out); Maldonado (8,7th inning off Langston, 0 on, 0 out)

BASERUNNING
SB: Maldonado (4, 2nd base off Langston/Santovenia)

Montreal Expos	AB	R	H	RBI	BB	K	PO	A
Da. Martinez cf	4	0	0	0	0	0	1	1
Brooks ph	1	0	0	0	0	0	0	0
Nixon cf	0	0	0	0	0	0	0	0
Foley 2b	2	0	0	0	1	0	3	3
Hudler ph-2b	1	0	0	0	0	0	0	2
Galarraga 1b	3	0	1	0	1	1	8	0
Raines lf	4	1	1	0	0	1	2	0
Wallach 3b	3	1	0	0	1	0	0	3
Walker rf	1	2	1	0	3	0	4	1
Santovenia c	4	0	0	0	0	0	8	0
Owen ss	2	0	0	0	2	1	1	2
Langston p	2	0	0	0	0	1	0	0
W. Johnson ph	1	0	1	1	0	0	0	0
Burke p	0	0	0	0	1	0	0	0
Totals	28	4	4	1	9	4	27	12

FIELDING
DP: 3

BATTING
2B: Raines (23, off Lefferts)
IBB: Owen (23, by Bedrosian)

BASERUNNING
SB: Raines (27, 3rd base off Bedrosian/Manwaring)

PITCHING

San Francisco Giants	IP	H	HR	R	ER	BB	K
LaCoss	6.2	3	0	1	0	5	3
Lefferts	1	1	0	1	0	0	1
Bedrosian L(2–6)	0	0	0	2	0	4	0
Knepper	0.1	0	0	0	0	0	0
Totals	8.0	4	0	4	0	9	4
Montreal Expos	IP	H	HR	R	ER	BB	K
Langston	7	6	2	2	2	5	8
Burke W(7–2)	2	1	0	0	0	0	0
Totals	9	7	2	2	2	5	8

IBB: Bedrosian (4, Owen)
Umpires: Terry Tata, Dana DeMuth, Steve Rippley, Bruce Froemming
Time of Game: 2:54 Attendance: 24,719

smacking six home runs in 15 games—numbers that are, by the way, each divisible by three.

I had gone from Indianapolis to Montreal with my wife the night before, and I remember Tim Wallach welcoming me into the clubhouse. Having someone come right over to me took some of the edge off, which was totally appreciated.

It seemed like it took forever for the game to start, but once it did, I had three walks and a hit—a game against Mike LaCoss and the Giants. Will Clark was the Giants first baseman, and after I had walked those first two times, he came over to me and said, "Jeez, we're pitching you like you're Babe Ruth." I didn't know what to say to that, so I just kind of smiled. We won with a few runs late. My family didn't make it in, but I know they watched the highlights a bunch of times on TSN, which is kind of Canada's version of ESPN. It was a big deal that a Canadian guy was playing for a Canadian team. But in Montreal, it didn't really count until I proved myself, because I wasn't a *French*-Canadian. That makes all the difference there, until you produce. I might as well have been a Texan.

I got out slowly, hitting around .150, so they stopped running me out there after a while. Me and Dave Martinez started sharing time.

Also on August 16, 1989
Nolan Ryan strikes out his 4,994th career batter, setting the stage to get number 5,000 in his next start on "Arlington Appreciation Day" at his home ballpark in Texas.

AUTHOR'S NOTE: Fifteen Augusts later, Walker would spurn the chance to become "Walker, Texas Ranger" when he vetoed a deal to Arlington, taking a trade to St. Louis instead.

David Wells
Born: May 20, 1963
Debut: June 30, 1987

David Wells has long been a walking, talking study in contrasts. With tremendous command of his high–80s fastball, a cutter, a change, and a curveball, he is all about control. On the other hand, his occasional off-field behavior and lack of conditioning leads one to believe he is totally out of control.

Actually, although Wells appears to be a portly, disheveled mess as he balloons out of his uniform, he is lauded by scouts as one of the most athletic big men in baseball. Despite lingering back problems that send him to the DL seemingly every other year, Wells continues to win and does so with an astounding walks-to-strikeouts ratio. In 2003 and 2004, he posted identical numbers: just 20 of the former, 101 of the latter. In his younger days, Wells was good for 160 or so punch-outs a season, but like another veteran with a nasty streak, Jack Morris, it was less about the K's and more about the W's. Through 2004, Wells had rolled up a major league record of 212–136, going 18–4 for Toronto in 1998 and then 20–8 in 2000 for the Yankees.

His days in pinstripes were, so to speak, both the best and worst of times. He won over Yankee fans with his devotion to the late Babe Ruth, wearing double-3 in his honor and then later purchasing a Babe Ruth game-worn cap and actually pitching an inning with it on his head. Wells also pitched a perfect game as a Yankee but later wrote in his autobiography that he had been half-drunk at the time. (David Letterman reported the next night that after retiring those 27 Minnesota Twins in a row, Wells celebrated by retiring 27 Heinekens in a row.) The image-conscious Yanks fined him $100,000, not believing Wells's excuse that, in his own autobiography, he had somehow been "misquoted." To borrow a line from the late Dick Young, it was a perfect game thrown by an imperfect man. (Young wrote that sentence about another Yankee from Point Loma High School in California, Don Larsen.)

Raised by a single mom who hung with the Hell's Angels biker gang, Wells says it was common practice for some of the Hell's Angels to attend his Little League games, gunning their Harleys. These days, Wells is a happily married father of two, although married life hasn't completely quieted the lefty. He listens to heavy metal music before each game to get "pumped up." AC/DC and Metallica are his two favorites. But it's a lyric from

BOXSCORE

New York Yankees 4, Toronto Blue Jays 0

Game Played on Tuesday, June 30, 1987 (Night) at Exhibition Stadium

New York	1	2	0	0	1	0	0	0	0	—	4	11	0
Toronto	0	0	0	0	0	0	0	0	0	—	0	7	0

BATTING

New York Yankees	AB	R	H	RBI	BB	K	PO	A
Henderson lf	4	0	1	0	1	2	2	0
Randolph 2b	4	0	1	2	1	0	5	2
Mattingly 1b	4	2	1	0	0	1	7	0
Winfield rf	4	0	2	0	0	1	0	0
Ward cf	4	0	2	2	0	0	2	0
Kittle dh	2	0	0	0	0	1	0	0
Washington ph-dh	1	0	0	0	1	0	0	0
Cerone c	4	0	1	0	0	1	10	0
Pagliarulo 3b	4	1	1	0	0	2	0	2
Tolleson ss	3	1	1	0	0	0	1	2
Zuvella ss	1	0	1	0	0	0	0	1
Guidry p	0	0	0	0	0	0	0	1
Stoddard p	0	0	0	0	0	0	0	0
Totals	**35**	**4**	**11**	**4**	**3**	**8**	**27**	**8**

FIELDING
DP: 1

BATTING
2B: Randolph (18, off Wells); Cerone (4, off Wells)

BASERUNNING
CS: Henderson (4, 2nd base by Wells/Moore)

Toronto Blue Jays	AB	R	H	RBI	BB	K	PO	A
Fernandez ss	4	0	0	0	0	0	5	5
Moseby cf	3	0	1	0	1	2	1	0
Barfield rf	4	0	1	0	0	2	1	0
Bell lf	4	0	1	0	0	1	0	0
Fielder dh	3	0	2	0	0	1	0	0
Mulliniks ph-dh	1	0	0	0	0	0	0	0
Gruber 3b	3	0	0	0	0	2	0	2
Leach ph	1	0	0	0	0	0	0	0
Iorg 2b	3	0	2	0	0	0	2	2
Whitt ph	1	0	0	0	0	1	0	0
Upshaw 1b	3	0	0	0	0	1	10	2
Moore c	3	0	0	0	0	0	8	1
Wells p	0	0	0	0	0	0	0	0
Eichhorn p	0	0	0	0	0	0	0	0
Lavelle p	0	0	0	0	0	0	0	0
Totals	**33**	**0**	**7**	**0**	**1**	**10**	**27**	**12**

FIELDING
DP: 2

BATTING
2B: Barfield (11, off Stoddard)

PITCHING

New York Yankees	IP	H	HR	R	ER	BB	K
Guidry W(1-3)	7.2	6	0	0	0	1	9
Stoddard	1.1	1	0	0	0	0	1
Totals	**9.0**	**7**	**0**	**0**	**0**	**1**	**10**
Toronto Blue Jays	**IP**	**H**	**HR**	**R**	**ER**	**BB**	**K**
Wells L(0-1)	4.0	9	0	4	4	2	4
Eichhorn	3.0	1	0	0	0	0	3
Lavelle	2.0	1	0	0	0	1	1
Totals	**9.0**	**11**	**0**	**4**	**4**	**3**	**8**

WP: Wells 3 (3)

Umpires: Ted Hendry, Ken Kaiser, Derryl Cousins, Mark Johnson

Time of Game: 3:03   Attendance: 45,297

Whitesnake's "Here I Go Again" that seems to fit him best: "Like a drifter, I was born to walk alone." Doing it his way all the way, Wells has pitched for nine different teams, going to the postseason ten times. His playoff record is 10–3 with a sparkling 3.19 ERA. He is now, of all things, a member of the Boston Red Sox, the arch-enemies of his beloved Yankees.

Doug Ault was our manager at [AAA] Syracuse, and I had gone out after the game that night. Imagine that, huh? I come in around one A.M. in Tidewater, a bunch of us, and I had a message in my phone back in the room from Doug, saying call him no matter what time it is. So I figure, "Uh-oh," but it was good news.

I debuted against the Yankees at Exhibition Stadium [against] Ron Guidry, one of my two favorite pitchers growing up. Steve Carlton was the other . . . Guidry was pitching for the Yankees, and I got to face him. I lost 4–0 but I did okay. I struck out Don Mattingly with Billy Martin watching from the dugout. The day before I pitched, the Blue Jays had lost like 14–7. I think [Dave] Winfield hit a grand slam, and suddenly things were goofy. Jimy Williams was our manager, and he comes over and says, "Go on down to the bullpen and warm up." And I reminded him I was

Also on June 30, 1987

Heavyweight boxer Mike Tyson officially enters adulthood (and reaches the legal drinking age), turning 21.

AUTHOR'S NOTE: Wells, himself a heavyweight, was drinking long before his 21st birthday. The concept of "adulthood" has, at times, eluded him.

pitching tomorrow—you know, against Guidry—and he says, "I don't give a sh—. Get your ass down there and warm up!" So I went down there, warmed up, but never got in, meaning I could still pitch the next day, and I was really glad about that. The Yankees were my favorite team growing up, Guidry my favorite pitcher. I was really looking forward to that. They were in first place at the time. The warming up the day before threw me a little, but I went out there, and even though I lost, I can always say I held my own against Louisiana Lightning [Guidry] in my big league debut.

Courtesy Detroit Tigers

Vernon Wells
Born: December 8, 1978
Debut: August 30, 1999

Vernon Wells III was introduced to big league baseball at an early age. His father, Vernon II, had been an athlete of some renown himself, and after a brief pro football career, he moved his family to Arlington, Texas, home of the Rangers. It was there that he began to market his accomplished oil painting skills, looking to capitalize on the LeRoy Neiman trend of painting sports stars' portraits. Wells offered his services to the visiting players who would come through Arlington Stadium, and ten-year-old Vernon would often tag along, befriending players like Rickey Henderson, Dave Parker, and Dave Stewart (who once made good on a promise to come watch one of Vernon's Little League games in person).

As Wells's own physical gifts developed, big league scouts began to replace big league players at his games. The Blue Jays made him the fifth overall selection in the 1997 draft, convincing him to spurn his scholarship to the University of Texas. Wells had planned to play baseball and football in Austin, having excelled in both sports at Arlington's Bowie High. He says he chose baseball, in part, because of the everyday challenge the sport presented, compared to the once-a-week aspect of football.

So, at 18 years old, it was off to A-ball and a fast track to the majors in Toronto. He offered skills and stats similar to those of Ellis Valentine, a fleet, strong-armed outfielder who had played a generation earlier for Canada's other team, the Expos. At the age of 24, he clocked in with a hundred-RBI season, the youngest-ever Blue Jay to reach that mark. He was an All-Star the following year, upping his RBI total to 117, with 33 home runs. He also led the league in hits, doubles, and total bases while playing Gold Glove–caliber defense.

An aggressive, line drive hitter, he and Carlos Delgado gave the Jays a vicious three-four punch in the middle of the batting order, each man receiving votes for MVP in 2003.

It was funny the way it was put to me that I was going up. My manager at Syracuse [Pat Kelly] called me at home and said, "Do you feel like going to the big leagues today?" I said, "Sure, I think I'd like that okay." So I had my wife, then my girlfriend, pack up all our stuff and drive it up to Toronto while I got on a plane and flew up.

I remember my first at bat of my first game. They put me right in there, batting second. Brian McRae, who they had just traded for, had gotten hurt, so there I was where he would have been, batting second and playing center. I had told everybody that I was going to swing at the first pitch no matter what, that I was ready to just jump on one. So I get up there against Joe Mays of the Twins [actually, it was Jason Ryan], and it was right down the middle, perfect, but I was, like, paralyzed. I took it for a called strike. I ended up striking out a couple times that game, but it was still cool. I threw out a runner trying to stretch a single into a double. My girlfriend had made it on time to see the game, and I was just as happy for her as I was for me. She had been following me all year, starting down at Single-A, and she had really sacrificed.

My dad didn't make it to that first game, but they watched it at Bobby V's restaurant on the big screen in Arlington. Bobby Valentine's restaurant was one of his favorite places, and I think he liked that, walking in there and telling the bartender to find the Blue Jays game on satellite so he could watch his son in action.

Also on August 30, 1999
Eric Gagne appears in his final Double-A game, cementing Texas League pitcher of the year honors before being promoted to the Dodgers.

AUTHOR'S NOTE: Four years later, Wells's base hit off Gagne started the rally that won the All-Star Game for the AL. Wells scored ahead of Hank Blalock, whose home run swung World Series home field advantage for his league.

BOXSCORE

Toronto Blue Jays 2, Minnesota Twins 1
Game Played on Monday, August 30, 1999 (Night) at Skydome

Minnesota	0	0	0	0	1	0	0	0	0	—	1	5	0
Toronto	1	1	0	0	0	0	0	0	x	—	2	2	0

BATTING

Minnesota Twins	AB	R	H	RBI	BB	K	PO	A
Jones cf	4	0	0	0	0	0	1	0
Allen lf	3	0	0	0	1	0	4	0
Lawton rf	4	0	1	0	0	1	1	1
Cordova dh	4	0	0	0	0	0	0	0
Walker 2b	3	0	1	0	0	1	2	0
Coomer 1b	3	1	1	1	0	0	8	1
Koskie 3b	3	0	2	0	0	0	1	3
Steinbach c	3	0	0	0	0	2	3	0
Hocking pr-ss	0	0	0	0	0	0	1	0
Guzman ss	2	0	0	0	0	0	2	3
Mientkiewicz ph	0	0	0	0	0	0	0	0
Hunter ph	1	0	0	0	0	0	0	0
Valentin c	0	0	0	0	0	0	1	0
Ryan p	0	0	0	0	0	0	0	1
Totals	30	1	5	1	1	4	24	9

FIELDING
DP: 1

BATTING
2B: Koskie (16, off Hentgen)
HR: Coomer (16, 5th inning off Hentgen 0 on, 0 out)

BASERUNNING
SB: Lawton (22, 2nd base off Hentgen/Fletcher)

Toronto Blue Jays	AB	R	H	RBI	BB	K	PO	A
Stewart lf	4	0	0	0	0	0	4	0
V. Wells cf	3	0	0	0	0	2	1	1
Green rf	2	0	1	0	1	0	2	0
Delgado 1b	1	0	0	0	2	0	12	0
Fernandez 3b	3	0	1	1	0	0	1	0
Fletcher c	3	0	0	0	0	1	4	0
Batista ss	3	1	1	1	0	1	2	5
Greene dh	3	0	0	0	0	0	0	0
Bush 2b	2	0	0	0	0	0	1	7
Hentgen p	0	0	0	0	0	0	0	2
Lloyd p	0	0	0	0	0	0	0	0
Koch p	0	0	0	0	0	0	0	0
Totals	24	2	2	2	3	4	27	15

FIELDING
DP: 1

BATTING
HR: Batista (21, 2nd inning off Ryan, 0 on, 1 out)
HBP: Bush (5, by Ryan)

PITCHING

Minnesota Twins	IP	H	HR	R	ER	BB	K
Ryan L(0–2)	8	2	1	2	2	3	4

Toronto Blue Jays	IP	H	HR	R	ER	BB	K
Hentgen W(9–10)	7.1	5	1	1	1	0	4
Lloyd	0.2	0	0	0	0	0	0
Koch SV(26)	1	0	0	0	0	1	0
Totals	9	5	1	1	1	1	4

HBP: Ryan (1, Bush)
Umpires: Mike DiMuro, Jim Reynolds, Durwood Merrill, Rocky Roe
Time of Game: 2:18   Attendance: 22,137

John Wetteland
Born: August 21, 1966
Debut: May 31, 1989

Right-hander John Wetteland induced the final out of the 1996 World Series, reaching the top of the Ferris wheel in what had been a tumultuous career. In his younger Dodgers days, he had been known as a renegade "wild man" type, quick with a practical joke and even quicker to indulge in the postgame nightlife. But in 1990, he found religion, and a suddenly spiritual Wetteland began a successful 12-year big league run.

As a potential addition to the Dodgers starting rotation in the late eighties, John Wetteland had shown just enough to merit consideration. As the Dodgers "swing man" in 1989 and 1990, he was 7–10 with an ERA near four. When L.A. dealt him to Montreal in 1992, the Expos anointed him as their closer, and his career took off, albeit in relative Canadian obscurity. It was the realization of a dream for his father, who had pitched in the St. Louis Browns system before becoming a musician. Edward Wetteland played with the San Francisco Symphony and was also was a conductor, arranger, and has written and played on albums. John inherited his father's musical talent, playing the clarinet in his youth and guitar since his professional baseball career began.

In 1992, the California native nailed down 37 saves and followed with 43 more in 1993. Overlooked for All-Star teams during his three-year run with the Expos, he benefited from the national spotlight upon joining the Yankees in '95. It was there that he began a run of six consecutive seasons with between 31 and 43 saves. His 43 saves in 1996 not only led the league, but they helped the Yankees to their first Fall Classic appearance in 15 years. Against Atlanta, he saved four more games, cementing World Series MVP honors.

Back trouble ended his on-field career at the age of 34, but he is now a valued member of the Rangers coaching staff, not to mention their best guitarist.

We were on the road in Triple-A. Las Vegas. Four in the morning, Kevin Kennedy tracks me down and says, "Wake up. You're on a plane to L.A. in two hours." Wow, that'll get your attention! I get in . . . still a little bleary-eyed, and the cab driver had no idea where Chavez Ravine was. We spent a while looking for it. I ran right into the clubhouse, day game, then took off on a two-week road trip needing to get some clothes. Orel [Hershiser] took me shopping in Cincinnati, and I loaded up on everything I'd need.

I actually got in the game that first day in L.A., only after a brawl. Pascual Perez was pitching for Montreal and was inciting our guys with that fist-pump stuff he did after strikeouts. Kirk Gibson triples off him and stands there at third base mimicking those fist pumps. Before you know it, Perez is throwing at Mike Scioscia, and I'm out on the field in the middle of a big pile before I had even gotten in the game. Now it's the ninth inning, and everything's settled back down, and I get the call. And I remember I was taking my warm-up pitches, throwing to Rick Dempsey, and my heart started skipping. I had to walk around that mound a little, trying to calm down. Dempsey comes over and asks if I'm okay, and I said, "Yeah, sure," but I can't say that I was sure of anything right then. He kind of smiled and said, "Let's just play catch here, okay?" I was on in relief of Orel, who I'm now proud to be coaching with. I threw a couple strikes to Tim Raines, but my next four pitches weren't even close. I got Hubie Brooks out, though, and Tim Wallach grounded into a double play. Time to exhale.

I was supposed to be up just until Ray Searage's back got better, but they sent out Tim Crews instead, because I was pitching too well. The big key was just getting through the first inning of that first game, shaking off the nerves. It was all good from there.

Also on May 31, 1989
Deion Sanders makes his big league debut for the Yankees.

AUTHOR'S NOTE: Wetteland and Sanders, each a couple of reformed "wild men," are now both born-again Christians living in suburban Dallas.

BOXSCORE

Los Angeles Dodgers 9, Montreal Expos 4
Game Played on Wednesday, May 31, 1989 (Day) at Dodger Stadium

Montreal	3	0	0	0	0	0	0	1	0	—	4	4	0
Los Angeles	0	0	0	1	0	0	7	1	x	—	9	13	2

BATTING

Montreal Expos	AB	R	H	RBI	BB	K	PO	A
Da. Martinez cf	3	1	1	0	0	0	4	0
Nixon ph-cf	1	0	0	0	0	1	0	0
Foley 2b-ss	3	1	1	0	0	0	1	4
Hudler ph-ss	1	1	1	1	0	0	0	1
Galarraga 1b	3	0	0	1	0	0	9	0
Raines lf	3	1	1	0	1	0	2	0
Brooks rf	3	0	0	0	1	0	1	0
Wallach 3b	3	0	0	1	0	1	1	3
Fitzgerald c	2	0	0	0	1	0	5	0
Owen ss	3	0	0	0	0	1	2	0
McGaffigan p	0	0	0	0	0	0	0	0
Frey p	0	0	0	0	0	0	0	0
B. Smith p	2	0	0	0	0	1	0	2
Hesketh p	0	0	0	0	0	0	0	0
Perez p	0	0	0	0	0	0	0	0
Garcia 2b	1	0	0	0	0	0	0	0
Totals	28	4	4	3	2	6	24	10

BATTING
2B: Raines (14, off Hershiser)
HR: Hudler (1, 8th inning off Horton, 0 on, 2 out)
SF: Galarraga (2, off Hershiser); Wallach (4, off Hershiser)
HBP: Brooks (1, by Hershiser)

BASERUNNING
CS: Fitzgerald (4, 2nd base by Hershiser/Scioscia)

Los Angeles Dodgers	AB	R	H	RBI	BB	K	PO	A
Gwynn lf-rf	4	1	1	0	0	1	1	0
Randolph 2b	5	1	3	3	0	0	1	4
Gibson cf	5	2	4	1	0	0	3	0
Wetteland p	0	0	0	0	0	0	0	0
Murray 1b	4	0	1	2	0	1	11	0
Davis rf	3	0	0	0	1	1	5	0
Horton p	0	0	0	0	0	0	0	0
Shelby ph-cf	1	0	0	0	0	0	0	0
Scioscia c	3	0	1	0	0	0	3	2
Dempsey pr-c	0	1	0	0	0	0	1	1
Hamilton 3b	4	1	1	2	0	0	0	1
Griffin ss	3	1	0	0	1	0	1	5
Hershiser p	2	0	0	0	0	1	0	0
Stubbs ph	0	0	0	0	0	0	0	0
Hatcher ph-lf	2	2	2	1	0	0	1	0
Totals	36	9	13	9	2	4	27	13

FIELDING
DP: 1
E: Gibson (2), Hamilton (6)

BATTING
2B: Murray (15, off B. Smith); Hatcher (6, off Hesketh); Randolph (4, off Perez)
3B: Gibson (1, off Perez)
HR: Hamilton (5, 7th inning off McGaffigan, 1 on, 2 out)
SH: Gwynn (2, off Hesketh)
SF: Murray (5, off Perez)
HBP: Scioscia (2, by Perez)

BASERUNNING
SB: Hatcher (1, 2nd base off McGaffigan/Fitzgerald)

PITCHING

Montreal Expos	IP	H	HR	R	ER	BB	K
B. Smith	6	6	0	2	2	2	3
Hesketh L(4–2)	0	1	0	2	2	0	0
Perez	0.2	2	0	3	3	0	0
McGaffigan	0.2	3	1	2	2	0	0
Frey	0.2	1	0	0	0	0	1
Totals	8.0	13	1	9	9	2	4

LosAngeles Dodgers	IP	H	HR	R	ER	BB	K
Hershiser W(7–4)	7	3	0	3	3	1	4
Horton	1	1	1	1	1	0	1
Wetteland	1	0	0	0	0	1	1
Totals	9	4	1	4	4	2	6

WP: Hershiser (3)
HBP: Perez (2, Scioscia); Hershiser (2, Brooks)
Umpires: Bill Hohn, Steve Rippley, Ed Montague, Randy Marsh
Time of Game: 3:00 Attendance: 22,858

Bernie Williams
Born: September 13, 1968
Debut: July 7, 1991

It seems an impossible question to ponder: How can an All-Star center fielder for a dynasty based in the country's largest city be underrated? The answer likely is grounded in the fact that Bernie Williams is so quiet, introspective, and so happy to fly under the radar in a city that clamors for its celebrities to soar above it.

When Williams first came to New York, he was so shy that his teammates nicknamed him "Bambi." Williams preferred to let his bat do the majority of his talking for him, and it spoke loudly. Off the field, he remained dignified and studious, looking the part as he thoughtfully strummed his guitar in front of his locker every day, playing everything from Debussy to Ozzy Osborne.

Williams didn't have the pure base-stealing speed to be a classic leadoff man, but with minor league (and later major league) manager Buck Showalter firmly in his corner, he would find his way into the Yankees starting lineup, and, in 1995, he helped the Pinstripes back to the postseason for the first time since 1981. In the team's ALDS heartbreak against Seattle, he excelled, hitting .429 and becoming the first player ever to homer from both sides of the plate in a single playoff game. His postseason exploits have mirrored those of his team; no player in big league history has hit more postseason home runs than the graceful Williams.

Williams was an All-Star each year between 1997 and 2001, winning Gold Gloves in four of those seasons. He also won the 1998 batting title, hitting .341 in the year in which the Yankees won 114 regular season games. At the time, he was just the seventh switch-hitter in big league history to have won a batting title and the only Yankee besides Mickey Mantle to have pulled off the feat. The following year, he became the first Yankee since Lou Gehrig to get 200 hits and 100 walks. Good stuff, especially from a guy who almost chucked it all to become a professional guitarist.

The day before I was in Louisville, playing in Triple-A. My wife was going to be meeting me down there for the All-Star Game. I took batting practice and then decided to walk around the stadium a little bit, because I had never seen it before. Columbus wasn't in Louisville's league at that time. Well, they're looking all over for me, to tell me that the Yankees are calling me up. Rick Down finally got to me, and he' s mad, like, "Where *were* you?" And you know me, I'm real calm, so I just told him I was trying to kill some time walking around because I had nothing else to do, and he kind of made a face and said, "Well, we do have something else for you to do now. They're expecting you in New York. You're getting called up, and your plane leaves in an hour. Pack your stuff and go."

I kept thinking I'd get ahold of my wife at some point, find a phone and tell her not to drive down after all, but this was before cell phones were real common. I never reached her. She drove from Columbus to Louisville, went to the hotel, and was told they had checked me out of my room. Whoops.

The first game I got in for the Yankees, I faced Jeff Ballard of the Orioles, got a sac fly. Then they brought their closer in, Gregg Olson, and I got an infield hit off him, which was nice. They stopped the game and gave me the ball, but right after that, he got the final out and we lost. It was still a very memorable and very cool time.

Also on July 7, 1991

AL umpire Steve Palermo is shot and seriously wounded attempting to stop a holdup outside Campisi's Restaurant in Dallas. Palermo had just worked the Rangers–Angels game, in which Nolan Ryan's no-hitter was broken up in the eighth on a single by Dave Winfield.

BOXSCORE

Baltimore Orioles 5, New York Yankees 3
Game Played on Sunday, July 7, 1991 (Day) at Yankee Stadium

Baltimore	0	0	3	0	0	1	0	1	0	—	5	13	0
New York	0	0	0	0	2	0	0	0	1	—	3	7	0

BATTING

Baltimore Orioles	AB	R	H	RBI	BB	K	PO	A
Devereaux cf	5	1	1	2	0	3	3	0
Orsulak lf-rf	5	1	2	0	0	0	2	0
C. Ripken ss	5	0	1	0	0	1	1	5
Horn dh	3	0	1	1	0	1	0	0
Milligan 1b	4	0	1	0	0	1	14	0
Martinez rf	4	0	2	0	0	1	3	0
Anderson pr-lf	0	1	0	0	0	0	0	0
Gomez 3b	3	1	1	0	1	0	0	1
Hoiles c	4	0	2	1	0	1	2	0
B. Ripken 2b	4	1	2	0	0	0	2	4
Ballard p	0	0	0	0	0	0	0	0
Flanagan p	0	0	0	0	0	0	0	2
Olson p	0	0	0	0	0	0	0	1
Totals	37	5	13	4	1	8	27	13

BATTING
2B: Orsulak (9, off Taylor); Horn (11, off Taylor); Gomez (8, off Taylor); Hoiles (7, off Habyan).
HR: Devereaux (10, 3rd inning off Taylor, 1 on, 0 out)
HBP: Horn (2, by Taylor)

New York Yankees	AB	R	H	RBI	BB	K	PO	A
Sax 2b	4	0	0	0	0	0	1	1
Velarde ss	4	0	1	0	0	1	4	5
Mattingly 1b	4	0	0	0	0	0	6	2
Barfield rf	4	1	1	0	0	0	1	0
Maas dh	4	1	2	0	0	0	0	0
Meulens lf	3	1	1	0	0	0	3	0
Hall ph	1	0	0	0	0	0	0	0
Nokes c	2	0	0	0	2	0	8	0
Williams cf	3	0	1	2	0	0	3	0
P. Kelly 3b	4	0	1	1	0	0	0	1
Taylor p	0	0	0	0	0	0	0	0
Habyan p	0	0	0	0	0	0	1	0
Totals	33	3	7	3	2	1	27	9

FIELDING
DP: 3

BATTING
2B: Maas (11, off Ballard)
SF: Williams (1, off Ballard)

PITCHING

Baltimore Orioles	IP	H	HR	R	ER	BB	K
Ballard W(5–9)	7	4	0	2	2	1	1
Flanagan	1	1	0	0	0	0	0
Olson SV(17)	1	2	0	1	1	1	0
Totals	9	7	0	3	3	2	1

New York Yankees	IP	H	HR	R	ER	BB	K
Taylor L(4–3)	5	11	1	4	4	1	4
Habyan	4	2	0	1	1	0	4
Totals	9	13	1	5	5	1	8

HBP: Taylor (3, Horn)
Umpires: Joe Brinkman, Derryl Cousins, Rocky Roe, Rick Reed
Time of Game: 2:46   Attendance: 43,505

AUTHOR'S NOTE: Palermo would make a partial recovery from paralysis, later working as an umpiring supervisor based out of New York, where he'd often watch Williams's games. Winfield's presence in the Yankee lineup in the late '80s and early '90s nearly drove Williams out of baseball. Seeing a Yankee outfield crowded by Winfield, Rickey Henderson, and Claudell Washington (and with Jay Buhner and Roberto Kelly blocking his path at Triple-A), Williams contemplated leaving the sport to pursue a career in music.

Dontrelle Willis

Born: January 12, 1982
Debut: May 9, 2003

With his exaggerated delivery and charismatic personality, Dontrelle Willis has drawn comparisons to both Mark Fidrych and Vida Blue. Willis's mom appreciates the comparison to Blue, as she was a huge fan of his in her youth. She says she was at the game when A's owner Charlie Finley presented him the blue Cadillac and Vida did laps around the Oakland Coliseum in it while in full uniform.

Blue, in his rookie season at age 21, went 24–8 with a 1.72 ERA, winning Rookie of the Year and MVP while striking out 301 batters. Willis, in his rookie season at age 21, fell short of all that, but 14–6, 3.30 was plenty good to help the Marlins into the postseason as the NL wild card.

More than the pitching comparisons, pundits pointed to Willis's unbridled joy, which was absolutely genuine. While he never did drive a Cadillac around the outfield waving to his fans, Willis did show the proclivity to launch that dazzling smile seemingly hundreds of times per day.

Not only can Willis pitch, he can swing the bat. He started the 2004 season 6-for-6, and although he harbored thoughts of trying to steal, like his boyhood hero, Rickey Henderson, cooler heads prevailed.

When I got the word I was going up, I really wasn't that enthusiastic about it, because I didn't really appreciate the scale of what was going on. See, our team was in Orlando, playing a Double-A game, and my manager, Tracy Woodson, told me I was getting promoted, which to me meant to Triple-A, and I'm thinking, "Okay, Albuquerque, that's cool and all. A promotion's always good." And sure enough, he starts going on about how nice the weather is in Albuquerque, but then he says, "But you're not going to Albuquerque, you're going to The Show." And I just break down. I'm like, "What!? What did you say?" He gathered my teammates and told them what he had just told me, and I remember Miguel [Cabrera] being more enthusiastic than I was. I was still numb. I got on a small, shaky little plane, and that's when it really hit me: I was going to Miami.

It happened so fast. I wanted to call my mom so she'd hear the news from me and not someone else. I left a message. And it took forever to get a cell phone signal because that clubhouse in Orlando is underground. I kept going outside, making calls, leaving messages for people, but all I would get back is messages in my voice mail. The cell phone service was so bad, my phone would never ring. So my mom and I kept missing each other, trading messages forever. I never really talked to her 'til after the game I pitched. I flew her and a bunch of people out and had to borrow the money to do it. Oakland to Miami on no notice is a real expensive flight!

I walked into that clubhouse, and Juan Encarnacion was the first guy I saw. He gave me a big hug, and that made me feel real welcome. I was pitching that same day. You talk about things happening fast. I went out to the bullpen to warm up, and I couldn't breathe, man. Warming up, it all hit me, it's a dream coming true.

Darren Oliver [later became] my teammate in Florida, and I was facing him in that first game, and he got a hit off me. I only gave up three runs, but two were because of his hit. And now every single day he brings that up. We may be one player short someday because I'm going to kill him over that. [Laughs.] Preston Wilson hit a home run off me, and I was amazed that he could hit a ball that hard. No one did that at Double-A! I kept Helton and Walker down, though, and we eventually won on a walk-off home run by Juan [Encarnacion]. I was out there, hugging him just like he had hugged me before the game. I'll never forget that day.

Also on May 9, 2003
Rapper 50 Cent ascends to the top of the charts with "In Da Club."

AUTHOR'S NOTE: Willis, who has been known to sing a rap lyric or two himself, finds himself "in da club" now too.

BOXSCORE

Florida Marlins 5, Colorado Rockies 4
Game Played on Friday, May 9, 2003 (Night) at Pro Player Stadium

											R	H	E
Colorado	0	0	2	0	0	1	0	1	0	—	4	9	1
Florida	1	0	0	0	0	2	0	1	1	—	5	7	0

BATTING

Colorado Rockies	AB	R	H	RBI	BB	K	PO	A
Stynes 3b	4	0	0	0	1	1	1	3
Payton lf	4	0	2	1	0	0	6	0
Helton 1b	3	0	0	0	1	1	7	0
Wilson cf	4	2	2	1	0	1	3	0
Walker rf	4	0	0	0	0	1	2	0
Hernandez ss	4	0	2	1	0	1	1	3
Johnson c	4	1	2	0	0	2	3	1
Butler 2b	3	0	0	0	0	1	0	0
Belliard 2b	1	0	0	0	0	0	1	0
Oliver p	2	1	1	1	0	1	0	1
Sweeney ph	0	0	0	0	1	0	0	0
Lopez p	0	0	0	0	0	0	0	0
Reed p	0	0	0	0	0	0	0	0
Norton ph	1	0	0	0	0	0	0	0
Speier p	0	0	0	0	0	0	0	0
Totals	34	4	9	4	3	9	24	8

FIELDING
E: Walker (1)

BATTING
2B: Johnson (6, off Willis)
HR: Wilson (8, 6th inning off Willis, 0 on, 1 out)

Florida Marlins	AB	R	H	RBI	BB	K	PO	A
Castillo 2b	4	0	0	0	0	0	1	3
Pierre cf	4	0	0	0	0	4	0	0
Lowell 3b	4	2	2	1	0	1	1	0
Rodriguez c	4	1	1	0	0	9	0	0
Lee 1b	3	1	2	0	1	1	6	0
Encarnacion rf	4	1	2	3	0	0	1	0
Banks lf	3	0	0	0	0	0	2	0
Levrault p	0	0	0	0	0	0	0	0
Almanza p	0	0	0	0	0	0	0	0
Spooneybarger p	0	0	0	0	0	0	0	0
Looper p	0	0	0	0	0	0	0	0
Mordecai ss	2	0	0	0	1	0	2	3
Willis p	2	0	0	0	0	0	0	0
Hollandsworth lf	1	0	0	0	0	1	1	0
Totals	31	5	7	4	2	3	27	6

FIELDING
DP: 2
PB: Rodriguez (5)

BATTING
2B: Encarnacion (7, off Oliver); Lowell (10, off Reed)
HR: Lowell (9, 1st inning off Oliver, 0 on, 2 out); Encarnacion (5, 9th inning off Speier, 0 on, 0 out)
IBB: Mordecai (3, by Oliver)

BASERUNNING
SB: Lee (11, 2nd base off Oliver/Johnson); Mordecai (2, 2nd base off Oliver/Johnson)
CS: Lee (1, 2nd base by Reed/Johnson)

PITCHING

Colorado Rockies	IP	H	HR	R	ER	BB	K
Oliver	6	5	1	3	3	1	2
Lopez	1.1	0	0	0	0	0	1
Reed	0.2	1	0	1	1	1	0
Speier L(2–1)	0	1	1	1	1	0	0
Totals	8	7	2	5	5	2	3

Florida Marlins	IP	H	HR	R	ER	BB	K
Willis	6	7	1	3	3	2	7
Levrault	1	0	0	0	0	1	0
Almanza	0.2	2	0	1	1	0	1
Spooneybarger	0.1	0	0	0	0	0	0
Looper W(3–1)	1	0	0	0	0	0	0
Totals	9	9	1	4	4	3	9

WP: Reed (1), Willis (1)
IBB: Oliver (1, Mordecai)
Umpires: Joe Brinkman, Derryl Cousins, Mike DiMuro, Lance Barksdale
Time of Game: 2:23   Attendance: 10,272

Kerry Wood
Born: June 16, 1977
Debut: April 12, 1998

The buildup for native Texan Kerry Wood was incredible. The Cubs had misfired in the 1983 draft, selecting a Texan by the name of Jackie Davidson rather than Roger Clemens. But in 1995, they chose the correct Lone Star right-hander, making Wood the fourth overall pick, behind Darin Erstad, Ben Davis, and Jose Cruz, Jr. His high school credentials were impeccable. Against tough Texas competition, he had gone 12–0 allowing 27 hits in 72 innings his senior year. There was concern when, two days after he was drafted, he threw a 175-pitch complete game to get his high school team into the state championship. But Wood, who had long admired Nolan Ryan's durability, swore he would be okay. At least at the beginning, he was great.

The confident but soft-spoken power pitcher made history in just his third big league start when, at 20 years old, he struck out his age. A record-tying 20 K's against a powerful Houston Astros club that was reduced to flailing helplessly against the sizzling fastball and zigzagging slider. On an otherwise unremarkable May afternoon in Chicago, Wood turned the city upside-down with a one-hit shutout, which was followed by an invitation to appear the next day on Letterman and Leno. He politely declined. (Three hours after the final out, Wood "celebrated" his accomplishment by eating dinner at Applebee's with fellow pitcher Terry Adams.)

Eight starts later, there were 11 different groups of fans hanging K's to record his strikeouts . . . and that start was in Cincinnati! He went on to finish 13–6 that year, holding hitters to a sub-.200 batting average and winning Rookie of the Year honors. Nolan Ryan proved prophetic, however, when that summer he said, "You just hope they don't overload him." Indeed, injuries robbed Wood of dozens of starts the next several seasons, but by 2003, he had recaptured ace status, leading the league in strikeouts and leading the Cubs into the final game of the NLCS. After failing to hold a 5–3 lead in Game Seven, Wood stood stoically in front of his Wrigley Field locker, telling reporters, "There is no curse. There is no jinx. The bottom line is that I choked. I let my teammates, the organization, and the city of Chicago down." He was applauded for taking responsibility and eventually rewarded with a long-term contract.

I was in the hotel in Iowa, sleeping, and I got a call from Dave Wilder, our minor league coordinator, and he apologized for waking me but said I had to

240

get a flight to Montreal to meet the team. At first I was sure he was joking. I really didn't think I was ready, just a week into the season. But he convinced me he was serious. I called my parents real quick and told 'em they had to get a flight to Montreal if they wanted to see my debut. Freaked 'em out a little because it meant getting passports, or so they thought.

I went over to the stadium, grabbed my stuff, and bolted for the airport. Off to Montreal and got hung up in customs for what seemed like forever. Two hours in that little room they send you off to if they have questions. I was 20; I was sweating that whole time.

Got to the ballpark and they fined me in kangaroo court for not being there the day before, for not making the team out of spring training, for about four or five other things. They seemed real eager to take my meal money from me.

Phil Regan was the pitching coach, and he kept a pretty close eye on me. I had a good bullpen session, went out there and faced Mark Grudzielanek, and somehow struck him out. I cruised for a little, then got in trouble in the fourth. Brad Fullmer got me with a double. Next inning, I left with the bases loaded, and they brought in Ben Van Ryn to face Fullmer instead. He doubled again, and I got hung with those three runs. Overall, though, it was a nice way to break in—not a lot of media or fans there in Montreal, very low key.

Also on April 12, 1998

The defending champion Florida Marlins lose again, dropping to 1–11 for the season.

AUTHOR'S NOTE: By 2003, the Marlins would once again be World Series champions, rallying off Wood in the decisive Game 7 of the NLCS.

BOXSCORE

Montreal Expos 4, Chicago Cubs 1

Game Played on Sunday, April 12, 1998 (Day) at Stade Olympique

Chicago	0	0	0	0	0	0	1	0	0	—	1	5	2
Montreal	0	0	2	0	2	0	0	0	x	—	4	9	0

BATTING

Chicago Cubs	AB	R	H	RBI	BB	K	PO	A
Brown cf	3	0	1	0	0	1	2	1
Hernandez ph-cf	1	0	0	0	0	0	0	0
Morandini 2b	3	0	0	0	1	1	1	3
Sosa rf	4	0	0	0	0	2	1	0
Grace 1b	4	0	1	0	0	1	10	1
Rodriguez lf	4	1	1	1	0	2	0	0
Blauser ss	4	0	0	0	0	2	0	6
Orie 3b	3	0	0	0	0	0	0	1
Servais c	3	0	2	0	0	0	10	1
Wood p	2	0	0	0	0	0	0	0
Van Ryn p	0	0	0	0	0	0	0	0
Pisciotta p	0	0	0	0	0	0	0	0
Houston ph	0	0	0	0	0	0	0	0
Mieske ph	1	0	0	0	0	0	0	0
Telemaco p	0	0	0	0	0	0	0	0
Mulholland p	0	0	0	0	0	0	0	0
Totals	32	1	5	1	1	9	24	13

FIELDING

E: Sosa (3), Orie (1)

BATTING

HR: Rodriguez (5, 7th inning off Hermanson, 0 on, 0 out)

Montreal Expos	AB	R	H	RBI	BB	K	PO	A
Grudzielanek ss	5	0	0	0	0	2	1	2
Santangelo cf	1	2	1	0	2	0	4	0
V. Guerrero rf	4	2	2	0	0	2	2	0
Fullmer 1b	4	0	4	4	0	0	7	2
White lf	4	0	0	0	0	0	0	0
Vidro 2b	3	0	0	0	0	2	2	2
Mordecai 2b	1	0	0	0	0	0	0	0
Widger c	4	0	0	0	0	1	9	0
Andrews 3b	4	0	1	0	0	2	0	4
Hermanson p	2	0	0	0	1	1	1	0
DeHart p	0	0	0	0	0	0	1	0
May ph	1	0	1	0	0	0	0	0
Urbina p	0	0	0	0	0	0	0	0
Totals	33	4	9	4	3	10	27	10

BATTING

2B: Fullmer 2 (7, off Wood, off VanRyn)
HBP: Santangelo (1, by Wood)

PITCHING

Chicago Cubs	IP	H	HR	R	ER	BB	K
Wood L(0–1)	4.2	4	0	4	4	3	7
VanRyn	0	1	0	0	0	0	0
Pisciotta	1.1	1	0	0	0	0	1
Telemaco	0.2	1	0	0	0	0	1
Mulholland	1.1	2	0	0	0	0	1
Totals	8.0	9	0	4	4	4	10
Montreal Expos	**IP**	**H**	**HR**	**R**	**ER**	**BB**	**K**
Hermanson W(1–1)	6.2	5	1	1	1	1	8
DeHart	1.1	0	0	0	0	0	0
Urbina SV(2)	1	0	0	0	0	0	1
Totals	9	5	1	1	1	1	9

HBP: Wood (1,Santangelo)
Umpires: Frank Pulli, Charlie Williams, Ed Rapuano, Bruce Dreckman
Time of Game: 2:37   Attendance: 18,506

David Wright
Born: December 20, 1982
Debut: July 21, 2004

With the weight of incredible expectations, David Wright shouldered the load his rookie season in New York. The Mets had already spat out 128 third basemen in 42 years of existence, but they felt that finally they had the (w)right fit.

The apple-cheeked slugger with the wide smile seemed almost too good to be true. He had grown up a Mets fan, seeing their Triple-A players up close in Tidewater, Virginia. The son of a Norfolk narcotics officer, he grew up well-mannered with respect for authority and a desire to one day represent the Mets organization at the big league level. He came across as the East Coast version of the Cardinals' Scott Rolen—great makeup, terrific defensively, picked approximately 40 players into the free agent draft, and needing 3 1/2 years to wade through the minors before bursting onto the scene.

A childhood teammate and friend of the Devil Rays' B. J. Upton, he arrived in The Show around the same time and immediately started smacking the ball around National League ballparks. In just 69 games, Wright hit 14 home runs and somehow garnered 40 RBI, playing for a team that was woefully inept at providing him runners to drive in. The Mets won just 25 of those 69 games in which he played, but as the Mets seemed to be crumbling around him, the mature-beyond-his-years Wright simply kept smiling, playing hard, and making every play. He ended his rookie season hitting .293, having hit .363 at Double-A and .298 at Triple-A before his July promotion. The onetime first-round draft pick appears to be the Chosen One, capable of burying the Mets' longtime third base curse, which has swallowed up everyone (alphabetically) from Edgardo Alfonzo to Don Zimmer.

John Stearns was funny when he told me I was going up. We had just gotten done playing Durham there in Norfolk, and I had gotten showered and dressed, and as I was on my way home—meaning my real home, to my parents' place in Norfolk—all I'm thinking is, "I wonder what's for dinner." Stearns says to come in his office, which isn't that unusual, but when I walked in, he shut the door behind me, which he had never done before. He says, "Sit down," and I didn't. I just said "Why? What's up?" He says, "Well, you're going to the big leagues." And I must have had this look on my face like I was going to faint or something, and he says, "Now don't you want to sit down?"

I got on my cell and my brothers and folks were going crazy. My dad answered the phone, and I couldn't even find the words to tell him what had happened. My mom got on the phone and said she had to do laundry so I'd have clean clothes to take with me. I flew up the next day to New York. I'm sure they felt like coming, too, but they gave me my space. They actually didn't come see me for another week or so.

I'll always remember coming out for stretching just before the game, and they're going through the starting lineups on the PA. Right when I stepped on the field, I saw my picture and name on the Jumbotron and heard myself being introduced. And if that wasn't cool enough, I got this tremendous ovation from the fans, and it just gave me chills. I mean, I hadn't even done anything yet, and already there's this big, long cheer from the crowd. Spine-tingling stuff, no exaggeration. I could actually feel it in my spine and all over my body.

Also on July 21, 2004
The Red Sox fall to nine games behind the Yankees in the AL East as Pedro Martinez suffers his worst start of the year, giving up eight runs in a 10–3 loss versus Baltimore.

AUTHOR'S NOTE: Three days later, the Sox's season would turn around when they won a fight-marred nationally televised thriller against the hated Yankees. Martinez would later spurn the Red Sox after their World Series win, joining Wright's Mets instead.

BOXSCORE

New York Mets 5, Montreal Expos 4
Game Played on Wednesday, July 21, 2004, at Shea Stadium

Montreal	0	0	0	0	1	0	3	0	0	—	4
New York	0	0	3	1	0	0	0	1	x	—	5

BATTING

Montreal Expos	AB	R	H	RBI	BB	K	LOB
B.Wilkerson lf	5	2	2	1	0	0	1
E.Chavez cf	5	1	3	3	0	0	0
J.Vidro 2b	4	0	1	0	1	1	0
J.Carroll pr	0	0	0	0	0	0	0
T.Batista 3b	5	0	2	0	0	0	4
T.Sledge rf	4	0	0	0	0	0	2
O.Cabrera ss	4	0	2	0	0	0	1
N.Johnson 1b	4	0	2	0	0	1	1
B.Schneider c	3	0	0	0	1	1	3
J.Patterson p	1	0	0	0	1	0	2
S.Kim p	0	0	0	0	0	0	0
H.Mateo ph	1	1	1	0	0	0	0
T.Tucker p	0	0	0	0	0	0	0
J.Rivera ph	1	0	0	0	0	0	1
J.Horgan p	0	0	0	0	0	0	0
L.Ayala p	0	0	0	0	0	0	0
Totals	37	4	13	4	3	3	15

FIELDING
E: O.Cabrera (8, throw); J.Vidro (5, throw); N.Johnson (4, catch)

BATTING
2B: E.Chavez (9, off Seo); O.Cabrera (12, off Seo)
HR: B. Wilkerson (17, 5th inning off Seo, 0 on, 0 out); E.Chavez (5, 7th inning off Stanton, 2 on, 0 out)
Runners left in scoring position, 2 out: T.Batista 1, J.Patterson 1, B.Schneider 1
GIDP: B. Wilkerson, J.Rivera, T.Batista

BASERUNNING
Team LOB: 9

New York Mets	AB	R	H	RBI	BB	K	LOB
J.Reyes 2b	5	0	1	0	0	1	3
K.Matsui ss	4	0	1	1	0	0	0
T.Wigginton 1b	2	2	0	0	3	0	0
C.Floyd lf	3	1	1	0	1	1	4
M.Stanton p	0	0	0	0	0	0	0
O.Moreno p	0	0	0	0	0	0	0
T.Zeile ph	1	0	0	0	0	0	1
B.Looper p	0	0	0	0	0	0	0
R.Hidalgo rf	5	1	1	3	0	1	5
M.Cameron cf	4	0	2	0	0	1	0
D.Wright 3b	4	0	0	0	0	0	0
V.Wilson c	3	0	1	0	1	0	1
J.Seo p	3	1	2	0	0	0	2
S.Spencer lf	1	0	0	0	0	0	1
Totals	35	5	9	4	6	4	19

FIELDING
DP: 3 (J.Seo-K.Matsui-T.Wigginton, K.Matsui-J.Reyes-T.Wigginton 2)

BATTING
2B: J.Seo (1, off Patterson)
HR: R.Hidalgo (14, 3rd inning off Patterson, 2 on, 1 out)
2-out RBI: K.Matsui
Runers left in scoring position, 2 out: C.Floyd 1, R.Hidalgo 2, J.Seo 1, J.Reyes 1

BASERUNNING
SB: M.Cameron (12, 2nd base off S.Kim/B.Schneider)
Picked off: J.Reyes (1st base by S.Kim)

PITCHING

Montreal Expos	IP	H	HR	R	ER	BB	K
J.Patterson	4.0	5	1	4	4	4	4
S.Kim	2.0	3	0	0	0	1	0
T.Tucker	1.0	1	0	0	0	0	0
J.Horgan L(3–1)	0.2	0	0	1	0	1	0
L.Ayala	0.1	0	0	0	0	0	0
Totals	8.0	9	1	5	4	6	4
New York Mets	**IP**	**H**	**HR**	**R**	**ER**	**BB**	**K**
J.Seo	6.0	8	1	3	3	3	1
M.Stanton BS(4)	1.1	3	1	1	1	0	2
O.Moreno W(3–1)	0.2	0	0	0	0	0	0
B.Looper S(20)	1.0	2	0	0	0	0	0
Totals	9.0	13	2	4	4	3	3

WP: L.Ayala
IBB: J.Vidro (by Seo); V.Wilson (by Kim)
Umpires: Jeff Nelson, Marty Foster, Joe Brinkman, Tim Tschida
Time of Game: 3:03   Attendance: 30,227

Ron Wright
Born: January 21, 1976
Debut: April 14, 2002

The tale of Ron Wright is the stuff of Shakespearean tragic comedy. "I guess it all depends on your point of view, which one it is," he says.

The Washington-state native was drafted by Atlanta in June 1994 (ahead of Carl Pavano, Wes Helms, Daryle Ward, Bubba Trammell, Ronnie Belliard, Corey Koskie, and Keith Foulke, to name a few). In his first full minor league season, he powered 32 home runs for the Braves' Sally League affiliate in Macon, driving in 104. He was the key component of the Braves' trade with Pittsburgh for Denny Neagle in 1996, although it should be pointed out the Braves nailed the "player to be named" in the deal, grabbing Jason Schmidt a few days later. From there, a series of waiver claims saw him bounce from the Pirates organization to the Reds, the Reds to the Devil Rays, and the Devil Rays to Seattle.

Wright began the 2003 season at Triple-A, in his home state of Washington, but stayed in Tacoma for only two weeks. When Edgar Martinez hurt his hamstring in series-opening game at Texas, the Mariners summoned the big first baseman to join them the following day. Manager Lou Piniella played Ruben Sierra at DH that afternoon, but the next day, a pleasant Sunday with a big crowd on hand, Piniella gave Wright a start against lefty Kenny Rogers (only after Jeff Cirillo had taken a ball off his ear during batting practice, on a ricochet).

His first at bat, Wright took a called third strike from ump Darryl Cousins, not knowing it would be the best thing to happen to him all day. Next time up, with the Mariners leading 1–0 in the fourth, Wright came up with runners at first and third and nobody out. Wright chopped a ball to the third-base side of the mound, but before it could get past Rogers and into center, the three-time Gold Glover speared it, starting a 1-6-2-5-1-4 triple play, with Wright being the third out, barreling into Texas's Michael Young near second.

Next time up, with Seattle now trailing 2–1, again he approached the plate with first and third, no one out, and proceeded to bang into a 6-4-3 double play. Three at bats, six outs, having made outs for the cycle (one out, two, and three). As the M's rallied with six in the seventh, Wright was lifted for pinch hitter Mark McLemore, and as it turned out, *never played in a big league game again*. He spent the 2004 season in the independent Northern League, as a Sioux Falls (South Dakota) Canary. He has now retired from

244

baseball, coaching junior college ball part-time and pursuing his bachelor's degree.

There was certainly no way of knowing that's how it would turn out. It was a lousy way to debut, going 0-for-3 with the triple play, but I sure figured I'd get a few more chances. But the team was off to a huge (12–3) start, and John Olerud and Ruben Sierra (14-for-his-first-28) were hitting a ton. There was really no place for me to play, so they sent me back to Tacoma. No promises, but they said they'd try and get me back at some point, but no one ever really got cold or got hurt again.

It's funny, but I had only signed with Seattle because I saw a great opportunity. Older team, someone's going to get hurt at some point, I figured. But Sierra stayed healthy all year, and Edgar came back and was back to his usual form.

The other thing that's funny is I really hit that triple play ball okay. Kenny Rogers made a great play to stab it, coming off the mound, and I'm not really sure what happened after that. For some reason, Ruben stopped running and got hung up between

Also on April 14, 2002
The Detroit Tigers fall to 0–11 by allowing eight runs in the last of the eighth at the Metrodome to lose 13–7. Seemingly, the Tigers could never again have an April that bad, but actually, the following year, they did, going 3–21.

AUTHOR'S NOTE: Wright was sold to the 2003 Tigers by the Indians organization but lasted just eight days at Toledo before he was released. The day the Tigers cut him loose, their record was 20–62.

BOXSCORE

Seattle Mariners 9, Texas Rangers 7
Game Played on Sunday, April 14, 2002 (Day) at The Ballpark in Arlington

Seattle	1	0	0	0	0	0	6	2	0	—	9	18	1
Texas	0	0	0	2	0	3	2	0	0	—	7	10	0

BATTING

Seattle Mariners	AB	R	H	RBI	BB	K	PO	A
Suzuki rf	6	2	2	0	0	1	2	1
Guillen ss	5	1	1	2	1	0	3	5
Boone 2b	4	1	2	2	1	0	1	5
Cameron cf	4	1	0	0	1	0	1	0
Sierra lf	5	1	5	1	0	0	0	0
Relaford pr-3b	0	1	0	0	0	0	0	0
Olerud 1b	4	1	4	2	1	0	13	2
Wright dh	3	0	0	0	0	1	0	0
McLemore ph-dh	2	0	0	0	0	2	0	0
Davis c	5	0	1	1	0	1	5	0
Gipson 3b-lf	4	1	3	1	1	0	1	0
Halama p	0	0	0	0	0	0	1	2
Franklin p	0	0	0	0	0	0	0	0
Hasegawa p	0	0	0	0	0	0	0	0
Sasaki p	0	0	0	0	0	0	0	0
Totals	42	9	18	9	5	5	27	15

FIELDING
DP: 1
E: Boone (1)

BATTING
2B: Suzuki (3, off Rogers); Sierra (4, off Rogers); Gipson 2 (2, off Rogers, off Woodard)
3B: Guillen (1, off Woodard)

Texas Rangers	AB	R	H	RBI	BB	K	PO	A
Young 2b	3	2	2	0	0	0	3	1
Catalanotto ph-2b	2	1	0	0	0	0	0	0
Greer lf	5	1	2	1	0	1	2	0
A. Rodriguez ss	3	2	2	5	0	0	1	4
Palmeiro 1b	4	0	0	0	0	0	10	0
I. Rodriguez dh	4	0	0	0	0	1	0	0
Kapler cf	4	0	2	0	0	0	3	0
Mench rf	3	1	1	0	1	1	2	0
Haselman c	2	0	1	0	1	0	4	1
Everett ph	1	0	0	0	0	0	0	0
Lamb c	0	0	0	0	0	0	1	0
Blalock 3b	4	0	0	0	0	2	0	5
Rogers p	0	0	0	0	0	0	1	4
Woodard p	0	0	0	0	0	0	0	0
Miceli p	0	0	0	0	0	0	0	0
Seanez p	0	0	0	0	0	0	0	0
Rocker p	0	0	0	0	0	0	0	0
Totals	35	7	10	6	2	5	27	15

FIELDING
DP: 1. TP: 1
PB: Haselman (1)

BATTING
2B: Young (1, off Halama); Kapler (4, off Hasegawa)
HR: A. Rodriguez 2 (4, 4th inning off Halama, 1 on, 1 out; 6th inning off Halama, 2 on, 0 out)
HBP: A. Rodriguez (3, by Hasegawa)

PITCHING

Seattle Mariners	IP	H	HR	R	ER	BB	K
Halama	6	8	2	5	5	0	2
Franklin	0	0	0	2	1	2	0
Hasegawa W(2–0)	1.2	2	0	0	0	0	2
Sasaki SV(3)	1.1	0	0	0	0	0	1
Totals	9.0	10	2	7	6	2	5

Texas Rangers	IP	H	HR	R	ER	BB	K
Rogers	6	8	0	1	1	3	1
Woodard	0	3	0	3	3	0	0
Miceli	0.1	3	0	3	3	0	0
Seanez L(0–2)	1.1	3	0	2	1	1	2
Rocker	1.1	1	0	0	0	1	2
Totals	9.0	18	0	9	8	5	5

WP: Seanez 2 (2)
HBP: Hasegawa (1, A. Rodriguez)
Umpires: Derryl Cousins, Martin Foster, Andrew Fletcher, Joe Brinkman
Time of Game: 3:39   Attendance: 32,866

third and home, and my first base coach said "Go to second," and next thing you know, I'm out and it's a triple play. But when it left the bat, I thought maybe I had a hit. It was kind of bad luck to draw Kenny for that start anyway. I was so geared up to hit the fastball, so pumped to be there, with my wife and parents having surprised me by flying in for the series. But if you know Kenny Rogers, crafty veteran, the last thing I was going to see that day was a fastball. I'll remember that day forever. I'm 0-for-3 lifetime, and I'll remember every detail of each lifetime at bat.

Courtesy Seattle Mariners

Michael Young
Born: October 19, 1976
Debut: September 29, 2000

When the Texas Rangers decided to deal Esteban Loaiza to the Blue Jays for pitcher Darwin Cubillan in July 2000, they were handed a choice of two infielders to even out the deal—either Brent Abernathy (one-time second-round pick, 13 homers at Double-A the year before) or Michael Young (one-time fifth-round pick, five home runs at Single-A the year before). Although the stats may have said to choose otherwise, the Rangers went with their positive scouting report on the right-hand hitting Young and have never looked back.

Young's numbers have improved with every year he's spent in Texas, topping out in an All-Star 2004 that saw him set a franchise record for hits (216) and drive in 99 runs, mainly from the leadoff spot in the order.

Developed as a shortstop, Young made the transition to second base with the arrival of Alex Rodriguez. He and the superstar became fast friends, and soon Young was as smooth as his mentor both on the field and off. ("No one wears the GQ look better than Michael Young," said an envious teammate.) By 2002, he had acquired the nickname "Slick," as much for his charisma off the field as his glove work on it.

When A-Rod was spun off to the Yankees, Young made the switch back to shortstop and assumed a leadership role on the young, swashbuckling Ranger team his buddy had vacated. The native Californian extinguished what could have been an explosive spring training situation by volunteering to shift back to short, allowing new teammate Alfonso Soriano to stay where he was most comfortable, at second base.

A boxing aficionado (and the cousin of onetime welterweight champion Zachary Padilla), Young scored a TKO over those in the Texas organization who doubted he could ever hit enough to be a regular. In 2002, he had to fend off Frank Catalanotto for a starting job, and in 2003, there was talk of moving Hank Blalock off third base to play Young's position so that Herbert Perry could play third. In the end, his combination of intelligence, speed, power, and ability to win out in two-strike at bats put him in the lineup to stay. With his friend A-Rod, the Rangers averaged 71 wins a season. Without him in 2004—led by Young's resolve—they went 89–73, narrowly missing an AL West title.

I was in Oakland, and of course a few years later, the Rangers would have some run-ins out there with their fans, with the whole bullpen, chair-tossing

247

BOXSCORE

Oakland Athletics 7, Texas Rangers 5
Game Played on Friday, September 29, 2000 (Night) at Network Associates Coliseum

Texas	1	0	0	1	0	1	0	2	0	—	5	12	2
Oakland	0	0	0	2	1	3	0	1	x	—	7	8	2

BATTING

Texas Rangers	AB	R	H	RBI	BB	K	PO	A
Alicea 2b	0	0	0	0	1	0	0	0
Sheldon pr-2b	3	3	2	1	1	0	3	3
Clayton ss	5	0	3	1	0	0	3	3
Palmeiro 1b	4	0	0	0	1	1	9	0
Curtis lf	4	0	0	3	1	0	1	0
Ledee rf	5	0	1	0	0	2	0	0
Sierra dh	5	0	0	0	0	1	0	0
Lamb 3b	4	1	1	0	1	1	3	4
Green cf	5	0	2	0	0	2	1	0
Knorr c	4	1	3	0	0	0	7	0
Valdes ph	0	0	0	0	1	0	0	0
Young pr	0	0	0	0	0	0	0	0
Rogers p	0	0	0	0	0	0	0	0
Cordero p	0	0	0	0	0	0	0	0
Johnson p	0	0	0	0	0	0	0	0
Perisho p	0	0	0	0	0	0	0	0
Sikorski p	0	0	0	0	0	0	0	0
Venafro p	0	0	0	0	0	0	0	0
Crabtree p	0	0	0	0	0	0	0	0
Totals	39	5	12	5	6	7	24	10

FIELDING
DP: 1
E: Sheldon (5), Lamb (33)

BATTING
2B: Sheldon (11, off Tam)
SF: Sheldon (2, off Olivares)

BASERUNNING
SB: Clayton (11, 2nd base off Mecir/Hernandez)
CS: Green (6, 2nd base by Mecir/Hernandez)

Oakland Athletics	AB	R	H	RBI	BB	K	PO	A
Porter lf	3	0	0	0	1	1	1	0
Stairs ph-rf	1	1	0	0	1	0	0	0
Velarde 2b	5	1	3	2	0	2	3	3
Ja. Giambi 1b	3	1	1	1	2	0	6	2
Saenz dh	5	0	2	1	0	1	0	0
Tejada ss	2	1	0	0	2	1	1	3
Long cf	4	0	0	0	0	0	1	0
Piatt rf	1	0	0	0	1	1	3	0
Je. Giambi ph-lf	1	0	1	0	0	0	0	0
Stanley ph	1	0	0	0	0	0	0	0
Christenson lf	0	0	0	0	0	0	0	0
Chavez 3b	3	1	0	1	1	1	1	2
Hernandez c	4	1	1	0	0	0	6	1
Byrnes pr	0	1	0	0	0	0	0	0
Fasano c	0	0	0	0	0	0	3	0
Olivares p	0	0	0	0	0	0	1	0
Mecir p	0	0	0	0	0	0	1	0
Tam p	0	0	0	0	0	0	0	0
D. Jones p	0	0	0	0	0	0	0	0
Isringhausen p	0	0	0	0	0	0	0	0
Totals	33	7	8	5	7	7	27	11

FIELDING
E: Velarde (12), Tejada (21)
PB: Hernandez (7)

BATTING
2B: Hernandez (19, off Venafro)
HR: Jason Giambi (42, 4th inning off Rogers, 0 on, 0 out)
IBB: Stairs (4, by Johnson)

PITCHING

Texas Rangers	IP	H	HR	R	ER	BB	K
Rogers	4.1	5	1	3	3	5	4
Cordero L(1–2)	0.2	1	0	2	2	1	0
Johnson	0.1	1	0	1	0	1	0
Perisho	0	0	0	0	0	0	0
Sikorski	0.2	0	0	0	0	0	1
Venafro	1	1	0	1	0	0	0
Crabtree	1	0	0	0	0	0	0
Totals	8	8	1	7	5	7	7
Oakland Athletics	**IP**	**H**	**HR**	**R**	**ER**	**BB**	**K**
Olivares	5	6	0	3	3	5	4
Mecir W(10–3)	2	2	0	0	0	0	1
Tam	0	3	0	2	2	0	0
D. Jones	1	1	0	0	0	0	0
Isringhausen SV(32)	1	0	0	0	0	1	0
Totals	9	12	0	5	5	6	7

WP: Johnson (2)
IBB: Johnson (2, Stairs)
Umpires: Rocky Roe, Ian Lamplugh, Brian Runge, John Shulock
Time of Game: 3:39   Attendance: 30,522

incident and all that. This was a few years before all that happened, but I already knew Oakland fans could be kind of tough because I knew about the Raider fans and how worked up they got.

I went out to pinch-run, and the PA announcer says, "Pinch-running at first, making his major league debut . . ." and then all I heard was booing. Couldn't believe it! Our first base coach, Bobby Jones, kind of laughed and asked me, "What the f——— did you ever do to these people?" I had no answer for him. But after the game I went out with my parents and my wife, who had made the trip in. No real celebration or anything because really, all I had done was pinch-run, and I knew there would be better things still to come in my career.

Also on September 29, 2000
Doc Gooden pitches in his last major league game, allowing a home run to the Orioles' Chris Richard in a ten-run Baltimore second.

AUTHOR'S NOTE: Young grew up a hardcore Dodger fan and fondly remembers watching Mike Scioscia's NLCS-saving ninth inning home run off Gooden in 1988.

Robin Yount
Born: September 16, 1955
Debut: April 5, 1974

Robin Yount's older brother, Larry, was a pitcher who appeared in just one big league game, and barely. Warming up to pitch the ninth inning in a Houston–Atlanta game, he felt a twinge in his elbow and had to leave without actually throwing a pitch, never to return to a big league mound. Robin, however, left his mark much more indelibly, with a Hall of Fame 20-year career as a Milwaukee Brewer.

Yount grew up a Giants fan in California, playing in his backyard, hitting against Larry and pretending he was Willie Mays, Orlando Cepeda, and Willie McCovey. Years later, an entire generation of Wisconsin little leaguers would play ball in their backyards, pretending to be Robin.

Proud to have played his entire career with the organization that drafted him (the third overall pick in 1973), he won MVP awards as both a short-stop and center fielder. Six times he eclipsed the .300 mark, including .331 to lead Milwaukee into the World Series in '82. He went 12-for-29 in the seven-game series against St. Louis.

A member of the 3,000 hit club (only Hank Aaron and Ty Cobb were younger when they achieved the feat), he would make it to Cooperstown on the first ballot, along with Nolan Ryan and his good friend George Brett.

Early in his Brewers career, he dabbled with chucking baseball for the pro golf tour, going so far as to miss spring training and all of April in 1977. Baseball's siren song lured him back soon enough, and he picked up where he had left off, becoming a true Milwaukee fan favorite until he retired in 1993. Yount's son, Dustin, was an Orioles ninth-round pick in 2001, and his daughter, Jenna, is an accomplished figure skater. And cry not for older brother Larry. He is now a successful business tycoon in Phoenix, where Robin has served as a coach for the Diamondbacks in recent years.

The first play I had to make, at shortstop, was a high chopper over the pitcher's head, with a runner at first base, Cecil Cooper, who later became a teammate of mine. I'm 18, have no experience, remember, and really wasn't familiar with making that play right near the bag. I went over real awkwardly and ended up getting spiked in the shin, then throwing the ball in the dirt so we didn't get the double play. So basically, because of the inexperience factor, I got my clock cleaned, first inning, Opening Day, and the next day, the coaches were out there going through what I should have done. That play

249

BOXSCORE

Boston Red Sox 9, Milwaukee Brewers 8
Game Played on Friday, April 5, 1974 (Day) at County Stadium

Boston	0	2	5	0	0	0	2	0	0	—	9	11	1
Milwaukee	3	1	0	0	0	4	0	0	0	—	8	6	0

BATTING

Boston Red Sox	AB	R	H	RBI	BB	K	PO	A
Harper dh	5	0	1	0	0	2	0	0
Beniquez cf	4	1	0	0	1	2	4	0
Cooper 1b	3	1	1	0	1	1	7	1
Yastrzemski lf	5	2	2	2	0	0	1	0
Petrocelli 3b	2	0	1	1	0	0	0	0
Kennedy pr-3b	2	1	0	0	0	0	0	0
Carbo rf	3	2	1	0	1	0	4	0
Miller rf	0	0	0	0	0	0	0	0
Montgomery c	4	2	2	3	0	0	8	0
Griffin 2b	3	0	2	3	1	0	1	0
Guerrero ss	4	0	1	0	0	0	2	1
Tiant p	0	0	0	0	0	0	0	0
Segui p	0	0	0	0	0	0	0	2
Totals	35	9	11	9	4	5	27	4

FIELDING
DP: 1
E: Cooper (1)
PB: Montgomery (1)

BATTING
2B: Griffin (1, off Bell)
HR: Montgomery (1, 2nd inning off Colborn 1 on, 2 out); Yastrzemski (1, 7th inning off Kobel, 1 on, 1 out)
HBP: Cooper (1, by Rodriguez)

BASERUNNING
SB: Harper (1, 2nd base off Rodriguez/Porter)
CS: Griffin (1, Home by Bell/Porter); Beniquez (1, 2nd base by Rodriguez/Porter)

Milwaukee Brewers	AB	R	H	RBI	BB	K	PO	A
Money 3b	2	0	1	1	1	0	1	5
Berry dh	5	1	1	0	0	2	0	0
May cf	5	0	0	0	1	2	2	0
Scott 1b	3	2	1	0	1	2	9	3
Briggs lf	4	1	1	3	0	0	1	0
Porter c	3	1	0	0	1	0	6	1
Coluccio rf	3	1	0	0	1	1	2	0
Garcia 2b	3	2	1	1	1	1	1	3
Yount ss	1	0	0	0	1	0	1	3
Alou ph	1	0	0	0	0	1	0	0
T. Johnson ss	1	0	1	0	0	0	2	1
Colborn p	0	0	0	0	0	0	1	1
Bell p	0	0	0	0	0	0	0	1
Kobel p	0	0	0	0	0	0	0	0
Rodriguez p	0	0	0	0	0	0	1	0
Totals	31	8	6	5	6	8	27	18

FIELDING
DP: 1

BATTING
2B: Money (1, off Tiant); T. Johnson (1, off Segui)
3B: Garcia (1, off Tiant)
HR: Briggs (1, 1st inning off Tiant, 2 on, 2 out)
SH: Money (1, off Segui)
SF: Money (1, off Tiant)

BASERUNNING
SB: Money (1, 2nd base off Segui/Montgomery)

PITCHING

Boston Red Sox	IP	H	HR	R	ER	BB	K
Tiant	5.1	5	1	8	7	5	1
Segui W(1–0)	3.2	1	0	0	0	1	7
Totals	9.0	6	1	8	7	6	8

Milwaukee Brewers	IP	H	HR	R	ER	BB	K
Colborn	2.2	4	1	7	7	4	3
Bell	3.1	4	0	0	0	0	2
Kobel L(0–1)	0.1	2	1	2	2	0	0
Rodriguez	2.2	1	0	0	0	0	0
Totals	9.0	11	2	9	9	4	5

WP: Segui 2 (2)
HBP: Rodriguez (1,Cooper)
Umpires: Jerry Neudecker, Ron Luciano, Art Frantz, George Maloney
Time of Game: 2:56   Attendance: 32,761

simply had never come up all spring training, but it came up immediately in my first game that counted.

They had made a decision late about my going north with the club. The Brewers had a tradition of inviting the previous year's number one draft pick to spring training, but it was supposed to be just a formality, so I was shocked when they said I had made the team. I had really just been the "go in in the eighth inning guy" to pick up the guy who had started at short for 'em the last year, Tim Johnson. But I started getting more and more playing time, and sure enough I made the team. Two days away from the end of spring training I found out, enough time to get my mom and dad there to see me play.

Also on April 5, 1974
A day after Hank Aaron ties Babe Ruth's record of 714 home runs, it is decided that Aaron will sit out the next day's game in Cincinnati so he can attempt to break the record once the Braves return home to Atlanta.

AUTHOR'S NOTE: Aaron would indeed set the record during the Braves' home opener three days later and would ultimately finish his career with Yount in Milwaukee two years later.

Barry Zito
Born: May 13, 1978
Debut: July 22, 2000

Not your average, run-of-the-mill lefty, Barry Zito possesses a cliff-diving curveball and the guts of a burglar, but that's hardly what separates him from the pack. The yoga-practicing California native arrived in the big leagues with his own satin pillow, a stuffed frog named Smoochie, and collection of scented candles . . . yet he bristles when he's called "eccentric."

Actually, Zito may be the most centered player in sports, not to mention the most eager student of Eastern philosophy and of "putting out positive energy." His general manager, Billy Beane, says, "He reminds you of those 1970s guys who read Psycho-cybernetics. In his mind, he's already pitched an entire game before he takes the mound."

Operating on a variation of Norman Vincent Peale's "power of positive thinking," Zito has been known to write himself Post-it notes in his apartment for positive affirmation. "All lefties fear me" is a Post-it that got him through a tough stretch in July 2001. That same summer, he and his dad, a former conductor and arranger for the legendary Nat King Cole, worked through the book *The Creative Mind*, written decades earlier by religious philosopher Ernest Holmes. With the message of not letting the external affect the internal, Zito channeled himself into a pitcher who won 34 of his next 40 decisions.

With the paralyzing curveball always at the ready, Zito zipped to a Cy Young Award in 2002, going 23–5, placing third in the league in ERA, and first in wins. Remarkably, he developed the curveball (stop reading, Little Leaguers) at age ten, when his dad paid for private lessons from Cy Young winner Randy Jones. Out of high school (where he was much more of a skateboarder than a ballplayer), he was drafted in the 59th round by Seattle. He went off to college instead. The Rangers made him their third-round pick two years later, but he turned down their offer and went back for another year of school (something the Rangers would rue for years, as Zito won his first 12 decisions against Texas). Finally, as the A's first-rounder in 1999, he signed a pro contract and has been delighting Oakland fans with his wicked stuff and winning personality ever since.

The nephew of Patrick Duffy (Bobby Ewing on *Dallas*), Zito has gravitated towards the entertainment culture as well, playing the guitar, writing songs, and occasionally sitting in with his sister's band, *The Sally Zito Project*. If indeed he's a trifle unusual, he's also incredibly talented on the mound.

BOXSCORE

Oakland Athletics 10, Anaheim Angels 3
Game Played on Saturday, July 22, 2000 (Day) at Network Associates Coliseum

Anaheim	0	1	0	0	0	1	1	0	0	—	3	5	0
Oakland	1	0	0	6	2	0	0	1	x	—	10	18	0

BATTING

Anaheim Angels	AB	R	H	RBI	BB	K	PO	A
Erstad cf	4	1	2	0	1	0	4	0
Gil ss	4	0	0	0	1	2	2	2
Vaughn 1b	3	0	1	1	0	1	3	1
Salmon rf	4	0	0	0	0	2	5	0
Anderson dh	3	0	0	0	1	2	0	0
Glaus 3b	2	2	1	1	2	1	2	1
Molina c	4	0	0	0	0	0	4	0
Clemente lf	4	0	1	1	0	1	2	0
Spiezio lf	0	0	0	0	0	0	0	0
Kennedy 2b	3	0	0	0	1	1	2	2
Cooper p	0	0	0	0	0	0	0	0
Fyhrie p	0	0	0	0	0	0	0	0
Turnbow p	0	0	0	0	0	0	0	0
Holtz p	0	0	0	0	0	0	0	1
Totals	31	3	5	3	6	10	24	7

FIELDING
DP: 1

BATTING
2B: Erstad (28, off Mathews)
HR: Glaus (29, 6th inning off Mathews, 0 on, 0 out)
HBP: Vaughn (9, by Zito)

BASERUNNING
CS: Erstad (7, 2nd base by Zito/Hernandez)

Oakland Athletics	AB	R	H	RBI	BB	K	PO	A
Long cf	5	1	2	3	0	0	3	0
Velarde 2b	5	2	3	0	0	0	0	0
Ja.Giambi 1b	3	1	0	0	2	0	6	1
Grieve lf	4	1	2	4	1	1	1	0
Christenson pr-lf	0	1	0	0	0	0	0	0
Stairs rf	5	0	3	1	0	1	1	0
Je.Giambi dh	5	0	1	0	0	1	0	0
Tejada ss	4	2	3	1	1	0	4	2
Chavez 3b	4	2	3	1	0	1	1	0
Hernandez c	4	0	1	0	0	0	11	0
Zito p	0	0	0	0	0	0	0	2
Mathews p	0	0	0	0	0	0	0	0
Magnante p	0	0	0	0	0	0	0	0
Totals	39	10	18	10	4	4	27	5

BATTING
2B: Velarde (16, off Cooper); Stairs (14, off Cooper)
HR: Grieve (19, 4th inning off Cooper, 3 on, 1 out); Tejada (18, 5th inning off Fyhrie, 0 on, 0 out)
SH: Hernandez (6, off Cooper)
SF: Chavez (4, off Holtz)

PITCHING

Anaheim Angels	IP	H	HR	R	ER	BB	K
Cooper L(4–4)	3.1	10	1	7	7	2	2
Fyhrie	2.2	5	1	2	2	1	2
Turnbow	1.1	3	0	1	1	1	0
Holtz	0.2	0	0	0	0	0	0
Totals	8.0	18	2	10	10	4	4

Oakland Athletics	IP	H	HR	R	ER	BB	K
Zito W(1–0)	5.0	2	0	1	1	6	6
Mathews	3.0	3	1	2	2	0	4
Magnante	1.0	0	0	0	0	0	0
Totals	9.0	5	1	3	3	6	10

HBP: Zito (1, Vaughn)
Umpires: Jim Wolf, John Shulock, Rocky Roe, Brian Runge
Time of Game: 3:09   Attendance: 20,111

Through 2004, his record was 72–40 with an ERA of 3.41. His postseason ERA is a sparkling 2.76, but, incredibly, he has won none of his five starts. "Doesn't get me down," he insists. "Nothing does."

I had heard rumblings about me coming up to pitch the week before, but instead they called up Marcus Jones. As I understand it, they didn't want my first start in the big leagues to be in Colorado, so they sacrificed poor Marcus Jones. It ended up being his only big league start. I got the call a week later and had the pleasure of pitching at home instead of at Coors Field.

The game was a whirlwind. Mo Vaughn, Tim Salmon. Darin Erstad, who was having a great year. I only gave up two hits, but it was a battle (50 balls, 50 strikes). I struck out the side in the fifth with a couple guys on. There was a big roar from the crowd when that happened.

Art Howe, being the gentleman that he was, let me go out there to take some warm-up pitches before the sixth because he wanted me to have the nice ovation from the crowd walking off the field. Had he taken me out after five like I'd expected, I never would have had that experience, and I'll always be thankful that he did that.

Also on July 22, 2000
Lance Armstrong moves to within a day of winning the 2,250-mile Tour de France for the second year in a row.

AUTHOR'S NOTE: Armstrong, courageously beating cancer, has a kindred spirit in Zito's beloved mother, who also beat long odds, fighting through biliary cirrhosis two summers prior.

Josh Lewin
Born: October 25, 1968
Fox Debut: June 1, 1996

Josh Lewin is an announcer for the Fox "Saturday Game of the Week" and the television voice of the Texas Rangers. His rookie game behind the mike for Fox was June 1, 1996, as Boston beat Seattle, 6–5. A graduate of Northwestern University's Medill School of Journalism, he worked Baltimore Orioles radio as well as TV play-by-play for the Chicago Cubs and Detroit Tigers before relocating to Dallas. This is his second book.

Doing a nationally televised game was beyond my wildest expectations . . . my goal had always been to be someone's number-two radio guy. I knew this wasn't the "A" game; that was Buck and McCarver. But working with Ken Singleton and having to have about seven production meetings before the actual game made me realize this was all pretty heavy. I worried most about my on-camera stuff, having come up in radio . . . I was incredibly self-conscious, and looking back, the owner of the worst haircut in American history. But they [Fox] kept bringing me back for more . . . I guess that first one wasn't a disaster. Mo Vaughn hit a long home run and somehow my voice didn't crack when I called it.

BOXSCORE

Boston Red Sox 6, Seattle Mariners 5
Game Played on Saturday, June 1, 1996 (Day) at Kingdome

Boston	0	1	0	0	4	1	0	0	0	—	6	9	0
Seattle	1	0	1	0	0	1	0	2	0	—	5	8	1

BATTING

Boston Red Sox	AB	R	H	RBI	BB	K	PO	A
Hosey lf	3	1	0	0	1	0	2	0
Valentin ss	4	0	0	0	1	1	2	3
Vaughn 1b	4	1	3	3	1	0	7	0
Canseco dh	5	0	1	0	0	2	0	0
Naehring 3b	4	1	1	1	0	0	1	2
Stanley c	3	1	0	0	1	1	7	1
Malave rf	4	0	1	1	0	1	1	0
Selby 2b	4	1	2	0	0	0	2	2
Cuyler cf	2	1	1	0	1	0	5	0
Wakefield p	0	0	0	0	0	0	0	0
Stanton p	0	0	0	0	0	2	0	0
Slocumb p	0	0	0	0	0	0	0	0
Totals	33	6	9	5	5	5	27	8

FIELDING
DP: 2

BATTING
2B: Malave (2,off Milacki).
HR: Naehring (6,2nd inning off Milacki 0, on, 0 out); Vaughn (21,5th inning off Milacki 2 on, 2 out).
SH: Hosey (1,off Carmona). HBP: Cuyler (3,by Carmona).
IBB: Vaughn (6,by Carmona). Team LOB: 7.

BASERUNNING
SB: Hosey (6,2nd base off Milacki/Marzano).
CS: Cuyler (3,2nd base by Guetterman/Marzano).

Seattle Mariners	AB	R	H	RBI	BB	K	PO	A
Cora 2b	2	2	1	0	1	0	3	2
Rodriguez ph, ss	2	0	0	0	0	2	0	0
Bragg lf	3	0	0	0	0	0	4	1
Hunter ph, lf, 1b	1	0	1	0	0	0	1	0
Strange ph	1	0	0	0	0	0	0	0
Griffey cf	4	1	2	2	0	1	4	0
E. Martinez dh	2	0	0	0	2	1	0	0
Buhner rf	4	1	1	1	0	2	1	0
Sorrento 1b	3	0	1	0	0	0	4	2
Amaral ph, lf	1	0	0	0	0	0	0	0
R. Davis 3b	3	1	1	1	0	1	3	0
Marzano c	4	0	0	0	0	0	5	1
Sojo ss, 2b	3	0	1	0	0	0	1	2
Milacki p	0	0	0	0	0	0	1	0
Guetterman p	0	0	0	0	0	0	0	1
Jackson p	0	0	0	0	0	0	0	0
Carmona p	0	0	0	0	0	0	0	1
Totals	33	5	8	5	3	8	27	10

FIELDING
DP: 1
E: Cora (5)

BATTING
2B: Griffey 2 (12,off Wakefield 2); Cora (8,off Wakefield); Sorrento (7,off Wakefield);
Hunter (2,off Stanton).
HR: Buhner (19,8th inning off Stanton 0 on, 1 out); R. Davis (5,8th inning off Stanton 0 on, 2 out).
HBP: R. Davis (2,by Wakefield); Sojo (1,by Wakefield).
Team LOB: 5.

BASERUNNING
SB: Cora (5,2nd base off Wakefield/Stanley); Griffey (7,3rd base off Wakefield/Stanley).

PITCHING

Boston Red Sox	IP	H	HR	R	ER	BB	K
Wakefield W (4–5)	6.1	5	3	3	3	3	0
Stanton	1.1	3	2	2	2	0	2
Slocumb SV (8)	1.1	0	0	0	0	2	0
Totals	9	8	5	5	3	8	2

Seattle Mariners	IP	H	HR	R	ER	BB	K
Milacki L (1–2)	5.1	8	6	2	2	2	2
Guetterman	1	1	0	0	2	0	0
Jackson	1.2	0	0	0	0	2	0
Carmona	1	0	0	0	1	1	0
Totals	9	9	6	2	5	5	2

HBP: Wakefield 2 (4,R. Davis, Sojo); Carmona (1,Cuyler).
IBB: Carmona (5,Vaughn).
Umpires: Larry McCoy, Dale Ford, Chuck Meriwether, Jim Evans
Time of Game: 2:54 Attendance: 34,822